THE BOUNDARIES
OF PLURALISM

THE BOUNDARIES OF PLURALISM

The World of the University of Michigan's Jewish Students from 1897 to 1945

By

Andrei S. Markovits and
Kenneth Garner

Published in the United States of America by
Michigan Publishing

DOI: https://doi.org/10.3998/mpub.11461932

ISBN 978-1-60785-552-1 (paper)
ISBN 978-1-60785-553-8 (e-book)
ISBN 978-1-60785-575-0 (open-access)

An imprint of Michigan Publishing, Maize Books serves the publishing needs of
the University of Michigan community by making high-quality scholarship widely
available in print and online. It represents a new model for authors seeking to
share their work within and beyond the academy, offering streamlined selection,
production, and distribution processes. Maize Books is intended as a complement
to more formal modes of publication in a wide range of disciplinary areas.
http://www.maizebooks.org

*In a letter from October 1918, Professor I. Leo Sharfman of the
Department of Economics—who, as readers of this book will discover,
plays a role in our story—provided an account of the impact of the
Spanish flu on Ann Arbor and on the University of Michigan. He
wrote, "churches, schools, and theaters are closed; and all public
meetings of whatever character are prohibited." As for the university,
while "the academic work has been all shot to pieces, and our capacity
for readjustments is being tested to the limit," Sharfman averred that
"all are maintaining their good nature in these trying times and are
doing their utmost in every respect."*

*A century later, as we completed the finishing touches on this book,
another pandemic ravaged the university community and the nation
as a whole: COVID-19. It is in the spirit of resilience expressed in
Professor Sharfman's letter that we dedicate our work to the memory
of the deceased, and to the selfless heroism of the countless health care
workers without whom the devastation wrought by the coronavirus
would have been much worse.*

- A.S.M. and K.G., May 2020.

CONTENTS

ASU   American Student Union
BHL   Bentley Historical Library, University of Michigan
BBHN   *B'nai B'rith Hillel News*
HN   *Hillel News*
JSC   Jewish Student Congregation
MCAF   Michigan Committee for Academic Freedom
MD   *Michigan Daily*
NSL   National Student League
SRA   Student Religious Association
VPSS   Vice President of Student Services
ZBT   Zeta Beta Tau

Please note that the *B'nai B'rith Hillel News* and *Hillel News* were alternating names for the Michigan Hillel chapter's bulletin.

A Note on Sources

The footnotes cite all sources in short form style. The bibliography provides complete publishing information. For archival citations, the first instance of an archival source is presented complete, subsequent citations are given in short form.

child of a Holocaust-ravaged, Hungarian-speaking Jewish family and having grown up in western Romania, Vienna, and New York), I have devoted parts of my academic career to the study of subjects central to Jewish life, none more so than certain aspects of postwar German, but also Austrian—indeed European—politics. Although my interest in both of these countries included a wide array of topics, from trade unions and social democracy to new social movements and governance, I paid particular attention to Jews and antisemitism. Even though I had always been deeply interested in American Jewry's history and contemporary affairs, I had never done any serious research or writing on any of its important subjects. This changed abruptly during my four-month stint teaching in the wonderful Michigan in Washington program from early January to late April 2015 when I decided that, upon my return to Ann Arbor in May, I wanted to study the history of Jewish students at my very own University of Michigan. In particular, spurred by my interest in Benny Friedman, Michigan's legendary quarterback of the 1920s, and sports at Michigan, I was eager to study Jewish student-athletes at the university, thus adding another angle to the story.

And that is exactly what happened. The first Monday back home in Ann Arbor, I drove to the Bentley Historical Library knowing nothing about its resources but being fully aware that this was the one and only place where all my sources lay. The first person I met upon entering this amazing place was the now-retired Karen Jania. The rest is history, as they say. After telling Karen my vague and completely uninformed ideas, she did not ridicule or turn away from me but did exactly the opposite: In the most welcoming and encouraging manner possible, she went to work immediately, telling me to contact this and that person, read this book and that article. She kept bombarding me with materials and sources. My head spinning from all this information, I headed for lunch when I noticed through a half-opened door Terrence McDonald seated at a fancy desk in a corner office. I suddenly realized that Terry was no longer my long-serving dean but had in the meantime become the director of the Bentley. I knocked on the door and—just as he had done as dean—Terry welcomed me here, too, with warmth and openness. When I told him what had brought me to the Bentley Library, he not only expressed genuine interest and real enthusiasm for my project but also promised me that I could always count on him and his staff to help me as best they could. Have they ever! *Tout court*, this project would be nowhere without Terry and his Bentley crew. Many thanks to them indeed!

But I needed a seasoned historian to assist me in this endeavor. Enter Kenneth Garner. From our very first meeting, I knew that Ken was special. His knowledge of history, literature, politics, music, theater—in short, his *Bildung*—was exemplary and provided the contours of our early acquaintance. But it was his formidable familiarity with the Bentley and his mastery of its materials that rendered him an indispensable research assistant on this project. However, in the course of working together, it soon became clear to me that Ken had departed from his position as my assistant and developed into that of my full-fledged coauthor. The journey of this project not only yielded two books but, more important, Ken became a dear friend whose work I admire, whose advice I cherish, and whose company I enjoy.

Ken and I first set out to write a book on Jewish students at the University of Michigan from the late 1890s until 1945. Along the way, we published a companion volume entitled *Hillel at Michigan 1926/27–1945: Struggles of Jewish Identity in a Pivotal Era.* While originally part of the present book, we extended our material on the Hillel Foundation's activities at Michigan to form a book all its own. We published it literally on the very day in December 2016 that coincided with Hillel's founding on the Michigan campus in December 1926, thus feting this institution's ninety-year existence at the University of Michigan.

As with *Hillel at Michigan*, with this book too, I owe deep gratitude to Jason Colman and Patrick Goussy from Maize Books who chaperoned the manuscript expertly from beginning to end through the usual maze of academic publishing. Even a relatively low-budget project such as this requires some funding and once again, I am most grateful to the small but immensely helpful research support that the University of Michigan accords me annually via my Deutsch Collegiate and Thurnau professorships.

As with all my writings, I dedicate this book, too, to my beloved Kiki, our late Cody, and our darling Emma, without whom none of this would be possible!

Andrei S. Markovits
Ann Arbor, August 2019

In the more than four years that Andy and I worked on this project, he has been a wise teacher, an encouraging mentor, and above all a generous friend. Under his careful direction, I gained the confidence to follow wherever the archival documents led us, and Andy was unfailingly supportive even during the rough patches and dry spells that all such research projects endure. When Andy decided to promote me from research assistant to coauthor, I had some doubts about the wisdom of his decision; not having trained in either Jewish history or the history of American education, I was unsure if I could truly help him to realize his ambitions for this endeavor. His patient guidance, and his deeply insightful reading of the documents, however, enabled us to make constant progress. Andy and Kiki's warm generosity, our animated conversations while enjoying Kiki's tasty desserts during my visits to Onondaga Street, and Andy's enthusiasm will remain my fondest memories of this long and winding road.

If Andy and Kiki deserve my primary thanks, I am also grateful to many others who have given me support and friendship during the long research and writing process. While some are mentioned in the acknowledgments, I want to especially thank my family and friends, too numerous to list in this short preface; they listened to me recount the emerging narrative in this book many times and helped me to clarify ideas that Andy and I developed during the course of the writing. Chris Johnson gave me valuable advice and encouragement at different stages in the project. My father, Kenneth Garner, Sr., played an especially important role by taking publishable quality photos of almost all the images in this book. In a strange way, considering the role he plays in our narrative, I also feel that this project owes a considerable debt to President Alexander Grant Ruthven himself. His decision to collect and preserve scrupulously the documents cited throughout this work, including those that are sharply critical of him and his administration, made it possible for us to develop and write this study.

Finally, my deepest and abiding gratitude goes to Heather, who patiently endured many nights of me sitting in front of a computer instead of watching films or reading with her. Her love and kindness have added so much to my life: *Ti amo più qualsiasi cosa al mondo.*

Kenneth Garner
Ann Arbor, August 2019

gnant insights as to what the Michigan campus was like during the late 1930s and early 1940s.

Michelle McClellan provided us with photos of archival documents from her own research as well as secondary source recommendations. Her generosity enabled us to flesh out our account of the Willis Ward and Pretzel Bell controversies. Moreover, she gave us photos of letters that two of the dismissed students sent to Ruthven's biographer, Peter Van de Water. We owe Michelle many thanks. Greg Dooley kindly shared his collection of news articles about Harry Kipke with us at an early stage in the project. Above all, we wish to thank Ed Lawson for his time in helping us to devise the onomastic method of assessing Jewish student enrollment in chapter 1.

Many students assisted us with researching, and even writing, different facets of this project. We would like to thank Sam Woodbury, Charles Sorge, Jackson Bunis, and Jillian Victor for their hard work and the impressive research that they produced. Olivia Divak, Julia Ebben, and Adam Stone researched and wrote important sections on Jewish student life. Our thanks to all of them and especially to Adam for his thorough work in helping to conduct the extensive analysis on Jewish surnames, which contributed immensely to the core of chapter 1. While we could not have written this book without the assistance of all the people mentioned above, any errors in our account are ours alone.

INTRODUCTION

D eep in the archival boxes of Ira M. Smith, who served as registrar for the University of Michigan from the mid-1920s to
the mid-1950s, are two folders with the same seemingly innocu-
ous name: "Interview reports for New York applicants, 1938."[1]
While conducting interviews of prospective university students
is hardly a noteworthy event, a careful reading in these two folders reveals a more complicated, and fascinating, story. In one, we
meet Arlene E. Lazansky from Brooklyn, New York. Described as
an "ambitious young woman" who was "bright, cheerful, and com-
panionable, and yet attractively modest," she had just graduated
cum laude from the Adelphi Academy, Brooklyn's oldest private
preparatory school, in the summer of 1939, when she learned that
Michigan had rejected her application for admission.[2] Shocked,
she penned a note to Smith, expressing disappointment not just
over her rejection but also because "there was no explanation
accompanying the refusal."[3]

1. Ira M. Smith Papers (hereafter cited as Smith), box 4, folders 42 and 43, Bentley
Historical Library, University of Michigan (hereafter cited as BHL).

2. Edward Lazansky to Alexander Ruthven, letter dated July 11, 1939, Smith, box 4,
folder 42, BHL. On Adelphi, see www.adelphi.org. Lazansky's story is also recounted
in Alan Gongora's senior honors thesis, "The Changing Function of Public Education: Selective Admissions at the University of Michigan, 1920–1940."

3. Arlene Lazansky to Ira M. Smith, letter dated June 28, 1939, Smith, box 4, folder
42, BHL. For Smith's affirmation of the committee's decision, see Smith to Arlene
Lazansky, letter dated July 5, 1939, Smith, box 4, folder 42, BHL.

When Smith's reply restated the Committee on Admissions' decision and failed to provide any explanation, the Lazansky family
marshaled its connections to force the university to change its
mind. Arlene's great-uncle, Edward Lazansky, a presiding judge
in the appellate division of the New York State Supreme Court,
wrote a letter to the university president, Alexander Grant Ruthven, forcefully laying out Arlene's qualifications as well as his own
prominent legal career and his position as a trustee of the City
College of New York (CCNY). Judge Lazansky informed Ruthven
that a recommendation letter from John Huston Finley, a former
CCNY president and an emeritus editor at the *New York Times*, was
about to be sent to the University of Michigan pleading Arlene's
case. Lazansky also handwrote below his signature that he "omitted to state that Arlene's father served in the army as a volunteer
for two years, one of which was in France at the front."[4] Finley's
own letter emphasized, if it were still needed, Judge Lazansky's
prominence as "one of our foremost citizens" and expressed surprise at his great-niece's rejection by the University of Michigan
given that she had "so high a record in college entrance subjects."[5]
The intervention of these two prominent New Yorkers made the
university quickly reconsider its decision. Smith wrote back to Finley thanking him for the "supplementary information" that he had
provided (which was nothing beyond his incredulity at Arlene's
rejection). The same day, Smith also wrote a letter to Arlene that
finally explained to Arlene the committee's initial decision: the
state of Michigan could not bear the costs of admitting all out-of-
state students—in other words, a purely economic rationale for
her initial rejection. Smith then inquired as to whether she had
already made living arrangements in Ann Arbor for the upcoming academic year.[6] The registrar's 180-degree reversal continued

4. Edward Lazansky to Ruthven, letter dated July 11, 1939, Smith, box 4, folder 42,
BHL.
5. John Finley to Ruthven, letter dated July 11, 1939, Smith, box 4, folder 42, BHL.
6. Smith to Arlene Lazansky, letter dated July 22, 1939, Smith, box 4, folder 42, BHL.
Arlene's family made arrangements in early June of 1939 for her to live in a rooming

when Smith cabled Arlene's mother to request an interview with Arlene in Ann Arbor in late July, after which, unsurprisingly, the Committee on Admissions reversed its original decision. Smith's letter, informing Arlene of the good news, was far more conciliatory than before: "I sincerely hope that you will find your work here both pleasant and profitable. I also trust that your return trip to New York from your recent visit to Ann Arbor was entirely without accident or near accident."[7] Lazansky proceeded to play an active role in the University of Michigan's campus social life, with her name mentioned a few times in the student newspaper, the *Michigan Daily*, in connection to dances and sorority life.[8]

By itself, Lazansky's story may appear insignificant. Many students find themselves rejected by their dream schools. Moreover, in Arlene's case, her predicament ended most fortuitously by her being eventually admitted to her desired institution. Thus, the whole thing seemed to have had a happy ending. Yet the folder in which we find Arlene's story also shows that the initial decision to reject a student with such strong qualifications was likely for reasons that were additional to the expense incurred by the Michigan taxpayer in support of an out-of-state applicant's presence at the university. Some clues appear on the blank interview form that follows the Lazansky correspondence.[9]

This form [Figure 0.1], used by University of Michigan representatives at the interviews, asked prospective students both for their father's and mother's birthplace. More tellingly, the form also inquired whether these students were members of the National Student League (NSL), the Student League for Industrial Democracy (SLID), or the American Student Union (ASU),

house at 814 East University. See the Western Union telegram from Mrs. Charles Lazansky to Smith, received July 26, 1939, Smith, box 4, folder 42, BHL.

7. Smith to Arlene Lazansky, letter dated August 2, 1939, Smith, box 4, folder 42, BHL.

8. "League Dance Most Fun . . . ," *Michigan Daily* (hereafter cited as *MD*), November 12, 1940; and "The Pledges Do Their Bit," *MD*, August 25, 1941.

9. Registrar's Office, Interview Blank, Smith, box 4, folder 42, BHL.

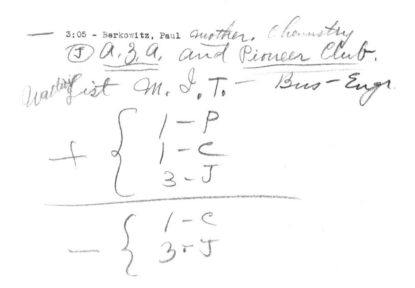

2:30 - Leavitt, Harold Jack

2:45 - Palmer, Osna Rosalind

3:00 - Galas, Eduardo

3:05 - Berkowitz, Paul

Figure 0.3 [Interview Sheet - June 3, 1939 (back)], Ira Smith box 4, folder 42, Bentley Historical Library, University of Michigan

blank interview form. Both folders contain many pages of hand-written notes that accompany typed lists of prospective students, organized by the date and session in which they were interviewed. Looking at just the first page for one of these sessions—for Saturday afternoon, June 3, 1939, in Boston [Figure 0.2]—one notices

UNIVERSITY OF MICHIGAN
ANALYSIS OF SEPTEMBER, 1935 APPLICANTS FROM NEW YORK AND VICINITY

FIELD OF INTEREST	SEX	JEWISH APPLICANTS								GENTILE APPLICANTS								TOTAL APPLICANTS	
		Both Parents Foreign		One Parent Foreign		Both Parents American		TOTAL		Both Parents Foreign		One Parent Foreign		Both Parents American		TOTAL			
		A	R	A	R	A	R	A	R	A	R	A	R	A	R	A	R	A	R
LIT	Men	2	1	1	-	2	-	5	1	-	-	-	-	1	-	1	-	6	1
	Women	2	-	1	2	2	-	5	2	-	-	-	-	2	-	2	-	7	2
SCIENCE	Men	1	2	1	2	3	-	5	4	-	-	-	-	1	-	1	-	6	4
	Women	1	-	-	-	2	-	3	-	-	-	-	-	-	-	-	-	3	-
EDUC	Men	-	-	-	-	-	-	-	-	-	-	-	-	-	-	-	-	-	-
	Women	-	-	1	-	-	-	1	-	-	-	-	-	-	-	-	-	1	-
ENG	Men	1	-	-	2	2	-	3	2	1	-	2	-	2	-	5	-	8	2
	Women	-	-	-	-	-	-	-	-	-	-	-	-	-	-	-	-	-	-
ARCH	Men	-	1	-	-	-	-	-	1	-	-	-	-	-	-	-	-	-	1
	Women	-	-	-	-	-	-	-	-	-	-	-	-	-	-	-	-	-	-
BUS	Men	-	1	-	-	-	-	-	1	1	-	1	-	-	-	2	-	2	1
	Women	-	-	-	-	-	-	-	-	-	-	-	-	-	-	-	-	-	-
LAW	Men	-	2	-	-	-	1	-	3	-	-	-	-	-	-	-	-	-	3
	Women	-	-	1	-	-	-	1	-	-	-	-	-	-	-	-	-	1	-
MED	Men	7	12	2	2	-	2	9	16	-	-	-	-	-	-	-	-	9	16
	Women	1	-	-	-	1	-	2	-	-	-	-	-	-	-	-	-	2	-
TOTAL	Men	11	19	4	6	7	3	22	28	2	-	3	-	4	-	9	-	31	28
	Women	4	-	3	2	5	-	12	2	-	-	-	-	2	-	2	-	14	2
	Total	15	19	7	8	12	3	34	30	2	-	3	-	6	-	11	-	45	30

Figure 0.4 [University of Michigan, Analysis of September, 1935 Applicants from New York and Vicinity], Ira Smith box 4, folder 42, Bentley Historical Library, University of Michigan

that the University of Michigan representative, in conducting the interview, drew a circled *J* next to the names of four students— Melvin Klayman, Robert Rakofsky, Myrtle Calmas, and Esther Finn—two of whom had pluses (admits), and two minuses (rejects).

On the next page [Figure 0.3], the interviewer, possibly Smith himself, tallied up his admits and rejects and then divided them by *P, C,* and *J*: Protestant, Catholic, and Jew.

That these letters served as religious designations is confirmed by what follows the interview sheets: typed spreadsheets analyzing and comparing the number of students admitted and rejected during these interviews (unfortunately, we do not have the analysis for June 1939). An example is the spreadsheet for the potential fall 1935 applicants who were from the New York area [Figure 0.4].

What is telling in these and other such sheets is the way the students are compared. The analysis does not divide them by Jewish, Catholic, Protestant—as the handwritten notes scrawled into the interview sheets do—but simply by "Jewish Applicants" and "Gentile Applicants." What appears quite surprising on closer look is the total number of Jewish to Gentile students interviewed: sixty-four (thirty-four admits and thirty rejects) to eleven (all admits), respectively. In both categories, the results are further divided into whether one, or both, of the applicant's parents were foreign-born.

At least one of Arlene Lazansky's parents was born and raised in the United States; her great-uncle, Judge Edward Lazansky, made a point to Ruthven that Arlene's great-grandfather—his father—immigrated to the United States from Bohemia in 1868 and "was a resident of Brooklyn from the time he came from abroad, and was a successful merchant." Lazansky himself had studied at Columbia Law School before embarking on his prestigious legal career.[10] The judge's letter offered Ruthven a brief, encapsulated assimilationist narrative, stressing the extent to which the Lazansky family had conformed to the American aspirational ideal and had thrived in doing so. Even without direct proof, one suspects that Edward Lazansky understood the actual reason for his great-niece's rejection from Michigan. Indeed, if one thumbs through the sheets in the second folder, one encounters a circled *J* next to the name "Lazansky, Arlene Elise" on the sheet dated Saturday afternoon, April 22, the date she interviewed as a prospective freshman [Figure 0.5].[11]

10. Edward Lazansky to Ruthven, Smith, box 4, folder 42, BHL.

11. "Interview sheet: Saturday Afternoon—April 22," Smith, box 4, folder 43, BHL.

SATURDAY AFTERNOON

April 22

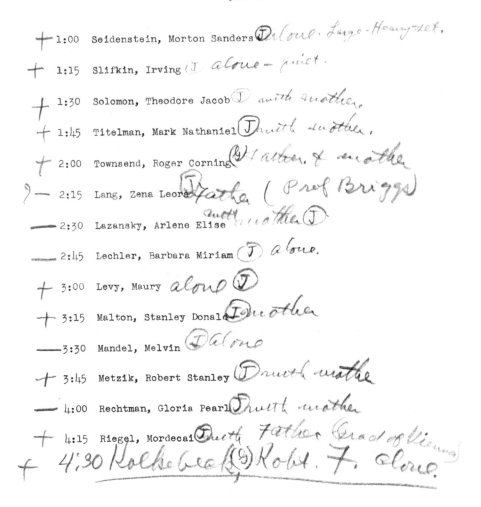

1:00 Seidenstein, Morton Sanders *J alone. Large - Heavy-set.*

1:15 Slifkin, Irving *J alone - quiet.*

1:30 Solomon, Theodore Jacob *J with mother.*

1:45 Titelman, Mark Nathaniel *J with mother.*

2:00 Townsend, Roger Corning *J father & mother*

2:15 Lang, Zena Leora *Father (Prof Briggs)*

2:30 Lazansky, Arlene Elise *with mother J*

2:45 Lechler, Barbara Miriam *J alone.*

3:00 Levy, Maury *alone J*

3:15 Malton, Stanley Donald *J mother*

3:30 Mandel, Melvin *J alone*

3:45 Metzik, Robert Stanley *J with mother*

4:00 Rechtman, Gloria Pearl *J with mother*

4:15 Riegel, Mordecai *J with Father (Grad of Vienna)*

4:30 *Kolhberg J Robt. F. alone.*

Figure 0.5 [Interview Sheet - April 22 (1939)], Ira Smith box 4, folder 43, Bentley Historical Library, University of Michigan

but not debunk. As will be evident in our book, Michigan was, indeed, a university that fostered social and intellectual pluralism. But it was a pluralism that had boundaries which were articulated and solidified in the 1930s. Significantly, the University of Michigan drew the boundary lines for both types of pluralism across one single subset of students: Jews from the East Coast, specifically from the New York and New Jersey area. In the spring of 1935, Alexander Ruthven's administration extended the practice of using personal interviews, which had previously been limited to admissions to the Medical School, to the broader population of East Coast undergraduate applicants.[17] It thus served as a means of defining those boundaries by filtering out students whom the university's admissions officials and policies deemed "undesirable." The Ruthven administration came to regard Jews from the New York and New Jersey region as potential carriers of a particularly noxious intellectual virus—a radical leftism that encompassed those who held either socialist or communist values. These left-wing views, which themselves ran outside the boundaries of pluralism established by Ruthven, became associated with East Coast Jews through the latter's visibility in the radical student organizations on campus in the 1930s: the NSL (1931–35) and its successor organization, the ASU (1936–41).

In effect, the administration defined this subset of Jewish students as outside the boundaries of the University of Michigan's pluralist culture. Through their high visibility as campus leftists, Jews from the East Coast reinforced the already common belief that the NSL and ASU were *Jewish* groups, even though both had numerous Gentile members. This also led to the view that socialism and communism, more broadly, were Jewish phenomena. Leftism, and political radicalism, became associated with East Coast Jewish students, which prompted the Ruthven adminis-

17. On the use of personal interviews for Medical School admissions, see Borst, "Choosing the Student Body." The authors would like to thank Michelle McClellan for providing us with this reference.

tration's efforts to limit their numbers. Other non-radical Jews recognized the risk that campus leftism had for tarnishing *all* Jews and either encouraged moderation or avoided associating with left-wing Jews altogether. Dr. Bernard Heller, director of the Michigan chapter of the Hillel Foundation, wrote worriedly in the *B'nai B'rith Hillel News* that "if one feels that he must be radical, by all means let him be radical. . . . What distresses me, however, is the tendency of these Jewish students to protrude themselves to the leadership or forefront of such groups."[18]

This relegating of a select group of East Coast Jewish students outside the boundaries of pluralism, as demarcated by the Ruthven administration and other organs of institutional life at Michigan, indicated that the university as well as Jewish organizations on campus did not include communist sympathies and socialist tendencies among Jewish students in the larger tenet of accepted cultural pluralism. In his fascinating study, *The Jewish Origins of Cultural Pluralism* (2011), Daniel Greene describes how, at the turn of the century, a group of Jewish students at Harvard University founded the Menorah Society, which sought to articulate a distinct Jewish identity while facilitating Jewish students' assimilation into the broader American culture. One of the Menorah Society's founding members, Horace Kallen, in attempting to resolve this seeming paradox, was the first to advance the idea of cultural pluralism.

As Greene writes, "pluralism emerged alongside two contentious and related debates: a universal debate about the meaning of American identity and a particular debate about the proper expression of Jewish identity within America. First, pluralism rejected the argument that cultural groups had to abandon their cultural particularity in order to become Americans. Second . . . it sought a way to make space for Jews in the United States to articulate a new form of Jewish identity that would allow them to fully enter

---

18. Heller, "Director's Column," *B'nai B'rith Hillel News* (hereafter cited as *BBHN*), April 15, 1935, Hillel News folder, BHL. The name of the Michigan Hillel's newsletter changed during the 1930s. It was variously named *Hillel News* and the *B'nai B'rith Hillel News*.

into American polity and yet still self-identify as Jewish."[19] Applying this framework to the Michigan case, it is clear that in the 1930s Jewish institutions like Hillel sought to promote precisely this type cultural pluralism, whereas the left-wing NSL and ASU ultimately undermined, or were seen to undermine, such efforts because they enabled non-Jews to associate Jews with political radicalism, making them, in some sense, unassimilable.

Among other features delineating the presence of Jewish students at the University of Michigan in the five decades framing this study, our book seeks to explain how left-wing East Coast Jewish students found themselves at risk for being outside the Ruthven administration's boundaries of pluralism. By focusing on boundaries, we hope to avoid some obvious pitfalls and accrue some methodological advantages in the telling of our story. For one, we seek to avoid the easy assumption that President Ruthven and his administration acted because of antisemitism when they filtered East Coast Jewish students out of the university. Such a charge is easy to make, given that antisemitism was generally recognized as an "acceptable" prejudice at this time, but the historical record does not bear this out. Ruthven, indeed, was an ardent and passionate advocate for Hillel, remained on largely good terms with its directors, and sought to incorporate this organization, and Jews more generally, into his vision of a religiously pluralistic university community. Such a vision exacted an ecumenical approach to religion in which Judaism was accorded pride of place and which Ruthven viewed as an essential ingredient for a complete education. Nor will it do to say that Ruthven sought merely to silence or eliminate radical student activity on the Michigan campus. He actually tolerated a considerable degree of radical agitation until a combination of factors compelled him to move against student radicals. Nor, frankly, can it be said that those who applied pressure on Ruthven—such as former football coach and Board of Regents member Harry Kipke—were neces-

---

19. Greene, *Jewish Origins*, 7.

sarily antisemitic although some, like the notorious pamphleteer Elizabeth Dilling and Kipke's patron, the automobile magnate Henry Ford, clearly were. Still, Ruthven and his administration targeted a specific group—East Coast Jews—and caused qualified students like Arlene Lazansky to master additional hurdles that had nothing to do with the applicant's academic qualification to gain admittance to the University of Michigan. But worse still, the Ruthven-led administration also dismissed enrolled students from the university, even when they were in good academic standing, and provided only the most meager and arbitrary grounds for such drastic actions.

East Coast Jews were not, of course, the only student population that found itself outside "the bounds of pluralism." Recent research conducted by Tyran Kai Steward has also revealed the ways in which African American students were "at but not of the university."[20] Stewart painstakingly details the university's long-standing policy, especially under Michigan's legendary football coach and athletic director Fielding Yost, of restricting African American participation to specific sports from the early 1900s to the mid-1920s. As he writes, "at Michigan, lodging restrictions, institutionalized racial quotas, and racist ridicule from professors in the classroom, among other forms of racial prejudice, stood as salient reminders to the school's black population of the gulf between their integration into a northern white institution and their attainment of full equality. Inclusion had its limits."[21] Although Jewish students by and large did not suffer from open hostility and ridicule to the same extent that African American students did, they too experienced discrimination in the form of being barred from Gentile fraternities and sororities and the use of admissions quotas—well established at the Medical School—that blocked the aspirations of students like Arlene Lazansky. Their

20. Steward, "At the University," 35–70. The phrase comes from Behee, *Hail to the Victors!*

21. Steward, "At the University," 36.

effects of the Great Depression and endured budget cuts that led to reductions in faculty salaries and a severe tightening of support for working-class students.[25] Ruthven was at the mercy of conservative state legislators who looked with dismay at the rising tide of campus radicalism that was sweeping the country, from City College of New York (CCNY) to the University of California, Los Angeles (UCLA), not sparing the University of Michigan, from 1933 onward.[26] He also found himself under pressure from the aforementioned right-wing ideologue Dilling and Henry Ford's operative Bennett as well as conservative regents who saw Ruthven's pluralism as too permissive. They demanded that Ruthven crack down on those who espoused radical sentiments and policies that Dilling, Bennett, and conservatives regarded as politically dangerous and incompatible with their views of what the University of Michigan ought to represent. Targeting East Coast Jews by either filtering them out while they were still applicants or removing them once they were enrolled students offered Ruthven and the university administration a relatively simple way of placating a suspicious and often vociferous Right that was a priori hostile to public and higher education especially when socialist and communist tendencies were articulated in its institutions, as was clearly the case on the University of Michigan's Ann Arbor campus. As much as our book is about what these Jewish students said and did, then, it is even more about how their gentile environment perceived them.

Our goal is that this book make several contributions to the literature both on the University of Michigan itself and on Jewish students in particular. The current official university history, Margaret and Nicholas Steneck's early 1990s update of Howard Peckham's *The Making of the University of Michigan* (originally published in 1967), treats the activities of the NSL and ASU, as well

25. Peckham, Steneck, and Steneck, *Making*, 198.
26. The most comprehensive treatment of the student movement of the 1930s remains Cohen, *When the Old Left Was Young*.

as Ruthven's dismissal of its members, rather cursorily and fails to account for the predominant number of Jews in the dismissals of 1935 and 1940 and in the interview practices of 1935–39.[27] The only full-length study of President Ruthven and his administration, Peter E. Van de Water's *Alexander Grant Ruthven of Michigan: Biography of a University President* (1977), is more careful and thorough in its discussion of Ruthven's crackdown on student radicals in the 1930s. But, because the author based his analysis both on archival research and on interviews with the aging emeritus president, he is generally sympathetic to Ruthven's interpretation of these events and also misses the Jewish dimension to the story.[28]

More recently, the history of the Michigan chapters of the NSL and the ASU, and President Ruthven's actions against them, have been fleshed out by honors theses from Michigan's Department of History. LaLonde's excellent 1991 thesis, "Student Activism and the Student Newspaper: The University of Michigan in the 1930s," recounts the histories of the NSL and ASU in much greater detail than does Van de Water. But LaLonde's thesis also fails to account for the fact that many of the dismissed students were Jewish and ultimately devotes more space to Ruthven's struggles pertaining to control over the student newspaper, the *Michigan Daily*, than the dismissals or the two political groups. Susan Horowitz's 2005 thesis, "Peace, Protests, and Parties: The Radical Student Movement against War and Fascism in America, 1933–1939," focuses largely on the anti-fascist dimensions of the movement and the development of students' anti-fascist views.[29] Indeed, given the frequent association by right-wing critics of Jews to communism and socialism, it is quite surprising how little is made of this in the

---

27. Peckham, Steneck, and Steneck, *Making*, 215–16, 222.

28. Van de Water, *Alexander Grant Ruthven*. Van de Water's book, published six years after Ruthven's death, is more critical of the president than his dissertation, which he defended when his subject was still alive. See especially Van de Water's comments in *Alexander Grant Ruthven*, 154.

29. LaLonde, "Student Activism"; and Horowitz, "Peace, Protests, and Parties."

historical literature on the 1930s student movement.[30] Cultural histories of the Left in the 1930s make passing mention of the role of Jewish students in fostering leftist campus movements. Two of the most notable among them are Robert Cohen's *When the Old Left Was Young: Student Radicals and America's First Mass Student Movement, 1929–1941* (1993) and Ellen W. Schrecker's *No Ivory Tower: McCarthyism and the Universities* (1986). Neither of these works, however, focus either on Jews or the University of Michigan.[31]

Still, some scholars have attempted to challenge Michigan's vaunted pluralist reputation. We previously mentioned Steward's investigations into African American students at the university and how these students faced a northern version of Jim Crow in Ann Arbor.[32] With respect to Jews, it has been well established that the university's Medical School restricted the number of incoming Jewish students beginning in the 1920s. Even Hollinger concedes that the Law School accepted a large donation from the notorious antisemite William W. Cook.[33] Yet, as these were professional schools, their actions did not manifestly challenge Michigan's overall pluralistic narrative. Although Gongora's work remains conjectural, his senior thesis certainly refers to an indirect quota system but ties it mainly to the university's selective admissions policy, which had been an ongoing project since the early 1920s.

By moving the frame to the 1930s and the presidency of Alexan-

---

30. See, e.g., Kaplan's 2011 senior thesis, "A Forgotten History." The absence goes in both directions: Jospe's classic article on "Jewish College Students in the United States" recounts the development of Jewish student organizations but does not mentions Jewish students' roles in left-wing political organizations. See Jospe, "Jewish College Students," 131–45.

31. Schrecker, *No Ivory Tower*.

32. See Steward's dissertation, "In the Shadow"; and Steward, "At the University."

33. For the Medical School, see Borst, "Choosing the Student Body"; and Davenport, *Not Just Any Medical School*. On the Cook donation, see Hollinger, "Academic Culture," 91.

der Grant Ruthven, we contend that a much richer story emerges. Although Ruthven was a conservative, he had a vision of building a pluralist university community through the creation of different spheres of interfaith dialogue and faculty-student interaction. Ruthven was a scientist by training and not particularly religious. Yet, as his biographer, Peter Van de Water, asserts, "his rejection of dogma, mysticism, and blind faith, his optimistic belief in the worth of the individual and humanity, and his endorsement of the methods of science showed his religious attitudes more nearly akin to Universalism than [his native] Methodism. . . . It was these somewhat liberal attitudes, tempered by traditional ethical standards that Ruthven sought to impose on the Michigan students of the thirties."[34] As part of his vision to create a pluralist campus community, Ruthven cultivated Hillel, even going so far as to solicit funds for it personally in the dark days of the Depression. Ruthven saw Jews as integral to the realization of his vision of a great university's educational mission.

But the Depression had the effect of politicizing parts of the student body. The Spring Parleys, which the Office of Religious Education, a Ruthven creation, organized near the end of every school year to foster a structured dialogue between faculty and students, moved away from its more philosophical origins toward an active engagement with the more hot-button issues of the time such as labor conflict, socialism and communism, the civil war in Spain, and sex education, to mention some prominent topics. Groups like the NSL staged events that called into question Ruthven's stewardship of the university among some conservatives. Ruthven's desire to foster a pluralist university community in both senses of the term—in which all types of students and opinions were tolerated, if not always welcomed—risked damaging his legitimacy. Either Ruthven had to abandon his pluralist initiatives or pinpoint and eliminate the source of his headaches or some combination of both. Hence, Jews from the East Coast/

34. Van de Water, *Alexander Grant Ruthven*, 126.

Michigan faculty, for appointing a delegation to attend the 550th anniversary of Heidelberg University in Nazi Germany in 1936. Secondly, his administration rebuffed an appeal for a one-hour closure of the university in the wake of *Kristallnacht* in November 1938. More important, it was during this time that the university's practice of interviewing almost exclusively East Coast Jewish applicants continued apace. While Jewish organizations like Hillel and ZBT were unaffected by these developments, the ambiguity of the university's relationship to its Jewish students was one of the characteristics of this era.

Chapter 6 moves beyond the direct involvement with Ruthven and Jewish students to consider some of the larger forces that were shaping university policy. Specifically, by the late 1930s, the university was facing an increasingly right-leaning political environment with the defeat of the Democratic Michigan governor Frank Murphy in 1938 and the hardening conservatism among the Right as typified by the beginning of the Dies Committee's investigations into "un-American activities." Closer to home, former football coach Harry Kipke was elected to the Board of Regents for an appointment beginning January 1, 1940. Kipke's close friend was Harry Bennett, the head of Ford's Service Department, dispenser of Ford patronage (i.e., jobs and commissions), Ford's disciplinarian on the shop floor, and leader of his own private police and spy network. Many right-wingers believed that Michigan harbored "anti-American" elements, and Bennett sent the notorious antisemite Elizabeth Dilling to "investigate" the campus. Ruthven, then, found himself in a hostile climate with Kipke on the board and Bennett and Dilling seeking to paint the university as a redoubt of radicalism. We contend that it was this "rightward drift" that influenced the president's decision to dismiss another, larger, round of students in 1940, the majority of them Jewish.

Our seventh and final chapter profiles the controversy surrounding the dismissal of, initially, seventeen students from the university in June of 1940. While some of these students were allowed to return with a warning, the majority of those who were not permitted to return were Jewish students from the East Coast. Unlike in 1935, there was a much more concerted effort on the part of left-wing groups to challenge the president's arbitrary decision to remove students, most of whom were in good academic standing. A Michigan Committee of Academic Freedom (MCAF) was formed largely under the auspices of the Civil Rights Federation in Detroit, which worked with both the national office and Michigan chapter of the ASU. Although some non-Jewish students as well were affected by the university's measures, there were suspicions that the university had acted out of resentment toward East Coast Jewish radicals. Evidence exists that President Ruthven received from Harry Kipke secret reports from Bennett about radical students, and that these reports insistently highlighted that these students were Jewish or black. When the Board of Regents refused to reconsider Ruthven's decision, the MCAF attempted to organize a nationwide response by hosting an "open trial" of the dismissed students. This, however, failed to generate more than a transitory interest in the students' case, and the university barred the Michigan chapter of the ASU from campus soon thereafter. By 1940, the boundaries of pluralism were well entrenched: Jews were welcome on campus as long as they were the *right* kind of Jews (non–East Coast/non–left-wing). Again, while the main bodies of Jewish student life (Hillel/ZBT) were largely unaffected by these events, nevertheless the university— responding to pressure from the Right—ensured that a specific subset of Jewish student was not to be tolerated on campus.

While our story attempts to paint a compelling portrait of Jewish student life on the University of Michigan campus, it is equally concerned with the university's relationship to its Jewish students. Again, we are not claiming that Ruthven was himself antisemitic or that his administration followed an antisemitic policy. Indeed, for the vast majority of Jewish students, Michigan truly offered a space of tolerance and belonging. However, in his administration's interactions with radical Jewish students, Ruthven's otherwise commendable (for the era) policy of pluralism—designed to

throughout the 1850s and 1860s by expanding their tannery business to New York and Chicago, to which the Ann Arbor–based family members departed leaving Ann Arbor with no Jews as of the late 1860s.[3] In 1895, William Lansky and his family arrived in Ann Arbor. The Lanskys owned a junkyard and were soon joined by the Levys, who were shoemakers. Most important was the arrival at this time of Osias Zwerdling, who came to work for Mack and Co. furriers and was to become a leading furrier himself and, significantly, the patron of arguably Ann Arbor's most important Jewish family for the ensuing decades well into the 1960s. There were very few Jews in Ann Arbor at the turn of the twentieth century.

The beginning of the twentieth century saw a growth of Jews in the United States almost exclusively by dint of massive emigration of Jews mainly from Russia and Eastern Europe. While most of these immigrants settled in large cities mainly on the East Coast, some, of course, made their new homes in small towns all across the United States, Ann Arbor included. The 1920 census recorded a population of 19,500 in Ann Arbor, with approximately 300 as identifiably Jewish. During the 1920s, the Jewish population in Ann Arbor dropped by half, and it did not reach 300 again until the 1950s.[4] It is important to understand that throughout this entire period, Ann Arbor's Jewish population had virtually nothing to do with the University of Michigan. Moreover, in contrast to the current situation, which commenced heavily in the late 1960s, most Jews living in Ann Arbor at this time did not pursue any intellectual professions nor were they wealthy. They were neither lawyers nor doctors. Instead, they were typically members of the petite bourgeoisie by owning shops and small businesses of various kinds. However, there lived three Jews in town who represented what at the time was an exception: Jewish university professors.

3. There have been consistent rumors to this day that the reason for the Jews' absence in Ann Arbor at this time was a pogrom. Neither Helen Aminoff nor Richard and Ruth Adler in *Jewish Ann Arbor* found any evidence for this alleged occurrence.

4. Adler and Adler, *Jewish Ann Arbor*, 33.

Most American universities in the nineteenth century, the University of Michigan among them, had few if any Jewish faculty. But in the 1890s, "at least three Jewish scholars joined the faculty; each would play a significant role in the development of the institution in the new century."[5] They were Max Winkler, who was appointed assistant professor of German in 1895 and promoted to full professor in 1902 as well as department chair, a position he held until his death; Moritz Levi, who joined the faculty in 1890 as an instructor in French earning the title of professor emeritus in that field by the time he retired in 1923; and possibly the most prominent among them, Moses Gomberg, a native of Elizabethgrad in Russia and a graduate of the University of Michigan in 1890 as well as holder of this university's doctorate in chemistry, which he attained in 1894. In 1904, Gomberg achieved the rank of full professor with his research and publications reaching over a wide array of chemistry.[6]

Indeed, growth in the number of Jewish students and their campus organizations, and student-centered organizations more generally, occurred at the same time that the University of Michigan was undergoing significant transformation. As Christopher Lucas points out in his history of American higher education, the 1910s were the pivotal decade for the entrance of Jews into American universities: "Jewish students . . . were first admitted in large numbers in the second decade of the new century. Their arrival occasioned considerable controversy at some institutions; and in the wake of nativist prejudice that swept the country immediately after World War I, anti-Semitism became a conspicuous feature of the collegiate landscape."[7]

Under the long presidency of James Burrill Angell from 1871 until 1909, the University of Michigan's total student enrollment increased nearly fivefold, from 1,100 at the start

5. Adler and Adler, *Jewish Ann Arbor*, 22.

6. Adler and Adler, *Jewish Ann Arbor*, 22–24.

7. Lucas, *American Higher Education*, 213. See also Zeitlin, "Jewish Learning," 582–616.

of his term to over 5,300 by 1910, making it "the third rank-
ing university in size, surpassed by Columbia and Chicago."[8]
To accommodate the increasing numbers, the Angell administration introduced important changes that gave the university
the foundations for its modern organizational structure. As
the university's official history states, "the traditional 'departments' were reorganized as 'colleges' under deans with growing
autonomy. Similar courses of study were grouped into subject
departments under chairmen."[9] In 1890, graduate education
was first organized as a separate department within the Literary College.[10] The very next year, the Angell-led institution
created Michigan's first four-year medical school program and
within a few years an engineering department was introduced
to campus as well.[11]

These and similar changes both reflected the university's
growing national stature and also represented a continuation of
the goals set out by its first president, Henry P. Tappan (1852–
63), who had sought to make Michigan into a major research
institution. As much as Angell introduced important institutional
changes, his administration was marked, especially in its latter
years, by the wholesale development of student life. According to
the University of Michigan's official history, "From 1891 to 1909
was the period not only of intercollegiate athletic growth, but
of the proliferation of sororities and fraternities, the Michigan
Union movement, the establishment of various honor societies,
the rise of student publications, and the organization of music
and dramatics."[12] Although student activities and clubs existed
before the turn of the century, it is important to appreciate not

8. Peckham, Steneck, and Steneck, *Making*, 127.

9. Peckham, Steneck, and Steneck, *Making*, 99.

10. Peckham, Steneck, and Steneck, *Making*, 102.

11. Under Angell, engineering education was housed in the West Engineering Building, completed in 1904, which to this day remains a key feature of campus as the
gateway to the Diag.

12. Peckham, Steneck, and Steneck, *Making*, 117.

only their astonishing growth at this time but also how quickly they became embedded within both the university administration and in the broader campus culture. There were various kinds of games as early as 1870 with some precursors reaching into the 1860s. Football, which saw the Wolverines play their first intercollegiate game in 1879, was brought under university administrative control formally with the creation of the Board in Control of Athletics in 1894 by the University Senate.[13] The senate also put the student newspaper, the *Michigan Daily*, founded in 1890, under the control of a Board in Control of Student Publications in 1904.[14] Administrative oversight was twofold: on the one hand, it aimed to regulate the activities of these groups; on the other, it offered de facto, official recognition of their place in campus life.

Growing numbers of sororities and fraternities also meant

13. Peckham, Steneck, and Steneck, *Making*, 107. Two years later, Michigan would be one of the founding members of the Intercollegiate Conference of Faculty Representatives, later known as the Western Conference and ultimately the Big Ten Conference. The Board's name changed to the Board in Control of Intercollegiate Athletics during the spring of 1926. Earlier that year a faculty committee headed by Edmund Day, Dean of the School of Business Administration, was formed both to consider the construction of a new football stadium and to evaluate the role of intercollegiate sports at Michigan more generally. The Day report both endorsed the construction of a new stadium—a long-held goal of the university's athletic director Fielding Yost—and affirmed the importance of intercollegiate athletics at the university. However, the Day committee also recommended reconstituting the Board of Control with more faculty representatives in order to wrest it from Yost's iron grip. In effect, the price for Yost getting his stadium was to lose his control over the Board—at least formally. Although the authors could not identify the precise date of the name change, the first appearance in the *Michigan Daily* of the name "Board in Control of Intercollegiate Athletics" was on April 23, 1926—the very day that the newspaper announced the Regents' approval of the new stadium. The same article mentions that the new, reconstituted board would go into office on May 1. It is therefore probable that the name change occurred as a result of the university's decision to follow the Day committee's recommendations to affirm intercollegiate athletics and to reconstitute the Board in Control. See "Stadium Approved: Regents Authorize Building of New Football Structure, Leaving Details to Board," *MD*, April 23. 1926. For more on the Day committee and its recommendations on intercollegiate athletics and the Board in Control, see Soderstrom, *The Big House*, 261-279.

14. Peckham, Steneck, and Steneck, *Making*, 118.

by undergoing a massive building program that included the Law Quadrangle and new dormitories. Its administration also introduced measures to raise the University of Michigan's academic standards. Yet the increasing numbers of students—total enrollment surpassed 10,000 by the 1923–24 academic year—were not only intensifying long-term problems such as housing but were also producing seismic changes in the broader campus culture. As the University of Michigan's official history describes, "these were the years that fraternities boomed. Local clubs and fraternities were quickly formed and after a year of satisfactory existence usually sought national affiliation. By the end of 1924, Michigan had sixty national and local social fraternities, twenty-one professional fraternities, and twenty-two sororities. They claimed about 32 percent of the men students, and about 22 percent of the women students."[28] These produced exponential changes in the university's social life—more organizations meant more activities, such as dances and mixers—including the full blossoming of football culture as Michigan Stadium was completed and inaugurated in 1927. Michigan's long-serving coach, the legendary Fielding Yost, cultivated such players as Harry Kipke, who later became the Wolverines' coach and then a regent; Bennie Oosterban; and Benny Friedman, the team's first Jewish quarterback.

There were, of course, downsides to the increase in both enrollment and fraternities. Among them were hazing rituals, drunkenness, and public misbehavior, including vandalism of two Ann Arbor cinema houses after a victorious football game.[29] In addition, many students struggled to find adequate housing and part-time jobs to meet their expenses. Burton's untimely death in 1925 meant that these problems were inherited by his successor, Clarence C. Little, who had previously served as president of the University of Maine and as an assistant dean at Harvard, where he had earned three degrees. Little had broad sympathy

28. Peckham, Steneck, and Steneck, *Making*, 168.
29. Peckham, Steneck, and Steneck, *Making*, 171.

for the plight of poorer students who struggled to find housing and earn money and advocated both the building of dormitories and increasing scholarship opportunities.[30] Unlike his predecessor, however, he had little patience for the fraternity culture and quickly banned liquor and excessive hazing rituals in the fraternities.[31] Moreover, President Little wanted to change the admissions policy to go beyond academic proficiency and to include questions about an applicant's character. In his view, "a real and lasting education cannot be obtained by an individual whose character and personality are not worth educating."[32]

However, Little's belief in the importance of character assessment for an effective admissions policy was most likely not a product of his disdain for fraternities. During the 1920s, many American higher education institutions, especially the elite universities on the East Coast, began to introduce selective admissions policies to limit their numbers of Jewish students. Although Jews had been admitted to these universities in the past, including during and after the First World War, their increasing numbers at these institutions began to appear problematic to university administrators. Researchers have long seen the 1910s and 1920s as a pivotal shift in Americans' view of Jews.[33] The influx of Eastern European Jews "aroused distaste among native Americans from the moment they landed."[34] Jews whose families had already assimilated found themselves increasingly the victims of antisemitic prejudice at summering places and social organizations like the masons. More pertinent, elite eastern universities experienced an influx of Jewish students who sought to demonstrate their academic prowess. The extant fraternities and sororities refused to admit Jews into their ranks, leading to the creation

---

30. Peckham, Steneck, and Steneck, *Making*, 185.
31. Peckham, Steneck, and Steneck, *Making*, 188–89.
32. Peckham, Steneck, and Steneck, *Making*, 186.
33. Higham, "Social Discrimination," 1–22; and Wechsler, *Qualified Student*.
34. Higham, "Social Discrimination," 14.

the B'nai B'rith Foundation severely curtailed, thus threatening Hillel's very existence. Like the JSC and ZBT, Hillel functioned primarily as an *integrative* body: fostering its members' sense of their Jewish identity while, at the same time, providing them with a space for socializing and a means of integrating into the broader campus culture. As presented in detail in the next chapter, Hillel had come to play a central role in Ruthven's vision of an ecumenical campus in which the fostering of the Jewish religion assumed pride of place.

Here, however, we will deal with Jewish student life at Michigan in the pre-Ruthven period. In particular, we aim to provide clear documentation of Jewish students' presence in the late nineteenth century and the first two decades of the twentieth century, both of which preceded any meaningful organized Jewish life on the University of Michigan's campus. One key piece in Ruthven's correspondence surrounding his attempts to raise funds for the beleaguered Hillel Foundation featured Henry Wollman, an eminent lawyer in New York and senior partner of Wollman & Wollman, a respected Wall Street firm. Wollman received his law degree from Michigan in 1878. Ruthven's correspondents also included Captain Charles E. Riegelman, class of 1899, who at this juncture was the president of Michigan's New York Alumni Association, and Moritz Rosenthal, a member of the banking firm of Ladenburg, Thalman & Company who, prior to his successful banking career, "stood extremely high as a lawyer when he practiced at the bar in Chicago."[42] Moritz Rosenthal had been graduated from Michigan in 1888.

In Ruthven's attempt to constitute a Committee on Jewish Religious Programs, Ruthven intended to go beyond the immediate issue of Hillel's very survival and furnish a structure to advise him on matters relating to integrating Jewish life on campus. We found a memo from the Bureau of Alumni Relations dated Feb-

---

42. Letter from Henry Wollman to Alexander Ruthven, January 11, 1933, Alexander Ruthven Papers (hereafter cited as Ruthven), box 7, folder 27, BHL.

ruary 14, 1933, in which Ruthven clearly requested the names of prominent Jewish alumni in a number of locations across the country. In addition to Wollman, Riegelman, and Rosenthal, the New York contingent also included Hilton Livingston, class of 1901, and a much younger Valentine Davies, who had just been graduated in 1927. The Detroit group featured Henry M. Butzel, class of 1891 and 1892 Law School; his younger brother Leo, class of 1894 and 1896 Law School; the famous Michigan football player Joe Magidsohn, class of 1910; Mrs. William Brown, class of 1906; and Leo I. Franklin, class of 1924, Law School in 1926, son of the legendary Rabbi Leo M. Franklin, whom Ruthven had contacted in this endeavor and who played a crucial role in assisting the president by, among others, inviting Ruthven to address the rabbi's Detroit congregation. The Sonnenschein brothers, Hugo and Edward, were Chicago's only representatives on this list, Hugo having been graduated in 1905 and receiving his law degree two years later, and Edward belonging to the class of 1904. David E. Heineman from Leland, Michigan, received his bachelor's degree in 1887 and was bestowed an honorary degree in 1912.

Thus, there exists clear evidence that individual Jews attended the University of Michigan in the latter part of the nineteenth century and made their education there the stepping-stone for solid, even prominent, careers in law and business in cities such as New York, Detroit, and Chicago. Interesting, too, is the presence of two women among this group. Ruthven's list provides the only known definitive document specifying the presence of actual Jews on campus. Along with Ruthven's list, we found information on the overall Jewish student body at the University of Michigan compiled in 1940 by the Student Religious Association (SRA):

> It is rather a well-known fact that the Jewish population in America is mainly in the East and in large cities. From University figures and figures compiled by the Bureau this condition is reflected in the campus enrollment, with a bulk of the Jewish students coming from outside the State of Michigan and three quarters from cit-

ies over 100,000. While 14% of the student body went home on a particular weekend last year, only 7% of the Jewish students went home. It is reported that the Jews represent 3.5% of the total population of the U.S. and only 1.99% of the State of Michigan. The Research Bureau of the B'nai B'rith Hillel Foundations reports that in colleges [of] over 5000 enrollment in the U.S. and Canada the average Jewish enrollment is 21% of student bodies and 9.13% for all institutions of higher learning. This condition seems to exist to a lesser degree at the University of Michigan, with approximately a 10% Jewish enrollment reported by the University."[43]

Rather than merely featuring individual examples of prominent students or reporting on only the demographics of Jewish students, we needed a more systematic approach to uncovering the extent to which Jews were present on the University of Michigan campus in the late nineteenth and early twentieth centuries.

This chapter proposes to do just that. We embarked on an attempt to determine which students on the Michigan campus were Jewish. To complicate matters, we also wanted to evaluate the scope and range of their social lives on campus thereby trying to gauge whether these Jewish students were integrated into the social life of the campus and if so, how and to what extent this was the case. Thus, to attain this information in the absence of extant student records, which have not been preserved, and the lack of admissions reports that classified the student population by religious affiliation (for which extant copies do not begin in essence until the 1930s), we undertook a survey of the university's yearbooks, the *Michiganensian*, from its earliest year in 1897 until 1923, by which time we have more sources that assess the extent of Jewish students, and their integration, on campus.

For each year, we surveyed the list of graduating students and

43. James Vicary, "A Survey of the Relations of Jewish and Gentile Students at the University of Michigan" (1940), 3 (hereafter cited as "Survey"), Student Religious Association (hereafter cited as SRA), box 8, BHL.

sought to determine, based on their family name, whether it was more likely than not that they were Jewish. This method is, by its nature, imprecise, especially as Jewish identity is traditionally passed through the maternal line. Nonetheless, as we will describe in the methodology section below, utilizing specific techniques, including onomastics—the study of the origins of family names—as well as statistical analysis, we located a range of probability for the number of Jews on campus in the early twentieth century. Thus, our conclusions are predicated on a determination that a specific surname was, in fact, more likely to be Jewish than not.

In addition, for each student that we identified as likely Jewish, we also collected information on their society affiliations—which the yearbooks provided—to surmise the extent to which Jews were integrated within the broader campus community. Thus, we sought not only to determine the extent to which Jewish students were represented as a percentage of the university population but also to provide some sense of the quality of their presence on campus as a distinct group. By this method, we hoped to gauge the Jewish students' integration on the University of Michigan campus.

Here are some baseline characteristics of those students whom we ultimately determined to be Jewish and thus important for our larger study. By our calculations, 5.694% of students graduating from the University of Michigan from 1897 to 1923 were Jewish. Of those students, 58.92% were involved in some extracurricular or social activity outside of their studies. At the outset of our study, we assumed the Jewish enrollment at the University of Michigan to be in the 5%–7% range. Moreover, we also assumed that a good portion of these students participated in extracurricular activities, bespeaking a relatively integrated on-campus existence on the part of these Jewish students. We are pleased that our assumptions were largely confirmed by data that we collected for this study. Let us now proceed to delineate our methodology.

The determination of whether a particular student was possibly, or likely, Jewish was problematic. Until the 1930s, there are no extant records which show that the university administration registered or tracked students by ethnic or religious affiliation. Thus, we needed to devise a method for determining likely Jewish identity among all university graduates. We began with an online list of Jewish surnames obtained from the Avotaynu website, which bills itself as "the leading publisher of products of interest to persons who are researching Jewish genealogy, Jewish family trees, or Jewish roots" including selling "books about Jewish surnames."[45] Given Avotaynu's position in the field of Jewish genealogy (it has published a journal on Jewish names and family trees for the last thirty-three years as well as seventy-five books on the topic since 1991), the list of surnames can be considered both comprehensive and reliable as a guide for determining Jewish ethnicity or affiliation.

We then compared the surname of every University of Michigan graduating senior from 1897 to 1923 against Avotaynu's list. We contained Avotaynu's list within a single Microsoft Word document and utilized the Search in Document function to compare names found in the *Michiganensian* to those on the list of Jewish surnames. All surnames entered into the Search in Document bar that had results that either matched exactly with, or had a close derivation to, the name included on Avotaynu's list were recorded in Microsoft Excel. Close derivation refers to names such as Zimmerman (Zimmermann was on Avotaynu's list) and Heineman (Heinemann). In this sense, our process of culling names from *Michiganensian* yearbooks was completely inclusive, excepting names that are historically non-Jewish.[46] Jews at this time gener-

45. See http://www.avotaynu.com for more resources on Jewish genealogies.

46. Names excluded from the search on the surnames document were those beginning with Mc, Mac, or Van, such as McDonald, MacAulay, or Van Dijk, which are historically, Irish, Scottish, or Dutch, not Jewish. Although it cannot be universally accepted that there are no Irish, Scottish, or Dutch people that are also Jewish, it is highly unlikely that any were Jewish, so they were excluded from consideration.

ally did not marry outside of their faith or ethnic group. Given the prevalence of endogenous marriage within Jewish communities in the early twentieth century, we felt reasonably confident to exclude evidently non-Jewish surnames from consideration. The inclusivity of this process is important to note because of its ability to include as many potentially Jewish students as possible, allowing for the assimilation of Jews into American society. Because we included nearly all students in the search for Jewish students, even those strongly assimilated had a chance to be found and included in this study.

After we collected and recorded the initial group of names for each year, we decided that a further level of specificity was necessary to differentiate between three groups: those students who were rather unlikely to be Jewish, although we collected their names based on Avotaynu's list; those who were somewhat likely to be Jewish; and those who were almost certainly Jewish. Given that our aim was to elucidate the quality of Jewish students' lives and the extent of their social assimilation on the University of Michigan campus, we found it necessary to produce this hierarchy to narrow our initial population into more distinct groups of having a *less likely*, *likely*, or *highly likely* Jewish affiliation. That is, to provide a holistic picture of Jewish student life on campus, we first needed to find those students who were highly likely to be Jewish. Speculation on the lives of students that were in fact not Jewish would lead to conclusions that were not representative of Jewish life, which was not our goal.

To differentiate further among students contained within the Excel spreadsheets, we consulted several sources within a specialized field that studies the development and origins of words and proper names: onomastics.[47] Then we availed ourselves of published scholarship in the subfield of Jewish onomastics, or

47. The Merriam-Webster definition of *onomastics* is in part: "1 (b): the science or study of the origin and forms of proper names of persons or places," https://www.merriam-webster.com/dictionary/onomastics.

the study of the origins and development of Jewish proper names and surnames.[48] The two most influential sources in this endeavor proved to be Edwin D. Lawson, Emeritus Professor of Psychology at SUNY Fredonia, the premier expert in the field of Jewish onomastics, and the late Benzion C. Kaganoff, a rabbi from Chicago who devoted much of his life to the study of Jewish surnames and their changes, particularly in America. Kaganoff and Lawson shaped much of the literature concerning the assimilation of Jews into American society and the changes found within Jewish surnames as families entered the United States.

Other pieces inspired by Lawson's work that also had an impact on our understanding of onomastics and the issues surrounding Jewish names more generally came from a series of volumes on Jewish onomastics entitled *These are the Names: Studies in Jewish Onomastics*, that were published papers from a conference at Bar-Ilan University in Ramat Gan, Israel.[49] Harvey E. Goldberg's "Names in Their Social Contexts: An Anthropological Perspective" provides an understanding of Jewish names in the United States and Israel from a basis in the social context of each nation. Goldberg argues that the composition of Jews' names in different cultures often varies to fit the social construct of each culture, a clear signal of the use of changing names as a part of Jewish assimilation into American culture.[50] Similarly, and more thoroughly, Stanley Lieberson's "Jewish Names and the Names of Jews" discusses how Jewish naming practices reflect the political, social, religious, and economic situations in each Jew's country of residence.[51] Lieberson cites a rapid shift in the preferences of given names and surnames from the grandparent to the parent to the child in a three-generation path that Jews often used to assimilate into various cultures with the aid of changing names.[52]

---

48. These sources included Gorr, *Jewish Personal Names*; Kaganoff, *Dictionary of Jewish Names*; Hook, *Family Names*; as well as Jewish onomastics expert Professor Ed Lawson from the State University of New York at Fredonia.

49. See Demsky, et al, eds. *These are the Names.*

50. Goldberg, "Names in Their Social Contexts."

51. Lieberson, "Jewish Names," 155.

52. Lieberson cites an array of names that Jewish men often used to help assimilate

After careful study of the major works in the field of Jewish onomastics and personal communication with Lawson, we recognized the enormous difficulty of pinpointing the precise nature of an individual's Jewishness with only their name (surname and given). The impeding factors include the fluid nature of Jewish immigrant surnames in America, Jewishness being passed from generation to generation through matrilineage in a patriarchal society that almost always gave children the father's surname, and the relative popularity of many Jewish first names—particularly of Biblical origin—in broader American culture. Due to these difficulties, we decided, with Lawson's generous help, to devise a scale by which to rate students on their likelihood of being Jewish—determined by not only their first and last names but also their hometown and extracurricular activities.

The scale we devised for this purpose—which we have come to call the "Lawson scale" as a token homage to our gratitude for Lawson's support of our work—places students at one of three levels in a "1, 2, 3 decision making process": (1) the student is less than 50% likely to be Jewish and therefore is not under consideration as part of the Jewish community during this study; (2) the student is greater than 50% likely to be of Jewish heritage but less than 85%–90% likely (i.e., more likely than not the student is Jewish, but one cannot be totally certain on the determination so the inclusion of 2 rated students in the study's understanding of Jewish life is one of probability rather than certainty); and (3) the student is 90%–95% likely to be Jewish and would be considered certainly or nearly certainly Jewish by her or his environment. After consulting with Kaganoff's publication and Lawson's understanding of Jewish names, we fully understand that there is no way to be 100% certain of a student's Jewish identity with-

into American society, often first names that were American in nature but were so prevalently used to assimilate that they became known as Jewish names: Ira, Irving, Marvin, Morton, Stanley, and Seymour. Although these names do not encompass all of the names that Jews used to help assimilate into American society, they joined distinctly Jewish names such as Moses, Solomon, and Isaac to help provide an understanding of who was Jewish by name outside of surnames.

Table 1.B: All Students Collected to Total Number of Graduates, 1897-1923

All Students Collected to Total Number of Graduates, 1897–1923			
Graduating Year	Jewish Seniors	Total Seniors	% of Jews to Total
1897	41	291	14.08934708
1898	81	497	16.29778672
1899	78	513	15.20467836
1900	71	534	13.29588015
1901	91	505	18.01980198
1902	102	578	17.64705882
1903	86	610	14.09836066
1904	97	621	15.61996779
1905	125	684	18.27485380
1906	135	799	16.89612015
1907	145	837	17.32377539
1908	175	887	19.72942503
1909	161	840	19.16666667
1910	148	777	19.04761905
1911	163	910	17.91208791
1912	167	996	16.76706827
1913	172	993	17.32124874
1914	203	992	20.46370968
1915	189	1019	18.54759568
1916	173	1005	17.21393035
1917	222	1224	18.13725490
1918	160	903	17.71871539
1919	142	711	19.97187060
1920	211	1069	19.73807297
1921	257	1280	20.07812500
1922	248	1443	17.18641719
1923	359	1821	19.71444261

18.09% is much too inclusive to be representative of students that were Jewish at the University of Michigan at that time.[53]

As can be seen in Table 1.B, the rates of students recorded yearly reflect a consistent trend within a range of 13.3% to 20.5%, show-

53. http://www.hillel.org/college-guide/list/record/university-of-michigan (calculated from number of Jewish undergraduates and graduates divided by total number of undergraduates and graduates).

ing that the culling method originally used consistently yielded similar percentages of students, even as numbers of total students increased. Because we expected the historical percentage of Jewish attendance at the University of Michigan to be approximately 7%–10% during this time period and the initial findings indicated a set of students roughly double that size, we decided to pursue the 1, 2, 3 decision process previously described to differentiate the data further and attempt to arrive at a more exact subset of Jewish students attending the university in this era.

The act of deciding if a student was likely to have been Jewish or not without major clues such as membership in a Jewish fraternity such as ZBT, or a Jewish club like Menorah or the Zionist Society, was particularly subjective. For this reason, both Lawson and Markovits completed ratings of students in 1897 and 1908 to provide a basis for comparison of our subsequent ratings of all years from 1897 to 1923. Totally independent from each other, Lawson and Markovits made a series of 216 decisions over those two years. Thereafter, we calculated an inter-rater reliability coefficient (known as Pearson's r) to compare the deviation between the two raters. Pearson's r can range from -1.0 to $+1.0$, from a perfect negative correlation to a perfect positive correlation, indicating the correlation between the agreements of two or more raters. Stated more simply, Pearson's r gives one solid indication of the likelihood of the two raters agreeing on any one 1, 2, 3 decision. For the 216 trials that Markovits and Lawson completed, Pearson's r equates to .3117. An r value of .3117 indicates a weak, positive correlation between the two raters. However, when this r value is understood in terms of the numerous subjective measures considered while making each decision, the positive correlation between Markovits's ratings and Lawson's is an important point in affirming our work's reliability.

Furthermore, when these results are more meticulously analyzed, one can see the overlap between each rater's decisions regarding 3s, far and away the most important category for determining the certainty of a student's Jewish identity. Markovits tended to produce more 2s and 3s than Lawson. This is born out in the data, as Markovits produced 44 3s to Lawson's 14 and 123 2s compared to Lawson's 39 over the two years. Yet this abundance of 2s and 3s does not invalidate our rating style. When Lawson rated a student a 3 (14 times), Markovits agreed 11 times, and rated the other three students 1, 2, and 2, respectively. These results indicate that our reliability in recognizing a student as a 3 and rate that student as a 3 was very high, selecting a student as a 3 as often as Lawson 78.6% of the time and selecting them as a 2 or 3 as often as Lawson 92.9% of the time. Although Lawson was more restricted in his assigning of 3s and Markovits was more inclusive, the underlying agreement on what characteristics constituted a 3 student remains robust, despite subjective differences of interpretation.

Breakdowns of the students rated 3 and the students rated 1 and 2 follow in the next two sections.

3s Results

The 1,329 students rated a 3 equates to 5.964% of the total number of students that were graduated between 1897 and 1923.

As evident in Table 1.C, the percentage of 3s in each graduating class slowly builds, especially after 1910, to its highest level of 7.908% in 1923. This increase follows our understanding of the patterns of Jewish enrollment at the University of Michigan, especially in the 1920s as Jews became systematically discriminated against by East Coast universities' admissions, especially those that later became members of the Ivy League. Although the rate of 5.694% does not exactly follow our expected 7%–10% hypothesis comprising the percentage of Jewish students of the University of Michigan's student body, the 1923 figure of 7.908% does, and the large proliferation of 2s (to be discussed in the next section) indicates that it is likely that about 7%–10% of students graduating from the University of Michigan from 1897 to 1923 were Jewish.

Not only does the general trend of students who were certainly Jewish follow our initial hypothesis and the pattern we expected,

Table 1.C: Yearly Totals of 3s Collected to Total Number of Graduates, 1897-1923

Graduating Year	3s Collected	Total Collected	% of 3s to Collected
1897	6	291	2.06185567
1898	22	497	4.42655936
1899	27	513	5.26315789
1900	29	534	5.43071161
1901	21	505	4.15841584
1902	31	574	5.40069686
1903	26	610	4.26229508
1904	25	621	4.02576490
1905	24	684	3.50877193
1906	41	799	5.13141427
1907	42	837	5.01792115
1908	38	887	4.28410372
1909	36	840	4.28571429
1910	35	777	4.50450450
1911	48	910	5.27472527
1912	47	996	4.71887550
1913	69	993	6.94864048
1914	68	992	6.85483871
1915	55	1019	5.39744848
1916	66	1005	6.56716418
1917	80	1224	6.53594771
1918	57	903	6.31229236
1919	49	711	6.89170183
1920	74	1069	6.92235734
1921	86	1280	6.71875000
1922	85	1443	5.89050589
1923	144	1821	7.90774300

but the social and academic makeup of the students collected does as well. As shown in Table 1.D, we list students from 1897, 1902, 1905, 1907, 1911, 1914, 1917, 1921, and 1923 to showcase both the variety and range of Jewish students at the University of Michigan as well as the general composition of their social lives at the time. This creates a random assortment of students that we chose

and strengths of our initial process of collecting and selecting names.

We categorized 597 or 14.1% of names that we collected as 1s. Of the total number of graduating students from 1897 to 1923, the students labeled 1 made up 2.558%. While the data concerning these students do not provide further insight into the social milieu of Jews at the University of Michigan, they do give information concerning the parameters of this study. Socially, 1s must be considered along with their fellow Gentiles, as we deemed this group specifically non-Jewish. While this may seem unimportant upon first inspection, these data offer a valuable sample of non-Jewish students and their social composition during the period of this study. If these 1s are inspected further, as the data on the 3s have been, they may well produce a good contrast to Jewish students and greater context to the social lives of all students at the University of Michigan. Currently, the 1s provide important data in support of the process by which we performed the initial data collection: of the 4,224 names collected, only 14.1% do not have any chance of providing insight into Jewish social life at the University of Michigan. This means that over 85% of data collected have the potential to provide the information that we sought.

We categorized 2,298 of the 4,224 names collected as 2s. Given that the designation of 2 indicates a greater than 50% but less than 90% likelihood of being Jewish, there is the potential that many of these students could actually have been Jewish. This gives us two helpful insights. First, because the percentage of total students that were 3s was 5.694%, it is very likely given the number of 2s that the expected historical percentage of Jewish students at the University of Michigan (7%–10%) was well represented in the data collected from 1897 to 1923. Future years may see a rise in 3s to match the historical record, but given the number of 2s that we collected, it is safe to assume that Jews contained within this category likely bridged the 1%–4% gap between 3s recorded in our study and the expected historical rates of Jews at the University of Michigan mentioned in the previous section. Second, the large swath of 2s provides credence to the understanding set forth by Benzion Kaganoff and others studying Jewry in America that Jews were often strongly assimilated into American culture and that their naming practices reflected this phenomenon. These data provide analytic backing for the previous examples concerning assimilation of Jews in America because of the large number of potential Jews in the general student population.

A Systematic Sampling

After compiling the preceding data on Jewish students at the University of Michigan from 1897 to 1923, we decided that to enhance our method's overall reliability it was necessary to provide a baseline against which we could check our procedure of identifying Jewish students at the university. To solidify our methodology concerning the data between 1897 and 1923—the focal point of this chapter—we resorted to a method of verification, which, *prima facie*, might appear confusing. Concretely, by utilizing official data to verify independently our results from 1897 to 1923, we selectively sampled four years in which we could verify our methodology with the help of the University of Michigan's own data on its Jewish students. Prior to our collection of the data on students from the *Michiganensian*, we recorded data gathered by the University of Michigan Registrar's Office in the 1920s, 1930s, and 1940s on the religious affiliation of students attending the university. This official university record of the percentage of Jewish students on campus serves as our baseline test for the accuracy and reliability of our procedure identifying Jewish students from yearbook records. We chose the four following years to act as a blind test of our methods: 1927, 1934, 1936, and 1940. Garner, who was not involved in the collection, rating, and categorization of students in this chapter, which were performed solely by Markovits and Stone, chose these four years randomly without knowing the official university percentages gathered during each year. Thus, our sampling method of the four years remained blind throughout our collection and evaluation process.

Although we utilize the university's records as an official base-line against which to measure our efforts, administrators at the University of Michigan were, of course, fully aware of the great difficulty in finding an appropriate definition of what constituted a "Jew." A major study entitled "A Survey of the Relations of Jewish and Gentile Students at the University of Michigan," conducted by the university's Bureau of Student Opinion during two weeks in February 1939 and published in 1940, shows that there existed a significant discrepancy between the percentage of Jewish students that listed their affiliation as Jewish in response to the university's official question of "What is your religious preference?" and those that identified as Jews to the interviewers conducting the survey. "First, four surveys made by the Bureau of Student Opinion show a larger number of Jewish-preference students in the student body than the official records show. This situation is recognized by the Religious Counselor for the University and may be attributed to the fact that some students would rather not be listed officially as a Jew, and that in our oral interviews no name is attached to the schedule. This increase is estimated to be from 2 to 4% of the student body."[54] Moreover, the Bureau of Student Opinion research-ers were also aware of the fact that Jews might well exist among respondents that identified with the "no preference" category when asked to list their religion. "If this 12% is spread evenly over the 82% who state a preference, the Jews would have an added 1% of the student body. If a greater proportion of Jewish students have [sic] left the church than Gentiles, as Mrs. Van Tuyl of the Psychology Department reports, the figure could be doubled to include such a trend, making the group 2% of the campus."[55]

Although we recognize the limits of the university's attempts to determine the religious affiliation of students, they remain the most comprehensive account of students who self-identified as

54. Vicary, "Survey," 1.
55. Vicary, "Survey," 1.

Jews available as a basis for comparison for our study. To gauge our results against the official records, we compared the percentage of students that we categorized as 3s in each of the four years sampled to the percentage recorded by the Registrar's Office. A breakdown of the yearly results and a discussion of the effectiveness of our procedure follows.

1927 Results

According to our results, 140 out of 1,806, or 7.752%, of the total graduating seniors in 1927 had a high likelihood of being Jewish, that is, those students who were marked as 3s. The official registrar record from 1927 indicates that Jewish students composed 7.13% of the total graduating class. Our sample found that 0.62% more of the 1927 class comprised Jewish students than the official registrar record indicates.

1934 Results

We marked 97 out of 1,104, or 8.786%, of the total graduating seniors in 1934 as 3s. The official registrar record from 1934 states that Jewish students composed 8.9% of the total graduating class. In our analysis, 0.114% fewer of the 1934 class comprised Jewish students than the official registrar record indicates.

1936 Results

In our systematic sampling of 1936, 135 out of 1,200, or 11.250%, of the total graduating seniors were marked as 3s. The university's registrar record in 1936 asserts that Jewish students comprised 10.3% of the total graduating class. Our analysis found that 0.9% more of the 1936 class included Jewish students than on the official registrar record.

At this point we pause to give another example of our categorization technique. Among the graduates of the 1936 class,

we encountered numerous "Millers." Here is how we categorized them: We assigned a 1 to Miller, James Walter from Berrien
Springs, Michigan, and to Miller, Barbara Eyre from Grand Rapids,
Michigan. In contrast, we assigned a 3 to Miller, Morris Bernard
from Staten Island, New York, and to Miller, Sarah Katherine from
Westfield, New Jersey. Not only did we gauge the respective first
names assuming a greater probability of being Jewish for "Sarah"
and "Morris" as opposed to "Barbara" and "James," but we also
took their place of origin into consideration, once again believing
that hailing from New York and New Jersey enhanced one's probability of being Jewish as opposed to being from a small town in
Michigan.

1940 Results

Those who had a high likelihood of being Jewish, that is, those
students in our sample who were marked as 3s, accounted for 167
out of 1,466, or 11.392%, of the total graduating seniors in 1940.
The official registrar record from 1940 indicates that Jewish students composed 10.1% of the total graduating class. Our analysis
found that 1.292% more of the 1940 class comprised Jewish students than the official registrar record indicates.

Procedural Conclusions

After comparing our random sample of four years—1927, 1934,
1936, and 1940—to the registrar's record of those same years, we
found promising results for the procedure with which we evalu-
ated how likely a given student graduating from the University of
Michigan between 1897 to 1923 was Jewish. For each of the four
years, our procedure resulted in percentages of Jewish students
within each graduating class that were comparable with the Registrar's Office records. The percentage of Jewish students compos-
ing the graduating class expected with our procedure was within
1% for 1927, 1934, and 1936 and 1.3% higher in 1940 of the figures

Table 1.E: 1, 2, 3 Decision Process Examples from 1936

1, 2, 3 Decision Process Examples from 1936

Year	Lawson Scale	Lname	Fname	Degree	Hometown	Club/Group Affiliations
1936	1	Miller	Barbara Eyre	AB	Grand Rapids, MI	Delta Gamma, Junior Girls' Play, Theater and Arts, League Social Committee, Orientation Committee
1936	1	Miller	James Walter	AB	Berrien Springs, MI	Alpha Kappa Kappa, President Medical Class
1936	3	Miller	Morris Bernard	BS	Staten Island, NY	Baseball
1936	3	Miller	Sarah Katherine	AB	Westfield, NJ	Pi Beta Phi, Choral Union

reported by the university. Given that our percentages matched so closely with the official records in these four years, we can safely assume that our procedure for the years featured in this chapter (from 1897 to 1923) occurring before official university records existed, also produced similarly accurate results.

Conclusion

Research presented in this chapter has effectively gathered data on over 4,000 students at the University of Michigan in the 1897 to 1923 period and provides a unique look at the lives of graduating students during that period. We verified the soundness of the methodology with which we undertook this research using official records in 1927, 1934, 1936, and 1940. Our research drew on methods housed in the academic disciplines of history, sociology, and onomastics to provide a foundation for future analysis and gathering of data on the lives of Jewish students at the University of Michigan. Importantly, we also devised and tested a process by which subjective information regarding individual students can be analyzed and interpreted to make conclusions about religious affiliation during a time when no such official records existed.

Although having only completed the first twenty-six years of a forty-eight-year study, this research provides a baseline of comparison for our expectations and initial hypotheses. It also sheds some valuable light on Jewish student life at the University of Michigan during an era when many of the first Jewish student organizations at the university were still non-existent or in their infancy. The data collected show not only that the expected historical rates of Jewish enrollment actually occurred during this time period but also that the diversity of Jewish students in terms of hometown and extracurricular activities was as wide and varied as that of their Gentile peers. From the Jews rated among the 3s, one was class president, another was on the football team, and a third was not involved in any extracurricular activities at all. This spread of involvement was not unusual and, in fact, common among both Jews and Gentiles. Although Jews were perhaps more engaged in extracurricular activities than their Gentile peers (and more so with the creation of Jewish-specific organizations from the 1910s onward), there is no discernable difference between Jews and Gentiles socially, at least until the mid-1920s.

If the growth of Jews at the university continued at the rate seen in Table 1.C, the extrapolation of this trend would lead to a noticeable increase in the number of Jewish students by the mid- to late 1920s. This increase occurred right when the Jewish admissions to the University of Michigan's Medical School were restricted and when the Registrar's Office introduced a new application form and process that sought information on an applicant's identity, such as family origin and languages spoken at home. As presented in the evaluation of our methodology beginning with 1927, we can see that such an increase in the number of Jewish students did, in fact, occur in each of the four years that we sampled. By verifying our methodology, we can confirm the results of this chapter's larger motivation and aim: to provide insight into the lives of Jewish students at the University of Michigan and evidence of their integration into the broader university community at a time previously not studied in a systematic manner partly due to the absence of available student data and Jewish student organizations on campus. The ensuing chapters will concentrate on an environment in which this had changed. By the late 1920s, Jewish students gained the opportunity to express their Judaism in organizations, not all of which were explicitly Jewish yet all of which became spaces where Jews played an important role. In the next chapter, we turn our attention to arguably the most prominent among these: ZBT, the first Jewish fraternity on campus, the JSC, Hillel, and Avukah. We will also devote some space to the presence of Jewish athletes at the University of Michigan, a world in which they played by far the most salient role in the history of the university past and present.

Chapter Two

Integrating Jewish Students at Michigan, 1910–30

When Jewish students began to enroll in larger numbers at the University of Michigan, it was inevitable that they created organizations and associations that allowed them to build a sense of belonging on campus as well as solidarity among each other. Unlike the City College of New York, which had its first Jewish fraternity—Zeta Beta Tau (ZBT)—as early as 1898, the first known durable Jewish institutions at Michigan were not founded until the 1910s.[1] In February of 1910, a chapter of the Menorah Society, an organization for the study and advancement

---

1. *ZBT 1898–1923, The First Twenty-Five Years* (New York: Zeta Beta Tau, 1923), in the papers of Isaiah Leo Sharfman, professor of political economy (later economics) at Michigan from 1912 to 1955, I. Leo Sharfman Papers (hereafter cited as Sharfman), box 10, BHL. Born in the Ukraine, Sharfman (1886–1969) attended Boston Latin School and Harvard, where he was a founding member of Harvard's Menorah Society. After earning his LL.B. from Harvard Law School, he taught law and political science at the Imperial Pei-Yang University in Tientsin, China, before accepting the position of assistant professor of economics at Michigan. Sharfman served as chairman of the Department of Economics from 1927 until his retirement in 1955. A specialist in railroad and public utility problems and regulation, Sharfman's major scholarly achievement was a five-volume study of the Interstate Commerce Commission (1931-38). To this day, the Department of Economics maintains the endowed I.L. Sharfman Economics Fellowship Fund. For more on Sharfman, see http://faculty-history.dc.umich.edu/faculty/isaiah-leo-sharfman.

founded on February 27, 1910.[3] The first Menorah Society had been founded four years earlier at Harvard University by a small group of Jewish students, most of whom were the children of Eastern European immigrants.[4] As some of the first Jewish students to attend what had long been a Protestant institution, they sought a means to retain their Jewish identity in the face of pressures to assimilate to Harvard's broader culture. Menorah's main objective was to advance the study of Jewish history and culture in order to cultivate Jewish students' appreciation of their heritage. "Rather than viewing the college experience as one in which Jewish students should downplay either private or public identification as Jewish," Daniel Greene writes, "the Harvard Menorah Society's philosophy rested squarely on the premise that particular culture, in this case Hebraic culture, should be studied and celebrated."[5]

The founding group of students that included Horace Kallen, the future philosopher and founding member of the New School for Social Research; Henry Hurwitz, later president of the Intercollegiate Menorah Association and publisher of its journal; and Isaiah Leo Sharfman, who spent his entire career as economics professor at the University of Michigan following his initial appointment in 1912; deemphasized the role of religion as being the single constituent of Jewish identity. Rather this group promoted a "renaissance" in Jewish humanities through the study of Jewish literature and culture that would provide the basis for cultivating its members' identity while, at the same time, winning acceptance from the campus as a whole. The founders sought "to build an organization that would promote the serious academic study of Jewish culture in the university and serve as a platform for the nonpartisan discussion of Jewish problems.

3. Irving Katz provides the date of February 27, 1910 in his "A History of the Menorah Movement in U.S., at U-M." A list of Menorah Societies on American campuses appears in the *American Jewish Yearbook*, volume 17 (Philadelphia: The Jewish Publication Society of America, 1915), 304.

4. Greene, *Jewish Origins of Cultural Pluralism*, 14-34.

5. Greene, *Jewish Origins of Cultural Pluralism*, 16.

Hurwitz aimed to liberate the Jewish college student from the feeling that his Judaism diminished his American identity."[6] This was a conflict-laden issue that remained central to the lives of Jewish students—indeed American Jews, or should it rather be Jewish Americans—at Michigan and elsewhere throughout much of the twentieth century.[7] "Menorah's primary purpose was thus intellectual—the study of the history and culture of the Jewish people, so conceived that nothing Jewish should be alien to it. It was to be a nonpartisan and nonsectarian open forum. Nonactivist, as well, it would neither sponsor purely social functions nor engage in philanthropic or social-service activities. Its energies were to be concentrated upon its cultural purpose."[8]

When the Michigan Menorah Society was founded in early 1910, it followed the Menorah mission "to build an organization that would promote the serious academic study of Jewish culture in the university and serve as a platform for the nonpartisan discussion of Jewish problems."[9] Menorah sought to "liberate the Jewish college student from the feeling that his Judaism diminished his American identity"—that is, it was created in the spirit of what Kallen would later articulate as 'pluralism.'[10] Its founder was a sophomore named Samuel Levin, class of 1912, who became an instructor in American and European history at Detroit Central High School.[11]

6. Jospe, "Jewish College Students," 135.

7. Jospe, "Jewish College Students." Our juxtaposition of "American Jews" to "Jewish Americans" offers an American analogy to the well-known dichotomy between "deutsche Juden" and "jüdische Deutsche" in the German context, particularly in this era, with the former denoting a more assertive identity of being Jewish and the latter of being German.

8. Jospe, "Jewish College Students," 136.

9. Jospe, "Jewish College Students," 135.

10. Jospe, "Jewish College Students," 135.

11. "University Menorah Society to Give Smoker," Jewish Chronicle, March 31, 1916. Along with Levin, another prominent early Michigan Menorah president was Samuel J. Rhodes, class of 1915, who, according to the Jewish Chronicle, "did much to arouse the Jewish students to a greater interest in the literature and the culture of

While the *Michigan Daily* described Michigan Menorah as part of a movement "in collegiate circles for the dissemination of Jewish history and ideals," the chapter was in fact largely dormant for its first two years, failing to announce any activities in the *Michigan Daily* until April 1912 (this was Menorah's only appearance in the newspaper until November of that year).[12] Sharfman's arrival in Ann Arbor in the fall of 1912 marked a turning point. He discovered that many Jewish students, and especially the leading Jewish students on campus, held Michigan Menorah in low regard and saw it as nothing more than a social club. According to the historian Irving Katz, the society's "activities were for the most part social, it met off the campus, it received little recognition or encouragement from the University authorities or from the community at large."[13] As Sharfman wrote to Henry Hurwitz, who had just been named the first resident of the newly formed Intercollegiate Menorah Association in January 1913:

> Owing to the special conditions prevailing here [at the University of Michigan] the notion became deep rooted at the very beginning of the society's existence that social activities rather than cultural aims were at the bottom of the Menorah idea. The error of this conception is becoming clearer to members from day to day.[14]

their faith. Under his leadership the Menorah chapter of Michigan became one of the most influential in the country." After graduation, he became the first editor of the *Jewish Chronicle*, a position that was later assumed by another former Michigan Menorah president, Philip Slomovitz. "Prominent Jewish Young Men Enlist," *Jewish Chronicle*, May 18, 1917. Jackie Headaphol, "A Century of Our History," *Jewish News*, July 29, 2015: https://thejewishnews.com/2015/07/29/a-century-of-our-history/

12. See "Menorah Society to Hold Annual Assembly Tonight," *MD*, April 28, 1912. Katz also states that the Michigan Menorah only became an active organization in the 1912-13 academic year; see "History of the Menorah Movement in the U.S., at U-M."

13. Katz, A History of the Menorah Movement in U.S., at U-M."

14. Sharfman to Henry Hurwitz, letter dated March 29, 1913. Responding to Sharfman, Hurwitz concurred that many Menorah societies at western U.S. universities

Sharfman not only sought to align Michigan Menorah according to the Society's cultural objectives but he also attempted to raise its profile by admonishing these leading Jewish students on campus to dismiss their indifference to the society:

> If, therefore, these leaders are really mindful of themselves and the Jewish cause, they cannot afford to stay away from the Menorah. They must join and participate actively in the work and policies of the society and labor unceasingly to change the complexion of the organization in those respects in which change seems necessary. Not a few are beginning to comprehend the situation.[15]

Sharfman and Hurwitz discussed several strategies for raising the profile of Michigan Menorah, including developing funds to bring in speakers, arranging for the distribution and dispatch of Menorah publications to Ann Arbor, finding sponsors among prominent Jews, promote student achievements through prizes and awards, and developing contacts with Jewish graduates.[16] Sharfman and

"have not quite understood the cultural purpose of the Menorah, dissociated as it is from social activities. . . . Some personnel influence seems necessary to steer them in their true course and attract to them the best students, wherever these are not already identified with the Menorah." Hurwitz hoped that the Intercollegiate Menorah Association, which was formed at a meeting of all the Menorah societies in Chicago in January 1913, clarified Menorah's cultural program to the student ambassadors. Hurwitz to Sharfman, letter dated April 24, 1913. Sharfman, box 10, folder Henry Hurwitz 1, BHL.

15. Sharfman to Hurwtiz, letter dated March 29, 1913. Although it is not entirely clear who these "leading" Jewish students were, Sharfman's simultaneous involvement with the fraternity, Zeta Beta Tau (see below), suggests that he was attempting to foster greater cohesion between the two organizations. Sharfman also refers to the social exclusivity of ZBT in his letter to Hurwitz on October 14, 1913. Sharfman, box 10, folder Henry Hurwitz 1, BHL.

16. Sharfman to Hurwitz, letter dated March 29, 1913, and Hurwitz to Sharfman, letter dated April 24, 1913. Sharfman, box 10, folder Henry Hurwitz 1, BHL. For example, Menorah announced the creation of an essay prize of $100 in the *Michigan Daily*. See "Chicagoan Offers Prize for Essay," *MD*, February 25, 1913. Sharfman, Rabbi Leo M. Franklin and philosophy professor Robert M. Wenley served as judges, see "President Names Judges to Award Menorah Prize," *MD*, March 18, 1913.

Hurwitz's correspondence regarding the latter's proposed trip to Ann Arbor in December 1913 shows how successful the young economics professor had been in building Michigan Menorah among the campus' Jewish students in little over a year. During Hurwitz's stay, Menorah sponsored an informal meeting at the Zeta Beta Tau (ZBT) house, the Jewish fraternity on campus, and an open session where Hurwitz gave a speech "supplemented by a reply from [University of Michigan] President Hutchins and by one or two addresses of faculty members who are interested in our work, influential on the campus, and popular with the students."[17] In the same letter, Sharfman could not help but boast to Hurwitz at how completely Michigan Menorah had turned itself around since his arrival in Ann Arbor:

> I think you are coming to a rejuvenated Menorah Society here at the University of Michigan. Within the space of one year remarkable progress has been made. The society now has a clearer and loftier conception of its purpose, and it is proceeding with commendable energy to carry out its purpose . . . I believe the society stands on a much higher plane on the campus today than at any time since its foundation.[18]

The rejuvenated Michigan Menorah held its meetings in Newberry Hall that featured discussions on Hebrew literature and culture, and talks by invited speakers such as Rabbi Dr. Leo M. Franklin, who headed Temple Beth El in Detroit from 1899 to 1941;

17. Sharfman to Hurwitz, letter dated November 22, 1913, Sharfman, box 10, folder Henry Hurwitz 1, BHL. Hurwitz's visit was reported in the *Michigan Daily*. See "Henry Hurwitz To Address Menorah Meeting Tonight," *MD*, December 7, 1913.

18. Sharfman to Hurwitz, letter dated November 22, 1913, Sharfman, box 10, folder Henry Hurwitz 1, BHL. Unfortunately, Sharfman's subsequent correspondence with Hurwitz does not address the Michigan Menorah, focusing instead on issues concerning the Intercollegiate Menorah Association, and the publication, *Menorah Journal* and its various controversies, all of which are outside the scope of this study. Thus, these few letters from 1913 provide the only inside look at the campus' first organization for Jewish students.

Kallen and Hurwitz, as well as noteworthy journalists, prominent attorneys, academics, and religious figures.[19] Overall, under Sharfman's careful stewardship Michigan Menorah aimed to foster a greater awareness and appreciation for Jewish culture among its members. Like its Harvard predecessor, Michigan Menorah was intellectual but not sectarian. "Menorah's primary purpose was intellectual—the study of the history and culture of the Jewish people, so conceived that nothing Jewish should be alien to it. It was to be a nonpartisan and nonsectarian open forum."[20] As one of the original Menorah chapters, the Menorah at Michigan was one of the founders of the Intercollegiate Menorah Association in 1913.

Michigan Menorah remained active throughout the teens and into the early 1920s, sponsoring not only prominent speakers but also essay competitions on Jewish history, for instance, or lectures on topics related to Jewish history or contemporary issues.[21] The chapter played a prominent role in the Intercollegiate Menorah Association, and Sharfman was elected as its second national president.[22] For a brief time, from the mid-teens until the United States entry into the war in April of 1917, Michigan Menorah played

19. Franklin is mentioned as a guest speaker in "Menorah Society to Hold Ânnual Assembly Tonight" *MD*, April 28, 1912; while the reading of Hebrew literature is noted in "Menorah Society to Hold Annual Smoker on Nov. 12," *MD*, November 1, 1912. For Kallen, see "Prof. Kallen Speaks to Tonight," *MD*, March 18, 1916; for Hurwitz, see "Hurwitz to Address Menorah," *MD*, November 12, 1916; "Prominent Men Address Michigan Society," *Jewish Chronicle*, May 19, 1916.

20. Jospe, "Jewish College Students," 136.

21. Indeed, Menorah organized a welcome event for Sharfman when he was first hired by the university. See "Menorah Society Extends Welcome to Mr. Scharfman,"*MD*, February 25, 1913. The article mentions that Sharfman was one of the original founders of Menorah while he was a student at Harvard. For the essay contest, see: "President Names Judges to Award Menorah Prize," *MD*, March 18, 1913 and "Menorah Society Starts Prize Essay Competition," *MD*, January 9, 1914. Sharfman is listed as speaker in several talks including "Menorah Society to Assemble Sunday," *MD*, October 7, 1914; "What's Going On" *MD*, October 16, 1915; "Prof. I.L. Sharfman To Speak Twice At Y" *MD*, March 9, 1919.

22. Katz, A History of the Menorah Movement in U.S., at U-M."

a central role in fostering a nonsectarian and cultural program to develop its members' appreciation of their identity as Jews. In addition to essay competitions and invited speakers, Michigan Menorah also organized study circles. Lecture and study circle topics included "The Philosophy of Job," discussions of the Russian author Turgenieff [Turgenev] and his attitude toward Jews; the role of Old Testament heroes and prophets in art; studies in Jewish personality; as well as those concerning "current Jewish problems."[23]

Following the outbreak of European hostilities in August 1914, Michigan Menorah also sponsored talks about the world war and its potential impact on Jewish life and culture.[24] Sharfman himself, in one of his many speeches to the society, encouraged Menorah members to support the war effort and to commend them for their engagement in such activities as the Liberty Loan campaign.[25] After the U.S. declaration of war in April 1917, Menorah would also sponsor a talk on "The Jew in the Great War."[26]

Like other student groups, Michigan Menorah's membership dropped significantly as many of its young men were called up for the war. In February 1918, the chapter took the unprecedented step of electing a woman, Rebecca Greenburg, as its president for the first time.[27] The outgoing [male] president commended the

23. See "Campus in Brief," *MD*, April 17, 1914; "Menorah Society to Study Turgenieff," *MD*, November 14, 1914; "Prof. Cross to Lecture on Art Before Menorah Society," *MD*, April 25, 1915; "Rabbi to Address Menorah Society," *MD*, February 19, 1916; "Menorah Society to Discuss Problems," *MD*, March 14, 1915.

24. A representative sample of these talks: "Menorah Society to Discuss World War," *MD*, November 28, 1914; "Talks on 'the Jew and the War'," *MD*, May 14, 1916; "Professor Sharfman Speaks Tonight," *MD*, November 18, 1917; "Jews in the War, Subject of Menorah Society Lecture," *MD*, April 27, 1918.

25. See "Menorah Meets Sunday Night: Prof. Sharfman to Speak on 'Jewish Duty in Present Crisis,'" *MD*, October 27, 1916; "Society Outlines Year's Policy" (which mentions a recent talk on "The Jew in the World War"), *MD*, October 30, 1917; "Prof. I.L. Sharfman Tells Menorah Society of Duty," *MD*, November 20, 1917.

26. "Jews in the War, Subject of Menorah Society Lecture," *MD*, April 27, 1918.

27. "Woman Elected to Head Menorah," *MD*, February 26, 1918. Hailing from Mey-

choice stating, "During the past semester the Menorah Society has lost two-thirds of its male membership. It will now be up to the women of the organization to continue our work. Miss Greenburg, as the winner of last year's Menorah essay prize, and as one of the most active members of the society, was therefore the most logical candidate for the position."[28] Greenburg would not be Michigan Menorah's only woman president. The 1920 *Michiganensian* yearbook featured one Ida Esther Mines from Fall River, Massachusetts, who served as president the year after Greenburg.[29] Nevertheless, the loss of members appears to have affected the chapter's viability: during the 1918-19 academic year, it did not meet until early March.[30]

Paradoxically, it was just at the moment when Michigan Menorah was beginning to weaken that the chapter staged the highest-profile event of its existence. In May 1918, the chapter hosted the Baltimore-based soprano and expert on Jewish folk songs, Elizabeth Gutman, who gave the campus' first-ever performance of

erstown, Pennsylvania, Rebecca Greenburg (1896-1988) completed her bachelor's degree at the University of Michigan. She appears in the 1918 *Michiganensian* yearbook as one the Literary Seniors for that year, and also as a member of Menorah, Deutscher Verein, Stylus, and as the recipient of the Menorah Prize Essay for 1916 and 1917. After finishing her studies, she married the accountant and art collector Bernard Reis (1895–1978) and, with her husband, became prominent in the New York art world. See University of Michigan. *Catalogue of Graduates, Non-Graduates, Officers, and Members of the Faculties, 1837-1921* (Ann Arbor: University of Michigan, 1923), 244. In 1980, the Smithsonian Institution extensively interviewed her about her husband's and her life and relations with prominent artists. Although she makes almost no mention of her college years, she recalls taking a degree at Michigan, saying "I think it was the year 1919" and that she went to Michigan because "I thought I was discovering the West, I think." She makes no mention of her involvement with Menorah. See Smithsonian Institution, "Oral History Interview with Rebecca Reis, 1980" https://www.aaa.si.edu/download_pdf_transcript/ajax?record_id=edanmdm-AAADCD_oh_215644.

28. "Woman Elected to Head Menorah," *MD*, February 26, 1918.

29. "University of Michigan Notes: Active Woman Student Heads Menorah Society at the University of Mich.," *Detroit Jewish Chronicle*, March 19, 1920. See also the 1920 *Michiganensian*, 122.

30. "Menorah Society Holds First Meet," *MD*, March 6, 1919.

Yiddish and Russian folk songs before a university audience.[31] The event was headlined in the *Michigan Daily* that described the audience as filled to its capacity, and Gutman as having "the sympathy of an artist who felt and understood the emotions and inner spirits of her art."[32]

Following its five-month hiatus in late 1918 and early 1919, Michigan Menorah was reorganized and, according to the *Detroit Jewish Chronicle*, "[from] present indications the society will have the largest membership in the history of the organization. Several study circles have been organized to meet on Wednesday and Thursday nights."[33] By the 1919-20 academic year, and now installed in Lane Hall with the campus' other religious organizations, the chapter appears to have resumed its full roster of activities.[34] Indeed, it was following Menorah's reorganization that the *Detroit Jewish Chronicle* praised the society, as well as the Jewish Student Congregation, for creating a viable cultural life for Jews at the University of Michigan:

> Until a very few years ago, students attending such an institution as the University, situated as it is in a town with a very small, indeed almost a negligible resident Jewish community, were in effect cut off during the four most important years of their life from contact with Jews and from influences essentially Jewish.
>
> At our great State University, fortunately, this condition has been very largely counteracted during the past several years through the organization there of the Jewish Student Congregation and of the Menorah Society, both of which from very different angles have

31. "Famous Soprano to Sing Tonight," *MD*, May 12, 1918.

32. "Jewish Singer Pleases Audience at Concert," *MD*, May 14, 1918. The *Michigan Daily* also reported that Sharfman entertained her at his house after the concert.

33. "U. of M. Menorah to Hear Rabbi Hershman," *Detroit Jewish Chronicle*, March 21, 1919.

34. See the photo caption for "The Home of the S.C.A.," *MD*, November 21, 1920.

been eminently successful in keeping alive the Jewish consciousness of the student body and in implanting within the young men
and women a sense of decent pride in their religious heritage.[35]

Yet, for all its postwar aspirations, and despite the praise lav-
ished upon it, Michigan Menorah never completely recovered
from its wartime loss of members. The society disappeared from
the pages of the *Michigan Daily* after May 1922 (other than an
announcement of a Menorah study circle meeting in the November 15, 1922 issue). In February 1924, the *Detroit Jewish Chronicle*
featured an exchange between Hurwitz and Philip Slomovitz, a
former president of Michigan Menorah and now reporter at the
Chronicle, entitled "Is the Menorah Society Dead?"[36] While Hurwitz argued that the Intercollegiate Menorah Association was
still viable on over sixty college campuses, Slomovitz detailed the
failed effort to breathe new life into the Michigan society after
the war. Quoting a letter that Slomovitz received from another
former Michigan Menorah president, he writes:

"Not even a Menorah society on paper exists here any longer. The
older boys—some of us rounding up our fifth, sixth, or seventh
year on the campus—have witnessed with keen regret the passing
away of this institution, but its passing has been unmistakable."[37]

35. "Student Day in Detroit," *Detroit Jewish Chronicle*, May 14, 1920.

36. "Is the Menorah Society Dead?" *Detroit Jewish Chronicle*, February 1, 1924. Philip
Slomovitz (1896-1993) was born in Minsk and emigrated to the U.S. in 1910 where he
studied journalism. In 1918, he became a reporter and night editor for the *Michigan
Daily*, and served as president of Michigan Menorah. After working at the *Detroit
News* from 1918-20, he worked as editor of the *Detroit Jewish Chronicle* beginning in
1921. He stayed at the *Chronicle* until 1942 when he formed his own paper, *The Jewish
News*, which he ran until 1984. See *MD*, January 18, 1918; "What's Going On," *MD*,
April 23, 1919. Slomovitz briefly mentions his presidency of Michigan Menorah in an
interview with Robert Rockaway. See Rockway, "To Speak Out Without Malice: An
Interview with Philip Slomovitz, Jewish Journalist," 8.

37. "Is the Menorah Society Dead?" *Detroit Jewish Chronicle*, February 1, 1924.

The letter then goes on to state what had caused Michigan Menorah to fall apart:

> "An attempt was made two years ago to resurrect the local [University of Michigan] chapter, but it was only too obvious that its apparent life would be co-terminous [*sic*] with the period of exhaustive stimulation. . . . I am inclined to believe that the pursuit of the Greek letter fraternity has crowded out or precluded this interest, and my conversations with men of other universities impress me further still that the Hellenic influence is not local."[38]

Thus although the disappearance of Menorah from Ann Arbor was in part due to the campus' specific environment of "exhaustive stimulation," it was also part of a national trend that saw membership decline throughout the 1920s.[39] "Its program," according to Alfred Jospe, "which had been geared to the intellectual interests of a small minority, lacked a mass base on which to draw for new leadership and support."[40] Although we cannot determine what

38. Is the Menorah Society Dead?" *Detroit Jewish Chronicle*, February 1, 1924.

39. Michigan Menorah's precise membership numbers are impossible to tabulate. The society was only once given its own page in the *Michiganensian* yearbook (for 1917) where it listed roughly forty members. Significantly, this was the last academic year (1916-17) before the U.S. entry into the First World War affected their numbers. With one exception, the final year that any students listed membership in Menorah in their yearbook profile was in the 1924 *Michiganensian* (for the 1923-24 academic year) suggesting that the club persisted into 1923 or 1924 even though no Menorah activities were announced in the *Michigan Daily* in those years. The one exception was one Edward Reuben Robbins who was listed in the 1926 *Michiganenisan* as Menorah Society, President (2). The (2) indicates that Robbins held this position in his sophomore year (1923-24) which meant that the club was active to some uncertain degree during those years although no record of their activities remains. Menorah is completely absent from the *Michiganensian* from 1927 as Michigan Hillel took over its role as the leading Jewish student society on campus.

40. Jospe, "Jewish College Students," 136. Slomovitz told Irving Katz that the chapter stopped functioning in 1919 or 1920, although the *Michigan Daily* articles shows that it was in existence through 1922. See Katz, "A History of the Menorah Movement in U.S., at U-M."

specific factors led to the cessation of Michigan Menorah, the increasingly sports- and socializing-centered attitudes on university campuses in the roaring twenties were not particularly conducive to fostering higher-minded cultural programs. In a letter to the Intercollegiate Menorah Association Board of Governors in 1928, Hurwitz lamented what he regarded as the trivialization of Jewish organization and student life on American campuses:

"One fails to see how this essential task [promoting Jewish history and culture] is helped by having, for instance, Jewish basket-ball teams on a campus; nor how many spent on providing ice-cream parties for Jewish students, male and female, can be said to be advancing the religious interests of Judaism among them, whatever delectable uses such parties may otherwise have. And insofar as immature students are given the notion that just living together, playing by themselves, joining a Jewish club or congregation, going through the hocus-pocus of organization and 'activities', is admirable preparation for their future careers as 'Jewish leaders', a positive harm is done to them and certainly to Judaism."[41]

In truth, Menorah was also being supplanted by a new organization founded at the University of Illinois in 1923: Hillel.[42] While Michigan Hillel cannot be said to have taken over Michigan Menorah, the former's chapter founded in 1926 shared defunct

41. Hurwitz to the Menorah Board of Governors, letter dated September 28, 1928. Sharfman, box 10, folder Henry Hurwitz 2, BHL. Although the Michigan Menorah folded around 1922–23, Sharfman remained on the Menorah Board of Governors into the early 1930s as his correspondence to Hurwitz shows.

42. This was not a welcome development for everyone. Slomovitz, in the pages of the *Detroit Jewish Chronicle*, stated that "we would prefer to see the revival of Menorah rather than the formation of a new student organization, in the form of the newly planned Hillel Foundation. Sixty-one Menorah chapters should be able to exert enough of an influence to bring about a revival of things in Ann Arbor; 61 chapters should speak in argument against the formation of a duplicate student organization." Is the Menorah Society Dead?" *Detroit Jewish Chronicle*, February 1, 1924.

Michigan Menorah's objective of promoting Jewish culture as a means of encouraging Jewish students to embrace and cultivate their identity. Yet, Hillel also was more open to the socializing and 'activities' that Hurwitz found inimical to fostering a mature Jewish identity among students. While Michigan Menorah failed to endure, its legacy would continue through the long and successful career of Hillel at the University of Michigan.[43]

Zeta Beta Tau

As it did on many campuses in the country, ZBT was to become a focal point of Jewish life at the University of Michigan as well. Although we do not know much about the Michigan chapter in its early years, publications from the national organization provide a clear sense of this fraternity's overall mission to foster its members' sense of their Jewish identity while, at the same time, to dispel antisemitic prejudice and promote a successful integration with campus life: "It is the mission of the Jewish student to have contact with his non-Jewish comrades on the athletic field, in journalism, debate, dramatics, and in every field of campus activity which afford expression to that moral and physical courage, that capacity for sportsmanship, generosity, sociability, and social conscience which form part and parcel of the Jewish racial heritage."[44] ZBT defined itself as spearheading this missionary effort to combat antisemitic prejudice and argued that this mainly set it apart from other fraternal organizations: "This group of socially congenial Jewish collegemen banded together to demonstrate by their every word and deed in public and in private the

43. As late as 1939, Hurwitz was writing quixotically to Sharfman that Menorah could serve as a valuable support to Hillel. "I know that Hillel has taken the place of Menorah at Ann Arbor," he wrote, "nevertheless . . . I believe Menorah can serve the Michigan Hillel, and indeed all the Hillel Foundations. . . . After all, why not utilize—that is, enable—Menorah to serve Jewish life in these of all challenging times?" Sharfman's reply is not preserved. See Hurwitz to Sharfman, letter dated January 31, 1939. Sharfman, box 10, folder Henry Hurwitz 2, BHL.

44. ZBT 1898–1923, *The First Twenty-Five Years*, Sharfman, box 10, BHL.

best of which Jewish manhood is capable and the inherent excellence of the Jewish character."[45]

The Michigan chapter—named Phi—was founded on May 19, 1912; its first house was located at 114 North Division Street. An early history of the Michigan chapter was featured in ZBT's 25th anniversary book, see [Figure 2.1]. Sharfman, who arrived at the university to teach in the Department of Economics in the fall of 1912, became its first honorary member and served as faculty advisor while he simultaneously developed Michigan Menorah from an inchoate to an active organization. From ZBT's beginning, Sharfman was intent to foster an ethic of scholarship and service in this organization as well as develop ZBT's cooperative ties with Michigan Menorah.[46] In the fall semester of 1914, he wrote to ZBT's national organization "for the ways and means of raising the standard of scholarship among our men."[47] His suggestions mirrored those that he had suggested to Hurwitz with respect to Menorah: develop the cultural and service ethic of the organization and promote student development through academic prizes. The national ZBT wholeheartedly endorsed Sharfman's ideas and proposed the creation of a series of academic prizes, believing that "a movement of this kind will not only be of tremendous benefit to the members of the Fraternity, but will greatly improve our standing among the outside world."[48] High academic achievement

45. ZBT, Sharfman, box 10, BHL.

46. Sharfman's correspondence suggests that, at least initially, he found ZBT to be too socially exclusive to play an effective role in promoting the Jewish cultural and service ideals that he hoped to propagate among the campus' Jewish students. When Hurwitz proposed the creation of a Jewish University Club, Sharfman was hesitant about "fighting the social exclusiveness of our neighbors by an equally narrow social exclusiveness of our own." But he went on to tell Hurwitz that, should such a university club be formed, "I strongly hope that it will be launched on a much broader basis than that provide by the Zeta Beta Tau fraternity." See Sharfman to Hurwitz, letter dated October 14, 1913. Sharfman, box 10, folder Henry Hurwitz 1, BHL.

47. Alvin Sapinsky to Sharfman, letter dated September 29, 1914, Sharfman, box 10, BHL.

48. Ultimately the national organization adopted the plan to award fraternity prizes on the basis of scholastic merit. Sapinsky to Sharfman, letter dated November 3, 1914, Sharfman, box 10, BHL.

Phi

FOUNDED May 19, 1912.
Charter members: Jack Goldman, Morris Feldstein, Harry Rabinowitz, Jess Fishman, Harry Fisher, Louis W. Greenstein, Jack Levenson.

First house at 114 North Division Street.

First honorary member—Prof. I. Leo Sharfman.

Second house at 644 East University Street.

Representation in Interfraternity Conference, 1912-1913.

With the advent of '17-'18, the roll of Phi was greatly depleted. The chapter house was thrown open and men enrolled in the S. A. T. C. were accommodated in the house. At the end of the semester the house was given to the government as a barracks for soldiers attending the trade schools at the University of Michigan.

By October 1918, practically all the active members were in the S. A. T. C. During this period, Phi lost Brother Walter Atlas, whose memory was perpetuated by a library donated by his parents.

The following Fall, the men returned to the chapter house at 807 South State Street, eager for the annual eight month vacation. The house was too small and plans were made for the building of a new house.

In '20-'21, the chapter was presiding fraternity of the Interfraternity Conference.

In '21-'22, a Parents' Day was instituted. In March plans were made to purchase the Zowski Home on Washterman Avenue and largely through the efforts of Joseph Hirschman the project was successful. With the new house came a new interest in all types of campus activity and the chapter entered upon the most brilliant period of its entire career.

Tau

YOU can't do it." They protested. "Harvard isn't a fraternity college."

"We can; we will," we replied. And, in 1912, we did.

Those charter members who took the initial plunge prepared for a hard struggle. And they had it, too, with Harvard sentiment

Figure 2.1 [Early History of Michigan ZBT Chapter, Phi, from *ZBT: The First Twenty-Five Years 1898-1923*], I. Leo Sharfman box 10, Bentley Historical Library, University of Michigan

would become one of the characteristics that defined membership not only in the Phi chapter but also in the national organization more broadly. The *Detroit Jewish Chronicle* noted in 1919
that ZBT placed fourth among fraternities in terms of scholarly
achievement.[49] A 1951 retrospective of ZBT's history notes that
"the [Phi] chapter has established an outstanding record at
Michigan and in ZBT. Its achievements and scholarship, individual leadership by chapter members and group participation
in all campus activities have made it the equal of the most successful and respected of the thirty-nine fraternities of this campus. University records for the past twenty-six years testify that
scholastically Phi has been consistently the highest of all Michigan fraternities."[50]

Yet ZBT's twin goals of encouraging cultivation of their members' Jewish cultural heritage and intellectual identity and aspir-
ing to integrate them more fully into campus life through high
academic achievement often crashed against the recalcitrance of
its members. A jauntily written pledge initiation from November
1917, for example, titled "At Ease, Men!" as well as the program for
the initiation ceremony itself make absolutely no reference to any
aspect of Judaism or scholarship, choosing instead to revel in the
debauchery often associated with fraternity life by promising to
show the initiates "the goldarnest, highfalutinest old time you've
had since buck was a calf."[51] The ZBT national office wrote Sharfman in January 1920, when the fraternity was effectively reconstituting itself after the First World War, to inform him of a program
established by the fraternity's education committee to awaken
the "Jewish consciousness of our college men."[52] The program
itself sought to "overcome the indifference and prejudice to, and

49. "Local Notes," *Detroit Jewish Chronicle*, October 10, 1919.

50. Stuart Winkelman, "Phi (Michigan)," *Zeta Beta Tau Quarterly*, October–
December 1951, 7, Sharfman, box 10, BHL.

51. "At Ease!" Sharfman, box 10, BHL.

52. George Hyman to Sharfman, letter dated September 20, 1926, Sharfman, box 10,
BHL.

arouse interest and enthusiasm for things Jewish on the part of Zeta Beta Tau men."[53] Such proposals included encouraging ZBT men to "assume leadership in Jewish affairs at their local colleges and universities as in Menorah, Zionist Societies, etc." or requiring a pledge to "acquaint himself with a certain amount of Jewish history, such as the reading of Goodman's Jewish history," among other ideas.[54] These admonishments appeared to have had some effect: a letter from the national organization in 1924 claimed that a recent survey among Jewish fraternities showed that "Z B T seems to be the only one which actively leads its members into Jewish activities."[55]

If cultivating members' sense of their Jewish identity was, at times, a struggle, apparently so was the goal of inculcating high academic achievement within ZBT's culture. In 1926, the national organization amended its rules in order to suspend any member who was not able to maintain an average academic standing.[56] In a letter responding to the ZBT national organization, Joseph Bursley, Michigan's Dean of Students, approved the amendment, stating that "if this regulation is rigidly lived up to it cannot help but raise the scholastic standing of Zeta Beta Tau wherever it has a chapter."[57] Whether grade-based membership qualifications proved to be decisive is impossible to say given the scant evidence.

---

53. "Suggestions for Educational Activities," attached to Hyman to Sharfman letter, Sharfman, box 10, BHL.

54. "Suggestions for Educational Activities." Even at the national level, ZBT's leadership were routinely frustrated by their chapter members' lack of interest in Jewish culture and heritage. See, e.g., Mark Waldman, "Reminisces of the First Generation," *Zeta Beta Tau Quarterly*, December 1925, 6–11. Debates continued throughout the later 1920s as to the best methods for developing ZBT members' sense of their Jewish identity, with some arguing that the religion itself needed to be modernized in order to attract students. See "The College Man's Religion," *Zeta Beta Tau Quarterly*, May 1928, 34–35.

55. George Macy to Sharfman, letter dated September 23, 1924, Sharfman, box 10, BHL.

56. Macy to Dean Joseph Burley, letter dated September 23, 1926, VPSS, box 4, BHL.

57. Bursley to Macy, letter dated October 2, 1926, VPSS, box 4, BHL.

By 1928, in fact, Sharfman himself had grown frustrated with the fraternity's lack, in his view, of a genuine culture of intellectual curiosity and pluralism that had been the motivating impetus behind Menorah, and his earlier efforts to encourage ZBT leaders to become involved with Menorah and thus with Jewish culture in any serious manner. In a letter to the Michigan ZBT chapter's president that October, Sharfman ended his affiliation with the group: "You may recall that I was elected an honorary member of the fraternity some fifteen years ago, when Zeta Beta Tau was the only Jewish group on the Campus. My primary purpose in joining was to do what I could from the inside in molding the ideals and activities of our Jewish students in the most worthwhile direction. . . . The entire fraternity set-up does violence to standards of sympathetic understanding and democratic intercourse which I deem vital to genuine educational progress among students and university men."[58]

Sharfman's personal objections notwithstanding, both the Phi chapter and ZBT's national organization developed a reputation for, and defined themselves by, their members' high academic performance. Responding to an inquiry from Dean Joseph Bursley in 1935, the Phi's president defended the chapter against insinuations about alcohol in the house by stressing that the "Phi Chapter has always prided itself on its scholarship record. I believe that you are well acquainted with our standing so I shall not go into detail here. The officers of the house have always stressed scholarship as one of the ideals of our chapter."[59]

However imperfectly, both academic achievement and cultivating their members' sense of Jewish heritage in order to integrate with the campus culture remained ZBT's consistent goals. The fraternity also prided itself on its members' service in the US armed forces. Writing to a ZBT alumnus who had joined the US

58. Sharfman to Richard Meyer, letter dated October 8, 1928, Sharfman, box 10, BHL.
59. Jack Efroymson to Bursley, letter dated February 12, 1935, VPSS, box 4, BHL.

Army, in December of 1917, Sharfman stated to young Lieutenant Henry Weinstein, "In my opinion, Phi has done itself proud this year, in spite of the unusual situation and many distractions— perhaps because of the abnormal conditions. The boys are certainly awake to the significance of these critical days, and they are acting like men."[60] Sharfman enthused about, and named, the young ZBT members who had enlisted, claiming that "they all are going with a fine spirit and the boys who remain also have their teeth set." Almost inevitably, some ZBT members did not return home from the war. Sharfman wrote to Lt. Weinstein again in October 1918 to inform him of the death of Walter Atlas, a Phi chapter member who died after a five-week struggle against the Spanish flu in Camp Sherman.[61] Atlas's family donated his life savings to Michigan's ZBT chapter in order to purchase a larger house.[62] The pride that ZBT would take in its members' military service would also be evident during the Second World War.

Myron E. Chon: ZBT and Assimilation in the Free-Spirited Twenties

While the members of ZBT, like all student organizations, were not shy in espousing their fraternity's core values such as high academic achievement and public service, it is much more difficult to discern what day-to-day life was like for these fraternities' individual members. Fortunately, one such member, Myron Edward Chon (1902–87) deposited his scrapbook with the University of

60. Sharfman to Weinstein, letter dated December 12, 1917, Sharfman, box 10, BHL.

61. Sharfman to Weinstein, letter dated October 18, 1918, Sharfman, box 10, BHL. According to Sharfman's letter, the university was particularly hard hit by the Spanish flu. "We have some 1500 cases now, and there have been many deaths. Churches, schools, and theaters are closed; and all public meetings of whatever character are prohibited. The University work is continuing, but we are all wearing gauze marks, in the classroom, as well as on the street." See also Peckham, Steneck, and Steneck, *Making*, 149.

62. Sharfman to Emanuel Atlas, letter dated May 21, 1919, Sharfman, box 10, BHL.

Michigan's archives at the Bentley Historical Library. Chon came to Michigan in 1919 and became a noted saxophonist on campus. In February 1920, in the middle of his freshman year, he was initiated into ZBT. He participated in ZBT's social activities as both a musician and a skit performer, playing one of the "Great Balkan Tragedians" presenting their famous novelty act, "Ask Me and I'll Tell You," at the fraternity's house party in April of that year according to the preserved playbill. Chon also played an overture in one of ZBT's annual "Vodvil" (vaudeville) gigs and was a featured saxophone artist at another "Spotlight Vaudeville" that ZBT performed at the University of Michigan's vaunted Hill Auditorium. One of the small news scraps that Chon saved contained a mention that "Mike Chon's saxophone is a byword on the campus. No vaudeville, spotlight or dance is complete without it. In addition Chon's creative ability produced one of the song hits of the opera."[63]

Excepting his ZBT activities, however, there is little in the scrapbook to indicate that Chon was particularly focused on Jewish history and culture or on anything related to cultivating his Jewish identity. Indeed, all the events that Chon collected were secular in nature—dances, vaudevilles, concert, the annual junior hop ("j-hop"). If anything, the scrapbook suggests quite solidly that Chon felt himself well integrated into the broader campus culture in an era when social activities and sports were seen as more important markers of a student's life on campus than his coursework. "To a growing number of American undergraduates in the first third of the twentieth century," writes Christopher Lucas, "attending college marked a pleasant interlude between the end of adolescence and the assumption of adult responsibilities. The college years in some cases amounted to little more than a prolonged childhood: a time to develop friendships, to socialize, and to indulge in good fun. . . . The situation was little changed

63. The material in this and the following paragraphs, unless otherwise cited, is from Myron Chon's scrapbook, BHL.

in the 1920s—the age of flappers and bootleggers, coonskin coats and bathtub gin, hot jazz and new dance crazes. On college campuses across the country, academics took a decided back seat to the electing of beauty queens, popularity contests, and adulation of football heroes."[64] Photos of Ferry Field, the precursor to Michigan Stadium, of the Little Brown Jug and the crowd at the 1921 Michigan-Minnesota game, of Michigan's All-Americans and clippings of photos of football players like Doug Roby, Herbert Steger, and Harry Kipke show that Chon was well taken with Michigan sports. The scrapbook contains a photo of Michigan's president, Marion Leroy Burton, and a picture of Chon in a large crowd of sophomores before a tug of war match.

Chon seemed proudest of his role as a co-composer and actor in the musical comedy, "In and Out," that was performed by the Mimes of the Michigan Union and was even staged at Detroit's Orchestra Hall and in Indianapolis's Murat Theater. In one of the numerous notices that Chon preserved, his acting is listed as "entertaining in his easy ways of falling 'in and out' of love." Clearly, this is not the scrapbook of someone who felt apart from, or alien to, the university—quite the opposite. Chon seemed to revel in his life at the University of Michigan. Judging by what Chon decided to preserve, he emerges as a student who both held a strong allegiance to his beloved fraternity but was also very much a part of the broader university culture. ZBT provided Chon with a sphere in which he could develop his talents—as a composer, saxophone player, and actor—that allowed him to carve out a reputation for himself on campus. In other words, Chon's scrapbook shows how a student like him assimilated through his association with ZBT into the larger world of the University of Michigan. In fact, this appeared to have happened to such an

64. Lucas, *American Higher Education*, 208, 210. Robert Cohen, a historian of the "Old Left," generally agrees that the 1920s were an apolitical era marked by a focus on social activities and a sense of elitism among undergraduates. "The traditional attitude of the affluent student majority was if you could not afford college, you did not belong there." See Cohen, *When the Old Left Was Young*, 3–15; quote is on 13.

extent that Chon's religion or ethnicity is never once mentioned in the entire scrapbook.[65] Indeed, while Chon was hardly indifferent to his academic performance—he included a grade sheet in his scrapbook showing he earned two As, two Bs, and one C for the second semester of 1920–21 (well above a gentleman's C)—nothing in his scrapbook would indicate that he was much different from a popular, fun-loving, highly sociable student that was a fixture on campus during this era. Not once do we read anything about his being Jewish, let alone even a hint of his suffering any slights or experiencing any disadvantages or hostilities by dint of his Judaism. Chon's scrapbook portrays his student life at Michigan as a largely free-spirited one without any evident self-consciousness of being Jewish nor any sense that his Jewish origin set him apart from his peers.

The Jewish Student Congregation
(co-authored with Julia Ebben)

While both Menorah and ZBT shared a similar orientation toward promoting Jewish cultural awareness and serving as spaces for socializing with a generally nonsectarian focus, a more religiously oriented group was also organized on campus during the teens. On February 26, 1914, Jewish students at the University of Michigan, under the guidance and direction of Dr. Leo Franklin, rabbi of Detroit's Temple Beth-El, established their very own congregational community that had no chapters or presence anywhere else in the country.[66] They named it the Jewish Student Congregation

65. After graduating from Michigan in 1923, Chon went to work in advertising in Chicago and became an executive creative director for Arthur Meyerhoff Associates. His younger brother was William Shawn, long-time editor of the *New Yorker* magazine, who studied at Michigan from 1925 to 1927. On Chon, see https://quod.lib.umich.edu/b/bhlead/umich-bhl-2016010?view=text.

66. The date of February 26, 1914 comes from Stiefel, "Early Jewish Life." There are some indications that the congregation may have been founded slightly earlier. A mid-1916 article in the *Jewish Chronicle* states that the organization was founded three years prior. See "S.D. Frankel Elected Head of U. of M. Jewish Students." *Jew-*

fact that they were held at the University of Michigan's venerable Hill Auditorium, which had opened in 1913. During these services, "'all churches in the city [of Ann Arbor were] closed on this evening, the congregations thereof being invited to participate in the Jewish service. So far, as we can learn, this is the first time in the history of American cities when all other churches have closed their doors even for a single service for such a purpose.' . . . An estimated 5,000 residents, students and guests filled the auditorium for the event. Another service was held a year later, on January 16 at Hill Auditorium. The Christian congregations of Ann Arbor again closed in order to participate."[74] As the *Jewish Chronicle* stated on the occasion of the fourth annual service in January 1918: "The service is unique, as no other instance is on record where practically all the churches of a community suspend their own services to permit their congregations to participate in a Jewish service of worship."[75]

The JSC established Sunday services—spurning the Jewish tradition of having services on the Sabbath—as an attempt to reach as many Jewish students as possible, including those who did not identify their Judaism religiously but socially. As such, the organization saw its main mission as providing a social home to Jews who otherwise had none on campus since the university's main social organizations, namely its fraternities and sororities, did not accept Jews as members. Before the establishment of Ann Arbor's Beth Israel Congregation in 1916, the city's first and oldest Jewish house of worship, the JSC served as a place of worship for Ann Arbor residents in addition to University of Michigan students.

In April of 1914—mere months after the founding of the JSC—Julius Rosenwald of Chicago, the president of the Sears-Roebuck

74. "Churches Combine for Annual Union Service."
75. "All Churches in Ann Arbor to Close for Jewish Service," *Jewish Chronicle*, January 11, 1918. The annual service appeared in the *Chronicle* (later the *Detroit Jewish Chronicle*) until March 1926, the very last service organized by the JSC. "Hill Auditorium Service," *Detroit Jewish Chronicle*, March 26, 1926.

Company, offered a "considerable sum of money" to the organization so that it may be able "to secure speakers and lecturers, and to assist in meeting the running expenses."[76] Relating to the securing of speakers, the congregation purported in the *Michigan Daily* that its meetings would feature talks from "many of the most prominent rabbis of the country" prior to its first meeting of the 1914–15 academic year.[77] On at least two occasions, however, the leadership of the organization invited a prominent Christian minister to be the speaker at its weekly meetings: Ann Arbor minister Reverend Lloyd C. Douglas addressed the organization on both March 4, 1917, and March 30, 1919.[78]

Early on in the JSC's existence, the *Michigan Daily* clarified that this organization was "distinctly religious and [would] engage in no social activities whatsoever."[79] Furthermore, in April 1914, the JSC was differentiated from another (older) University of Michigan Jewish organization, the Menorah Society. The *Michigan Daily* again described the JSC as being "purely religious" and "a local body."[80] Although not a socially focused organization, the JSC did host more social events as the years passed in an effort to procure new members and to welcome its existing membership back to campus.[81] Beginning in the fall of 1918 and continuing in the following years, the JSC even partnered with the Menorah Society at least once annually to host social events in an effort to bring "together all the Jewish students on the campus," much like Hillel and Avukah would later do in the 1930s and 1940s.[82] The JSC

76. "Chicago Merchant Offers Fund for Jewish Speakers," *MD*, April 28, 1914.

77. "Rabbi Franklin to Speak on Sunday," *MD*, October 7, 1914.

78. "Jewish Student Organization Will Hear Rev. L. C. Douglas," *MD*, March 4, 1917; and "Lloyd Douglas to Address Jewish Students Tonight," *MD*, March 30, 1919.

79. "Fixel Elected President of Jewish Congregation," *MD*, February 28, 1914.

80. "Jewish Clubs Are Unrelated," *MD*, April 19, 1914.

81. "Jewish Students Begin Year's Athletics," *MD*, October 24, 1917.

82. "Jewish Students Will Meet Sunday," *MD*, October 15, 1918; "Jewish Society to Hold Social," *MD*, November 16, 1918; and "Sharfman to Speak before Meeting of Jewish Students," *MD*, October 18, 1919.

also had some ties with the university's Zionist Society, given that the president of the JSC once addressed the society.[83] In May of 1920, the three aforementioned organizations even jointly met "to commemorate the occasion of the granting of the mandate to Great Britain for Palestine, and the consequent assurance of a Jewish homeland."[84] Temple Beth El in Detroit also graciously hosted an annual Student Day for the JSC in which approximately 150 members of the organization attended special services in the city; members of the temple also generally entertained the students for a dinner in the evening.[85]

By 1918, the JSC had been so successful in establishing itself within the campus community that the *Jewish Chronicle* proudly stated that "The organization is far beyond the experimental stage and has come to take a definite and important part in the life of the student community at Ann Arbor."[86] Another *Jewish Chronicle* article went further in its approbation. Describing the JSC at Michigan as a pioneer and "the model of which similar organizations have been established at a number of the larger universities of the country," the article enthused that ". . . it is gratifying that many a young man indifferent to Judaism when he entered college has gone forth upon graduation to become a leader in the Jewish life of his community and congregation. Moreover, the Jewish Student Congregation has served to give to the Jewish student a new respect in his own eyes and in the eyes of professors and fellow-students."[87] The fears that had haunted the JSC at its founding—that it would serve to segregate Jewish from their non-Jewish peers—had been largely allayed. "There is absolutely no organization anywhere," declared an editorial in the *Detroit Jew-*

83. "Zionist Society Meets Tonight," *MD*, November 17, 1917.

84. "Jewish Societies to Meet Jointly," *MD*, May 11, 1920.

85. "Many Jewish Students Will Attend Services in Detroit," *MD*, March 23, 1918; and "Jewish Students Take Part in Detroit Entertainment," *MD*, March 26, 1918.

86. "Thousands Hear Jewish Message at Ann Arbor," *Jewish Chronicle*, January 25, 1918.

87. "Judaism's Appeal to the College Man," *Jewish Chronicle*, January 25, 1918.

ish Chronicle, "that is doing more not only to conserve the Jewish spirit among our young men but also to prepare earnest and intelligent young people to assume the reins of leadership in our various communities than is the Jewish Student Congregation of the University of Michigan."[88]

Although decidedly not a Christian organization, the JSC also came to be incorporated under the larger umbrella of Michigan's Student Christian Association (SCA); through its affiliation with the SCA, the JSC secured a meeting place in Lane Hall, which it used from the fall of 1918 onward for its weekly gatherings.[89] Nevertheless, the organization's growth prompted some to call for the JSC to acquire its own chapel. In a speech at Temple Beth El, Abraham Gornetzky, a graduating law senior and JSC president for 1918-19, importuned the audience for funds.[90] No official decision was ever announced in the *Michigan Daily*, however, and it seems that the organization never moved forward with this project.[91]

The JSC continued to receive warm praise from the *Detroit Jewish Chronicle* in that the paper noted that the organization had "steadily grown from season to season in numbers and in influence."[92] Not only had the group succeeded in encouraging its members to take up work within their communities, but it had also attained an influence on non-Jews as well:

> Any one who was privileged to attend the magnificent service that
> was held in the great Hill Auditorium on the evening of March

88. "Religion and the College Man," *Detroit Jewish Chronicle*, January 23, 1920. Note: the paper's name changed from the *Jewish Chronicle* to the *Detroit Jewish Chronicle* beginning March 7, 1919.

89. "Jewish Students to Have Meeting," *MD*, December 4, 1918; "Student Christian Association Absorbs Campus Religious Work," *MD*, November 21, 1920; and University of Michigan Alumni Association, *Michigan Alumnus* 27 (1921): 484.

90. "The Bogy of Segregation," *Detroit Jewish Chronicle*, May 16, 1919.

91. "Jewish Students to Discuss Project for Chapel House," *MD*, May 25, 1919.

92. "Jewish Work in Universities," *Detroit Jewish Chronicle*, March 28, 1919.

Michigan Zionist society appears in an article in the *Jewish Chronicle* from May 1916 that profiled one Abraham Levin, who was both president of Menorah and vice-president of the Michigan Zionist Society.[99] The *Michigan Daily* also reported that Menorah had hosted a talk by a former president of the Intercollegiate Zionist Association in January 1917; however, only in October 1917 and thereafter would a Michigan-based student Zionist group appear in the *Michigan Daily*.[100] That the Michigan club was a chapter of the Intercollegiate Zionist Society is evident as it appeared under that name in the pages of the *Michigan Daily* on October 10, 1917; however, it changed its name to the University Zionist Society by the very next week.[101] Based on the scant evidence that exists, it seems likely that a section of Menorah members either broke away to form their own group, or founded the new organization while remaining part of Michigan Menorah.

Whereas Greene's *The Jewish Origins of Cultural Pluralism* depicts Zionist organizations as competitors with Menorah and other groups on campus, the situation at Michigan did not appear to be quite so polarized. Leaders of the Jewish Student Congregation spoke at Michigan's Zionist Society meetings and Leo Sharfman, a strong proponent of Menorah's nonpartisan and nonsectarian philosophy, also addressed the group on several occasions.[102] Rebecca Greenburg, who

99. "Detroit Boy Honored at College," *Jewish Chronicle*, May 5, 1916.

100. "Levin to Address Menorah: Speaker is Professor of Torts in University of Detroit," *MD*, January 7, 1917.

101. See What's Going On," *MD*, October 10, 1917, and then the brief meeting notice at the bottom of the fifth column on page 1 of *MD*, October 17, 1917. The group reverted to the name Intercollegiate Zionist Society in February 1920 when it posted meeting notices under that name in the *Michigan Daily*. Because there is no way of determining why these name changes occurred or what they indicted about the group in terms of its policies or composition, the authors have decided to use the blanket name Zionist Society (or Michigan's Zionist Society) in order to avoid confusion.

102. "Zionist Society Meets Tonight," *MD*, November 15, 1917; What's Going On," *MD*, November 7, 1917. Sharfman, however, did support the aims of the Zionist society and Zionism more broadly. As he told the group in a December 1917 talk: "Professor Sharfman said that a Jewish state in the East would in time add to the orient

was soon to be elected Michigan Menorah's first woman president, also read her Menorah prize-winning essay on "The Preservation of Jewish Nationality in America," to the Zionist society.[103] Moreover, Michigan Menorah, the JSC and the Zionist Society also jointly sponsored events such as a commemoration of the announcement of the British Mandate in Palestine in May 1920.[104] The *Michiganensian* yearbooks even show that some students held joint memberships among these organizations.[105] While we have no knowledge of the relations among Menorah, the JSC, and the Zionist Society; it does not appear that there was the same degree of contestation among these groups at the University of Michigan that Greene reported to have existed on other college campuses.

Whereas Michigan Menorah witnessed a decline in activity during the war years, the Zionist society went through prolonged stretches of apparent inactivity: no meeting announcements were posted in the *Michigan Daily* between the end of March 1918 and the end of February 1919 and then from March to October of 1919.[106] Like Menorah and all other "religious" groups, the Michigan Zionist society had its home in Lane Hall by 1919. Despite the

the materialism of the occident, and would in turn give the West the dreams of orientalism." See "Jews Can Help Civilization," *MD*, December 8, 1917.

103. "Zionist Society Will Meet Tonight," *MD*, October 19, 1917.

104. "Jewish Societies to Meet Jointly," *MD*, May 11, 1920. The ZSC and the Zionist Society also held a joint meeting in October 1920, see "Interesting Services Planned by Ann Arbor Churches for today; Music Features Many Programs," *MD*, October 10, 1920.

105. On page 368 of the 1919 *Michiganensian*, Abraham Gornetzky, a law senior, is named as president of both Menorah and the Jewish Student Congregation; while in the 1921 yearbook, page 46, Sara Gertrude Caplan is named Vice President of Menorah and of the Intercollegiate Zionist Society.

106. Between March and April 1919, announcements in *Michigan Daily* on Zionist-themed events were sponsored by the Zionist Circle of the Menorah Society. This suggests that Michigan Menorah, in an effort to bolster their numbers, attempted to bring the Zionist students into their tent. However, by the fall of 1919, an independent Zionist society was once again posting meeting announcements in the paper. See the "What's Going On" columns in *MD*, March 13, 1919; March 20, 1919; April 2, 1919; and April 23, 1919.

fact that the society was described as "one of the largest intercollegiate societies of its kind in the country," in truth it brought fewer speakers to campus than Michigan Menorah and its appearances in the *Michigan Daily* during the 1919-20 academic year were for the most part merely meeting and election notices.[107] Given the Society's fairly narrow thematic focus—compared to the Michigan Menorah's more expansive cultural approach—it is not surprising that the Society's roster of activities was more limited. The Society was obviously concerned with the condition of Jews in Palestine and one of its few speakers that year discussed in French the ongoing peace negotiations with the defeated Ottoman Empire.[108] Nonetheless, even in The *Detroit Jewish Chronicle*, notices about specific Zionist society-sponsored events and activities are slim. Indeed, the Michigan Zionist Society made only a few brief appearances in the *Chronicle*, such as this rather generalized description that says that the society "has study groups in Hebrew, Jewish history, Palestine and Zionism. The society arranges public forums and lectures for its own members and quite often for the general public. In addition, the Michigan chapter has done a noble work by making a large contribution to the Palestine Restoration Fund."[109]

The following academic years were much the same: mostly meeting announcements and the very occasional speaker on issues related to Palestine. Indeed, at the same time in the early 1920s that Michigan Menorah disappeared, the Zionist Society also suffered from a slow decline. Only meeting and election notices appeared in the *Michigan Daily* during the academic years 1921-22 and 1922-23, and the final mention of the Michigan Zionist Society was an essay contest announcement in mid-May

107. "Ann Arbor Notes," *Detroit Jewish Chronicle*, April 2, 1920.
108. "Levine Talks to Zionist Society," *MD*, November 4, 1919; "Zionist Society Discusses Turkey," *MD*, January 9, 1920.
109. "Form Branch of Intercollegiate Zionist Society," *Detroit Jewish Chronicle*, October 19, 1920.

1923.[110] During that time, the society seems to have neither sponsored nor hosted any outside speakers.[111] Indeed, the group does not even appear in the news reports on a visit by a prominent Jewish leader, Rabbi Stephen S. Wise, founder and first secretary of the Federation of American Zionists, in January 1921. With the exception of a second visit by Rabbi Wise in April 1926 that was sponsored by the Round Table Club, no activity even remotely related to Zionism was reported in the *Michigan Daily* until the summer of 1929.[112]

The Zionist Society's attenuation was no doubt due to the collapse of the national Intercollegiate Zionist Association earlier in the decade which had happened following the withdrawal of the latter's funding by its main sponsor, the Zionist Organization of America (ZOA).[113] But the Society also suffered from the broader decline in interest that had afflicted all the Jewish student organizations formed during the teens. In an apolitical era when college students focused increasingly on football, hi-jinks, sex and socializing, Menorah's high intellectualism, the JSC's religiosity, and the Zionist Society's political focus were distinctly unfash-

110. "Prizes Offered in Essay Contest," *MD*, May 13, 1923. On May 29, the *Michigan Daily* reported the election of officers to the University of Michigan Zionist Association. Whether this was yet another rechristened name or a competing organization is unknown. See "Zionists Elect Officers," *MD*, May 29, 1923. This group is only mentioned once more in late 1924: see Paul A. Elliott, "More Than Three Hundred Organizations Provide Extra-Curricula Activities For Students; A List of Michigan Societies," *MD*, December 24, 1924.

111. The group was not even mentioned in the news report on a visit by a prominent Jewish rabbi, Stephen S. Wise, Founder and First Secretary of the Federation of American Zionist, in January 1921. See "Wise Will Speak on Americanism." *MD*, January 26, 1921.

112. Significantly neither of Wise's two speeches at Michigan involved Zionism. The January 1921 speech was on "Americanism" and the April 1926 speech was on "The Revolt of Youth—Against What?" See "Wise To Talk On Revolt Of Youth in Speech Today," *MD*, April 7, 1926.

113. Jospe, "Jewish College Students," 137-38. Jospe mentions that several campus chapters persisted for awhile after the collapse of the national organization.

ionable; all three of these groups were effectively defunct by the mid-twenties.[114]

Indeed, it would not be until the later 1920s that a new Zionist club was formed on campus named the American Student Zionist Federation or Avukah. Although we do not have a precise date when this organization was created, Michigan Avukah became active approximately during the fall 1927 semester, roughly one year after the founding of Michigan's Hillel chapter.[115] The national Avukah had been founded in Washington, D.C. in July 1925 following the collapse of the national Intercollegiate Zionist Association.[116] Its founding occurred at the annual convention of the Zionist Organization of America and it would become an autonomous affiliate of the ZOA.[117] Avukah's organizers professed to have a more activist spirit than the previous Intercollegiate Zionist Association or Menorah. The very name Avukah (meaning "Torch") "was deliberately chosen to contrast with the milder emblem of Menorah ("candelabra",) betokening a new militant and aggressive spirit."[118] Avukah's constitution stated the organization's goals as promoting the Basel program of the First World Zionist Congress and "to study the life and literature of our people from the positive, creative Jewish national standpoint; to arouse

114. A HathiTrust-generated search of the *Michiganensian* yearbooks for the twenties shows that the last mention of the Michigan Zionist Society in a yearbook profile was in 1922; and the final mention of the Jewish Student Congregation was 1924. Neither the JSC nor the Michigan Zionist Society ever had their own page in the *Michiganensian* during their respective existences.

115. Although the precise date is not certain, a *Hillel News* article from October 1930 states that the Michigan Avukah "will begin its fourth year of existence on the campus under the leadership of Herman M. Pekarsky." See "Avukah Sponsors Zionist Lectures," *Hillel News* (hereafter cited as *HN*), October 8, 1930. The earliest mention of Avukah in the *Michigan Daily* is June 25, 1929, announcing that the University of Michigan would host Avukah's annual convention on June 28 and 29, 1929. See "College Zionists to Convene Here," *MD*, June 25, 1929.

116. Jospe, "Jewish College Students," 138.

117. "Student Zionists Form New Body at Recent Convention," *Detroit Jewish Chronicle*, July 17, 1925.

118. "Student Zionists Form New Body at Recent Convention," *Detroit Jewish Chronicle*, July 17, 1925.

the Jewish national consciousness of our youth; to establish contact with the spirit and work of the Chaluzim ("pioneers") of Palestine; to aid in the development of the Hebrew University of Palestine, and to co-operate with student Zionist bodies throughout the world in carrying out the aforesaid purposes."[119]

The University of Michigan was not represented among the fifty-one Jewish student leaders who attended the Washington D.C. conference. A campus Avukah chapter was not formed until two years later when the number of Avukah campus chapters doubled.[120] By the fall of 1928, Avukah was sponsoring invited speakers to the University of Michigan's campus.[121] The chapter's growing role within the national organization can be gauged by the fact that the University of Michigan would host Avukah's annual convention in late June 1929 in Lane Hall.[122] Although the Michigan chapter was a branch of the national Avukah, the organization was effectively intertwined with Hillel: Avukah and Hillel shared the same building (615 E. University), and the *Hillel News* would announce Avukah-related events and other news associated with the club. The close relations between Hillel and Avukah were already evident by 1929 when the *Hillel News*—first published in the 1929–30 school year—provided a summary of Avukah's June 1929 national convention, claiming that it was the university's "first convention of peculiarly Jewish interest."[123] The two

119. "Student Zionists Form New Body at Recent Convention," *Detroit Jewish Chronicle*, July 17, 1925.

120. Jospe, "Jewish College Students," 138. The first mention of Avukah in relation to Ann Arbor is a December 1927 notice of an upcoming Jewish student musical performance and visit by a Baltimore-based rabbi on behalf of Hillel and Avukah. "Jewish Students in U. of M. Play," *Detroit Jewish Chronicle*, December 2, 1927.

121. "Kay Addresses Avukah Meeting," *Detroit Jewish Chronicle*, October 29, 1928.

122. "Zionist Student Organization Will Meet Here This Week End," *MD*, June 26, 1929. The *Detroit Jewish Chronicle* reported that the decision to host the national Avukah convention in Ann Arbor was due to the fact that a national Zionist convention was to be held in Detroit at the same time. "Ann Arbor Chosen for Avukah Meet," *Detroit Jewish Chronicle*, May 24, 1929.

123. "Michigan Men Elected Executives of National Student Zionist Group, Ann Arbor Convention," *HN*, October 3, 1929.

organizations' close relationship is further evident in the joint hosting of lectures and other events, such as Oneg Shabbat, the joyous celebration of the Sabbath's arrival on Friday evening.[124] A bureaucratic measure that even further solidified this interactive relationship was that Avukah's president automatically became a member of the Hillel Council.[125] At Hillel's annual spring dance, Avukah also benefited from Hillel's generosity as it was able to sell corsages in an effort to raise money for the Jewish National Fund: an effort that Avukah seemingly often undertook.[126] U-M's Hillel Foundation consistently supported and collaborated with the university's chapter of Avukah.

Although its purpose was to promote the idea of a Jewish homeland, Avukah also had broader aims. In the *Hillel News* of October 1929, Avukah is described as "a gathering of those who wish to think seriously about the place and function of Jewish youth in the world about it."[127] This in practice meant the formation of study groups to consider works of Hebrew literature, open forums on Zionism, and banquets.[128] The Michigan Avukah chapter even prided itself on creating "probably the first [study group] in an American University that had as its sole purpose in the speaking and reading of Hebrew."[129] The key events that Avukah sponsored—and would continue to do so during this period— were visiting speakers such as prominent rabbis who spoke on Zionist-related issues or provided eyewitness accounts of events

124. "Announce Hillel Lecture Program," *MD*, January 11, 1930; "Julius Chajes to Play Here," *MD*, May 3, 1941; "War Events Topic of Hillel-Avukah Talk," *MD*, December 5, 1942; and "Hillel, Avukah Jointly Sponsor Party Saturday," *MD*, February 18, 1943.

125. "Hillel Chooses New President," *MD*, May 4, 1939.

126. "Hillel to Begin War Loan Drive at Spring Dance," *MD*, April 20, 1945.

127. "Avukah," *HN*, October 3, 1929; and "Avukah Banquet Proves Success," *HN*, January 23, 1930.

128. "Achad Ha-am and Hebrew Groups Form Part of Avukah's Varied Program of Activities," *HN*, November 27, 1929.

129. "Avukah Closes Busy and Successful Year; Wise, Butzel, Samuels, Fram Address Group," *HN*, May 22, 1930.

in Palestine.[130] In order to provide its members with the maximal extent of Zionist educational opportunities, the national organization hosted an annual "Avukah summer school."[131] In 1942, the *Michigan Daily* announced that University of Michigan students— along with students from nine other universities—would be attending the Midwest Avukah Region Summer School and Cooperative Camp.[132] Additionally, the national body organized the Palestine Work-Fellowships—a yearlong fellowship opportunity during which the selected students would fully immerse themselves "in the life of the agricultural collective, and is afforded special facilities for the studies of the problems of Palestine"— for which Avukah members could apply.[133] The *Michigan Daily* also announced in the summer of 1941 that "Avukah, student Zionist organization, will continue its educational and social program for two weeks at the end of June, and two weeks at the end of September, in national summer cooperative camps."[134] The promotion of a Jewish homeland and furthering of Zionist education were clearly quintessential to the Avukah organization.

Despite its serious, even scholarly, orientation, Avukah was not devoid of social activities. A blurb in the *Michigan Daily* in late November 1931 advertised an upcoming Avukah meeting in which "movies will be shown and there will be dancing between reels."[135] Throughout its years at the University of Michigan, Avukah hosted not only movie nights but also dances, parties celebrating Jewish holidays—Purim, Chanukah, Passover, Succoth (generally accompanied by traditional food, dances, and songs)— teas, picnics, and communal suppers.[136] Nonetheless, the majority

130. "Avukah Closes Busy and Successful Year; Wise, Butzel, Samuels, Fram Address Group," *HN*, May 22, 1930.

131. "Scholarships to Camp Offered Jewish Students," *MD*, June 2, 1934.

132. "Students Invited to Avukah Camp," *MD*, August 22, 1942.

133. "Palestine Work Prizes Open to Applicants," *MD*, March 31, 1939.

134. "Zionist Group Plans Activity," *MD*, June 8, 1941.

135. Daily Official Bulletin, *MD*, November 29, 1931.

136. "Events Today," *MD*, March 20, 1938; "Coming Events," *MD*, December 9, 1939;

of Avukah's activities centered naturally upon Zionism. By the fall of 1930, Avukah sponsored lecture series and conducted seminars on the history of the Zionist movement.[137] It organized its yearly activities according to some predominant theme. Thus, for example, for the 1931–32 academic year, the group chose "Zionism and the American Scene," which was "designed to allow ample opportunity for those interested in the Jew's relation to the rest of the world to express their views, as well as to interest those individuals who at the present time have but a rudimentary idea of Jewish nationalism."[138]

During wartime, Avukah attempted to address current issues facing not only its membership but also the wider world. Already in late 1938, the organization held a discussion of the "present Jewish refugee situation."[139] Furthermore, in the fall of 1942, Avukah collaborated with the War Manpower Board to organize a work holiday, during which the organization's members harvested farm crops.[140] Following the bombing of Pearl Harbor, Avukah and Hillel were quick to respond and engage by organizing a lecture that would address "the course of events since the bombing."[141] In early 1944, shortly before Jewish immigration into Palestine was to end as stipulated in the British government's White Paper of 1939, Avukah circulated petitions—which it intended to send to the British ambassador in Washington—in an effort to extend the

"Today's Events," *MD*, April 27, 1940; "Herbert London to Talk," *MD*, October 16, 1940; "Jewish Film Will Describe Zionist Feats," *MD*, December 15, 1940; "Picnic to be Given," *MD*, October 25, 1941; "Avukah Will Hold Purim Celebration," *MD*, March 8, 1942; "Daily Official Bulletin," *MD*, June 20, 1942; "Avukah to Hold Freshman Tea," *MD*, March 19, 1944; and "Avukah Will Show Movie on Palestine," *MD*, April 28, 1945.

137. Avukah Sponsors Zionist Lectures," *HN*, October 8, 1930; and "Zionist Class Will be Conducted by Avukah," *HN*, October 22, 1930.

138. "Avukah Organization to Hear M.B. Pekarsky," *HN*, October 8, 1931.

139. "Avukah to Discuss Refugee Situation," *MD*, December 8, 1938.

140. "Avukah Work Holiday to Aid Manpower Board," *MD*, November 13, 1942.

141. "War Events Topic of Hillel-Avukah Talk," *MD*, December 5, 1942.

immigration period past that specified in the document.[142] Similarly, Avukah once again appealed to the campus the year after, asking "students of all faiths . . . to sign a petition . . . protesting the Anglo-American decision on Tuesday denying the immediate entrance into Palestine . . . of more than 4,500 homeless European Jews."[143] There is no doubt that during the war years, Avukah sought ways to engage its membership in a discussion of war-related issues, especially those that pertained to Jewish concerns.

In its focus on Jewish statehood, Avukah was probably the least integrative institution among those surveyed in this chapter with respect to helping Jewish students negotiate the balance between their Jewish identity and the broader campus culture. By its very nature of placing Zionism at the core of its existence, Avukah represented the "exit" option for Jewish students, not the "voice" or the "loyalty" options of other organizations on campus. Indeed, Avukah saw its role as linking the campus student to the broader issue of Palestine rather than cultivating Jewish life at the university. As one editorial put it, "Avukah is but a singularly small part of a huge active organization which has for its purpose the nationalization of Palestine. This local student organization is the connecting link between the young student and this ideal."[144] While generally focused on its deeply political goal of having Jews leave the Diaspora for Palestine, Avukah did not completely spurn its presence as a social body on campus. It made a concerted effort to collaborate with other organizations both on and off the University of Michigan campus to attract Jewish students in that venue as well. Thus, for example, the University of Michigan chapter of Avukah once hosted the Wayne State chapter of the organization for a social party to which "all [were] welcome."[145] At least two of the aforementioned film evenings that Avukah hosted were staged in collaboration with

142. "Petitions Ask Revocation of White Paper," *MD*, February 11, 1944.
143. "Student Petition," *MD*, November 16, 1945.
144. "Avukah," *HN*, October 14, 1931.
145. "Events Today," *MD*, April 2, 1938.

other organizations, such as the United Palestine Appeal and the Jewish National Front.[146] In terms of being involved on the University of Michigan campus, Avukah recurrently functioned as a joint sponsor for events: co-sponsoring an Armistice Day program in the fall of 1938, partnering with the local chapter of Hadassah to host a German rabbi for a lecture, and joining a "Co-operative Council" with 22 other University of Michigan student groups upon the council's founding in 1933.[147] Furthermore, given its very close ties with Hillel, there existed most certainly much overlap in membership and joint participation in these two organizations' respective events.[148] Hillel, without a doubt, was by far the most important Jewish organization on campus and the only one among those presented in our study that survived the period until 1945 and continues to thrive to this day.

Hillel and Its Origins[149]

There is something very telling in the fact that Hillel emanated from the country's Midwest and its great public universities rather than from the East Coast, which has consistently embodied the core of Jewish life in the history of the United States. It was not at the City College of New York (CCNY), where in 1918/19 the student body comprised 78.7% Jews; nor at neighboring New York University, with its student body consisting of 47.5% Jews; and not even at elite Columbia University, where 21.2% of students were

146. "Coming Events," *MD*, May 4, 1940; and "Zionists Sponsor Movies," *MD*, January 11, 1942.

147. "Two Meetings Will Celebrate Armistice Day," *MD*, November 11, 1938; "Jospe to Talk on American Jews Today," *MD*, February 4, 1945; and "Groups Name New Council for Campus," *MD*, December 12, 1933.

148. For example, Josephine Stern presented a talk at Avukah on "Zionism and the American Scene," *MD*, January 12, 1932.

149. Our earlier book considers the history of Hillel at the University of Michigan in greater depth. What we provide in this section is both a summary of some of our earlier findings and additional discussion on Hillel's midwestern origins. See Markovits and Garner, *Hillel at Michigan*.

Jewish at this time. Neither was Hillel first established at Harvard (10% Jewish student population), Johns Hopkins (16.2%), Boston University (9.9%, University of Pennsylvania (14.5%), nor the University of Chicago (18.5%). Rather, it was in the Midwest's public university powerhouses—the University of Illinois with 4.2% of the student body being Jewish right after the First World War, the University of Wisconsin with 4.1%, the Ohio State University with 4.5%, and the University of Michigan with 4.0%—that Hillel organizations were established in 1923, 1924, 1925, and 1926, respectively.[150]

We see two reasons for this development. One reason, of course, has to do with the fact that various Jewish organizations preceded Hillel, mainly at East Coast universities, due to the large number of Jewish students there. The first among these was the ZBT fraternity founded under the Hebrew name (Zion Be-mishpat Tip-padeh; "Zion shall be redeemed by justice" [Isaiah 1:27]) at CCNY in 1898 "to encourage the study of Jewish history and culture among Jewish students, but shortly afterwards converted into a Greek-letter fraternity."[151] The transition from Hebrew to Greek letters signaled to the world very clearly that the young

150. Rubin, *Road to Renaissance*, 5. The percentages of Jewish students at these universities right after the First World War come from Jospe, *Jewish Students*, 6, 7, 8. Other than Rubin's work, which provides some useful information on Hillel in an otherwise cursory treatment of it in a brochure-like publication full of photographs, and Jospe's "Jewish College Students", which, too, offers fine data on Hillel but has the appearance of a typescript manuscript rather than that of a published book, we only found one book on Hillel: Webber and Sacks, *B'nai B'rith Hillel Foundation*. This book deals almost exclusively with British Hillel. Our research did not yield any work on individual chapters of any Hillel Foundation in North America or anywhere else in the world.

151. Jospe, "Jewish College Students," 135. To be sure, Pi Lambda Phi, founded at Yale University in 1895 by three Jewish students, preceded ZBT by three years. But "Pi Lam," as it was called, "was completely non-sectarian and its leadership refused to acknowledge any other classification. Nevertheless, until World War II its non-Jewish members never numbered more than a handful, and it was almost invariably classified as 'Jewish' by the rest of the world." Sanua, "Jewish College Fraternities,"10.

men who had created this organization were at least as interested in its social aspects as they were in its Jewish ones. By switching from Hebrew to Greek, this fraternity conformed fully to the prevailing mode. It was a Jewish entity that embraced the cultural codes of the dominant Gentile world around it. Other similar Jewish organizations followed rapidly: "the first professional fraternities, Sigma Epsilon Delta for dental students in 1901, and Phi Delta Epsilon for medical students in 1904. The first sorority, Iota Alpha Pi, came in 1903, as the Jewish girls began to follow their brothers into the collegiate world."[152]

As we have seen in our account of the situation at the University of Michigan, there were other organizations as well, such as Zionist societies at CCNY in 1902 and at Harvard and Columbia in 1905; "the University Jewish Literary Society at Minnesota in 1903; Menorah societies at Harvard in 1906 [the first one of its kind] and at Missouri in 1907; the Ivrim at the University of Illinois and the Society for the Study of Jewish Literature at the University of Texas in 1907; the Hebraic Club at Yale in 1909, and the Calipha club for the Study of Jewish Culture and Questions at the University of California in 1910."[153] Most of these organizations merged into the growing Menorah movement founded at Harvard by Henry Hurwitz, Horace Kallen, Leo Sharfman and others. There were other Jewish student organizations beside those in Menorah, among which, perhaps, the Zionist outfit Avukah, founded in Washington, DC, in 1925, became the most prominent. Closely associated with the Zionist Organization of America (ZOA) and Hadassah, Avukah—just like Menorah—proliferated among Jewish students on America's campuses, Michigan's included. All these organizations shared one important thing: they were almost exclusively student-run and student-dominated institutions with virtually no connection to the Jewish community off campus. Despite Avukah's affiliation with ZOA, the former ran its own

152. Levinger, *Jewish Student*, 2.

153. Jospe, "Jewish College Students," 135

affairs completely independent of the latter and indulged in major ideological conflicts between Revisionists and Labor Zionists that was to split Avukah in 1934 and lead to its demise in 1942.

As Marianne R. Sanua's pioneering work so convincingly shows, Jewish fraternities and sororities were the main places at American universities where Jewish students could congregate and socialize unencumbered by a hostile world whose fraternities and sororities, more often than not at the time, remained closed to Jews.[154] These organizations became crucial places for Jewish students to find a home away from home during their years in college. Moreover, they played a decisive role in the Jewish marriage market, because through these fraternities and sororities young Jewish students had a chance to meet one another. Fraternities and sororities replaced the famed matchmaker of yore for many Jewish students certainly until the end of the Second World War, which also forms the end focus of this project. But fraternities and sororities never had the comprehensively cultural, decidedly intellectual, and broadly inclusive social mission or self-understanding that Hillel was to assume. They were closed entities that chose their membership according to certain criteria that—by definition—emphasized some exclusivity, some special characteristic, and some particularity that remained incompatible with the all-purpose organization of Hillel's model. Moreover, fraternities and sororities constructed, experienced, and practiced their Jewishness very differently from how Hillel envisioned its Jewish identity, leading to tensions between the two.

The second reason for Hillel's midwestern roots concerns Jews' position in society—and society's reaction to Jews—being different in the Midwest from that on the East Coast. Because fewer Jews were in the Midwest, their fear of losing their Jewish identity—be that mainly of an ethnic, religious, or cultural variety or, as frequently the case, an undefinable mixture of all three—was more pronounced in the Midwest than on the East

154. Sanua, *Going Greek*; and Sanua, *"Here's to Our Fraternity."*

Coast. Jewish students at midwestern universities, virtually all of whom hailed from this region in the early 1920s, had to remain more closely associated with their larger communities outside the walls of academia if they were to continue their active Jewish identity. Thus, the town-gown separation that emerged on the East Coast would have been less viable in the Midwest.

But there was another major difference between the Midwest and the East Coast: the role of their respective institutions of higher learning. Whereas private institutions—with few exceptions, most notably CCNY—dominated on the East Coast, it was, again with some exceptions (University of Chicago and Northwestern University), the large public state universities that characterized higher education in the Midwest. These institutions were creations either of the Northwest Ordinance, as in the case of the University of Michigan and Indiana Seminary, later to become Indiana University in Bloomington; or mainly, of course, of the Morrill Land-Grant Act, as in the case of Michigan State University, the University of Illinois at Urbana-Champaign, the University of Minnesota, the University of Wisconsin at Madison, and the Ohio State University. These midwestern universities developed a completely different relation to the public trust than their East Coast counterparts, featuring a much greater sense of obligation to the community whose intellectual and cultural guardianship they assumed.

Put differently, the cultural and institutional boundaries that these universities had vis-à-vis the publics of their respective states were much less rigid and formidable than those denoting the identities of private East Coast institutions, especially of the elite variety that were later to form the Ivy League. Thus, not surprisingly, it was a non-Jewish professor of biblical literature at the University of Illinois named Edward Chauncey Baldwin "who, troubled by the attrition of Jewish knowledge and loyalty which he observed among his Jewish students, pleaded with rabbinical and lay leaders in Illinois to develop"[155] a college program

155. Jospe, "Jewish College Students," 139.

that was to cast a wide net in which Jewishness—however vaguely defined—was to flourish on campus with the active help of the larger American Jewish community. Baldwin asked Rabbi Louis Mann, a prominent leader of the Chicago Jewish community, "Don't you think the time has come when a Jewish student might educate his mind without losing his soul?"[156]

If not at Baldwin's behest then certainly in cooperation with him and as a consequence of his intellectual influence did his colleague Benjamin Frankel, familiar with the three hundred Jewish students at that institution and their mainly tenuous relationship to Judaism, develop at the University of Illinois in 1923 what was to become the very first Hillel in the world. By all accounts, Rabbi Frankel was the ideal person to establish such an all-encompassing organization whose mission it was to include all Jewish students—regardless of political ideology, religious proficiency, or any other intellectual disposition or ability—in all things Jewish broadly conceived and implemented. Of warm disposition and respected as a man of great intellect and learning—for example, Abram Sachar credited the birth of this organization to Frankel's "remarkably expansive, lovable personality, his genius for friendship, his courageous idealism and love for a great cultural heritage"[157]—Frankel envisioned a place on campus that would offer Jewish students an emotional home, a social haven as well as an intellectual resource during their four years at university. Above all, this structure was to provide a crucial bridge between the university and the outside world, not least in the funding of the former by the latter. For that purpose, Frankel constituted a board of lay leaders from outside the university who were to assist him in his endeavors right from the beginning. Moreover, Frankel included his University of Illinois colleague, the esteemed historian Abram I. Sachar, who would later—upon Frankel's untimely death in 1927 at the age of thirty—become Frankel's successor as the leader of this organization at the University of Illinois in 1928, the first full-time director of such an organization in the country and, in many ways, Hillel's most important national figure of all time.

By any measure, Sachar emerged as one of American Jewry's foremost leaders and most prominent public figures in the twentieth century. He had been graduated Phi Beta Kappa from Washington University in St. Louis, received a PhD from Cambridge University, and began his teaching career at the University of Illinois in 1923. In addition to his directorship of the Hillel Foundation at the University of Illinois, Sachar became Hillel's first national director in 1932. As is well known, Sachar became Brandeis University's founding president in 1948, leading it to a world-class research university in his twenty-year tenure there. After his retirement as president of Brandeis University in 1968, Sachar continued his active involvement with this institution first as its chancellor and later as its chancellor emeritus. In our research for this book, we also encountered two additional names of people who seem to have been very influential in the founding and initial formation of Hillel: Alfred M. Cohen and Boris D. Bogen. According to the Michigan chapter's publication, *Hillel News*, Cohen and Bogen joined Rabbi Frankel "as the three men who made the Hillel Foundation a reality."[158]

Frankel decided to name this new entity "Hillel": "It was a felicitous choice. Hillel is a symbol of the quest for higher learning. It was a beautiful name, too. It appealed to the Christian fellowship that pioneered the foundation, since Hillel was virtually a contemporary of Jesus. In those days the Jewish community still felt the need for the Christian imprimatur."[159] Perhaps most crucially, Frankel and Sachar succeeded in having B'nai B'rith adopt Hillel at the University of Illinois, thus opening the door for a con-

---

158. *HN*, October 24, 1929.

159. Rubin, *Road to Renaissance*, 5. Hillel, of course, was also one of the Jewish people's most pronounced sages and one of its major scholars and teachers whose name therefore fit the world of higher education as modern society's major locus of learning, research, and teaching.

struct in which a non-university-based charitable institution was to fund a good portion of a university-centered entity's activities and existence. Frankel was instrumental in opening the second Hillel at the University of Wisconsin in 1924 with Ohio State's and Michigan's to follow in 1925 and 1926, respectively. Not until 1939 did Hillel open its first facility on the East Coast by establishing the Brooklyn College Hillel, which, with an enrollment of 8,000 Jewish students, formed a hitherto unprecedented challenge that Abram Sachar personally oversaw.[160]

Five decisive principles guided the establishment and maintenance of Hillel student organizations. First, bespeaking the seriousness of Frankel's institutional commitment and his acute awareness of the inadequacy of previous amateurish efforts on the organizational firmament of Jewish student life, Frankel insisted that Hillel be run by a permanent professional staff. "Every Foundation operates under the guidance of a Hillel Director, usually a rabbi who combines Jewish academic competence with experience in youth work. Hillel Counselorships—Hillel's extension service units—are served by a rabbi in the community near the campus, an educator or group worker, or a Hillel Director from a nearby Foundation."[161]

The second principle pertains to the broad, indeed ecumenical, nature of Hillel's purpose and mission. All Jewish students, regardless of their theological orientation or sophistication or their ideological predilections, are welcomed by Hillel. The organization is not to address itself to any particular intellectual or political or religious segment of the Jewish campus population. It is not to favor any group or orientation over any other. Hillel "is designed to serve all Jewish students regardless of their backgrounds, Jewish ideologies or denominational preferences, and it seeks to meet student needs on the very intellectual levels on which they may exist. Nor does Hillel sponsor or endorse any

160. Rubin, *Road to Renaissance*, 7.
161. Jospe, *Jewish Students*, 30.

partisan view of Jewish life. It is hospitable to every wholesome expression of Jewish interest or concern that may exist in the campus community. Hillel Directors respect genuine differences of conviction but seek to create a sense of community that will eschew divisiveness and relate the Jewish student to the totality of Jewish group experience in time and space."[162]

The third principle pertains to the quality of instruction and discourse set by the organization, which, simply put, must happen on an intellectually high level commensurate with the exigencies and rigor expected at an institution of postsecondary education:

> Jewish values must not remain frozen on the Sunday school level. The development of a college approach to Jewish life and experience is the *raison d'être* of a mature program for Jewish college students. . . . The Hillel program is designed to fill the vacuum that is created when the immature childhood notions concerning religion and Judaism which many students bring along when they enter college are shattered by the intellectual challenge of the university. . . . [The Hillel program] requires the use of educational methods and the development of resources which are geared to the intellectual needs of the academic community.[163]

The fourth principle addresses the synthesis of information and knowledge on the one hand with participation and involvement on the other. Although the acquisition of the former is an obligation in any environment of learning and forms the basis of any communal discourse, without its deployment in moral deeds and actual activities in the real world, it might very easily disintegrate into abstract, even futile, sterility:

> Hence it is a principle of Hillel work to relate the study of Jewish values and ideas to an effort to discover the moral and Jewish

162. Jospe, *Jewish Students*, 30, 31.
163. Jospe, *Jewish Students*, 31.

basis of actions which students may want, or should be encouraged, to take on basic issues of Jewish or general concern. Discussions of past or present Jewish needs are related to a study of Jewish relief agencies and stimulate the formation of a student campaign for their support. And a study of the values of the prophetic tradition can be applied fruitfully to contemporary issues of social significance and stimulate students to express their convictions in socially responsible action.[164]

The fifth principle demands that students run their own Hillel chapters by electing student leadership groups that help plan and administer the program: "The Director is the guide and counselor, but the students are given the opportunity to share responsibility in Hillel's operation and program development."[165] Students must staff every committee, write and edit all publications, and decide all featured programs, from dances to lectures and from excursions to socials. Students choose whom to invite as guest lecturers and what books and records they want in their Hillel's library. In other words, even though the director and the staff lent a much-needed professionalism to this overall endeavor, Hillel never departed from being a student-centered organization, where it remains firmly to this day. Finally, Hillel's financial support broke down as follows: "seventy percent . . . came from B'nai B'rith, 20 percent from community sources (mainly federations and welfare funds), and the rest from student registration fees and activities income."[166]

In an untitled typescript of eight pages that we found in our archival research at the University of Michigan's Bentley Library, written by a rabbi who was clearly a director at one of the eight Hillel branches that existed at American universities by the early

164. Jospe, *Jewish Students*, 32.
165. Jospe, *Jewish Students.* 32.
166. Jospe, "Jewish College Students," 40.

1930s, we find the following four justifications for Hillel's existence. These coincide and overlap with the five principles just listed but are of additional value because they were not written as a matter of an organization's founding policy in distant Washington or New York or Cincinnati or any other place that was home to large Jewish organizations at the time but rather reflected the tone of a hands-on practitioner in the field. We have reason to believe that the author of these pages was the then University of Michigan Hillel Foundation's director Bernard Heller, but we simply cannot be certain.

In this author's view, Hillel's first *raison d'être* is its educational mission.

> In the first place, it [Hillel] constitutes a vital and indispensable link in our system of Jewish education. . . . There was a time when such Jewish education ended with the Bar Mitzvah and Confirmation. We have now begun to realize, however, that Jewish education is more than a preparation for a juvenile ceremony. . . . The Jewish education of our boys and girls ceases, however, with their entrance into the Colleges and Universities. . . . The years of college have created a gap in their spiritual and cultural strivings. They return to their homes and communities skilled in their respective professions and perhaps laden with information of the way and views of other people, but they are bereft of the knowledge of their own civilization and contribution to the storehouse of human learning. They attended strange vineyards, but left their own to neglect. The Hillel Foundation bridges over this gap. Side by side with a college education it intends to offer the Jewish student courses in Jewish history and literature and philosophy so that when he graduates, his education will not be lop-sided, but well-rounded.[167]

167. Untitled typescript, Ruthven, box 7, folder 27, BHL.

The second purpose pertains to Hillel as a spiritual source for students in an increasingly secular world.

> Secondly, the Hillel Foundation has come to promote the spiritual nature of the Jewish student. . . . To be truly educated one needs to be able not only to manipulate a Bunsen burner, but also must be able to guide himself by those beacons which have kept burning throughout the ages, and whose light illumined the course of many a ship on the stormiest and darkest nights. Education implies the ability to perceive and esteem those intangible realities which lie at the heart of life and the Cosmos. It is religion which strives to give us that vision and sense of value of the things that are eternally true and good and beautiful. . . . The Hillel Foundation . . . has come to see that the student goes through these critical periods of his life without being torn away from the spiritual moorings of his fathers. The Hillel Foundation wishes to guide him safely through the Scylla of former dogmatism and the Charybdis of his present doubts. The Foundation desires that the Jewish student should educate his mind, but not lose his soul in that process.[168]

The third purpose was Hillel's contribution to the universalistic values of an enlightened humanism, its "contribution not only to Israel, but to mankind."[169] After discussing the ill effects and adversities created by the particularisms that beset the age, the document suggests the following cure in which Hillel was to be accorded pride of place: "What is greatly needed today is a new insight and a new interpretation which will lead us out of this labyrinth of creeds and cross-purposes. We need a new point of view and philosophy which will collect the bits of truth that come to us from various sources and blend them into a harmonious whole."[170]

168. Untitled typescript, Ruthven, box 7, folder 27, BHL.
169. Untitled typescript, Ruthven, box 7, folder 27, BHL.
170. Untitled typescript, Ruthven, box 7, folder 27, BHL.

Hillel's fourth and final purpose according to this unnamed practitioner centers on the contribution of the foundation to "the cultural make-up of the University in which it is domiciled."[171] In other words, one of Hillel's missions is to be a good citizen at the university in which it operates and to enhance its host institution's intellectual and spiritual horizons and standing beyond its services to Jews and Judaism. Way beyond its particularistic tasks as a service organization for Jewish life on campus, Hillel was to see itself and function as an agent of universalistic values. The author writes,

> Judaism, as I have shown you, is more than a mere religion. It is a culture and civilization. Furthermore, it is a living culture and a living civilization. . . . The average American university, with the exception of Harvard and Columbia, includes in its circulum [sic] only courses in the Bible and its tenets. It is deficient in Rabbinics and Midaeval [sic] Jewish history and philosophy. The Hillel Foundation comes and supplies this need until that time when a definite chair will be provided for such instruction and this procedure supplements the cultural work of the University. . . . The Hillel Foundation helps, therefore, to make real the prophecy of a modern writer who, in speaking of America's cultural future, said, "In this infancy of our adventure America is a mystic word. We go forth all to seek America. And in the seeking, we create her. In the quality of our search shall be the nature of the America that we create."[172]

There could be no clearer statement of Hillel's central vision of itself as the core institution for providing an enlightened Judaism as a foundational element in the American republic.

In the following section, we will present a short summary of Hillel's founding years at the University of Michigan and highlight

---

171. Untitled typescript, Ruthven, box 7, folder 27, BHL.
172. Untitled typescript, Ruthven, box 7, folder 27, BHL.

its major contours in the late 1920s and throughout the 1930s. (For a much more detailed treatment of this matter, please consult our book *Hillel at Michigan 1926/27–1945: Struggles of Jewish Identity in a Pivotal Era*). An overarching conclusion analyzing the work and impact of Michigan's Hillel Foundation will end this chapter followed by a brief presentation of the involvement of Jewish students in three key team sports on the varsity level.

Hillel at the University of Michigan

According to the annotated chronology for the Hillel chapter at Michigan,

> first mention of The Michigan B'nai B'rith Hillel Foundation can be found in the hand-written minutes of the Executive Committee of the Independent Order of B'nai B'rith. 1925—Monday afternoon, December 7, the minutes record that Rabbi Leo M. Franklin of Detroit requested that a B'nai B'rith Foundation be established at the University of Michigan. 1926—December 12, the minutes (in part) read 'At the beginning of the scholastic year, the B'nai B'rith Michigan Hillel Foundation was founded at Ann Arbor.' This would strongly suggest that Hillel was on campus in 1926–1927. However, the University of Michigan index card in the National Hillel Office indicates that service began in 1927.[173]

Although it can be safely argued that Hillel at the University of Michigan was founded in late 1926, it is also evident that real operations in any meaningful sense did not commence until 1927. Hillel itself seems to have been torn about the date of its origin on the Michigan campus; we encountered some instances in which the fall of 1926 was mentioned as the founding date, but we saw other occasions in which 1927 was mentioned as such. It is quite

173. "B'nai B'rith Hillel Foundation at the University of Michigan, An Annotated Chronology," Hillel Collection (hereafter cited as Hillel), box 1, BHL.

clear, though, that the latter year must have been the foundation's first truly operational one at the University of Michigan. This is perhaps best reinforced by the fact that Hillel at Michigan celebrated its Bar Mitzvah in 1940 and not in 1939.

Michigan Hillel's foundation in late 1926 was also a matter of auspicious timing. The chapter was created not long after all the wartime-era Jewish organizations—Menorah, the Michigan Zionist Society, and the Jewish Student Congregation—had finally gone at least de facto if not de jure defunct. Hillel had no rival organization competing for members. Under the directorship of Rabbi Adolph Fink, Hillel hit the ground running to become a viable social forum for Jewish students on campus. Toward that end, mixers and dances became regular features, as did lectures and discussions on various topics relating to Jews. Already in the foundation's first two years, the catholicity of Hillel's approach to Jewish life became evident in its establishing nine committees that ranged from organizing discussions and debates to religious services and from fostering musical interests and literary circles to that of sports.

On the academic-intellectual side, the Educational Committee's achievements could not have been more impressive. Lectures on many aspects of Jewish history and religion appeared prolifically, as did discussion groups on topics that focused on general interest matters not immediately related specifically to Jews. The Literary Committee's eagerness to satisfy the deep and broad cultural literacy and engagement that the Jewish students on the University of Michigan campus clearly possessed manifested itself in many activities, not least in the establishment of a publication called the *Literary Comment*, which was to become a forum for budding poets and writers of all kinds. Prominent faculty members as well as President C. C. Little spoke at Hillel's many events that were often, though not always, chaired by Director Fink. Nationally prominent figures such as Abba Hillel Silver also came to campus to speak at Hillel. In its commitment to fostering all aspects of American life and culture—beyond the intellectual, literary, and religious—among Jewish students at Michigan, Hillel established an Athletics Committee whose most important innovation was the introduction of women's athletics to the community of Jewish students on campus. Hillel organized women's teams in basketball, baseball, and golf. Perhaps no endorsement offered Hillel greater legitimacy in its early years among Jewish students at the University of Michigan than rousing praise of its existence and activities by the legendary varsity football player Ray Baer, guard extraordinaire of the Wolverines and teammate of Benny Friedman, perhaps Michigan's greatest quarterback of all time, who had graduated in the spring of 1926, thus a few months before Hillel's establishment on campus. Baer went so far as to deliver a speech in the fall of 1927 "in which he asked the student body to support Hillel with the same enthusiasm in which they support the Michigan football team."[174]

From Hillel's very beginning, the organization had to demarcate its profile in contrast to that of the Jewish fraternities and sororities that flourished on campus at this time. Hillel faced the difficult task of having to appeal to all Jewish students. As such, it had to toe a fine line among all constituents of the Jewish student community: Hillel had to value religion without being too religious. It had to express a clear Jewish identity without becoming too tribal. It also had to extol the larger context of the Gentile world but not let it swallow the Jews into the pit of assimilation.

While Hillel's target audience was clearly young Jewish men on campus, Hillel, to its credit, also included women from its very beginning, as evident in the organization's Athletic Committee's commitment to have women participate in sports. In a remarkably progressive editorial entitled "The Date System," the *Hillel News* featured the problematic issue of the stigmatization of women who dared appear with no man by their side at various Hillel-organized events.

174. *HN*, October 6, 1927.

Library, dance, and theatre dates play an important and justifiable part in university life. But—when the influence of the system extends to a point where a college girl fears loss of social caste if she appears at any kind of mixed function without an attentive male escort at her beck and call, it has gone beyond its limits. Hillel Foundation affairs are intended for men and women. Yet, women are conspicuously absent at most educational and religious functions, seemingly from a fear of appearing unattended. Women are the exception at discussion groups and classes and are absolutely never seen at Friday evening services. Before the recent committee banquet, several feminine members expressed timidity at the prospect of going undated. Appearance in public unescorted was looked upon askance in the Mid-Victorian period. *Today, however is an age of women's rights, and these rights are particularly advocated by college feminists. At every opportunity they are militantly advanced. Freedom of dress, of vocation, of the use of the cigarette are fought for at every step of the way.*[175]

We chose to italicize the last three sentences because both in form and content they could have been written by second-wave feminists of the late 1960s and early 1970s, excepting perhaps the touting of the positive markers of cigarettes as welcome symbols of gender equality. Hillel picked up this topic at later dates as well.

Already during Rabbi Adolph Fink's leadership as the foundation's director as well as under the subsequent directorships of Rabbi Bernard Heller, Rabbi Isaac Rabinowitz, and Rabbi Jehudah Cohen, Hillel became a center for a variety of activities that are immensely impressive in their intellectual breadth. During the school year, there was a bevy of regular lectures on topics of interest to Jewish students that often reached way beyond the scope of Judaism proper. These featured speakers from the University of Michigan's community of students and faculty, but they also included many guest lecturers from all over the country as well as abroad. There were many student forums, debates, musical

175. *HN*, April 26, 1928; emphasis added.

events, and, of course, dramatic performances, particularly those of the Hillel Players who attained a national prominence and importance way beyond Ann Arbor and the University of Michigan. Mention should also be made of the many courses that Hillel offered, on subjects from Judaism and Modern Thought, to Elementary Yiddish; from The History of Zionism to Jewish Ethics; from Post-Bible Literature of the Jews to Medicine among the Jews during the Ages, to name but a few.

And yet, despite Hillel's remarkably rapid growth and the scope of its activities, there were those who felt that both Avukah and Hillel were not succeeding in cultivating Jewish students effectively. One editorial in the *Detroit Jewish Chronicle* in 1928 complained that:

> "Of the 8,951 who registered their religious affiliations at the University of Michigan, 718 were Jews. This number, the largest Jewish student body to our knowledge ever to be recorded at Ann Arbor, again places to the fore the problem of the Jewish student.
>
> . . . young Jews of today are least informed about all the centuries of history that are personified in the Jew. The wise Jewish people has permitted its youth to become estranged from its traditions and romances; it has permitted young Israel to become orphaned from everything that is beautiful about their people and their people's story . . .
>
> . . . But being as they are, ignorant of Jewish tradition and Jewish history, uninformed on Jewish needs and aspirations, there is left for the Hillel Foundation and Avukah the difficult task of at least retaining in the breasts of the Jewish college youth a spark of interest and devotion to Jews and Judaism, in the hope that the ablest among them will eventually become leaders of a people starved for leadership."[176]

176. "The Jewish Student and Leadership," *Detroit Jewish Chronicle*, October 26, 1928.

woman attends one of the Foundations' social functions minus a male escort, she is immediately placed among those who come to Hillel merely 'to catch herself a date'; when she doesn't attend, she's not showing any spirit. It is because of this opinion of the men that more women do not come to Hillel."[184] By the spring of 1932, Stern and another female student, Jane Cohen, were invited to give Hillel's Sunday Service "inasmuch as the campus women were taking part in the affairs of the Foundation, it would be an excellent plan if the women were to be given their turn at the Sunday services."[185] Indeed, an editorial in the final issue of the *Hillel News* for the 1931–32 academic year specifically highlighted Stern's Educational Committee as the most active of that year; Stern herself was also elected to the vice presidency of the Hillel Student Council for 1932–33.[186]

In her career at Hillel's Michigan chapter, Stern played an important role in developing a sphere in which women students could play an active role in the organization. Her strong sense of civic engagement continued after she received her master's degree from Michigan in 1934 and later a teacher's certificate from Wayne University. She married an attorney, Leonard Weiner, and in 1934, founded a Junior Council in Detroit for the National Council of Jewish Women (NCJW). She became a member of the NCJW's national board in 1953 and finally president of the national organization from 1967 to 1971. She also became a board member of Hebrew University in Jerusalem, the National Foundation for Jewish Culture, and the United Community Services Women's Committee of Metropolitan Detroit.[187] For her charitable work, Stern received a key to the city of Detroit in 1960 and a lifetime achieve-

184. "A Plea for More Women at Open Houses by a Woman," *BBHN*, November 5, 1930.

185. "Women to Give Sunday Service," *BBHN*, May 8, 1932.

186. "In Retrospect" and "Paul Wermer New President," *BBHN*, May 19, 1932.

187. Unpublished biography page from the National Council of Jewish Women in the Stern & Weiner Family Collection, box 1, TBE.

ment award from the Anti-Defamation League.[188] Stern's career at the University of Michigan could not have been more emphatically different than Myron Chon's: he was a secular Jew with little seeming interest in Jewish history and tradition, whereas she, in contrast, was steeped in many aspects of Jewish learning derived from her father's teachings and her experiences at Temple Beth El. However for both Stern and Chon, their very different Jewish experiences in their very different Jewish associations—Hillel and ZBT—provided each of them the opportunity to integrate within the broader campus community and to enjoy the solidarity and sense of belonging within a Jewish-specific organization.

An Overall Assessment of Hillel's Presence at the University of Michigan

Hillel commenced with the modest, even shaky, establishment of a new institution under totally uncertain conditions in 1926–27 and flourished to organize 90% of Jewish students on the University of Michigan campus, thereby becoming the largest branch of any Hillel Foundation at any North American institution of higher learning less than twenty turbulent years later. The organization's overall tally must be gauged a rousing success because the Michigan Hillel Foundation was able to thrive and offer Jewish students a sense of belonging in an era and a geographic environment in which antisemitism was not only rampant but indeed accepted public discourse.

As will be demonstrated in the ensuing chapters of this study, southeastern Michigan was at this time the home of two of the most vocal and virulent antisemites in the United States: Henry Ford and Charles Edward Coughlin. Ford's *Dearborn Independent* was his most pronounced medium for the dissemination of his vile antisemitism replete with all the common stereotypes of this

---

188. See her obituary, "Extraordinary Volunteer" [n.d.; but approximately October 25, 2000], in the Stern & Weiner Family Collection, box 1, TBE.

ancient human hatred: from the venal to the subservient, from the communist to the capitalist, from the cowardly to the devious Jew forever engaged in all kinds of conspiracies designed to spread his evil and conquer the world. Although this publication's very last issue appeared on December 31, 1927, thus at the end of the Hillel Foundation's first year on the Michigan campus, Ford's antisemitism did not diminish in subsequent years. Ford's influence over important political developments on the Michigan campus via his operative Harry Bennett's close connections to Michigan football coach and subsequent Regent Harry Kipke, if anything, increased in the second half of the 1930s, lasting well into the 1940s. Ford's profound connections to the University of Michigan in this era cannot be overstated. Charles Edward Coughlin, better known as Father Coughlin, was a Canadian-born Roman Catholic priest whose weekly broadcasts, filled with the vilest antisemitic bile extolling the policies of Adolf Hitler and Benito Mussolini, reached up to thirty million listeners throughout the 1930s.

One should also mention in the context of this geographic area's national prominence in antisemitic discourse and virulent antipathy toward Jews the presence of Gerald K. L. Smith, a clergyman and right-wing political organizer who founded the America First Party in 1943 and was a serious voice on the American Right and a prolific advocate of unbridled antisemitism, which he coupled with his hatred of communism. Both sentiments formed the core of Smith's authoritarian isolationism and his wish "to build a moral America based upon Christian morals, good citizenship, and patriotism—but with an authoritarian leader."[189] Smith moved to Michigan in 1939, where he came to base his operations during the years of the Second World War. He established close relations with Henry Ford, who initially admired Smith considerably and supported him financially before Smith wore out his welcome with Ford. Smith entered politics by running for a seat in

189. Jeansonne, *Gerald L. K. Smith*, 70.

the United States Senate from Michigan as a Republican in 1942, although this proved to be unsuccessful.[190]

Although there was antisemitism on the Michigan campus, there can be no doubt that the Jewish students, and Hillel in particular, had a potent advocate and defender in President Alexander Ruthven.[191] The president had nothing but great respect, even affection, for Hillel, which he saw as the most important, indeed possibly the only legitimate, representative of Jewish students on campus. Ruthven visited Hillel mostly, though not exclusively, for festive occasions. The president regarded Hillel as so important to the University of Michigan that he went out of his way to procure funds for the Hillel Foundation during a period of dire need. It is safe to say that Ruthven's intervention either saved Hillel from outright foreclosure or from experiencing a financial crisis that would have seriously curtailed its activities on campus. Hillel had an important part to play for Ruthven not only as a center for Jewish life on campus but also as one of the pillars of Ruthven's ecumenical vision of a religiously pluralistic University of

190. Jeansonne, *Gerald L. K. Smith*, 70–75.

191. We could not gauge how deep and widespread antisemitism was in Ann Arbor during this time, but there can be no doubt of antisemitism's existence on the Michigan campus, indeed its open articulation. After all, Jewish students at Michigan responded to a nationwide survey in 1939 to assess how Jewish students at an array of American universities categorized their institutions' feelings toward them with the verdict "strongly anti-Jewish." To be sure, it could have been worse if "severely anti-Jewish," the most negative of the four categories provided by the researchers, which was received by many of Michigan's peer institutions, among them prominent universities such as Columbia. Then again, it could have been better if Jewish students had characterized Michigan as exhibiting "none or little anti-Jewish feelings" or only "some anti-Jewish feelings," the first and second of the four categories in the study, respectively. We have no idea of the survey's methodological robustness and cannot vouch for its solid grounding in the social sciences of the era, but given the large number of universities appearing in the reported results, which thus permits some degree of comparison, we are reasonably certain that the Jewish students' perception of the atmosphere toward them at the University of Michigan in 1939 as "strongly anti-Jewish" has some validity.

Michigan. Indeed, we see Ruthven's assessment of Hillel as completely congruous with what Hillel saw as its own ideal: a broad-based, multipurpose, catch-all organization that provided a home for Jewish students; was their most effective representative on campus vis-a-vis all the university's constituencies; and remained deeply committed to being a place of learning, ideas, debates, reading, writing, acting: in short, of being an organization that cultivated the mind and was worthy of its surroundings furnished by the University of Michigan. Ruthven seemed not to have had similar affection for the Jewish fraternities and sororities mainly because of their role as primarily social institutions rather than intellectual ones, an issue that also posed a problem for Hillel. Ruthven certainly had much fewer, if any, sympathies for Jews who happened to have been radicals of one sort or another, particularly if they were members of Communist-affiliated organizations and hailed from the East Coast, whom the president actively fought as enemies of the University of Michigan's educational and moral mission.

In this context of ecumenicalism, so dear to Ruthven's heart and his vision of a proper university, Hillel's regular engagement with institutional representatives of Protestantism and Catholicism needs positive mention. Hillel made a concerted effort to reach out to these two faiths by organizing joint lectures, hosting jointly sponsored events, and engaging in regular contact. There is no question that this ecumenically positive and integrative dynamic existed on the leadership level of the institutions representing these three faiths. Alas, we do not know how deeply this reached into the world of regular Michigan undergraduates, meaning how closely students of these faiths encountered one another beyond a superficial socializing in the university's classrooms.

On any metric measuring Hillel's cultural offerings, there can be no doubt that they attained a very high level of sophistication fully in accordance with the standards of a leading institution of postsecondary learning. We need to mention first and foremost the Hillel Players, who, from what we can gauge, must have been a truly extraordinary troupe of actors throughout the period that our study covered. We would not be surprised if indeed the players were among the leading amateur theater companies in the Midwest, perhaps the nation. The players' annual gigs at the Lydia Mendelssohn Theatre became campus- and Ann Arbor–wide events of genuine importance. Perhaps to the players' greatest credit, they staged four student-written plays on an annual basis in the late 1930s, Arthur Miller's *They Too Arise/No Villain* among them.

Hillel's acquisition of books, periodicals, journals, magazines, and newspapers bespoke a truly impressive commitment to "high" culture, reflecting the intellectual sophistication of the students that regularly visited the foundation's premises. We believe that the quality and quantity of the items that Hillel ordered as a matter of course for its library must have rivaled that of a small college's. From Kafka to Werfel, from Freud to Marx, from Mann to Feuchtwanger—just to keep the list among authors producing their original work in German—Hillel's library composed of towering intellectuals of culture-defining writing is truly impressive. We have no way of knowing how many of Hillel's members—or students in general—bothered to read these major works of Western civilization. Perhaps they were just parked on Hillel's shelves gathering dust, but we doubt this for two reasons: First, our research gave us the impression that the Hillel library was a major locus of socialization for many students. Kids just hung out there, meeting one another, having tea, schmoozing. Second, we believe that the cultural capital in which many of these students grew up and which they brought with them to the University of Michigan as students featured a certain well-rounded *Bildung* in which at least some knowledge and appreciation of literature of this kind constituted social currency. It was "cool" for many of these students to have read Tolstoy and know Dostoyevsky. We believe this to have also been the case with music. Hillel's collection in this area impressed us even more than the printed material that it possessed. We do not believe that the Hillel Foundation would have continued purchasing records of the works of Sibelius, Mahler, Wagner, Brahms, Mendelsohn, Schubert, Dvořák, and many others had the students not shown keen interest in consuming them. We do know for a fact that students listened to Beethoven symphonies with such frequency that Hillel had to replace these records regularly with new ones because the records wore out.

The Hillel-organized lectures by invited speakers from across the country as well as by faculty of the University of Michigan all exhibited a high level of expertise and sophistication of the invitees who spoke on a wide range of interesting and demanding topics, from philosophy to history, from current events in the United States to developments abroad. Finally, of course, Hillel—by its very nature and mandate—provided a bevy of courses on many Jewish topics, from Hebrew and Yiddish language to literature in both, from Talmud studies to that of the Bible, from Jewish history to Jewish philosophy. Hillel's offerings on Jewish subjects were broad and deep. They fully accomplished Hillel's original mandate that such an educational effort "not remain frozen on the Sunday school level"; that "the development of a college approach to Jewish life and experience [be] the *raison d'être* of a mature program for Jewish college students"; and that this effort require "the use of educational methods and the development of resources which are geared to the intellectual needs of the academic community."[192] Hillel created an Honors College based on the Oxford tutorial system. This became a kind of parallel university to Michigan's, teaching subjects on Jewish topics that the university most certainly did not. The Hillel Foundation at the University of Michigan was quite possibly the only such institution in the country engaged in such a high level of education. Again, we have no idea how many students availed themselves of these offerings, but it is evident that there must have been some need for them on campus among some Jewish students since the regular curriculum at the university offered very few, if any,

192. Jospe, *Jewish Students*, 30.

courses on any of these topics, and those that it did, like courses on ancient Hebrew, were hardly attended by Jewish students, who much preferred to study French, German, and Spanish to fulfill their language requirement. The Hillel Foundation at the University of Michigan created a small version of what a few decades later, particularly following the massive changes in American higher education propelled by events of the late 1960s, came to be known as centers of Jewish studies.

Let us conclude with this assessment: Hillel's role on the University of Michigan campus included the organization's consistently complex relationship with the Jewish fraternities and sororities, which entailed coming to terms with the larger issue as to what it meant to be Jewish in America. From the start, Greek organizations were an irritant to Hillel, who found their purpose and participants shallow on all levels that mattered to Hillel. The students belonging to these organizations were simply not sufficiently Jewish for Hillel's liking, or—put differently—wrongly Jewish in Hillel's eyes. By featuring their Jewishness primarily in a social manner, the Greek organizations irked Hillel on numerous dimensions, even though part of its own mandate was precisely to provide a social organization for Jewish students.

But Hillel's interpretation of "social" was completely different than that of the Greeks. Whereas Hillel saw its social mission firmly anchored in Jewishness, it perceived the Greeks as displaying a culture in which Jewishness played a secondary role, or even worse, a role based solely on exclusion from Gentile Greek life. Therefore, the Jewish fraternities and sororities suffered a double stigma for Hillel, who viewed Jewishness at the Greek organizations as only grounded on not being accepted by the Christian world, on exclusion rather than on conscious agency. For Hillel, students belonging to the Greek system represented a hybrid for which Hillel had little patience. These students wanted to jettison their Judaism, which Gentile society and culture would not allow, resorting to the creation of a world in which they emulated the shallowest aspects of the dominant culture, hoping to master those aspects in their four-year stay at college later to gain much-desired entry into what at the time were closed places. Worse still, the actual lived Jewishness in which the fraternities and sororities engaged was insufficiently Jewish for Hillel on many levels, but most profoundly on the intellectual. Hillel disrespected the shallow anti-intellectualism of the fraternities and sororities that it also perceived as being detrimental to living a meaningful Jewish life. There is also no question that another reason for Hillel's tension with the Jewish fraternities and sororities hailed from seeing these Greek organizations as direct competitors for the attention and ultimately the adherence of the so-called independent Jewish students at the University of Michigan who did not formally belong to any organization. Throughout the period of this study, Hillel had to navigate the treacherous waters dividing it from the Jewish fraternities and sororities that composed the absolute center for Jewish social life at America's universities of the era.

In addition, Hillel had to balance the constant battles of how best to confront antisemitism and what it meant to be a Jew. Although not calling for the total assimilation of Jews into American society and thus the Jews' disappearance in it, a conformist view held that a less explicit expression of Jewishness would be to the Jewish community's benefit in the United States, which, very explicitly according to conformism, was to be the Jews' sole concern after giving up on Europe's more vicious and ultimately murderous antisemitism. Indeed, the essentially benevolent and tolerant culture of America formed the basis for this view. Students subscribing to it believed that—at least in part—antisemitism was a function of the Jews' doing, pertaining particularly to their overtly Jewish mannerisms, behavior, comportment, and language, which, to no one's surprise, Gentiles disliked (as did, of course, most of these "conformists"). Giving this voice further complexity (and power) was a generational and regional dimension that identified first-generation East Coast Jews—New York Jews in particular—as the most egregious representatives of these overtly Jewish mannerisms. If only the Jews would shed all these undesirable characteristics (Eastern European accents, loud-speaking voices, gesticulations with arms and hands, to name a few), anti-semitism would abate. If Jews would only become more American as defined by mainstream Gentile, Anglo-Protestant America, antisemitism would diminish, if not disappear. This strategy and path represented the most pronounced "loyalty option."

Opposing this conformist view were equally emphatic voices arguing that antisemitism's presence had nothing to do with the Jews' actual and concrete behavior, mannerisms, and language. Antisemitism, in this analysis, had many reasons, from economic to religious, from political to cultural; it had existed for a long time regardless of the Jews' actions. However, we were surprised that we did not find any instance of the argument that antisemitism had been alive and well in the world without the presence of any actual Jews; that this most historic of hatreds thrives on imaginary not real Jews; that antisemitism exists, indeed flourishes, without the necessity of having any Jews at all, as Paul Lendvai has so eloquently informed us.[193] The question then became how to assert one's Jewishness. We witnessed many expressions of this assertion in Hillel's world that one can all categorize as "voice options."

The first could best be characterized as the democracy-is-a-Jewish-value option. Like the previously mentioned conformism, this strategy also extols America but not by dint of its wealth or culture or consumerism or any other trait associated with macro America, rather by virtue of America's democratic institutions. This argument holds that nothing is more Jewish than democracy, that being Jewish and democratic are almost by definition compatible and symbiotic, often citing Justice Brandeis's famous dictum that the twentieth-century ideals of America had been Jewish ideals for twenty centuries. In other words, the essence of a Jewish identity coincides with America's ideals. This version also is assimilationist and conformist in a way, although exactly

193. Lendvai, *Antisemitism without Jews.*

in the opposite direction from the conformist view: in the loyalty option, it is the Jew who needs to conform to America; in the case at hand, it is as if America needs to conform to the Jews, with their millennia of democratic values and morally commendable ideals.

The next voice option enhances the scope of democracy and America's virtues to include labor. This social democratic version of Jewishness was well represented among Hillel's voices, of which none was more pronounced than that of Director Jehudah Cohen, who repeatedly emphasized the importance of featuring labor in any politics that presumes to be progressive and—crucially—beneficial to the Jews. One step further was the radical version, the most pronounced of the voice options, which often departed from that radical path by assuming a clear "exit" strategy instead. The radical (mostly, but not exclusively, communist) version saw its task to raise its voice to such a level as to depart frequently from—indeed reject—both America and often Judaism. This study does not analyze the many reasons why Jewish students and intellectuals played such a disproportionally large role in this specific exit strategy well beyond the United States. It is well known that in Europe, too, Jews played a most prominent role in the myriad manifestations of the political Left, from the varied versions of social democracy to the different faces of communism.

The leftist exit strategy became a major problem for the Hillel Foundation on the University of Michigan campus twice in the period of our study, in 1935 and 1940. As discussed in detail in subsequent chapters, a disproportionately large number of Jewish students hailing from the East Coast—New York Jews in certain instances—were expelled by the university administration for radical political activities, both on and off campus, involving organizations close to or part of the Communist Party. While being tepidly critical of the university's actions in 1935, Director Bernard Heller made it clear that he (and thus the Hillel Foundation at the University of Michigan which he led) would have preferred that Jews not be the leaders of such organizations—but could be their avid followers and sympathizers—because by holding leadership positions the Jews would not only suffer the consequences that they did but also cause problems for the larger Jewish community, which, as a minority, must always be aware of its precarious standing in a Gentile-dominated world. Despite *Hillel News*'s silence concerning the events in 1940, there can be no doubt that among the three grand options that Hillel delineated in an editorial published in that same year—"rightists," "liberals," and "leftists"—Hillel was ideologically and normatively closest to the leftists; however, it emphatically disdained the Stalinists, who, according to Hillel's thinking and that of many others then and since, perverted and abused the real identity of the Left.[194] The most pronounced exit strategy was, of course, Zionism, which saw no possibilities for Jews to improve their lives in the Diaspora—the United States included—via either the loyalty or the voice option, both of which Zionists saw as completely futile because Gentile society desired and permitted neither.

The Hillel Foundation at the University of Michigan had to integrate all these disparate voices and wishes. As a catch-all organization, it had to pursue a balancing act that, we believe, was immensely difficult. Adding yet another layer in Hillel's existence was its role of becoming a locus of Jewish life in Ann Arbor beyond the university's boundaries. As we mentioned at the outset of chapter 1, Jewish life in Ann Arbor was virtually negligible until the 1960s. In contrast to Michigan's peer universities located in larger cities, most notably Boston, New York, and Chicago, where Jewish students availed themselves of the resources and support of the local Jewish communities, this was impossible for Jewish students at the University of Michigan. If anything, the opposite became a reality in that it was the Jewish resources of the university as embodied by Hillel that furnished needed help with its programs, services, and facilities to the local Jewish community of Ann Arbor. Bernard Heller, Hillel's director in the 1930s, noted

194. *HN*, March 1940.

this very fact emphatically in a report that he wrote to President Ruthven in 1935, summarizing his (Heller's) first five years as director of Hillel:

> Michigan lacks one advantage. It is that the city in which it is situated is practically devoid of a Jewish community and, therefore, Jewish institutions and life. This town has a population of about 35,000. There are but a handful of Jews in the town. With the exception of two or more families, they are small shopkeepers and scrap and iron dealers. In order to provide for the social, cultural and religious needs of the students, the Hillel must not be merely a "shadchen" [matchmaker] between the students and the Jewish families of the town but the Foundation must create the very instruments and facilities for their [the students'] social welfare and their cultural and religious expressions. The Foundation at Michigan is, for example, called upon to establish not only Reformed but also Orthodox Services for its students and not only for the High Holidays but throughout the year. In the last few years the Michigan Foundation has gone to the expense of hiring a house and engaging a caterer who had the endorsement of the most Orthodox Rabbis of Detroit for the purposes of providing Pesach [Passover] meals to the Jewish students not only on the nights of the Sedarim [the first two nights of the eight-day Passover holiday] but for the entire eight days, a service which was greatly appreciated by parents— and without which many students would have been subjected to great mental anguish.[195]

In addition to the organizations discussed above in which Jewish students at the University of Michigan realized their social lives and pursued their extracurricular activities, it is also appropriate to research the presence of Jews on Michigan's athletic teams. This is the case for three reasons: first, because few, if any,

195. Heller's report to Ruthven, dated March 5, 1935, Ruthven, box 12, folder 12; BHL.

other venues in American life have provided such a major road to social acceptance and upward mobility than sports; second, because in no country in the world have sports played anywhere near the central role in the identity of postsecondary education as they have at American colleges; and third, because for Jewish young men in particular, playing sports in a serious manner bespoke a conscious effort to counter the massively prevalent view that Jews were people of the book and not of the sports field, that Jews and sports simply did not match. Thus, for Jews in particular, participating in college sports on the varsity level really meant a social commitment to the university and its community.

Sports (co-authored with Olivia Divak)

This section will present data on Jewish athletes who played sports at Michigan from 1900 to 1939. In particular, we chose to focus on the big three sports of baseball, basketball, and football. We did not consider other varsity sports because these three were and still are mainstays of America's sports culture, meaning that they are those rare sports that attained a valence in society that reach way beyond the playing fields and courts and represent generally recognizable and valued cultural icons. Being a baseball, basketball, or football player in the United States in the twentieth century entailed social acceptance and a distinction that athletes in other sports attained to a much smaller degree, if at all. It is significant that first-generation male Jewish children emanating from the petite bourgeoisie with immigrant parents who worked as tailors and small shopkeepers used sports as a vehicle for upward mobility and assimilation. As a result, particularly beginning in the 1920s, Jews participated in varsity sports at Michigan in a surprisingly high number, especially given the fact that there are very few Jewish athletes at Michigan today.

In the early twentieth century, the vast majority of Jewish students' parents had immigrated to the United States from Russia or other Eastern European countries. As a result of having immigrant parents, the class composition of students during this time period looked different than it does of Jewish students today at Michigan. For example, many parents of these Jewish students, as those of famed Michigan quarterback from the 1920s Benny Friedman, were tradesmen, such as butchers or tailors, and sports offered a form of upward mobility for their children to escape from behind the counters and the sewing machines. Friedman hailed from a Yiddish-speaking lower-middle-class family in Cleveland to which he remained loyal throughout his life. His father, Louis, came from Russia and was a tailor and furrier. His mother, Mayme (Atlevonik), also immigrated to the United States from Russia and became a homemaker in Cleveland, where she raised Benny and four of his siblings. Benny joined Sigma Alpha Mu during his years at the University of Michigan, which, after ZBT, was perhaps the best-known Jewish fraternity at the time. Friedman's active involvement with Hillel, which was further evidence of his identification as a Jew, came mainly after his being graduated from the university and when he was already a famous professional football player, since the foundation arrived on the Michigan campus in the year of Friedman's graduation. As to whether Friedman encountered any antisemitism during his four years at Michigan, his superb biographer Murray Greenberg indicates in his book *Passing Game: Benny Friedman and the Transformation of Football* that Friedman did indeed confront antisemitism on a number of occasions from his fellow students, although not from his teammates and the coaching staff (with the possible exception of one person who really disliked Benny). Greenberg writes, "His [Friedman's] experience with the Wolverines had been free of antisemitism (though he had his suspicions about George Little). He'd always considered himself a football player who happened to be a Jew. The exchange with the students confronted Benny with the unpleasant reality that at least to some people, he was a Jewish football player. And no Jewish football player had ever captained the Michigan Wolverines."[196]

196. Greenberg, *Passing Game*, 103.

An equally stellar Jewish Michigan quarterback, Harry Newman, came from Detroit, where he grew up in a family in which both parents had already been born in the United States. Rather than being a tailor or a self-employed figure living precariously on the economy's peripheries (or its less salient segments), Harry Newman's father was a Lincoln/Mercury dealer on Detroit's east side while his mother was a homemaker. Tellingly, Newman, in contrast to Friedman, did not speak Yiddish. Even though Newman fully identified himself as a Jew throughout his life, his ties to Judaism were much less emphatic than Friedman's. While the *Hillel News* proudly mentioned Harry Newman's many heroics on the gridiron, he, unlike Friedman, was not particularly close to Hillel and does not appear to have been involved in any of its activities.

The athletes whom we researched were typically first-generation Americans looking to assimilate into American culture and society. In almost every case, at least one of their parents—and often both—had been born outside of the United States. Thus, in addition to providing class mobility to these young men of modest and insecure means, sports also offered a hopeful road for integration into mainstream America and a concomitant shedding of their immigrant backgrounds. Sports was then, and remains today, truly the most attainable form of assimilation for the children of immigrants in the United States as well as elsewhere.

Michigan's Jewish athletes defied the stereotype of a Jew. The well-worn cliché of the Jewish boy as weak and scholarly, studying to be a dentist or a lawyer, was, of course, rampant in American culture at this time (and does in fact persist to this day). Views such as the following were commonplace: "The background, heredity, history and environment of the Jew have developed in him a serious-mindedness and self-consciousness which do not go well with a whole-hearted surrender to the joys of sport and athletics. But when a Benny Friedman comes to the fore, we begin to doubt and wonder whether or not our theory is sound."[197]

197. Greenberg, *Passing Game*, 77.

Whereas many of the Jewish athletes on Michigan's varsity teams were in fact studying to be dentists or lawyers, these young men were also multidimensional; playing sports was one but not necessarily the predominant aspect of their lives on campus. As a result, these Jewish student-athletes used sports to break down barriers and define their new identity as strong, American men. Athleticism is usually not associated with Jews, but interestingly, there were more Jewish varsity athletes during this era at the University of Michigan than at any other time in the university's history. Furthermore, these Jewish athletes identified themselves primarily as students, for whom sports was just another extracurricular venue that exemplified their integration into undergraduate life during their four years at the University of Michigan. For these young men, prowess at sports, perhaps more than anything else, expressed to them (although maybe less to the larger outside world) their full integration into the mainstream of American culture and society.

From 1900 to 1939, we found 128 student-athletes at Michigan involved in varsity-level baseball, basketball, and football whom we deemed with a reasonable probability to have been Jewish. We used the exact same method described in detail in chapter 1 to ascertain an athlete's likelihood of being Jewish. We cast our net widely here by including those students whom we categorized in groups 2 and 3 in chapter one (with 2 representing a student whom we deemed greater than 50% likely to be of Jewish heritage but less than 85%–90% likely, and 3 categorizing a student whom we perceived 90%–95% likely to be Jewish). Confirming the excellent all-around athletic abilities that some of these young men possessed, 26 of these athletes represented the university in more than one of these sports during their time at Michigan. College sports at this time assumed a very different form than they do today. Players then were not being recruited to the university for their athletic abilities; instead, they were exclusively students, with athletics assuming the position tantamount to that of being a member of any other extracurricular club or activity. Of the 128 athletes whom we deemed to be Jewish, 71 played baseball, 58 played basketball, and only 10 played football. Perhaps bespeaking football's cultural predominance at the University of Michigan, it should not come as a surprise that the most well-known Jewish athletes at the University of Michigan and beyond hailed from the small group of football players and not the larger ones of baseball and basketball players. In addition to the oft-mentioned Benny Friedman and Harry Newman, names such as Joe Magidsohn and Ray Baer were famous on campus and in the sports world at large.

Here is a breakdown by decade of Jewish student-athletes at the University of Michigan: From 1900 to 1919, there were a total of 24 athletes with 18 baseball players, 4 basketball players, and only 2 football players. However, 1920 to 1929 saw a large increase to 63 total players. During this decade, there were 29 baseball players, 30 basketball players, and 4 football players. In the decade of the 1930s, there was a slight decrease in the number of Jewish athletes but still a relatively large showing. There were 52 total Jewish athletes from 1930 to 1939 with 24 baseball players, 24 basketball players, and 4 football players.

After collecting data on these Jewish student-athletes, we broke down the results for each individual sport by a number of factors. First, we were interested in the players' geographic origins. Among the 71 baseball players, 23 were from Michigan (8 from Detroit); 16 were from New York (4 from Buffalo and 3 from New York City); 16 were from Illinois (11 from Chicago); 7 were from Ohio (3 from Cleveland); 3 were from New Jersey; and the remaining 6 came from Massachusetts, Pennsylvania, Washington, Wisconsin, Connecticut, and California. Whereas we expected to see a majority of these players hail from the Midwest, we were actually surprised by the relatively large number of varsity baseball players coming from the Northeast. Since this predates the national recruitment processes followed by Division I universities like Michigan in today's world, meaning that we are quite certain that none of these students were recruited by the university's scouts to come to campus, these data offer further evidence of the University of Michigan's respected reputation and far reach on the East Coast.

In addition to these players' geographic origins, we were also interested in learning about their majors on campus. They were diverse and represented a wide array of fields. Baseball players majored in literature, engineering, medicine, pharmacy, pre-dental, pre-law, business, education, and history. We were also interested in finding out about these players' standing on the team as well as the positions they played. Of the 71 baseball players, 8 held leadership positions as captains of their respective teams. We found this immensely significant because this clearly testifies to their being not only fully accepted by their teammates and the coaching staff but indeed honored and trusted by them. We do not know how explicitly Jewish these players were, but regardless it is quite certain that they were often identified as Jews from their names: Clarence Enzenroth, George Dillman, Herbert F. Steger, William Pucklekwartz, Harvey Straub, Avon S. Artz, Fred L. Petoskey, and Merle Kremer. Of the players whose positions we were able to discern, we found more Jewish pitchers and outfielders on the teams than infielders and catchers.

The results of our data for basketball are fairly similar to those for baseball. While basketball had fewer Jewish players than baseball, the former's players also represented a wide display of hometowns and majors. Specifically, of the 58 Jewish basketball players, there were 25 from Michigan (8 of those players were from Detroit); 8 from Illinois (6 from Chicago); 7 from New York; 4 from Ohio (2 from Cleveland); 6 from New Jersey; 4 from Indiana; and the remaining 4 from Pennsylvania, Missouri, Washington, and Kentucky. Fascinatingly, there were far fewer players from the Northeast in basketball than in baseball, perhaps denoting the fact that baseball at this time was already a truly national sport, indeed the country's national pastime, whereas basketball, although played across the country, was still largely a local phenomenon in both its playing as well as its following. The academic majors of basketball players were quite similar to those pursued by baseball players. They included pre-law, pre-dental, engineering, physical education, education, and history. Of the 58 Jewish basketball players, 6 were captains of their teams. They were Howard Birks, Gilbert C. Ely, Norman J. Daniels, John A. Gee, Leo C. Beebe, and William J. Cartmill.

Finally, the results of our data for football were very similar to baseball and basketball but on a much smaller scale. Of the 10 football players whom we categorized as being Jewish, their hometowns included Oak Park, Michigan; Allegan, Michigan; Detroit, Michigan; Rochester, New York: New York, New York; Utica, New York; Cleveland, Ohio; Louisville, Kentucky; Pittsburgh, Pennsylvania; and Memphis, Tennessee. Similar to those in basketball and baseball, football players majored in a variety of fields including engineering, medicine, and pre-law. Ultimately, these results reveal multiple patterns. With virtually no exceptions (even among star football players like Friedman, Newman, Magidsohn, and Baer), Jewish student-athletes were at Michigan primarily to receive an extraordinary education in a field in which they hoped to pursue a professional career upon being graduated from the university. These athletes were serious students studying difficult and challenging subjects such as law, engineering, and medicine, who also happened to play baseball, basketball, and football more as a hobby and an avocation, not a vocation. In addition, it is not surprising that the majority of the Jewish student-athletes were from the Midwest and the Northeast regions of the United States, as most of Michigan's student population as well hailed from these areas at the time (and continues to today). Moreover, the vast majority of Jewish immigrants to the United States settled in those regions, specifically in urban environments.

In addition to sports, these Jewish student-athletes were involved in almost every other possible extracurricular activity imaginable. Forty-two of the 128 students were fraternity members. Some of the young men were student managers or assistant student managers of various sports teams besides the ones in which they performed as players. There were two Jewish student-athletes who were also members of the Michigan Marching Band. Both of these student-athletes played the trumpet. Many of these players also held positions of leadership at the university, such as class treasurer, class president, class vice president, class secretary, literary officer (president), senior engineering committee member, recording secretary of the Michigan Union, literary finance chairman, class advisory committee chairman, student council (secretary), and secretary of the business administration class. The fact that these young men held such often time-consuming leadership roles illustrated their multifaceted talents and interests among which sports was but one. It also underlined their desire to seize every opportunity offered by the University of Michigan to advance their own professional standing and economic fortunes beyond the petite bourgeois, often immigrant, milieu in which they grew up. Just as impressive were the numerous honors organizations of which these students were a part. These included Phi Alpha Delta (Legal Fraternity), Aristolochite (Honor Society in the College of Pharmacy), Tau Beta Pi (Engineer Honor Society), Aeronautical Society, A.S.M.E. (The American Society of Mechanical Engineers), and A.I.Ch.E. (The American Institute of Chemical Engineers).

Many of the student-athletes were also members of popular clubs on campus, such as the Prescott Club, Griffins, Meese, Druids, Gargoyle, Newark Club, Chess Club, Auditing Committee, Oratorical Delegate, Michigamua, Vulcans, Varsity Reserves, Alchemists, Scabbard and Blade, Sphinx, Blue Key, Scalp and Blade Club, "M" Club, Military Ball Committee, Frosh Frolic Committee, Sophomore Prom Committee, and Manager's Club, and, of course, last but certainly not least, Hillel. Additionally, many of these Jewish student-athletes worked for the *Michiganensian*, the university's yearbook, as well as the *Michigan Daily*, the student newspaper. Here, too, student-athletes held leadership positions. Thus, one student was the business manager of the *Michiganensian* and another was a lead sports editor of the *Michigan Daily*.

Through their involvement with sports at its highest level,

these young Jewish men climbed yet another ladder to their inclusion in American life besides the one offered by education in the classroom. While all of these young men were serious students, they were also athletes. But above all, they were well-rounded undergraduates who used sports as a stepping-stone to upward mobility and integration into American society. In so doing, they employed a venue in which their excellence countered expectations and destroyed stereotypes. There can also be absolutely no doubt that these Jewish student-athletes' exploits on the playing fields and courts gave most Jewish Michigan students enormous joy and confidence in their own Jewish identities. Thus, for example, an article in the *Hillel News* of October 20, 1927, bursts with pride in describing the exploits of Ray Baer, Sammy Babcock, and Harold Greenwald on the football team; praises Ralph Cole's and Joe Morris's performances on the golf team; mentions Mannie Schorr, Clarence Barter, Meyer Rosenberg, Richard Fecheimer, and Ralph Miller on the swim team; and delights in touting Victor Berkowitz as the middleweight boxing champion on campus and Joe Stein as its featherweight title holder. As it has done for all ethnic groups in the United States and elsewhere, none more so than for fearful and ill-accepted minorities, sports gave Jews, both as its consumers but also its producers, immense pride and joy and self-confidence, possibly more than any other aspect of public life. Just think what pride the legendary Hank Greenberg's stellar performance in baseball, playing just a few miles east of the Michigan campus for the Detroit Tigers, bestowed on the Jewish community, particularly in Southeast Michigan, although nationwide as well.

Conclusion

In this chapter, we delineated the social world of Jewish students at the University of Michigan roughly between 1910 and 1930. The picture that emerges is one of a plurality of options that offered Jewish students important venues to live a good life on campus

154 THE BOUNDARIES OF PLURALISM
THE BOUNDARIES OF PLURALISM

during their four years at the university. Perhaps there can be no better way to conclude this chapter than to feature an official study conducted by the university on Jewish-Gentile relations. A survey on Jewish-Gentile relations among Michigan undergraduates conducted by the University of Michigan in February 1939 confirmed the cultural proclivities and sophistication of Jewish students on the Michigan campus as described in this chapter. In numerous instances in which the survey measured the cultural consumption of Jewish and Gentile students, the former clearly exceeded the latter on most dimensions one would associate with "high" culture and underperformed on items associated with typical collegiate culture like drinking and partying:

> Participation of Jewish students in extra-curricular activities and their wishes in these matters were found to be proportionally somewhat different from non-Jews. . . . In such activities as attendance at concerts, movies and the theater where anyone may go who can pay the price, Jewish students attended as often as Non-Jewish students. Jewish students, however, wanted to attend concerts oftener and the movie and theater less than non-Jewish students. Jewish students participated less than Gentiles in Beer Garden and Bar attendance, attendance at athletic games as spectators and playing cars, checkers and chess. Jews date about as often and want to date about as often as the non-Jews, but would rather not attend dances and parties as much. . . . The Jews pursue hobbies to a greater extent, play pool and billiards and bowl, participate in athletic games more than non-Jews. They sing and play musical instruments more and want to do so to a greater extent than Gentiles. All of the Jewish students reported that they listen to the radio or the phonograph; proportionally more Jews than non-Jews report that they do "leisure reading" on campus. Jewish participation in dramatics and debate is a little more than non-Jewish participation, and the Jews want to do this kind of thing oftener than the rest of the campus. . . . In matters of drama, Hil-

lel Foundation has its own dramatic activities. The Jewish students attend club and campus organization meetings more often than non-Jews. Also, there are proportionally many more Jewish students who attended three or more such meetings during the particular week surveyed. . . . It would seem, however, that though there may be some student clubs that discriminate against Jewish students, the Jews are participating at least as much, and maybe more, in extra-curricular activities.[198]

The survey makes it also clear that the Jewish student body at the University of Michigan was a good deal more secular than its Protestant and Catholic counterparts. What emerges here also is that contrary to the adherents of the two Christian faiths who identify their relationship to these religions mainly, perhaps primarily, in religious terms, the Jewish students identify their belonging to Judaism in much broader cultural terms.

In matters of religion it has been found by Mrs. Van Tuyl of the Psychology Department that Jewish students have more crises and have left the church in greater proportion than the Gentile group. The bulk of the Jewish students, however, would give their children the same religious training that they received in their childhood, but proportionally, the non-Jews would do so oftener. Of those Jewish students who would give another kind of training a third would give stricter training and a quarter no training at all. On the campus the Jews attend regular church service and so-called young people's meetings about half as much as the non-Jews, while they attend religious lectures and discussions somewhat oftener than the non-Jews. For one thing, the young people's meeting is a Protestant institution and strictly speaking there is no parallel institution for the Jews. It is claimed by Hillel students that Judaism is a way of life, and that many activities

198. Vicary, "Survey," 5, 6.

other than regular worship services are considered having religious significance. These activities would include such things as producing a Jewish play, or preparing a Kosher meal, and so on.[199]

One of the key figures that would help to define Jewish life on campus in the 1930s would be the university's president, Alexander Grant Ruthven. Indeed, as explained in chapter 3, Ruthven's policy of endorsing a pluralist campus community helped to define the role Jewish students and their institutions played at the university. However, Jewish students also, to their detriment, ultimately encountered the boundaries of Ruthven's pluralist policy. The story of how Jewish students both existed within and beyond the boundaries of pluralism at Michigan and a discussion of Ruthven himself follows.

199. Vicary, "Survey," 4.

CHAPTER THREE

ALEXANDER RUTHVEN AND HIS PLURALIST VISION

With the rise in the number of student enrollments in the 1920s, many universities struggled to adapt to a growing student body that was putting pressure on their infrastructure and resources. As Christopher Lucas notes, "in 1870, about 52,000 students were enrolled in four-year post-secondary education, or less than 2 percent of the population . . . by 1900 it hovered around 4 percent . . . By 1920s, the percentage doubles; and it was to reach 12 percent in the next decade."[1] The University of Michigan itself was not immune from this growth: in the academic year 1900–1901, the university had a little over 3,700 students; by 1919–20, 9,400; and in 1929–30, the student population had just exceeded 15,000 for the first time.[2] As already mentioned, the university struggled to accommodate these burgeoning numbers. One way to do so was an ambitious building program to accommodate students.

Another issue that came to the forefront in the 1920s was the increasing diversity of the student population and how it was to be managed. "Many schools imposed special admission tests or

1. Lucas, *American Higher Education*, 213.
2. "The President's Report to the Board of Regents 1940–1941." Ann Arbor: University of Michigan, 1941.

quotas for Jews, fearful that their presence would alter the character of the schools involved, and for the worse."[3] With the exception of the Medical School, the University of Michigan placed no quota on Jewish applications in the 1920s, although, under the presidency of Clarence Cook Little from 1925 to 1929, the university made changes to its admission practices by centralizing and standardizing admission requirements.[4] This measure involved changes to the application process in which the university began to ask high school officials whether a particular applicant was truly "fit" to undertake university study.[5] While devising new methods for sifting applicants was one way of attempting to stem the flood of new students, the lingering question, of course, remained as to what to do with students who were admitted. How were they to fit into an increasingly diverse campus? This was the challenge shouldered by Little's successor as university president, Alexander Grant Ruthven (1882–1971; president 1929–51) [Figure 3.1].

Ruthven's origins could hardly have been different from that of his Boston-born and Harvard-educated predecessor. The son of Scottish homesteaders, Ruthven was born in the town of Hull in Sioux County at the far western edge of Iowa. His youth on the family farm there engendered a lifelong interest in animals, and, after completing high school in a one-room schoolhouse, he began his secondary education at the Methodist-run Morningside College,

3. Lucas, *American Higher Education*, 213. As the official University of Michigan history explains, Little "was not willing to make academic proficiency the sole criterion of admission to the University. He wanted some further information about the character of the applicants so as to judge whether they were actually worth educating, a jarring thought." Although the authors do not reference this in relation to Jewish students, scholars of Jews in higher education have shown that "character" and "fitness" questions were one way of attempting to limit the number of Jewish applicants admitted. Peckham, Steneck, and Steneck, *Making*, 186; and Wechsler, "Rationale for Restriction," 643–67, esp. 649–52.

4. Borst, "Choosing the Student Body." The authors would like to thank Michelle McClellan for providing us with this reference.

5. Undated history of the University of Michigan Admissions Policy by Ira Smith. Smith, box 2, BHL.

Figure 3.1—Alexander Grant Ruthven Portrait: University of Michigan Library

which was at the time of Ruthven's enrollment only five years old.[6] Ruthven made the acquaintance of Professor Charles Adams of the University of Chicago, who offered him a scholarship to attend the university as a graduate student following the completion of his studies at Morningside. By the time Ruthven graduated from Morningside, Adams had become the curator of the Museum of Natural History at Michigan. Adams offered Ruthven a graduate assistantship beginning in the fall of 1903. This became the start of Ruthven's lifelong association with the university.

6. The biographical detail comes from Van de Water, *Alexander Grant Ruthven*, 15–24 and *passim*.

Ruthven diligently worked to complete his PhD in zoology; once completed, he became, upon Adams' departure, the curator of the museum. Ruthven spent much time conducting fieldwork both to build his professional reputation as a scientist but also to develop the museum's collections. By 1912, he was director of the museum, and, during the twenties, his main ambition was to see to the construction of an entirely new natural history museum, a dream that came to fruition with the eager support of President Little. Ruthven became dean of administration under Little beginning in 1928. However, the following year, Little's presidency found itself foundering after he had endorsed the sterilization of certain types of criminals and mentally handicapped persons in a series of speeches.[7] Appointed by the Board of Regents, not without some controversy, as Little's successor, Ruthven proved to be a contradictory president. Whereas he cleaved to such old-fashioned notions as the importance of character formation; Ruthven was also a modernizer who sought to put the university's antiquated administration on a newer footing by, for example, shifting authority from the deans to the faculty, fully believing that the decentralization of academic governance was an absolutely fundamental necessity to a democratic institution such as Michigan. Ruthven also created the administrative level of vice president and appointed an array of them, much like a business corporation, each of whom had binding authority over their respective areas.[8]

Yet it was Ruthven's beliefs in "character education" that would have a profound influence over campus life. As his biographer stated, "Ruthven's attitudes and values were, not surprisingly, in keeping with his times and his Midwestern heritage. His parents were humorless, Bible-toting Methodists, and he had a well-developed ethical system in keeping with the religious instruction

7. See Van de Water, *Alexander Grant Ruthven*, 51–53.
8. For Ruthven's administrative accomplishments, see Van de Water, *Alexander Grant Ruthven*, 83–95.

he received as a boy."[9] As a scientist, Ruthven rejected religious fundamentalism and its many strictures—he rarely attended church—and his views were also tempered by his strong belief in democracy. "It was these somewhat liberal attitudes, tempered by traditional ethical standards," his biographer asserted, "that Ruthven sought to impose on the Michigan students of the thirties."[10] The core of Ruthven's student policy would be twofold: character education and religious education. Ruthven's conception of character development meant cultivating students' inchoate abilities toward both spiritual and intellectual development. With respect to religious education, Ruthven sought to revivify the university's moribund religious culture, which had lain dormant in the free-wheeling twenties, in order to provide students with proper ethical guidance to their lives and, as it turned out, also to appreciate the growing religious diversity of the campus community.

Ruthven, then, was to have a major influence on the university's conception and construction of religious life that, primarily, meant an active interreligious relationship among Protestants, Catholics, Jews, and adherents to what was then known as "Far Eastern Religions." As such, perhaps no president in the University of Michigan's history had a more decisive role in the shaping of Michigan's Jewish student community than Ruthven. After his assumption of the presidency, he proceeded with the implementation of "a concept of the relationship between religion and higher education which was to assure the university's concern for, and involvement in, the religious education of students. It was not his intention to take religious activities out of the hands of students, but rather to establish the principle that the state university, which could never afford to be sectarian, could not, on the other hand, afford to neglect religion."[11]

Tout court, the implementation of Ruthven's pluralist vision

9. Van de Water, *Alexander Grant Ruthven*, 125.
10. Van de Water, *Alexander Grant Ruthven*, 126.
11. Austin, *Century of Religion*, 39.

marked the University of Michigan's first proactive attempt to address the issue of student diversity.[12] This diversity was defined in terms of religious affiliation, not race or ethnicity. Ruthven's goal was to create an interfaith campus community in which the four great religious traditions of Protestantism, Catholicism, Judaism, and "Far Eastern Religions" were to create a conceptual but also spiritual synergy and synthesis that was to provide a cultural foundation for an actively experienced common humanistic value system. Despite his religious upbringing, Ruthven did not want to turn Michigan into a religious school. Rather, religion had an important educational mission that one could safely call "secular." He was committed to religion's intellectual and moral contributions to society, not its ritualistic or spiritual ones. Above all, religion, as Ruthven wanted it experienced, had to be profoundly ecumenical. Ruthven would later explain his vision of an ecumenical campus community in his autobiography: "I was not brought up in what conventionally would be known as a religious family, but while I was in college I was fortunate enough to take, in addition to my other work, courses in the Bible, Christian Evidences, and Natural Theology. There developed from this early introduction to the field an interest in comparative religion which with my work in science has been instrumental in forming my concept of the nature of the world and man."[13]

After Ruthven arrived at Michigan as a graduate student in 1903, he found the teaching and study of religion to be inadequate on account of there being few classes devoted to religious studies and few institutions on campus promoting religion save for the Student Christian Association, which was an independent organization unrelated to the university. "These were inadequate for the students who wished to pursue intensive studies of the reli-

12. By contrast, Ruthven's immediate predecessors focused more on building programs (Burton) and changes to admissions policies (Little) to address the greater number and diversity of students on campus.

13. Ruthven, *Naturalist in Two Worlds*, 121.

gious backgrounds of different faiths."[14] Yet, as mentioned above, Ruthven's goal was not simply to promote research and study of comparative religions but also to foster the values of religious pluralism and tolerance on campus:

> I hoped that through our student religious center and programs in religious studies the wide variety of faith represented in the student body could come together with opportunities for discussions and mutual understanding and respect. The process was slow, but in later years for those students who took advantage of the cultural opportunities presented in and about the center the hope materialized. It seems wrong for a University which purports to offer broad opportunities for the training of students for good citizenship to ignore an area of thought that has so greatly affected the consciences, ideals, and aspirations of mankind.[15]

To implement his vision, Ruthven proceeded to establish the position of Counselor in Religious Education in 1932. The university hired Dr. Edward W. Blakeman for this newly created and important position. Blakeman, who had served as Methodist University pastor at the University of Wisconsin in Madison, assumed an identically named position at the University of Michigan when he arrived in 1932. He was one of the "pioneers in student religious work"; Blakeman had also served as one of the early presidents of the Conferences of Church Workers in State Universities.[16] In short, he was a seasoned hand in matters of interreligious affairs on university campuses. Indeed, in a manuscript entitled "The Protestant View of Public Higher Education," Blakeman delineated how he saw religion's role in the curricular presence of universities. It is amply clear from this document that Blakeman very

14. Ruthven, *Naturalist in Two Worlds*, 121.
15. Ruthven, *Naturalist in Two Worlds*, 121–22.
16. Austin, *Century of Religion*, 39.

much shared Ruthven's view of having a policy of religious pluralism play a crucial role in a university's educational mission.

> Can a university (state or private) keep off the field of religion and be a university? If it can, then religion would seem to be an isolated aspect of society. We do not so view it. On the other hand, if it cannot keep off the field it should be allowed full freedom to move untrammeled, not only over civic and other subjects, but also over religious subjects. . . . We hold that more freedom, not less, will aid religion. We would go further and hold that to get at the truth, the University must call on religious groups, at least for certain historic data in religion and for those methods known as church life and polity. The University, then, if it desires to do so, can go far in the matter of enriching the curricula, providing we of the Churches supply to it a broad and generous freedom.[17]

Blakeman then proceeded in his writing to differentiate between the manner in which private universities such as Harvard, Yale, and the University of Chicago constructed religion's curricular presence on their campuses as opposed to public universities, among which he featured his former institution, the University of Wisconsin, but also the University of California and, of course, the oldest public institution in the United States, the University of Michigan, founded in 1817. Blakeman argued that the private schools compartmentalized religion in departments or groups or discernable units labeled "religion," whereas their public counterparts embedded religion in various departments in which it served to enhance those departments' epistemological and methodological catholicity.

> A study of the University of Wisconsin curriculum compared with that of Yale, and of the University of California curriculum with

17. Edward Blakeman, "The Protestant View of Public Higher Education," 26, 27, Ruthven, box 7, folder 4, BHL.

Harvard reveals the facts. We discover, in the main, that religion as presented at Harvard is grouped or labeled "religion". But in the University of California courses in religion are not grouped, but are scattered. For example, in Harvard, Comparative Religion and History of Religions under a department of religion. In California, or Wisconsin or Michigan the data involved are offered partly in the department of Oriental Languages and Literature, and partly as Philosophy. . . . One might go on and on to illustrate that religion as a curriculum matter is finding its way into the State University.[18]

Blakeman ended this fascinating document that so much reflected his and President Ruthven's vision of religion's role at a major state university with the telling words that underlined Blakeman's and Ruthven's emphasis on the implementation of policies and ideas: "Where shall we begin? We reply, begin with the University Pastors just as we expect our Jewish neighbors to begin with their rabbis at Hillel Foundations and our Catholic neighbors to begin with their priests at chapels or Newman Clubs and appeal to each State College and University President for recognition on the basis of educational wisdom rather than on a basis of mutual suspicion."[19]

Blakeman proceeded immediately to implement Ruthven's vision of a profoundly ecumenical approach to religion, not as a spiritual phenomenon but rather as an essential part of a civilized society. To Ruthven, knowing about religion was much more important than practicing it since he saw the deep knowledge and respect for these four religious traditions as a crucial ingredient of any serious education provided by a university of Michigan's stature. In 1935, Blakeman recommended that the Student Chris-

18. Blakeman, "Protestant View," 31, 32, Ruthven, box 7, folder 4, BHL. The underlining in both instances occurred in the original. Moreover, the omission of a verb in the sentence starting with "For example" also appears in the original text. The text is underlined in the original source.

19. Blakeman, "Protestant View," 36, Ruthven, box 7, folder 4, BHL.

tian Association be ecumenically reconstituted as the Student Religious Association (SRA), which indeed happened two years later. This organization's mission was stated very clearly in its founding document, entitled "Toward a Religious Education at the University of Michigan." It was to have a counselor; it was to offer courses in religion; and it was to include all students at the university. Under the headline "Student Religious Association," we read the following statement of purpose: "In order that Jewish, Catholic, Protestant and Oriental students may have a better understanding of their own faith and the religions represented on campus, the University sponsors the Student Religious Association. All students are considered members of this campus-wide 'Association' with headquarters at Lane Hall. All who wish to make full use of the educational opportunities at the University should include in their program the lectures, classes, discussion, and social service work provided by the 'Association.'" (Please note that "Jewish" commences the list of the four great faiths that formed the constituent parts of Alexander Ruthven's grand scheme of a campus based on an intellectual and cultural vision of an ecumenically constructed religious existence.[20])

Many kinds of ancillary projects and bodies appeared at this time, all of which underlined Ruthven's priority of fostering an ecumenical religious experience emphasizing the intellectual-cultural dimensions of religion as opposed to its spiritual-tribal ones. Among them was the establishment of the Spring Parley, an annual student-faculty weekend always held in the spring semester "designed to stimulate and measure social and religious interest on the campus."[21] There also arose entities such as the Student Council of Religion, "which was formed with representatives from the four religious traditions and with members-at-large and which served as the pattern for the Student Council of

20. Edward Blakeman, "Toward a Religious Education at the University of Michigan," Ruthven, box 21, folder 25, BHL.

21. Blakeman, "Toward a Religious Education," 40, Ruthven, box 21, folder 25, BHL.

the Student Religious Association, Group X, an interfaith symposium, Freshman Rendezvous, a Peace Council, the Chinese Student Christian Association, hospital visitation service, sociological trips, and retreats each semester."[22] All of these began as Blakeman initiatives only to be fully integrated into the Student Religious Association in 1937.

A fascinating although, alas, undated document's very title indicated Ruthven's vision of this entire project as an active process of intellectual enhancement based on the enlightened pillars of the humanities and not a mere exercise of passive or polite tolerance. "Good Will Not Tolerance Is Becoming to Us" discusses the importance of interfaith understanding and activism: "During the last decade at the University of Michigan we have been endeavoring to understand the aspirations of the religious and social traditions out of which our students come to us. . . . The Far-Eastern tradition includes students from the Orient; a variety of cultures. Jewish tradition, about ten percent of our student enrollment. The Catholic traditions [sic], another ten percent of our enrollment. The Protestant tradition, larger and more varied, but a single cultural tradition."[23] In the ensuing paragraph, the document proceeds to give concrete examples as to how speakers from all four religions arrived on campus to meet with students to discuss topics of interest pertaining to each of these religions. For Judaism, "On other occasions we have had Jewish Rabbis or teachers such as Professor Nathan Isaacs from Harvard, who was here a year ago. On such occasions the local Rabbi and his leading students were hosts. The lectures are open to the entire campus public."[24]

In another document entitled "Report of Progress in Religious Education, University of Michigan," Blakeman provides a detailed bullet-style chronology of all the events and endeavors that occurred at the university concerning this Ruthven-inspired

22. Blakeman, "Toward a Religious Education," Ruthven, box 21, folder 25, BHL.
23. Blakeman, "Toward a Religious Education," Ruthven, box 21, folder 25, BHL.
24. Blakeman, "Toward a Religious Education," Ruthven, box 21, folder 25, BHL.

interfaith activity. Starting in 1933, this document provides a detailed timeline of religious initiatives at the university in the 1930s. We find entries of faculty names whom Ruthven and Blakeman consulted on their project and in an entry mentioning the Interfaith Symposium in 1935 we read of "Studies introduced as to Various Constituencies: Protestant, Catholic, Jewish, Eastern, with a view to institutionalizing each in some definite manner. Goal set up of a 'Hall of Religion' to house many types of religious and social expressions. Central feature, - Type of Worship and Study of Religion. This flanked on the left by 'Aesthetics' expression through drama, music, sculpture, and flanked on the right by 'Socio-religious Activities,' Social action, etc."[25]

In addition to the important social and cultural campus-wide components of Ruthven's ecumenical mission, Blakeman also implemented serious curricular ones. This aligned with Ruthven's vision of the state university's model of teaching religion across and within departments as mentioned above and not the autonomous religion-department-centered method implemented by private schools like Harvard and Yale. Fifty-three courses arose at the University of Michigan at this time, strewn across departments and even schools, all with the purpose "to emphasize the fact that religion is an aspect of civilization, of thought, and of social relationships and institutions."[26]

The Role of Jews and Hillel in Ruthven's Pluralist Vision

It is also interesting to note that Blakeman and Ruthven took the presence and welfare of Jewish students at the University of Michigan very seriously. In a letter dated February 1, 1939, addressed to a Dr. George Watt of Gramercy Park in New York

25. Edward Blakeman, "Report of Progress in Religious Education, University of Michigan, June 1938," Ruthven, box 21, folder 25, BHL. The text is underlined in the original source. We are not quite sure what Blakeman meant with flanks on the left and right in this context.

26. Blakeman, "Report of Progress," 41, Ruthven, box 21, folder 25, BHL.

City, Blakeman mentions a general study on Jews that he conducted from which he draws two important conclusions: "The first element to be considered is the eagerness of any minority for Education. In this the Jews and Armenians and similar groups surpass majority groups. 2. The Jewish religion is an intellectual motivation in the home, which the Christian religion has ceased to have upon its children."[27] It is fascinating that, as we noted in our delineation of Hillel's founding principles in chapter 2, Jewish leaders, just like their Christian counterparts, apparently worried that, analogous to Christian youth, the young generation of Jews was distancing itself from the key ingredients of Judaism and thus needed a corrective in college, which Hillel was to offer optimally. Blakeman also provided Watt with some interesting data concerning the presence of Jewish students on the Michigan campus compared to its peer institutions. "Relating to the percentage of Jewish students at the University of Michigan, we have given some attention. As Universities go, our ratio of 10% is very low. The College of the City of New York's enrollment is 85% Jewish. University of Pennsylvania, which might be similar to Michigan in many respects, is 20% Jewish."[28] Blakeman concludes his letter by highlighting what he (and by extension Ruthven in all probability) viewed as the disproportionate intellectual achievements and scholarly excellence of Jewish students on the Michigan campus. "Our Jewish students, per hundred, produce a rather large number of high grade scholars. Our youth in other faiths seldom make a similar showing per hundred."[29]

As the Jewish side's main representative in the many venues of this interfaith pluralism on campus, Hillel participated vigorously with the Student Religious Association. One of the tangible benefits that this cooperation yielded for Hillel was for the SRA to offer its facilities in Lane Hall to the annual Passover meals

27. Blakeman to Watt, letter dated February 1, 1939, Ruthven, box 21, folder 25, BHL.
28. Blakeman to Watt, Ruthven, box 21, folder 25, BHL.
29. Blakeman to Watt, Ruthven, box 21, folder 25, BHL.

because Hillel's own facilities could not accommodate that many students. Other Hillel activities, too, such as the occasional lecture and dances, occurred at Lane Hall. Isaac Rabinovitz, Hillel's director at the time, also led numerous discussions there. Additionally, "several members of the Hillel Foundation also participated in the study of antisemitism carried on by SRA. . . . Relations from the first between Hillel and the Student Religious Association were most cooperative."[30]

In a summary of the SRA's activities from 1937 to 1939, Kenneth W. Morgan gives Hillel pride of place as the sole Jewish organization offering a meaningful voice to the Jewish students on the Michigan campus. In highlighting the SRA's overall mission, this document states at its outset that

> during the first two years, the program of the Student Religious Association has been experimental. Our goal is clear: we wish to help the students at the University to a better understanding of religion and ethics than they had when they entered, and to provide them with a motivation strong enough to enable them to live up to their best insights. Our work was started with few conscious presuppositions as to how that goal could be attained. . . . At the outset, of course, there were very few students interested in the Student Religious Association. The program is now concerned with two areas: cooperation with local religious organizations and the development of a University religious program.[31]

Under the heading "COOPERATION WITH LOCAL RELIGIOUS ORGANIZATIONS" [all capital letters in the original], the first entry is "Jewish" preceding the one on "Roman Catholic" and "Protestant." This detailed paragraph indulges in praising Hillel's existence and its activities.

---

30. Blakeman, "Report of Progress," 48, Ruthven, box 21, folder 25, BHL.

31. Kenneth W. Morgan, "The Student Religious Association, 1937–1939," Ruthven, box 26, folder 28, BHL.

Under Dr. Heller, and under his successor Dr. Rabinowitz, the Hillel Foundation has at all times expressed a willingness to cooperate with the University. The Foundation has done noteworthy work in raising funds for refugee relief, conducting classes and forums, and providing recreational opportunities. Their present building is not large enough for the many activities carried on by the Foundation, nor do they have adequate facilities for Orthodox, Conservative, and Reformed synagogue services. During the years, the Association helped the Foundation to bring to the campus one Jewish lecturer, Dr. Cronbach, provided a place for the Hillel Players to practice, a place near the campus for their election and an occasional meeting, and gave them the use of the basement for serving Passover meals. There was also a quiet study of antisemitism in which several members of Hillel participated. Twice during the years, Dr. Rabinowitz led discussions at Lane Hall.[32]

On page 7 of this document, we read that Hillel conducted thirty-four play rehearsals at the SRA's facilities at Lane Hall during the academic year. The foundation also held its Passover meals there.[33] But not all was fine for Jewish students on campus as is evident from an entry on page 4 of the document, where we see a headline "Concerning Anti-semitism" under which appears "Jewish and Gentile students met to consider anti-semitism at Michigan and designed the poll which was taken later."[34] Under the entry "number of meetings" we read "7"; under the rubric "Approximate Attendance" we see "10 to 30."[35]

Interestingly, the diversity of the Protestant groups rendered the representation of that religion less cohesive than those of the Catholics and Jews respectively, leading the Protestant denomina-

32. Morgan, "Student Religious Association," Ruthven, box 26, folder 28, BHL.

33. Morgan, "Student Religious Association," Ruthven, box 26, folder 28, BHL.

34. Morgan, "Student Religious Association," Ruthven, box 26, folder 28, BHL.

35. Morgan, "Student Religious Association," Ruthven, box 26, folder 28, BHL.

tions to coalesce and emulate the organizational presence exhibited by the other two religions. In February 1939, an interreligious Advisory Board was established that featured representatives of the major faiths consisting of Protestant ministers, Catholic priests, and the director of the Hillel Foundation as well as laymen from each of these organizations. "This group met with the Board of Governors periodically to discuss the religious problems of the University and to clarify relationships between the University and the local religious organizations. During this period, cooperative relationships were also maintained with the Christian Science student organization and the local chapter of the Inter-Varsity Christian Fellowship, both of which met regularly in Lane Hall."[36]

This was also the exact moment (February 1939) in which the SRA conducted its study on Jewish students at the University of Michigan. Entitled "A Survey of the Relations of Jewish and Gentile Students at the University of Michigan," the existence of this study testifies to the university's major concern with the increasing antisemitism on the University of Michigan campus at this time. The university's awareness of this growing problem had not only international causes, such as the growing bellicosity of fascism in Europe best exemplified by *Kristallnacht*, but also campus-related ones anchored in the growing activism of left-wing students at Michigan, many of whom were Jewish (this will be thoroughly discussed in forthcoming chapters). Bottom line: Jewish students were solidly represented in all the university's decisive bodies at this time and, without any doubt, their most representative agency was none other than Hillel.

There is ample evidence that Ruthven personally cared deeply about the Jewish students' full integration and welfare on the Michigan campus. In a letter dated April 21, 1939, written to Blakeman and sent from the headquarters of the National Conference of Christians and Jews in New York City, Ruthven was singled out

36. Blakeman to Watt, letter dated February 1, 1939, 48, 49, Ruthven, box 21, folder 25, BHL.

by the author as a prospective recipient of something called the "Badge of Tolerance." The same honor had just been bestowed on Eleanor Roosevelt and New York City Mayor Fiorello La Guardia in the conference's national endeavor to launch a nationwide campaign "to help direct the attention of Americans of all faiths to the necessity of supporting democracy, freedom and tolerance."[37] The badge symbolized the importance of this nationwide campaign. The letter continues, "Our college secretary, Dr. Herbert L. Seamans, suggested my writing you concerning arrangements for a similar presentation to Dr. Alexander G. Ruthven, President of the University of Michigan, as representing the mid-West. His activity in favor of tolerance and democracy places him alongside of McCracken of Vassar, Sproul of California and Graham of North Carolina, the other university presidents to receive this presentation for their respective sections."[38]

Ruthven's Commitment to Michigan Hillel

President Ruthven's belief that Hillel had an important role as one of the pillars of his pluralist policy was underscored by his support of the organization, both publicly and behind the scenes. Already at commencement in the spring of 1932, Ruthven delivered a speech on intolerance to the attending seniors. Henry Wollman, one of Michigan's most illustrious and active Jewish alumni in New York, found the address a "splendid pronouncement" of such merit and importance that he later wrote on September 26, 1932, to Dr. Samuel Schulman—rabbi of New York's venerable Temple Emanu-El congregation on Manhattan's Fifth Avenue, arguably Reform Judaism's most eminent place of worship—that the rabbi "probably would desire to quote from it in a sermon

37. Letter of the National Conference of Christians & Jews, April 21, 1939, Ruthven, box 21, folder 25, BHL.

38. Letter of the National Conference of Christians & Jews, April 21, 1939, Ruthven, box 21, folder 25, BHL.

that you will deliver."[39] Wollman enclosed a copy of Ruthven's commencement address for good measure. In Ruthven's letter to Wollman dated September 29, 1932, the president first states his delight that "there is one alumnus at least who reads what I have to say."[40] Ruthven then mentions the three things that he wanted his commencement address to note: "First, I would like to give a little more attention to the orientation of students than has been done recently in our educational institutions; second, I feel that it is an opportune time to restate some of our educational problems; and third, I have been attempting to redefine the field of our institutions of higher learning."[41] In addition to Ruthven's closeness to Jewish alumni of Henry Wollman's stature, this correspondence clearly underlines Ruthven's commitment to educating Michigan students on a scale much beyond the materials comprising the conventional curricula of the various disciplines that constituted the university.

It was from the very beginning of 1933 that Ruthven's deep commitment to Hillel can be amply documented. Due to the Depression's profound impact on many aspects and institutions of American life—not least on the country's universities—there emerged serious considerations to curtail Hillel's activities in a substantial manner or even have its operations cease entirely on the University of Michigan's campus. Enter Ruthven to the rescue. In a letter written on January 5, 1933, to Rabbi Leo M. Franklin, arguably the Detroit area Jewish community's most prominent leader, Ruthven's plea for Hillel's continued flourishing couched in the president's vision of the foundation's role in his larger concept of Judaism's central importance for a proper university education cannot be more explicit. Ruthven writes,

39. Henry Wollman to Samuel Schulman, letter dated September 26, 1932, Ruthven, box 7, folder 27, BHL.

40. Ruthven to Henry Wollman, letter dated September 29, 1932, Ruthven, box 7, folder 27, BHL.

41. Ruthven to Wollman, letter dated September 29, 1932, Ruthven, box 7, folder 27, BHL.

I am very much distressed to learn that there is a possibility that the Hillel Foundation of the University of Michigan may be compelled to disband or at least greatly curtail its activities this year. I am sure that you agree with me that this Foundation has been of vital interest and importance to the students of the University. The contributions which it has made to the cultural, social, and religious development of the students can scarcely be overestimated. . . . The University can directly contribute to the professional training of the individual. It can also provide the raw materials for the development of a proper concept of life. This, however, is not sufficient. Education, especially in its spiritual aspects, must be experienced. In the experience of education we need not only formal instruction but opportunities for individual initiative to express itself, both in thought and action. I am most anxious that the several religious denominations have proper facilities in Ann Arbor to take the student beyond his study of the broad essentials in the religious field. It is my opinion that the abandonment of the Hillel Foundation work would be a disaster, not only for the Jewish students but indirectly for the whole student body.[42]

This letter attained such importance in the Jewish community well beyond the greater Detroit area that it was published with virtually no changes under the headline "Hillel Must Go On," authored by Dr. Alexander G. Ruthven, in the nationally circulated *B'nai B'rith Magazine: The National Jewish Monthly* of February 1933.[43] As mentioned in chapter 2, B'nai B'rith served as all the Hillel organizations' main benefactor.

On the very same day, January 5, 1933, Ruthven wrote an even more detailed letter to Wollman, the distinguished New York lawyer and prominent Michigan alumnus, and included a copy

42. Ruthven to Leo M. Franklin, letter dated January 5, 1933, Ruthven, box 7, folder 27, BHL.

43. "Hillel Must Go On," *B'nai B'rith Magazine: The National Jewish Monthly*, February 1933, Ruthven, box 7, folder 27, BHL.

of his letter to Leo Franklin. Ruthven writes, "I am very much distressed and I am turning to you for assistance. Briefly, apparently owing to some differences in opinion or lack of interest on the part of Jewish people, the Hillel Foundation is about to be wrecked."[44] Ruthven then proceeds to praise Hillel's director at the time, Rabbi Bernard Heller, whom he would like to send to New York for a meeting with Wollman to discuss the Michigan Hillel's predicament.

> We have been very fortunate at the University in the last few years in having a Rabbi who is not only a scholar but also a man who has splendid ideas as to the orientation of students. Together we have made substantial progress in changing some erroneous ideas which have prevailed here. . . . I want to ask you if you are sufficiently interested to give me permission to send Rabbi Heller to you for a conference. What he desires at the present time is your advice and counsel. I know you will enjoy talking with him and I also know that he will be able to give you a clear and concise account of what is happening on the campus. I have felt free to make this request of you because I know your interest in the institution and I also feel that it is not improper for me to do so because of your membership on the Alumni Advisory Council.[45]

In his letter to Wollman, Ruthven also revealed many of the reasons he found Hillel's existence on the Michigan campus so crucial for the implementation of his ecumenical ideas that, in Ruthven's view, were the foundation of any serious university.

> As always, I want to be frank with you. In previous years there has from time to time been voiced in the administration at Ann Arbor anti-Jewish as well as anti-Catholic and anti-every other religion [the original omits a noun such as "attitude" or "feeling" or "ori-

44. Ruthven to Wollman, letter dated January 5, 1933, Ruthven, box 7, folder 27, BHL.
45. Ruthven to Wollman, letter dated January 5, 1933, Ruthven, box 7, folder 27, BHL.

entation" that one would expect in this context]. I am standing solidly on the ground that we do not want in Ann Arbor a Jewish university or a Catholic university or a Methodist university or any other one kind of school. Our institution must be Jewish and Catholic and Protestant, and so forth. In other words, we want a real university, - a university that is as catholic in religion as it is catholic in the intellectual fields. I can give myself credit for very little but I do feel that this idea has become firmly rooted in the minds of our faculty and students at the present time. Never have we had such a tolerant spirit and more than this, never have we had such cooperation among the several religious groups as we have now. My thought is that the University should teach the fundamentals of religion. We should not try to run our own church nor should we bring the churches as such into the administration of student affairs. On the other hand, on the basis of a fundamental training in religion, which all of the denominations represented in Ann Arbor agree with me can be taught in the University, we should lead the students toward the student pastors according to the preferences which we find. We are not interested in making a Jew into a Catholic or, in fact, in leading the students in any direction. Neither are we desirous of putting any stumbling block in their way. What we want is to make our Jewish students better Jews, to make our Catholics better Catholics, and to make our Protestants better Protestants, with the thought that, after all, these several faiths lead to one common concept of the duty of man.[46]

Tellingly, both of Ruthven's interlocutors responded to the president's concerns posthaste. In a letter dated January 9, 1933, Leo Franklin writes to Ruthven,

I assure you that I agree with you in every particular as to the influence that this organization [i.e., Hillel] exerts upon the Jew-

---

46. Ruthven to Wollman, letter dated January 5, 1933, Ruthven, box 7, folder 27, BHL.

ish student body in particular, and perhaps as you say, upon the student body of the University in general. We have been much concerned about the financial condition surrounding the Foundation, and of the possibility of having to greatly curtail its activities, if not to disband it altogether. However, you may be definitely assured that we are taking the matter with all seriousness and that we shall attempt within the very nearest future to find some means of saving this great organization.[47]

In a letter dated February 6, 1933, Franklin went even further by inviting Ruthven for Sunday evening, February 26,

to address a meeting which we are calling at the Temple in behalf of the Foundation. It is our purpose to have as our speakers, yourself, Dr. Worrell and one or two other representatives of the University who know something of the work of the Hillel Foundation. We feel very sincerely that this work must go on. However, it is difficult in these times to put on a special drive, and we believe that with you as the principal speaker of the evening, we could get together a sufficient gathering of our people to secure then and there a very considerable part of the funds that we will require to carry on. . . . I need not tell you how greatly we will appreciate your acceptance of this invitation.[48]

Wollman, too, responded promptly. In a letter to Ruthven dated January 11, 1933, Wollman writes,

I want in every instance to do everything that you would like to have me do. . . . I suppose the object of the whole thing is to get money to help maintain the Ann Arbor branch of the Hillel Foundation. I do not know just how to go at this. I do not know whom to approach, but I am sending a copy of your letter and a copy of

47. Leo M. Franklin to Ruthven, letter dated January 9, 1933, Ruthven, box 7, folder 27, BHL.
48. Franklin to Ruthven, letter dated January 9, 1933, Ruthven, box 7, folder 27, BHL.

this letter to Captain Charles A. Riegelman, who at one time was president of the New York Alumni of the University of Michigan, and to Moritz Rosenthal, Esq., a member of the banking firm of Ladenburg, Thalman & Co., who stood extremely high as a lawyer when he practiced at the bar in Chicago, and now has a very firm standing as a banker. I am going to ask them to meet me at lunch, to confer with me with reference to your letter. Of course you and I appreciate what a dreadfully hard time it is to raise any money. Very many of the right are no longer rich, and those who are moderately rich have so many demands on them that it is impossible for them to comply with all of them.[49]

In his reply to Wollman's letter, Ruthven upped the ante and lent additional weight to the situation by wishing to meet Wollman himself rather than have Rabbi Heller handle the situation, as the president had originally wanted. Ruthven stated in a letter of January 19, 1933,

When I wrote you about the situation of the Hillel Foundation, it was not so much to get financial support, although this is badly needed, as it was to start you thinking on the general problem of the welfare of Jewish students on the campus. This is a matter that concerns me greatly. Perhaps we can have a visit when I come to New York in February. The Hillel Foundation has been an excellent agency in developing character in the Jewish group. . . . Now it seems that the Jewish students are going to be left entirely on their own because support has been withdrawn from the Foundation. I had thought that if our Rabbi could talk with you he could present the whole situation but, as I see it now, I would prefer to talk the matter over with you myself. If it is convenient, what would you think of getting together a few people who would be interested in the problem when I come to New York.[50]

49. Henry Wollman to Ruthven, letter dated January 11, 1933, Ruthven, box 7, folder 27, BHL.

50. Ruthven to Henry Wollman, letter dated January 19, 1933, Ruthven, box 7, folder 27, BHL.

In a note dated February 13, 1933, and addressed to Rabbi Franklin, President Ruthven mentions that "on a recent trip to New York, I was able to get prominent Jewish alumni of the University to form a committee which will interest itself in the work of the Foundation in Ann Arbor. I am quite confident that this group will be able to solve our problem."[51] Ruthven proceeds to add that given the New York developments, he thought it best not to address the Michigan Hillel matter publicly in Detroit at the end of February as Rabbi Franklin had initially wished: "I feel now that I might complicate matters for our alumni committee."[52] In response to the president's letter dated February 15, 1933, Rabbi Franklin concurred fully: "Of course I realize that it would be unwise at this time for you to make a general appeal in behalf of the Hillel Foundation in view of what you have so kindly done in New York. I spoke to Rabbi Heller over the phone this morning and he agrees with me that perhaps we had better go very slowly and very quietly about anything that we are now going to do in Michigan as our work here might possibly interfere with that of the committee which you have so thoughtfully arranged for in New York."[53]

In a lengthy letter dated February 15, 1933, and written to Charles Riegelman in which Ruthven summarizes Hillel's problems and predicament that he delineated at the New York meeting to a group of selected alumni, Ruthven expresses perhaps more than elsewhere his vision for Hillel at the University of Michigan. From the beginning of this document, it is amply evident how deeply Ruthven associated Hillel's welfare with that of the University of Michigan as a whole.

51. Ruthven to Franklin, letter dated February 13, 1933, Ruthven, box 7, folder 27, BHL.

52. Ruthven to Franklin, letter dated February 13, 1933, Ruthven, box 7, folder 27, BHL.

53. Franklin to Ruthven, letter dated February 15, 1933, Ruthven, box 7, folder 27, BHL.

Let me say that, in my opinion, the Hillel Foundation just now constitutes a problem which affects the whole University. I am not interested in the Foundation as a social institution. We do not need to encourage segregation. We need to discourage it. While the Foundation could be used to segregate the Jewish students, it can also be utilized to do away with such segregation. . . . I am developing a plan for religious education which will apply to the University as a whole. In my opinion, the whole plan will break down if we cannot provide for instruction in the Jewish religion. As I see it, this religion is the mother of all western faiths and will become increasingly important. . . . We have an excellent group of Jewish students and a Rabbi who is working with me and with the other religious leaders. The time is in every way opportune to knit the Jewish students into the general educational developments of the University and to place religious education on the sound foundation of the Jewish faith. As I understand it, you have consented to head a National committee of the Michigan alumni which will concern itself with the support of the Hillel Foundation in Ann Arbor. The amount of support which we need now is $12,000 a year, of which approximately $3,600 is promised by the Hillel Foundation. . . . If we had an endowment of $250,000, it would stabilize the whole University plan. I consider, then, that there are two objectives just now, first, the continuation of the Hillel Foundation work in Ann Arbor which, without support, must be discontinued this year and, second, a permanent basis of support in an endowment. I enclose a list of alumni who would, I believe, be willing to serve on the committee. You will think of others.[54]

A letter exchange between President Ruthven and the B'nai B'rith office in Cincinnati further confirms the president's deep commitment to rescuing Hillel and placing it on sound financial

---

54. Ruthven to Charles Riegelman, letter dated February 15, 1933, Ruthven, box 7, folder 27, BHL.

footing. Ruthven expressed great relief that Dr. I. M. Rubinow, secretary of the B'nai B'rith headquarters in Cincinnati, assured the president that even though funds to the Michigan Hillel— like to the other seven chapters in the country supported by B'nai B'rith at institutions of higher learning—had to be curtailed because of the difficult economic conditions, they were not going to be severed. "I am very glad to know that you have no intention of discontinuing the assistance you have been giving to the Hillel Foundation of the University of Michigan. As you know, I am working hard on this problem and I am confident that, with the assistance of Dr. Heller, we can save the Foundation in Ann Arbor although it is now in a very serious condition."[55]

The subject of antisemitism was never far from the surface during these crucial months for Hillel, as is best demonstrated by a letter from Rabbi Heller, the foundation's director, to Rubinow. Dated May 24, 1933, Heller responds to Rubinow who must have addressed the existence—perhaps even growth—of antisemitism on the Michigan campus in a letter to Heller that we do not have. Heller refutes the existence of such a negative phenomenon in no uncertain terms and makes it clear that any anti-Jewish sentiments on campus that might have been expressed on occasion had nothing to do with Jews per se but with members or sympathizers of what he misnames the "Student National League", (actually the National Student League) which had Communist leanings and Jewish students among its membership. In Heller's attempt to allay Rubinow's fears regarding the existence of massive antisemitism on the Michigan campus, Heller also took the occasion to praise the university administration's relationship to Jewish students. In fact, the letter is nothing short of a paean to the Ruthven administration's pro-Jewish attitudes and policies, as well as to the university as a whole. Heller writes,

> I haven't left Ann Arbor in the last three weeks for a single hour
> and yet I haven't heard of anything that justifies characterization

55. Heller to I. M. Rubinow, letter dated May 24, 1933, Ruthven, box 7, folder 27, BHL.

of an up-rising against Jews on the part of students. As I have told you on other occasions, I have found the administration most cordial and cooperative. Up to now no reasonable request that I have made has not been fully and whole heartedly granted to me. The attitude of Gentile students towards Jewish students, with exceptions of social matters, is no different than that between Protestants and Catholics. This rumor was born out of the wildest imagination. It may be the illegitimate offspring of the following incident. There is a group of students at our University called the "Student National League." I do not know exactly what their platform is. This much I do know.[56]

Heller then describes the demands that the group has made toward the university that Heller finds completely unreasonable and irresponsible. He also addresses the ever-present topic of the claimed overrepresentation of Jews among this organization's members:

I do not know how many members this society has or how many are Jews and how many are non-Jews. This I do know: that two individuals whose names are always in print and who are always making speeches on the steps of the library at inopportune as well as opportune times are Jewish and non-residents of Michigan. . . . In reply to one of the speeches made by one of these men, I understand one single student made some reference to this organizations [sic] as being manned and maneuvered by Jews. This had no effect, whatever upon the attitude and actions of the general student body. On the contrary, there appeared in the Daily, a letter which was written by a non-Jew protesting against this racial reference. These are all the facts of the case. If there were any beginnings or semblance of a student up-rising against fellow Jews, knowing the administration as I do, I am convinced that they would be most prompt and vigorous in its suppression. Please do your utmost to put an end to the rumor, not only

56. Heller to Rubinow, letter dated May 24, 1933, Ruthven, box 7, folder 27, BHL.

because it has no basis, but because it represents a calumny on an institution whose fairness matches its fineness.[57]

While Rabbi Heller was seeking to distance Hillel from the Jewish student radicals, he was also assiduously careful to maintain good relations with the administration and to show Ruthven that Hillel was active in promoting campus pluralism. In November 1934, a year after Ruthven's efforts to rescue Hillel from bankruptcy, Rabbi Heller forwarded Hillel's bulletin of activities to the president. In the accompanying letter, Heller made sure to point out that while the main objective of Hillel's activities was to cultivate the cultural and social life of Jewish students, they were open to all students. "My policy," he wrote, "has been to make the Hillel Foundation serve as wide a group as possible and particularly to contribute something distinctive to the already rich resources of our University . . . the action which the Hillel Players have taken last year in inviting non-Jewish students to take part in the dramatic ventures is also the result of that policy. The courses which we are offering will be thrown open to any and every student who may care to take them."[58] Heller closed his letter with his own defense of pluralism: "my action is prompted by my belief that the success and the welfare of a democracy such as ours depend on the various groups' sympathetic understanding of the others' history, literature and philosophy."[59] For Heller, as for Ruthven, meaningful pluralism had to be steeped in a kind of traditionalism in which different religious groups would come to appreciate the cultural traditions of others.

---

57. Heller to Rubinow, letter dated May 24, 1933, Ruthven, box 7, folder 27, BHL.

58. Heller to Ruthven, letter dated November 7, 1934, Ruthven, box 12, folder 12, BHL.

59. Heller continued to advocate interfaith activities, such as Jewish-Christian conferences to Ruthven. See his handwriting on the information bulletin of the National Conference of Jews and Christians, Ruthven, box 12, folder 12, BHL.

Conclusion

Ample evidence supports that President Ruthven cared deeply about Jewish students at the University of Michigan. As he wrote in one of his letters, the welfare of Jewish students on the campus "is a matter that concerns me greatly." Ruthven's commitment was the result of a confluence of factors that represented his core values: a clear liberalism that cherished the individual's autonomy as a prized contributor to society; and a belief in religious pluralism as an essential ingredient for an intellectually vibrant campus as well as an ecumenical education, which was the only option to create the moral foundation for a modern individual's ethical compass in life. Ruthven had nothing but admiration, even affection, for Judaism's towering contribution to Western civilization. He also fully believed that the presence of Jewish students at a place like Michigan was not only a moral must for an institution of stature but also a guarantor for its continued intellectual excellence. However, as shown in subsequent chapters, Ruthven's ecumenical inclusiveness and enlightened pluralism that reveled in giving Jews and Judaism pride of place had its definite limits.

CHAPTER FOUR

THE PARADOXES OF PLURALISM, 1931–35

The story of Michigan Menorah, Zeta Beta Tau (ZBT) the Jewish Student Congregation (JSC), the Zionist Society, Avukah, and Hillel, as well as Jewish participation in university sports, stresses the integrative and assimilative forces that existed for Jewish students at the University of Michigan in the 1920s and 1930s. Even before President Ruthven articulated his own philosophy of ecumenical pluralism, these bodies performed a similar role in that they sought to cultivate their members' sense of their Jewish identity through the promotion of Jewish history and culture, while at the same time facilitating their integration into the greater campus community and thus into mainstream American life. When Ruthven became president in 1929, his ideas accorded with those of these groups. Unlike the administrators at the elite universities on the East Coast, Ruthven was not a Brahmin of any kind. Rather, he was a Midwesterner who had spent his entire career, from graduate student to president, at Michigan. Consequently, he does not appear to have feared a "Jewish influx" in the same way that other university presidents had since the early 1920s. Indeed, as we saw in the previous chapter, Ruthven was immensely supportive of organizations like Hillel. As part of his pluralist approach, Ruthven wanted *integrative* associations, constituted along denominational lines, to foster a campus culture of tolerance. Moreover, Ruthven saw himself as a liberal who encouraged both freedom of thought and co-existence of minority groups on campus.

This, however, leads back to Arlene Lazansky's case and those vexing interview sheets with the circled Js discussed in the introduction to this book. How could Ruthven, a university president who, in many respects, was more open-minded than many of his peers, institute a specific practice—face-to-face interviews primarily targeted at Jewish applicants from the East Coast—that *prima facie* contradicted completely his pluralist and inclusive ideas since they were by definition designed to exclude? After all, we know with certainty that this interview process emerged as university practice with the president's approval in the spring of 1935. In May of that year, an Elisabeth Lawrie from the Admissions Office[1] submitted a memo to President Ruthven's office on "Suggestions for the Better Selection of Students." One of the four proposed policies stated that "some personal interview work be done in certain metropolitan centers, either using Michigan alumni who would be interested and qualified for such work, or using a man especially trained for such work." The latter, Lawrie suggested, "would be far the more satisfactory arrangement."[2] Using personal interviews as a means of filtering out "undesirable" students was not unknown, even at Michigan, where the Medical School had been conducting such interviews of East Coast applicants since the late 1920s.[3] As educational historian Charlotte Borst explains, "The personal interview was already in use in the 1920s by undergraduate institutions, particularly elite schools who were quite deliberate in their attempts to establish a racialized masculine ideal for their institutions. This ideal was predicated on the idea that those men with the wrong ethnic

1. See Lawrie's affiliation on p. 87 of the 1943 U-M Directory: https://books.google. com/books?id=mYOfAAAAMAAJ&printsec=frontcover&source=gbs_ge_summary_ r&cad=0#v=onepage&q&f=false.

2. Lawrie, "Suggestions," memo dated May 14, 1935, Ruthven, box 13, folder 19, BHL.

3. Borst, "Choosing the Student Body," 195.

backgrounds, usually meaning Jewish men, would have to be identified through personal inspection, as they might otherwise hide
their 'real' identity through changes in their surname, remaining
unidentifiable on paper."[4]

Ruthven approved Lawrie's suggestion to extend, in effect, the
Medical School's practice to the broader population of East Coast
undergraduate applicants to the University of Michigan's liberal arts programs. For that purpose, Ruthven dispatched a team
that included Dean of Students Joseph Bursley and the University Registrar Ira M. Smith to conduct interviews with prospective students from the New York City area that July at the Hotel
Pennsylvania in Manhattan. In their subsequent report back to
Ruthven, these men endorsed this interview process emphatically and unequivocally. They stated that it "is our consensus of
opinion that it was decidedly worthwhile to have this opportunity of obtaining such personal impressions" and that "the additional information to be gained from the personal interview is of
such vital importance that these personal interviews should be
held whenever it is possible."[5] They also averred that the statistical data report attached to their letter "reveals many interesting
points."

Interesting points indeed: the data report that emerged in September 1935, and that we first highlighted in the introduction of
our book, includes the list of prospective students organized by
area of interest (literary, scientific, engineering, etc.) along with
their residence, the birthplace of their parents, and their religious
affiliation. In this latter category, however, only two designations
appear—either "Jewish" or "Gentile."

President Ruthven later received, most likely from Registrar
Smith, an analytical survey of these interviews featuring the percentage of students accepted (A) and rejected (R), based on their

4. Borst, "Choosing the Student Body," 196.

5. Bursley et al. to Ruthven, letter dated August 3, 1935, Ruthven, box 15, folder 29,
BHL.

UNIVERSITY OF MICHIGAN
ANALYSIS OF SEPTEMBER, 1935, APPLICANTS FROM NEW YORK AND VICINITY
BY RACE

FIELD OF INTEREST	SEX	NUMBER OF APPLICANTS			PER CENT OF TOTAL APPLICANTS (75)			PER CENT OF APPLICANTS IN EACH SCHOOL OR COLLEGE		
		JEWS	GENTILES	TOTAL	JEWS	GENTILES	TOTAL	JEWS	GENTILES	TOTAL
LIT	Men	6	1	7	8.0	1.3	9.3	37.5	6.2	43.7
	Women	7	2	9	9.3	2.7	12.0	43.7	12.5	56.2
	Total	13	3	16	17.3	4.0	21.3	81.2	18.8	100.0
SCIENCE	Men	9	1	10	12.0	1.3	13.3	69.3	7.7	77.0
	Women	3	-	3	4.0	-	4.0	23.0	-	23.0
	Total	12	1	13	16.0	1.3	17.3	92.3	7.7	100.0
EDUC	Men	-	-	-	-	-	-	-	-	-
	Women	1	-	1	1.3	-	1.3	100.0	-	100.0
	Total	1	-	1	1.3	-	1.3	100.0	-	100.0
ENG	Men	5	5	10	6.7	6.7	13.3	50.0	50.0	100.0
	Women	-	-	-	-	-	-	-	-	-
	Total	5	5	10	6.7	6.7	13.3	50.0	50.0	100.0
ARCH	Men	1	-	1	1.3	-	1.3	100.0	-	100.0
	Women	-	-	-	-	-	-	-	-	-
	Total	1	-	1	1.3	-	1.3	100.0	-	100.0
BUS	Men	1	2	3	1.3	2.7	4.0	33.3	66.7	100.0
	Women	-	-	-	-	-	-	-	-	-
	Total	1	2	3	1.3	2.7	4.0	33.3	66.7	100.0
LAW	Men	3	-	3	4.0	-	4.0	75.0	-	75.0
	Women	1	-	1	1.3	-	1.3	85.0	-	85.0
	Total	4	-	4	5.3	-	5.3	100.0	-	100.0
MED	Men	25	-	25	33.3	-	33.3	92.6	-	92.6
	Women	2	-	2	2.7	-	2.7	7.4	-	7.4
	Total	27	-	27	36.0	-	36.0	100.0	-	100.0
TOTAL	Men	50	9	59	66.7	12.0	78.7	----	----	----
	Women	14	2	16	18.6	2.7	21.3	----	----	----
	Total	64	11	75	85.3	14.7	100.0	----	----	----

Figure 4.1 [University of Michigan, Analysis of September, 1935 Applicants from New York and Vicinity by Race], Ira Smith box 4, folder 42, Bentley Historical Library, University of Michigan

UNIVERSITY OF MICHIGAN
ANALYSIS OF SEPTEMBER 1936 APPLICANTS
FROM BOSTON, NEW YORK CITY, ROCHESTER AND BUFFALO

FIELD OF INTEREST	SEX	JEWISH APPLICANTS								GENTILE APPLICANTS								TOTAL APPLICANTS	
		Both Parents Foreign		One Parent Foreign		Both Parents American		TOTAL		Both Parents Foreign		One Parent Foreign		Both Parents American		Total			
		A	R	A	R	A	R	A	R	A	R	A	R	A	R	A	R	A	R
LIT	Men	1	3	4	1	3	–	8	4	1	–	–	–	3	–	4	–	12	4
	Women	2	3	4	1	5	1	11	5	1	–	1	–	5	1	7	1	18	6
SCIENCE	Men	2	1	2	–	–	–	4	1	–	–	–	1	2	–	2	1	6	2
	Women	1	–	–	–	–	1	1	1	2	–	–	–	–	–	2	–	3	1
EDUC	Men	–	–	–	–	–	–	–	–	1	–	–	–	–	–	1	–	1	–
	Women	–	–	–	–	–	–	–	–	–	–	–	–	–	–	–	–	–	–
ENG	Men	2	2	1	1	2	1	5	4	4	–	–	–	8	1	12	1	17	5
	Women	–	–	–	–	–	–	–	–	–	–	–	–	–	–	–	–	–	–
BUS.AD	Men	1	–	2	1	3	1	6	2	1	–	–	–	4	–	5	–	11	2
	Women	–	–	–	–	–	–	–	–	–	–	–	–	–	–	–	–	–	–
LAW	Men	–	4	1	–	1	2	2	6	–	–	–	–	2	–	2	–	4	6
	Women	–	–	1	–	–	1	1	1	–	–	–	–	1	–	1	–	2	1
DENT	Men	–	–	–	2	–	–	–	2	–	–	–	–	–	–	–	–	–	2
	Women	–	–	–	–	–	–	–	–	–	–	–	–	–	–	–	–	–	–
MED	Men	4	3	3	2	4	4	11	9	–	–	–	–	–	–	'–	–	11	9
	Women	–	–	1	–	1	–	2	–	–	–	–	–	–	–	–	–	2	–
TOTAL	Men	10	13	13	7	13	8	36	28	7	–	–	1	19	1	26	2	62	30
	Women	3	3	6	1	6	3	15	7	3	–	1	–	6	1	10	1	25	8
	Total	13	16	19	8	19	11	51	35	10	–	1	1	25	2	36	3	87	38

Figure 4.2 [University of Michigan, Analysis of September 1936 Applicants from Boston, New York City, Rochester, and Buffalo], Ira Smith box 4, folder 42, Bentley Historical Library, University of Michigan

gender, prospective major, and religious affiliation [Figure 4.1].
Remarkable here is not only the clear distinction made on this
analytical sheet between Jewish and Gentile applicants that were
interviewed (Gentiles are not broken down by denominational
affiliation) but also the choice to categorize the difference between
foreign- and American-born parents of prospective students and,
especially, the overwhelming number of Jewish applicants (64: 34
admits, 30 rejects) to Gentile applicants (11 admits, no rejects).[6]
Overwhelmingly, freshmen Jewish applicants for the fall 1935
semester had a disproportionately high number of either one or
both foreign-born parents (34 with both foreign born, 15 with one,
compared to 2 and 3, respectively, for Gentile applicants).

Although we have no document that directly describes the
criteria that applicants were expected to meet, Ruthven clearly
found the results satisfactory. For at least the next four years
(the archives only preserve interview forms up to the spring of
1939), the university sent representatives to New York City and,
ultimately, to other East Coast metropolitan centers to interview
prospective students. In September 1936, for example, Smith
compiled analytical tables for summer interviews conducted for
students in the New York City, Boston, and Buffalo and Rochester, New York, areas [Figure 4.2]. Again, the summary sheet shows
that Jewish applicants represented the overwhelming majority of
all the interviewed students: 69% of the total interviewees were
Jewish.[7] Whereas the numbers of Jewish and Gentile applicants
were roughly equal in the more interior cities of Buffalo and Rochester, a disproportionate number of applicants from the New York
(53 Jews [83%] to 11 Gentiles) and Boston (12 Jews [86%] to 2
Gentiles) metropolitan areas were Jewish.[8]

6. *University of Michigan: Analysis of September, 1935 Applicants from New York and Vicinity*, Ruthven, box 15, folder 29, BHL.

7. *University of Michigan: Analysis of September, 1936 Applicants from Boston, New York, Rochester, Buffalo and Vicinity by Race*, Smith, box 4, folder 42, BHL.

8. *University of Michigan: Analysis of September 1936 Applicants from Boston and Vicinity by Race; Analysis of September 1936 Applicants from New York and Vicinity by Race*; both in Smith, box 4, folder 42, BHL.

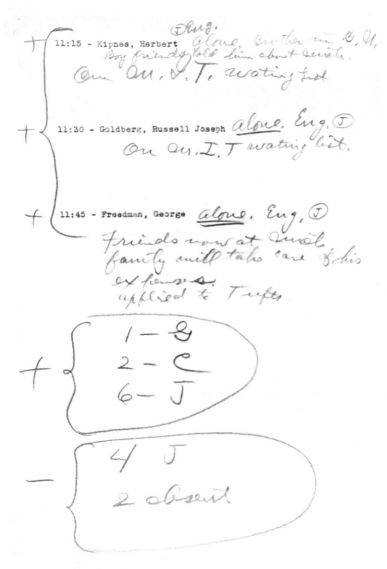

Figure 4.3: [Tally of applicants interviewed June 3, 1939], Ira Smith box 4, folder 42, Bentley Historical Library, University of Michigan

The fact that the applicants' ethnicities—and especially those of the prospective Jewish students—was a central concern in this procedure is best demonstrated by the surviving interviewers' sheets. These sheets, listed as dating from the 1938 and 1939 academic years, are preserved in Ira M. Smith's archives. Each of them features the typed names and meeting times for every

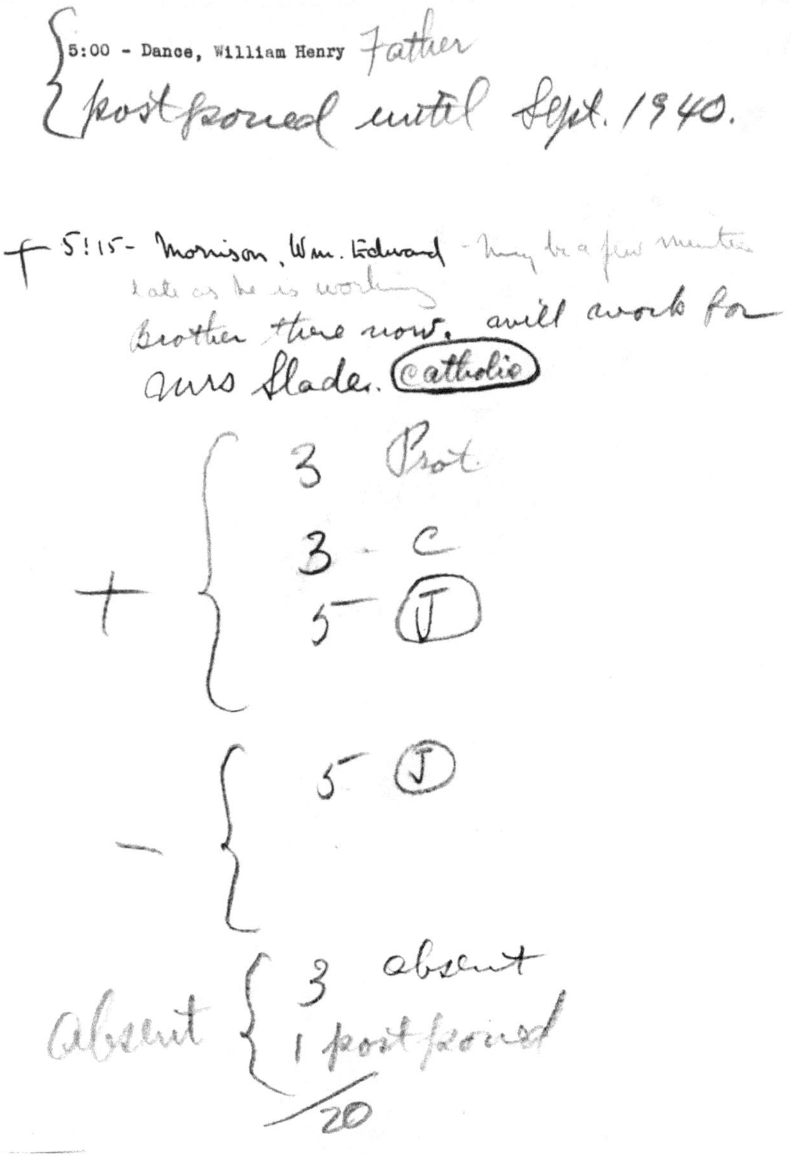

5:00 – Dance, William Henry *Father*
postponed until Sept. 1940.

5:15– Morrison, Wm. Edward – may be a few minutes late as he is working. Brother there now, will work for ours Slade. (Catholic)

+ { 3 Prot
     3 · C
     5 – Ⓙ

– { 5 – Ⓙ

absent { 3 absent
         1 postponed
         /20

Figure 4.4 [Tally of applicants interviewed June 5, 1939], Ira Smith box 4, folder 42, Bentley Historical Library, University of Michigan

interviewee. Prospective students were allotted fifteen minutes to meet with the university's representative, who wrote his or her comments in pencil in the space under their name. Students whom the representative deemed Jewish were designed with a handwritten letter *J* that was generally circled.[9]

At the end of a particular session—usually lasting about 3.5 hours and involving twenty interviews—the university representative tallied up the numbers of Jewish (*J*), Protestant (*P*), and Catholic (*C*) students. The interviewer scribbled a plus or a minus sign by each name, which likely meant accepted for admission or rejection. Not every session's remaining documents feature a tally at the end, and, at times, plus and minus designations are absent from students' names; thus, we will only consider those sessions for which we have clear plus and minus tallies at the end. As is evident from the above example from June 3, 1939 [Figure 4.3], while some Jewish applicants were admitted, the *only students who were rejected (having received minus signs) were Jewish.* Jewish applicants faced a higher likelihood of rejection than did their Gentile counterparts. This is consistent across all of the extant interview sheets and in the official tallies that were later reported to President Ruthven.

In only one case in the remaining documentation is a non-Jewish student rejected on the handwritten interview sheets. During the afternoon session of June 5, 1939, for example, one Catholic was rejected along with three Jews [Figure 4.4].[10] In all remaining handwritten sheets, and in the extant reports prepared for President Ruthven, Jewish applicants are consistently rejected at a greater rate than their Gentile counterparts. Thus, in both the interview sheets preserved by Smith and in the analytical reports that he prepared for the president, we see an impressive consistency across the 1935–39 period: Jewish students are identified *against* an undifferentiated mass of Gentile students.

We also know that this interview process occurred for at least

9. *Interview reports for New York Applicants, 1938*, Smith, box 4, folder 42, BHL.

10. *Interview reports for New York Applicants, 1938*, Smith, box 4, folder 42, BHL.

University of Michigan
ANALYSIS OF APPLICANTS FROM NEW YORK
AND VICINITY

Year	Sex	J			G			Total			Per Cent of Total		
		A	R	Total	A	R	Total	A	R	Total	J	Cr.	Total
1935	M	22	28	50	9	0	9	31	28	59	66.7	12.0	78.7
	F	12	2	14	2	0	2	14	2	16	18.6	2.7	21.3
	Total	34	30	64	11	0	11	45	30	75	85.3	14.7	100.0
1936	M	25	16	41	6	1	7	31	17	48	64.1	10.9	75.0
	F	8	4	12	4	0	4	12	4	16	18.7	6.3	25.0
	Total	33	20	53	10	1	11	43	21	64	82.8	17.2	100.0
1937	M	37	37	74	29	5	34	66	42	108	48.4	22.2	70.6
	F	26	10	36	7	2	9	33	12	45	23.5	5.9	29.4
	Total	63	47	110	36	7	43	99	54	153	71.9	28.1	100.0
1938	M	56	34	90	42	2	44	98	36	134	50.0	24.5	74.5
	F	20	17	37	9	0	9	29	17	46	20.5	5.0	25.5
	Total	76	51	127	51	2	53	127	53	180	70.5	29.5	100.0
1939	M	42	32	74	36	2	38	78	34	112	47.1	24.2	71.3
	F	20	10	30	14	1	15	34	11	45	19.1	9.6	28.7
	Total	62	42	104	50	3	53	112	45	157	66.2	33.8	100.0

Figure 4.5 [University of Michigan, Analysis of Applicants from New York and Vicinity 1935-1939], Ruthven box 23, folder 27, Bentley Historical Library, University of Michigan

five years. A five-year analytical summary sheet of New York based applicants[11] [Figure 4.5] that was provided to Ruthven proves that (a) the practice of interviewing East Coast applicants was consistently performed over the 1935–39 period; (b) Jews were numerically over-represented in these interviews compared to Gentiles (the distinction made between Protestants and Catholics was not retained in any of the extant semester reports or in the five-year summary); and (c) a higher percentage of Jewish than Gentile

11. *University of Michigan: Analysis of Applicants from New York and Vicinity*, Ruthven, box 23, folder 27, BHL.

applicants was rejected. Although we found no five-year summary sheet from another urban area, the New York vicinity was the region from which a majority of East Coast Jewish students hailed and, for reasons that will be explained later, the area of most concern to the Ruthven administration. Thus, the results listed in this five-year summary, we contend, reflect the deliberate effort by the Ruthven administration, acting through the Registrar's and the Admissions Office, to filter and thus limit the number of East Coast Jewish admits to the University of Michigan.

By observing the data on the five-year analysis, a few facts are strikingly clear. In no year were Jewish applicants fewer than two-thirds of the total interviewed, ranging from a low level of 66.2% in 1939 to a high of 85.3% in 1935. In every year, more than one-third of all Jewish applicants was rejected: from a low of 37.7% in 1936 to a high of 46.8% in 1935, with 1937, 1938, and 1939 at 42.7%, 40.1%, and 40.3%, respectively. By comparison, Gentile rejection percentages were negligible: Gentile applicants' worst year, 1937, saw a 16.2% rejection rate, whereas in 1935, 1936, 1938, 1939, the rates were 0%, 0.7%, 0.04%, and 0.056%, respectively.

Based on the data findings of the analytical reports and interview sheets, and on the way both were structured to compare Jews against Gentiles, it is evident that the interview sheets acted as a filter to eliminate a disproportionate number of East Coast Jewish applicants. Moreover, as Dean Bursley, Fred Wohr, and Ira Smith's August 1935 letter to President Ruthven acknowledges, the interviews were conducted "in accordance with your instructions."[12] It is thus clear that the president authorized this discriminatory practice and monitored its progress through the reports submitted by Registrar Smith.

If President Ruthven had instituted a screening interview process for *all* Jewish applicants to Michigan, one could argue that the university was covertly implementing a quota system much like the ones at the elite East Coast schools that later coalesced

12. Bursley et al. to Ruthven, letter dated August 3, 1935, Ruthven, box 15, folder 29, BHL.

into the Ivy League. Yet, as Lawrie's initial May 1935 proposal indicates, this interview process was created only for students "in certain metropolitan centers," specifically those on the East Coast. What was it about these East Coast students—specifically *Jewish* East Coast students—that differentiated them from other Jewish applicants and that compelled the university to limit their numbers in the latter 1930s? Why were they an exception to Ruthven's deeply felt ambition to foster a truly pluralist campus?

Although Ruthven's commitment to a pluralist university culture would have stopped him from instituting an overarching quota against Jewish students, this pluralism had definitive boundaries. Specifically, these boundaries encompassed student organizations that fulfilled the integrative functions that Ruthven and his administration desired: the creation of a religious-focused, yet ecumenical campus that promoted the pluralist values of interfaith tolerance. Associations that did *not* fulfill this necessarily integrative function were, at best, tolerated and, if they proved to be an irritant, fell outside the boundaries of Ruthven's pluralism. Moreover, *Jews* whose political activities were especially troublesome were singled out and subjected to arbitrary dismissal. To be sure, Gentile students could—and did—suffer the same fate, but not nearly in as large a proportion as did the Jewish students. This became the case in the early 1930s when a combination of factors, including the onset of the Great Depression, the ongoing struggles of many students to find acceptable housing and money to pursue their education, and the advent of political radicalism, certainly not among all but many Jewish students, ultimately challenged the president's pluralist visions. A new student organization, the National Student League (NSL), whose chapter in Ann Arbor was established in 1932, was not integrative in the sense that Hillel and ZBT were. The NSL espoused definitively left-wing, even Communist, views. It was profoundly secular, not oriented toward teaching its members any traditional or religious heritage and, frankly, by its very being posed a serious challenge to the Ruthven administration's vision of a university and society.

NSL's members pushed against the boundaries of Ruthven's pluralism to such an extent that many of them, disproportionately its Jewish members, and "innocent" Jews like Arlene Lazansky and others interviewed in the mid- to late 1930s paid a price.

Thus, it was not merely these applicants' Jewishness but rather their specific political associations that led Ruthven to single out one specific group for special scrutiny, open discrimination, and outright exclusion and rejection in the 1930s: Jewish students from the East Coast.

Edward Cheyfitz and the National Student League at Michigan, 1933–34

It so happens that the spring of 1935, when Lawrie first mooted the interview idea, was a pivotal moment in the university's relationship with a portion of its Jewish constituency. The Ruthven administration had been irritated for the previous year and a half by the Michigan chapter of the NSL, which was effectively a front for the promotion of Communism. Some of the NSL's most vocal members on the Michigan campus were Jewish students from the East Coast. Despite the presence of non-Jews in the group, Ruthven dismissed four members of the NSL from the university one month after Lawrie's proposal. All four of these students were East Coast Jews. Thus, the activities of the NSL's Michigan chapter play a pivotal role in understanding the articulation of Ruthven's covert discriminatory policy against East Coast Jewish students. Although previous histories of the University of Michigan, and the Ruthven administration, have recounted Ruthven's suppression of the student Left on campus, none have considered the role that the perception of the NSL as a *Jewish*-dominated group played in the larger impression of the chapter on campus and in the administration.[13]

13. Peckham, Steneck, and Steneck, *Making,* is the standard current institutional history but only offers a limited treatment of the political currents on campus in the

The NSL was founded at the City College of New York (CCNY) in December 1931.[14] Students at CCNY were largely working class and "came overwhelmingly from the city's ghettoes, which were enclaves of East European Jewish immigrants."[15] Unlike those at their elite-laden counterparts, like its close geographic neighbor Columbia, students at CCNY and other working-class institutions had started feeling the effects of the Depression by 1931 that had begun to reinvigorate the political Left, which remained largely dormant on American campuses throughout the 1920s. Some of these Jewish students of Eastern European origin who attended CCNY brought with them a background in political radicalism, including communism, and knowledge of working-class mobilization; indeed, many acquired experiences in organizing before they even entered college. When these students formed the NSL—first at CCNY and then very quickly at the other New York City area campuses—they sought to create a more activist organization than its rather genteel forerunners, like the League for Industrial Democracy, which had degenerated into becoming little more than debating societies during the politically apathetic 1920s. "The NSL's birth marked a new departure in campus politics not only because the group pioneered an innovative approach to student organization," writes historian Robert Cohen, "but also because the NSL's founders included communists."[16]

As Cohen explains, the majority of the NSL's members were also in the Young Communist League (YCL). As the new organization began to demonstrate its ability to organize around campus

1930s. Van de Water's *Alexander Grant Ruthven* is better in its detailing of the contest between Ruthven and the student left but overlooks the fact that Ruthven's dismissals fell disproportionately on radical Jewish students. Ruthven's own memoir, *Naturalist in Two Worlds: Random Recollections of a University President*, provides only a cursory discussion of the dismissals.

14. The following account of the NSL is derived mainly from Cohen, *When the Old Left was Young*, 22–41.

15. Cohen, *When the Old Left was Young*, 24.

16. Cohen, *When the Old Left was Young*, 34.

issues, the American Communist Party took an increasing interest in the group, to the extent that the NSL quite quickly became—and was seen as—a Communist front organization, although one that did not always pay fealty to Moscow. The organization's mobilizing activities, however, quickly raised the ire of college presidents whose institutions had already been burdened by the Depression. College presidents exercised paternalistic authority over their students based on the doctrine of *in loco parentis*, in which they and their faculty stood in place of the students' parents and could control their students—up to and including expulsion—accordingly. When Columbia's President Nicholas Murray Butler expelled the radical editor of the student newspaper, the *Columbia Daily Spectator*, the NSL organized protests and a one-day strike on campus in April 1932.[17] The following month, the NSL spearheaded a citywide protest against a fee increase at New York City's municipal colleges.[18] Many college presidents responded by banning radical organizations and expelling students from campus knowing full well that the courts would uphold their power of *in loco parentis*. Frederick B. Robinson, president of CCNY, expelled forty-three students and suspended thirty-eight between 1931 and 1934 and "haul[ed] hundreds of undergraduates before campus disciplinary boards, inquiring into their political associations, beliefs, and protest activity."[19] Ernest C. Moore, provost at the University of California, Los Angeles, engaged in his own "house-cleaning" activities, suspending five students whom he believed were involved in radical activity in 1934.[20]

Thus, when the Michigan chapter of the NSL was formed in late 1932, the national organization had already established over a year's experience in highly visible acts of campus political mobilization that had provoked stern and repressive admin-

---

17. See Cohen, *When the Old Left was Young*, 55–68.
18. See Cohen, *When the Old Left was Young*, 68–71.
19. Cohen, *When the Old Left was Young*, 108.
20. See Cohen, *When the Old Left was Young*, 118–29.

istrative responses.[21] The Michigan chapter's petition, written by its first president, Edward Cheyfitz (1914–59), a sophomore in the Literary College, defined the chapter's purpose as "to discuss student problems." It received university recognition in early May of 1933.[22] The chapter followed NSL's national platform that called for, among other things, the right to a free education, against "imperialist war and war preparations on the campus" (that also demanded the elimination of the ROTC from campus), anti-fascism, equal rights for minorities, and freedom of student thought and action.[23] The twenty-five signatures on the chapter's

21. The earliest mention of the Michigan chapter is "Radical, Liberal Book Stand Set Up by Students," *MD*, November 8, 1932.

22. See VPSS, box 5, folder National Student League (hereafter cited as NSL), BHL. Cheyfitz was a native of Toledo who joined the Young Communist League in 1932, according to the *Toledo Blade*. Following his graduation in 1934, according to the *Michigan Alumnus* (1945), he spent a year in the Soviet Union working in a chemical plant. He eventually obtained a law degree and, in 1939, broke with the Communists in 1939 over the Nazi-Soviet pact. Denounced by the *Daily Worker* in 1940, Cheyfitz became active in the anti-Communist faction of the CIO, particularly in its Casting Division of the Mine, Mill and Smelter Workers' Union before enlisting in the Army in 1943. In 1945, the *Michigan Alumnus* also records that Cheyfitz published an article in *Fortune* and was national chairman of the CIO's Mine, Mill and Smelter Workers, and was a national member of the CIO's Reconversion Committee. In 1946, he became an assistant to Eric Johnson, president of the Motion Picture Association of America and, in the following year, was investigated by the House Committee on Un-American Activities. In 1953, he became public relations director for the International Brotherhood of Teamsters and a lawyer for its president Jimmy Hoffa, a post he held for three years. According to *Life* magazine, Cheyfitz "conceived the proposal . . . by which Hoffa managed to get seated as president of the union after 13 dissident New York Teamsters accused him of rigging the election and got a court order barring him from the office." Cheyfitz died of a heart attack in May 1959. For Cheyfitz's brief bio, see *Michigan Alumnus* 51 (May 26, 1945): 390. See also George Zielke, "Eric Johnston Defends Edward Cheyfitz, Former Toledoan, Before Movie Inquiry," *Toledo Blade*, October 28, 1947, 2. On Cheyfitz's role as Teamster's public relations director, see "Cheyfitz Quits Teamster's Post," *Toledo Blade*, January 16, 1956, 8. On Cheyfitz's relation to Hoffa, see Paul O'Neil, "Star Attorney for the Defense," *Life*, June 22, 1959, 123.

23. *Building a Militant Student Movement: Program and Constitution of the National Student League*, VPSS, box 5, folder NSL, BHL.

petition do not suggest that Jews had a preponderant presence in the NSL.[24] While we find students with obvious Jewish surnames (our number 3 category) like Cheyfitz, Cohen, Levin, Moss, Perlmutter, and Raskin, we also encounter an array of surnames like Andrews, Bohland, Johnson, Matthews, and Way. Students with conventionally regarded Jewish surnames composed about a third of the petition's signatories.[25] A typed membership list, most likely made by the Dean of Students Office in the fall of 1934 or spring of 1935, shows that while the NSL chapter's numbers had increased to about forty-five members, the ratio of students bearing clear Jewish surnames to those with non-Jewish surnames remained roughly one-third.[26] Moreover, a handwritten note on this sheet's margins only counted three "acknowledged" Jews—and yet no other religious or ethnic affiliation appears in this handwritten tabulation.

Indeed, compared to the percentage of Jewish students per the entire university population (10% on average), the Michigan NSL chapter could be viewed as having a disproportionately large number of Jews compared to the student body's other denominational and ethnic affiliations. The handwritten marginalia in the 1934–35 typed list of NSL members also provides a clue as to the university's perception (or suspicion?) of the chapter as a redoubt of East Coast radicalism. Someone tabulated the students' geographic origins: Michigan (17), New York (11), New Jersey (3), Massachusetts (3), and miscellaneous/unknown (7/4). Fully two-thirds of the membership were not from Michigan and over one-third (NY, NJ, MA = 17/45) hailed from the East Coast. Thus, both "Jews" and "East Coast origins" provided the main categories of inquiry for whoever in the Dean of Students Office was compiling data on the NSL members in 1934.

The perception that the NSL's Michigan chapter was a bastion

24. VPSS, box 5, folder NSL, BHL.

25. VPSS, box 5, folder NSL, BHL.

26. VPSS, box 5, folder NSL, BHL.

of East Coast Jewish radicalism appears to have begun even before the group received official recognition from the university in May 1933. The group first attracted the attention of the *Michigan Daily* in January 1933 when Cheyfitz and another NSL member, Leon Gropper, a graduate student, held a protest in front of President Ruthven's office against the Student Good Will Fund, which was failing to provide relief for poor and starving students on campus. It was, as the *Daily* derisively noted, a protest "to which nobody came but several score of curiosity seekers."[27] Cheyfitz and Gropper denounced the university administration and the *Daily* as "reactionaries" on the steps of the library.[28] [Figure 4.6] That March, the Michigan chapter, following the example of other campus NSL chapters, hosted a series of meetings to demand that the Board of Regents grant a tuition payment moratorium for indigent students struggling in the depths of the Depression.[29] Surprisingly, the Board of Regents accommodated this wish rather quickly by providing a sixty-day moratorium after conducting personal interviews with many ("several hundred") of these financially needy students. The Michigan NSL chapter used its victory, which it attributed to its ability to "force the Board of Regents" to halt tuition increases, to forgo the dismissal of teaching assistants and instructors and to demand a democratically elected faculty committee for the upcoming 1933–34 school year.[30]

However, the Michigan NSL's actions on behalf of these poorer students provoked hostile responses in certain campus quarters, including, seemingly, with the leader of Michigan Hillel. In a letter to I. M. Rubinow, secretary of B'nai B'rith, of May 1933, Rabbi

27. "Students Protest Good Will Drive, All Two of Them," *MD*, January 11, 1933.

28. "Gropper Hits Good Will Fund Drive; Will Hold Mass Meeting," *MD*, January 12, 1933.

29. "Students Prevent Tuition Increase!" Michigan NSL flyer, April/May 1933, VPSS, box 5, folder NSL, BHL.

30. See the reprint of the *Michigan Daily* article in "Innocents Abroad: Tuition Moratorium," *Cornell Daily Sun*, March 3, 1933, 6. For the Michigan NSL's subsequent demands, see "Students Prevent Tuition Increase!" Michigan NSL flyer, April/May 1933, VPSS, box 5, folder NSL, BHL.

Anti-Good Will Fund Agitators Harangue 150 Students

Figure 4.6—Cheyfitz and Gropper in front of the library, *Michigan Daily*, January 12, 1933.

Bernard Heller, Hillel's director, responded to Rubinow's concerns that there had been hostile activities against Jews on the Ann Arbor campus.[31] After dismissing the rumor outright, Heller characterized it as "the illegitimate offspring" of the Michigan NSL's "stupid and objectionably vociferous" advocacy of the tuition moratorium. Heller pinpointed in his criticism the NSL's demands that the university support "indigent students irrespective of whether they hail from Pennsylvania, Connecticut, the Phillipine [*sic*] Islands, or China."

Turning to the issue of the NSL's membership, Heller demurred

31. This and following quotations in this paragraph: Heller to Rubinow, letter dated May 24, 1933, Ruthven, box 7, folder 27, BHL.

any knowledge of how many Jews to non-Jews there were in this organization, but he did offer that "two individuals whose names are always in print and who are always making speeches on the steps of the library at inopportune as well as opportune times are Jewish and non-residents of Michigan." Indeed, the supposed uprising against Jews, in Heller's view, was limited to a single student who "made some reference to this organization as being manned and maneuvered by Jews" and that this remark, Heller assured Rubinow, had no effect on the larger student body. While Heller sought both to reassure Rubinow that Michigan was a tolerant and largely safe campus for Jews—his letter described the university as an institution "whose fairness matches its fineness"—Heller's prose also reveals that some Michigan students connected radical agitation with Jews and that even Heller himself sought to attribute the NSL's "stupid and objectionably vociferous" actions to two out-of-state Jewish students.

The two vociferous students were undoubtedly Leon Gropper and Cheyfitz, the latter of whom was the Michigan NSL's president.[32] Press accounts portrayed Cheyfitz as "frequently a soap box orator on the campus" whose speeches and demonstrations were a feature of campus life.[33] Cheyfitz organized the chapter's May 19, 1933 campus demonstration on the library's steps against proposed tuition increases, which was advertised by a leaflet that proposed that the Board of Regents meet the University of Michigan's budget shortfall for the 1933–34 academic year by reducing faculty numbers and limiting the salaries of the deans rather than disadvantaging students, instructors, and assistants.[34] The *Michigan Daily*, whose editorial line was conservative in this era, took

32. An interesting sidenote: Gropper had actually spoken at Hillel services in December 1930 on science and religion. "Leon Gropper Speaks at Student Services," *HN*, December 16, 1930.

33. Library Clipping Files (hereafter cited as Clippings), box 46, folder Political Clubs—National Student League, BHL.

34. "Students Prevent Tuition Increase!" Michigan NSL flyer, April/May 1933, VPSS, box 5, folder NSL, BHL.

a dim view of Cheyfitz's and the Michigan NSL's suggestions that faculty numbers and administrative salaries be cut to maintain what the paper characterized as temporary employees.[35] Michigan NSL expressed high hopes for the May 19 demonstration, despite what it acknowledged as widespread campus apathy, claiming that Michigan students would copy the examples of mass political action at CCNY, Columbia, and New York University and that "the Regents also learn that it DOES matter if a few students have to drop out. . . . By this same mass pressure we can and will force the Regents not to raise tuition."[36] At the demonstration, a *Michigan Daily* editor, who was invited to provide an opposing view to the NSL speakers, "contented himself with a malicious reflection on the race and religion of some of these speakers," according to an eyewitness.[37]

In the following months, the *Daily* published an array of opinion pieces that were hostile to the chapter and that portrayed it as a minority faction composed of East-Coast–influenced "outsiders" who were out of step with the broader conservatism of the Michigan campus community. One writer, whose editorial was signed "Bourgeois" rather than a given name, claimed that "radical activities at New York City College, Columbia University, and other large schools in the East have progressed much farther than similar activities at Middle Western and Western institutions."[38] Nonetheless, the Michigan NSL members, in claiming to represent the broader student opinion in their speeches, have "dis-

35. "More Student League Petitions . . ." *MD*, May 17, 1933, Clippings, box 44, folder Political Clubs—National Student League, BHL.

36. Leon Gropper, "Co-Operative Apathy and Tuition Increase," *MD*, May 19, 1933.

37. That the speakers' Jewishness was the "race and religion" invoked can be inferred by the fact that the eyewitness, Arthur Clifford, begins his account of the incident by stating, "Being neither a Jew nor a member of the National Student League, I feel I may comment impartially." Clifford also suggested that the "Hitlerite editor" of the *Michigan Daily* be firmly rebuked. See Arthur Clifford, "Boorish Tactics at the Mass Meeting," *MD*, May 23, 1933, Clippings, box 44, folder Political Clubs—NSL, BHL.

38. This and the following quotation are from Bourgeois, "Campaigns of the National Student League," *MD*, July 25, 1933, Clippings, box 44, folder Political Clubs—NSL, BHL.

guised themselves as something they definitely are not." Another editorial from November 1933 draws a parallel between "the big city radicals as against the conservatives of the plains and the less populated regions, and the student radicalism at certain eastern universities obtaining at institutions like Michigan."[39] The NSL "apears [sic] to have a strong chapter at Columbia and C.C.N.Y. and there the League may represent some kind of opinion. But here it does not. It is an atomic minority. . . . The student body, traditionally ultra-conservative, is more than usually impregnable here in Ann Arbor—virtually the last citadel of Republicanism in the State of Michigan." Indeed, it appears that campus conservatives, for which the *Michigan Daily* provided a bastion at that time, repeatedly characterized the group as dominated by outsiders and East Coast Jews. A March 1935 profile of Michigan NSL claims that "the conservatives of the campus have charged the NSL variously with being a narrow sect of Eastern Semites, a band of Communists, a group of alien agitators whose tuitions are paid by someone or something, a 'bunch of publicity hounds,' and a 'gang of trouble-makers.'"[40]

The Michigan NSL's tuition-related demonstrations of spring 1933 attracted a hostile response among some conservative elements that publicly associated the chapter with Jews and East Coast political radicalism. Yet, as Cheyfitz and the Michigan NSL moved into the 1933–34 academic year, the organization's biggest problem was not conservative baiting tactics but dissension from within its own ranks. In September, some of its members departed to form a new organization called the Vanguard Club, and this confronted the Michigan NSL "with the serious problem of declining

39. This and the following quotation are from "Road Song of the Bandar-Log . . . ," *MD*, November 23, 1933, Clippings, box 44, folder Political Clubs—NSL, BHL.

40. Guy M. Whipple Jr., "What Is the National Student League? Statistical Analysis Makes a Reply," *MD*, March 31, 1935. See also the response from a Michigan NSL defender who, while impugning Whipple's motives for writing the article, neither refutes that the chapter's membership had a majority of out-of-state members nor clarifies the number of Jewish members in the chapter. See S.A.M., "Misplaced Sympathy?" *MD*, April 5, 1935, Clippings, box 44, folder Political Clubs—NSL, BHL.

membership."[41] Nonetheless, as the aforementioned membership lists from the 1934–35 academic year attest, the NSL managed to rebuild its numbers to about forty-five despite the defectors who now composed the Vanguard Club. Bridging whatever differences they had, the Michigan NSL and the Vanguard Club participated in each other's activities and coordinated actions together and even shared members. Both the Vanguard Club and the NSL committed themselves to actions that increasingly antagonized the administration. An early joint action in May 1934 produced the first serious confrontation between the campus radicals and the Ruthven administration.

That spring, Cheyfitz and Kendall Wood, president of the Vanguard Club, formed a United Front Committee to send a student delegation to participate in that year's May Day demonstrations in downtown Detroit. Renting a truck (most likely a bus)

41. Guy M. Whipple Jr., "Campus Red, White Present a Broken Front to the World," *MD*, November 1, 1933, Clippings, box 46, folder Radicals, BHL. Although the reason for the split has not been identified, a hint is provided in a June 1934 editorial that Kendall Wood, the Vanguard Club's president, along with other members, penned in the *Michigan Daily*. In it, they claimed that the Vanguard Club "was organized in September 1933, to enable all types of students to participate effectively in the study of economic, social, and political problems now before the world," suggesting that the NSL was, perhaps, too rigid. See Wood et al., "Explanation of Vanguard Club Activities," *MD*, January 26, 1934, Clippings, box 44, folder Vanguard Club, BHL. The Club, according to Whipple's November 1933 article, quickly allied itself with the Socialist Club and, in general, seems to have sponsored talks from prominent figures of the Left, including Norman Thomas, whom the Club brought to Ann Arbor in January 1934. See "Socialist Party Leader to Open Lecture Series," *MD*, January 5, 1934, Clippings, box 44, folder Vanguard Club, BHL. Yet the club was ultimately little different than the NSL, and its Communist leanings were apparent as well: in November 1933, they sponsored a film screening of "Thirty Days in Russia" that featured "interesting shots of peasant farms including some of the new 'collective' variety, views of industrial Russia in which the Stalingrad Tractor factory figured, and finally a picturization of 'young Russia'" (*MD*, November 24, 1933). Cheyfitz, in an interview with the Student Discipline Committee following the May Day 1934 incident, in fact, attested that the NSL and the Vanguard Club were largely organized for the same purposes. See Student Discipline Committee Records, box 1, Cheyfitz testimony, 10, BHL: 87112 Bimu C15 2. The Vanguard Club did not have a long life at Michigan, the *Michigan Daily* records its last sponsored activity—a speech by a political science professor on German racial ideology—in late April 1935. See *MD*, April 30, 1935.

from Alfred Lee Klaer, student pastor of Ann Arbor's Presbyterian Church, who also served as driver, roughly forty students drove from the university to Clark Park in downtown Detroit.[42] Sporting banners along the truck's sides that read, "University of Michigan Students Graduate to Unemployment" and "University of Michigan Students Show Solidarity With Workers," the group arrived at Clark Park about half an hour before a scheduled demonstration, only to encounter, in Klaer's account, "several hundred policemen." Ordered by the police to leave, the Michigan students re-boarded the truck and drove northeast to Grand Circus Park, which Detroit's Republican mayor, Frank Couzens, had declared off-limits to May Day–related activities, citing concerns over potential violence. As the truck drove around the park, the forty or so students sang a combination of the "Internationale" and the University of Michigan fight song "The Victors" while cheering on the crowds assembled around the park's perimeter.[43] A motorcycled escort of Detroit police quickly confronted the students and directed them away from the park and down to a point near the Detroit River. After the police ordered the participants to disembark from the bus, the officers roughed up and searched the students as they emerged. According to the event's account in the *Ann Arbor News*, some officers even entered the bus and forcibly ejected students with batons. The police then seized the emptied bus and ordered Klaer to remain in the cab while they escorted the vehicle back

42. Unless otherwise noted, the details of the event in this paragraph are taken from "Police Spoil Student Trip," *Ann Arbor News*, May 2, 1934, Clippings, box 46, folder Radicals—May Day Incident, BHL. Accounts of the number of student participants vary from thirty-five in the news accounts immediately after the incident to Michigan NSL's own figure of forty-two. For the former, see, e.g., "U. of M. Students and Tutor on Red Junket to Detroit Are Evicted from City by Policy; Ruthven to Investigate May Day Escapade," *Detroit Free Press*, May 2, 1934; for the latter, see Karl Cannon's letter to the editor, *MD*, May 16, 1934; both Clippings, box 46, folder Radicals—May Day Incident, BHL.

43. This detail is in the *Michigan Daily*'s immediate account, Paul J. Elliott, "Radicals Meet Detroit Police in Near-Riot," *MD*, May 2, 1934, Clippings, box 46, folder Radicals—May Day Incident, BHL. .

to Ann Arbor without the students, who had to hitchhike back to campus.

The group's confrontation with the Detroit Police ensured that the incident made the front pages of the Detroit and Ann Arbor papers. In response, Ruthven ordered that this occurrence be investigated immediately by the Student Discipline Committee. Faced with accusations that the Detroit Police had manhandled the students, its officers claimed that the students had violated several laws including having banners that were larger than what was permissible in the "loop" district around Grand Circus Park; that the students' "loud yelling" was a disturbance of the peace; and that they were driving contrary to traffic laws.[44] Cheyfitz and four other members of the excursion lodged a complaint with Detroit Police Commissioner Heinrich Pickert against members of his department who had clubbed several of the students.[45] Popular reactions to the May Day incident seemed to focus on the students' immaturity: "a few good spanks on the bodily part created for that purpose would do these infants a lot of good," one correspondent wrote.[46]

More telling was the way the conservative *Michigan Daily* reported on the incident. While the May 2, 1934, headlines in the *Detroit Free Press* and *Ann Arbor News* described it as a "junket" or even just as a "trip," the initial *Daily* article described it as a "near-riot."[47] Moreover, while the *Detroit Free Press* article identified both Cheyfitz and, mistakenly, Guy Whipple (a *Michigan Daily* reporter) as co-organizers of the trip, and the *Ann Arbor News* article did

44. "U. of M. Students and Tutor on Red Junket," *Detroit Free Press*, May 2, 1934, Clippings, box 46, folder Radicals—May Day Incident, BHL.

45. "U. of M. Students Who Charge Police Clubbed Them," *Detroit News*, May 3, 1934, 2, Student Discipline Committee Records, box 1, "May Day Incident 1934" Packet, BHL.

46. "Spank Them!" *Detroit News*, May 3, 1934, Student Discipline Committee Records, box 1, "May Day Incident 1934" Packet, BHL.

47. Elliot, "Radicals," *MD*, May 2, 1934, Clippings, box 46, folder Radicals—May Day Incident, BHL.

not mention either one, the *Daily* laid most of the responsibility for the entire operation from its very beginning to its end upon Cheyfitz.[48] Under a subheading that read "Cheyfitz Is Leader," the *Daily* article asserted that this student was "ostensibly in charge of the trip," that "Cheyfitz protested to the police inspector that as peaceable students they had a legal right to meet in the park," and that "Cheyfitz then had the group proceed downtown hoping to meet fellow demonstrators there."[49] Tellingly, perhaps, to emphasize Cheyfitz's leading role in the entire affair, the article did not mention Vanguard Club president Wood's participation in organizing the excursion, relying instead on the readers' obvious knowledge and recognition of Cheyfitz's being a Jew and Wood's a Gentile.[50]

The *Daily*'s hostility to Cheyfitz was even more evident in the subsequent editorial that the paper published about the May Day incident.[51] While taking the Detroit Police to task for their rough handling of the students, the editorial portrayed the trip as a willful provocation on Cheyfitz's part. "The student leader of the group, the well-known Mr. Cheyfitz," it said, "certainly has gained a reputation in local parts which should warn all students against participation in the activities which it is his wont to organize. None of his enterprises has borne fruit beyond the unpleasant type of publicity which this recent venture brought forth." Again,

48. Based on the testimony provided by Charles T. Orr to the Student Disciplinary Committee, it appears that Whipple was the *Michigan Daily* reporter assigned to the excursion, not an organizer of it. Orr testimony to Student Disciplinary Committee, May 1934, 5–6, Student Discipline Committee Records, box 1, 5, BHL.

49. Elliot, "Radicals," MD, May 2, 1934, Clippings, box 46, folder Radicals—May Day Incident, BHL.

50. The Vanguard Club's paper, *Michigan Tomorrow*, asserts that Wood played a role in forming the United Front Committee in order to organize the excursion. See "True Story of May Day," *Michigan Tomorrow* 1.2 (May 14, 1934): 1, Clippings, box 44, folder Vanguard Club, BHL.

51. Unless otherwise noted, this and the following quotations in this paragraph are from "Trouble Seekers Usually Find It . . . ," MD, May 3, 1934, Clippings, box 46, folder Radicals—May Day Incident, BHL.

the paper did not mention Kendall Wood's role as co-organizer of the excursion or as Cheyfitz's collaborator. Instead, while casting the other participants as naïfs who were "insensible enough to accompany a man like Mr. Cheyfitz in the first place," the editorial claimed that Cheyfitz deliberately engineered the event to provoke a reaction from the Detroit Police: "in the light of Mr. Cheyfitz's activities of the past, it seems more likely that the group found in Detroit about what it might have expected." Finally, the *Daily* encouraged the university to consider expelling Cheyfitz although, as a graduating senior, he had only one month left on campus. "We are certain," the editorial said in closing, "that very few tears would be shed if Mr. Cheyfitz were far enough removed from the campus that he would find it impossible ever again to lead others into the making of such unfortunate mistakes." Other papers picked up the tone and content of the *Daily's* editorial of which they must have had an advance copy since they published their pieces on the same day as the *Daily* ran its editorial. In the words of a *Detroit Free Press* article published on May 3 (one that also quoted extensively from the *Daily's* editorial), we read that Cheyfitz must have been "directing the organization of the group previous to its departure Tuesday afternoon" and had played a leading role in the group having "taken part in a number of demonstrations about the campus."[52] The *Ann Arbor News* characterized Cheyfitz as the "spokesman for the May Day group and frequently a soap box orator on the campus."[53]

Thus, the *Michigan Daily* sought to shape public perceptions of the May Day event by featuring Cheyfitz's role as organizer and spokesman and by de-emphasizing the collaborative nature of the excursion between Michigan NSL, the Vanguard Club, and those students who joined because of mere curiosity or, as some claimed, to engage in "sociological analyses." In other words, in

52. "May Day Trip Brings a Probe," *Detroit Free Press*, May 3, 1934, Clippings, box 46, folder Radicals—May Day Incident, BHL.

53. "May Day Trip Starts Probe," *Ann Arbor News*, May 3, 1934, Clippings, box 46, folder Radicals—May Day Incident, BHL.

the view of the *Daily*, naïve and sincere students were led astray into a police confrontation by a scheming — and Jewish — radical agitator. Arthur Clifford, whose editorial attacking the racial slurs made by a *Daily* editor during the May 1933 tuition freeze demonstration we already mentioned, again imputed malicious motives on the part of the *Daily*'s editorial staff for its unfair characterization of Cheyfitz's role in the May Day excursion. He claimed that the *Daily* assigned a reporter to cover the excursion with the instructions to "make the story as dirty as you can."[54] Clifford attributed this hit job on the May Day excursion to a "small political group who occupy some of the most important positions on The Daily, who have long ceased to reflect student opinion." For its part, the *Daily* responded by re-asserting the intellectual immaturity of the May Day participants and was unapologetic in demanding Cheyfitz's expulsion: "May we simply refer those who resent The Daily's stand on Mr. Cheyfitz to the stories which have appeared in The Daily in the last two years concerning him."[55]

Despite the *Michigan Daily*'s invective against the May Day participants, and Cheyfitz in particular, the administration's response was, for the most part, surprisingly mild.[56] The Student Discipline Committee conducted a brief week-long investigation, mainly by interviewing the excursion's leaders, including Cheyfitz, and several of the participants.[57] The committee found that the participating students exercised "bad taste, poor judgment and a regrettable immaturity of attitude, but that the episode has

54. This and the following quote are from Arthur Clifford, "May Day Expulsions," *MD*, May 6, 1934, Clippings, box 46, folder Radicals—May Day Incident, BHL.

55. John C. Healey, "May Day Demonstrators Clearly in Wrong . . . ," *MD*, May 9, 1934, Clippings, box 46, folder Radicals—May Day Incident, BHL.

56. Indeed, James Wechsler's *Revolt on the Campus* claims that the university was effectively indifferent to the fact that the Detroit police had attacked the students and that the administration was "irate because the students had become involved in so 'controversial' an incident." Wechsler, *Revolt*, 164.

57. The typed transcripts to the Discipline Committee's interviews with the May Day participants appears in the Student Discipline Committee Records, box 1, BHL: 87112 Bimu C15 2.

attracted much more attention and publicity than its importance warranted."[58] The committee concluded that the ridicule of fellow students "who routinely deplore sub-collegiate methods of obtaining cheap notriety [*sic*]" constituted sufficient discipline on its own, and yet its members also issued a warning to those they felt were primarily responsible for the demonstration. These individuals, so the committee held, merited not only ridicule but also censure and, in highly telling language, "to make it questionable whether they are desirable members of the student body of the University." The committee deemed these students responsible for flying a banner that seemed to indicate that they represented the Michigan student body and for conducting the demonstration that called for police interference. Any such future action "on the part of any student or groups of students by which they purport, without right, to represent the student body, or which reflects unfavorably upon the University will be cause for severe disciplinary action."

That Cheyfitz was the target of this specific censure seems evident by the Committee on Student Discipline's interviews. The committee asked Charles T. Orr, a teaching fellow in the Department of Economics and the excursion's faculty representative, if he realized the political tendencies of those who accompanied him:

Orr: I know Cheyfitz and wouldn't want to take part in any demonstration organized by him.
Committee: Didn't he organize this trip?
Orr: [Kendall] Wood and Cheyfitz were made a committee to get the truck.
Committee: You think Cheyfitz was the leader of the most radical group?

58. This and the following quotes in this paragraph are from "Board Assails Student Junket," *Detroit Free Press*, May 9, 1934, Clippings, box 46, folder Radicals—May Day Incident, BHL.

> Orr: Certainly, because he is a communist and pretended to be the leader of the whole thing. I know one other communist, who evidently let him be leader of their group.[59]

Cheyfitz, who appears to have been interviewed more extensively than the other participants, was asked if he was the leader of the May Day group and if he was the president of the Michigan NSL.[60] While he admitted to being one of the May Day leaders, he also claimed to have dropped out of the NSL "last year and a month of this" (a highly dubious claim since this would have meant that Cheyfitz quit the NSL in April 1933, when he had actually submitted the petition for the chapter's recognition in May 1933) because of the policies of "certain leaders of the organization." But he felt that, with an influx of new members, the "organization might come back to the purpose for which it was organized." He also mentioned that he had recently been selected for membership of the executive committee. Later Cheyfitz was asked what the NSL was, and he replied with deliberate vagueness that it was "a non-political organization, organized for specific things on every campus. On this campus they are organized now to hold open forums on certain things. I got into it because of its anti-war policies."[61] However, given Cheyfitz's history of political agitation on campus, the Disciplinary Committee must have known that his answers were willfully evasive. The committee's questions to Orr, the most senior person interviewed, clearly show that its members considered Cheyfitz to be the excursion's organizer. Moreover, Kendall Wood, the Vanguard Club's president whom

59. Orr testimony to Student Disciplinary Committee, May 1934, 5–6, Student Discipline Committee Records, box 1, BHL: 87112 Bimu C15 2.

60. The *Detroit News* had identified Cheyfitz as the Michigan NSL's president on May 2. "Students Charge Police Beating," *Detroit News*, May 2, 1934, 1, Committee on Student Discipline Records (CSDR), box 1, BHL: 87112 Bimu C15 2; Clippings, May Day Incident 1934 packet, BHL.

61. Cheyfitz's testimony to Student Disciplinary Committee, May 1934, 2, 10, Student Discipline Committee Records, box 1, BHL: 87112 Bimu C15 2.

Orr identified as having procured the truck with Cheyfitz, was not interviewed to the same extent, nor was he asked about his leadership role in either Vanguard or the May Day incident or his role in procuring the transportation.

Taken together, the evidence suggests that Cheyfitz was the person to whom the committee referred when it publicly stated that it was questionable "whether [certain students] are desirable members of the student body of the University." In other words, the Student Disciplinary Committee essentially accepted the *Michigan Daily*'s line that the May Day incident was largely the work of a known Jewish agitator—Cheyfitz—who led a group of largely immature students unwittingly into a police confrontation. The radical Jewish student Cheyfitz was censured by a university committee and publicly admonished by the student newspaper. The radical Gentile student Wood experienced neither of these punishments.

Cheyfitz's censure did not prevent him from graduating the following month and passing the leadership of the NSL chapter onto his successors. Although it is difficult to assess the general perception of the Michigan NSL on campus—which the *Michigan Daily*, no friend to the group, claimed was largely dismissive among the student body—it seems evident that Cheyfitz's reputation as a vocal and active radical agitator encouraged conservatives at the University of Michigan to view the chapter through the lens of Cheyfitz's actions and his Jewish ethnicity. Once the group ran afoul of the law in early May 1934, the university's own investigation followed the conservative line that Cheyfitz had been the prime instigator, despite the fact that the Vanguard Club's president Wood also played a significant coordinating role. Cheyfitz got away with only a censure, but the Discipline Committee's conclusion that those who led or organized political demonstrations risked their standing as desirable members of the student body, and the committee's promise that future such actions would lead to more stringent responses from the university, meant that later, specifically Jewish, members of the Michigan NSL were not as lucky.

"Perversive Activities" and Tumultuous Times: The 1934–35 Academic Year[62]

The committee's stern warning did little to deter the Michigan NSL from orchestrating future demonstrations and other activities in the 1934–35 academic year. Moreover, we need to note that the NSL was hardly the only group engaging in political activity on the Michigan campus that year. As the official history of the university describes, "on campus, pacifism and neutrality were the consuming issues, reflecting national concerns."[63] Along with the NSL, other groups formed such as the League against War and Militarism as well as the Student League for Industrial Democracy, the latter having splintered from the NSL arguing that the NSL "was made up of communists who were trying to capture other groups."[64]

Yet Michigan's NSL chapter remained the one that, in the eyes of the Ruthven administration, appeared most inclined to agitation. Indeed, the 1934-35 academic year witnessed an important change in the administration's approach to the NSL: from

---

62. The account of the NSL's activities and Ruthven's response to them is drawn from Van de Water, *Alexander Grant Ruthven*, 139–55. Van de Water's study is based upon his doctoral dissertation, "Peace Maker: President Alexander G. Ruthven and His Relationship to His Faculty, Students, and Regents." There are telling differences between the dissertation, which was based in part on extensive interviews with the former president and was defended while Ruthven was still alive, and the book, which came out after Ruthven died. The dissertation tends to take a more non-committal line toward Ruthven's handling of the NSL in 1934–35, whereas van de Water's book argues that "the feeling persists that to arbitrarily dismiss students without regard for established disciplinary procedures, without stated cause, and without hearing was, to borrow a word used by one of the dismissed students thirty years afterward, 'disgraceful.'" See Van de Water, *Alexander Grant Ruthven*, 154. Van de Water does not identify the name of the dismissed student in his dissertation or book. His files contain a letter from Abraham Stavitsky showing that he was the source. The official university history's account of the NSL's activities in the 1934–35 and the Ruthven administration's response is in Peckham, Steneck, and Steneck, *Making*, 213–16.

63. Peckham, Steneck, and Steneck, *Making*, 213.

64. Peckham, Steneck, and Steneck, *Making*, 213.

the relative restraint shown following the May Day event to a more active effort to curtail its activities. The decisive event that prompted this shift was the Willis Ward controversy that fall. At the beginning of the fall 1934 term, and under the Michigan NSL's new president William L. Fisch, a Jewish sophomore from Newark, New Jersey, the chapter immediately seized upon a racially motivated incident with which to mobilize against the university. There were rumors that Willis Ward (1912–83), an African American right end on the Michigan football team, was to be benched for the upcoming October 20 game against Georgia Tech, whose coaching staff had threatened not to appear on the field were Ward to play.[65] Willis Ward had joined the Wolverines in 1931 at the insistence of its coach, Harry Kipke (1899–1972), and over the objections of Fielding Yost, the university's athletic director, who had long barred African Americans from playing on the football team.[66] Although Yost had been Kipke's mentor when the latter played halfback and punter on the football team from 1920 to 1923, Kipke bravely challenged his former coach, and current supervisor, to allow Ward, who had also received an offer to play for Dartmouth, to join the team. Kipke marshaled the support of

65. "NSL Lays Plans for Coming Year," *MD*, September 28, 1934. Tyran Kai Steward's doctoral dissertation, "In the Shadow of Jim Crow: The Benching and Betrayal of Willis Ward," provides the most substantial account and analysis of this event. The controversy has also been subject of a recent documentary, *Black and Blue: The Story of Gerald R. Ford, Willis Ward, and the 1934 Michigan-Georgia Tech Football Game* (dir. Brian Kruger, 2012). Commemorative accounts tend to play up the relationship between Ward and the future president; see Mike Lopresti, "Michigan to Honor Black Player Benched 78 Years Ago," *USA Today*, October 19, 2012. Stephen J. Nesbitt provides a summary of Ward's background in "The Forgotten Man: Remembering Michigan Trailblazer Willis Ward," *MD*, October 18, 2012. See also John U. Bacon, *A Legacy of Champions: The Story of the Men Who Built University of Michigan* (CTC Sports, 1996). A brief discussion of the Willis Ward controversy can also be found in Peckham, Steneck, and Steneck, *Making*, 214–15.

66. Steward attributes Yost's racism to his southern origins and argues that Yost's barring of black athletes from the football team was part of a broad pattern of discrimination among southern US university administrators who held positions at northern institutions. On Yost, see Steward, "In the Shadow," 26–29.

prominent individuals, including a distinguished businessman and future University of Michigan regent, Frederick C. Matthei, president of the University of Michigan Club in Detroit, to pressure Yost into accepting Ward as a bona fide varsity player for the Wolverines.[67] In his first three years with the football team, Ward enjoyed considerable success on the gridiron in addition to being a renowned and successful member of the university's track team, on which he set multiple records and defeated the great Jesse Owens of Ohio State. But in the summer before his senior year, the coaching staff of the Michigan football team informed Ward that he would be benched for the forthcoming Georgia Tech game on October 20, 1934.

The decision to bench Ward drew widespread controversy both on and off campus.[68] Kipke, Yost, and President Ruthven were inundated with letters and correspondence opposing the university's willingness to defer to the dictates of the Jim Crow South. Michigan's NSL chapter was at the forefront of this protest. Indeed, it was the NSL, in league with other left-wing groups like the Vanguard Club, that brought the decision to bench Ward, which Yost had hoped to keep quiet, to public attention. NSL member Joseph Feldman was designated the NSL's representative in the Ward matter and personally sought an interview with Yost.[69] The chapter formed its own investigating committee to determine the truth and submitted an open letter to Yost and Kipke, "either to verify or deny these rumors within the next two

---

67. For his part, Kipke also tried to break down, with some success, the standard practice of lodging African American players away from white players while they were on the road. See Steward, "In the Shadow," 85.

68. See Steward, "In the Shadow," 120–70, for much of the detail in the following paragraphs. James Wechsler's contemporary account, *Revolt on the Campus* (1935), mentions the Ward case and claims that the University of Michigan "has concentrated its energies on athletic discrimination." Wechsler, *Revolt*, 365.

69. Steward, "In the Shadow," 123. A copy of this letter, dated October 4, 1934, is in Board in Control of Intercollegiate Athletics, box 20, folder 1, BHL. Our deepest thanks to Michelle McClellan for providing us with a copy of this letter.

or three days."[70] The NSL's open letter, published in the *Michigan Daily* on October 7 sparked a resolution from the Ann Arbor Ministerial Association condemning Michigan's acceding to the Jim Crow racism of the Georgia Tech team.[71]

Taking Kipke's and Yost's stony silence as a confirmation that Michigan was going to heed Georgia Tech's demand and not even dress Ward, let alone play him, the Michigan NSL—working together with the Vanguard Club and the Michigan League Against War and Militarism under the umbrella name of the Ward United Front Committee Against Negro Discrimination—launched a petition drive urging that either Ward be allowed to play or that the game be canceled.[72] By October 18, three days before the game, over 1,500 signatures had been collected, including by several faculty members; the University of Michigan's New York alumni chapter had even asked Benny Friedman, then playing professionally in New York, for a statement.[73] The Michigan NSL chapter was also pivotal in getting other NSL university chapters to send letters of protest to the Michigan Intercollegiate Athletic Department and the university's Board in Control of Intercollegiate Athletics.[74] The NSL also sent notices to Michigan alumni with its New York chapter announcing that it was contacting Michigan's former star quarterback Benny Friedman to provide a statement

70. "This Would Come Up," *MD*, October 7, 1934, Clippings, box 44, folder Political Clubs—NSL, BHL.

71. "Local Clergy Comment on Ward Rumor," *MD*, October 10, 1934, Clippings, box 27, folder Football 1931–35, BHL.

72. "Exclusion of Willis Ward Is Protested," *MD*, October 17, 1934, Clippings, box 27, folder Football 1931–35, BHL. See Steward, "In the Shadow," 132.

73. "Secure 1,500 Signatures on Ward Petitions," *MD*, October 18, 1934, Clippings, box 27, folder Football 1931–35, BHL. For Friedman, see "Exclusion of Willis Ward Is Protested," *MD*, October 17, 1934.

74. As Steward points out, the Willis Ward case was not the only instance in which the NSL fought for racial equality. The national NSL also hosted its annual convention at Howard University and "worked to enhance interest in the Scottsboro case, which they considered to be emblematic of an oppressive Jim Crow system." Steward, "In the Shadow," 134–36.

of support. Indeed, Friedman sent a letter the day before the game protesting the decision to bench Ward and arguing for the game to be canceled.[75] That same day, Joseph Feldman, the NSL's representative on the committee, provocatively sent Kipke and Yost a telegram inviting them to speak at a rally planned in support of Willis Ward on the eve of the game.[76]

The Ward United Front Committee, with NSL members generally out in front, played the most active role generating public awareness of the Ward case. While Yost and the team had hoped to keep the fact of Ward's benching quiet, the Ward United Front Committee, composed mainly of members of the NSL and the Vanguard Club, shined a spotlight on the controversy and brought the university unwelcome publicity. University officials, including Ruthven himself, grew exasperated at the public attention that the case was generating. Yost's ire was sufficiently strong that he determined to identify who were the individuals behind the agitation. The athletic director contacted the Pinkerton detective agency. He then proceeded to hire a detective to scope out the campus and inquire into the membership of both the NSL and the Vanguard Club.[77] Yost handed the Pinkerton detective the names of some individuals on Thursday, October 18, and also suggested that the detective attend the Ward United Front Committee's

75. On Friedman's response to the Ward controversy, see Steward, "In the Shadow," 139–40.

76. Board in Control of Intercollegiate Athletics (hereafter cited as BCIA), box 20, folder 1. The documents relating to the Pinkerton investigation is in BCIA, box 20, folders 1 and 2, BHL. Michelle McClellan very generously provided us with copies of these documents to which we owe her considerable thanks.

77. A letter of understanding between Yost and Pinkerton, dated October 19, 1934, is in BCIA, box 20, folder 1. A list of five student organizations was produced at some point in this investigation though the Pinkerton detective focused mainly on the NSL and the Vanguard Club; the other three were the Cosmopolitan Club, the Cooperative House, and the Socialist House. The Vanguard Club and the NSL shared members as is shown in the Vice President of Student Services' files where, in a letter from NSL organizational secretary Leo Luskin to Dean of Students Joseph Bursley, Fisch is also listed as the executive secretary of the Michigan NSL chapter. Luskin to Bursley, letter dated May 8, 1935. VPSS, box 4, folder NSL.

meeting/rally scheduled to be held Friday night—the eve of the game—in the Natural Science Auditorium.[78]

Through his inquires, the detective learned that William Fisch was chairman of the Ward United Front Committee and that he "was an active member of the Vanguard Club."[79] The Pinkerton detective also interviewed the *Michigan Daily*'s city editor who confirmed that the NSL and the Vanguard Club were sponsoring the Ward United Front Committee campaign but also opined that these organizations had little sympathy among the greater student body. "He [the city editor] stated," the Pinkerton man wrote, "that the University of Michigan acts as host to Georgia Tech on Saturday and that in his opinion practically all of the Michigan Students would welcome them in a most sportsmanlike and friendly manner in spite of their southern racial discrimination policies."[80] The detective received confirmation of the *Daily* editor's sentiments and assessments in random interviews that he conducted with students at the Michigan Union and at the Student Christian Association who believed "that the National Students' League and Vanguard Club are composed of students who are foreigners, some orientals, and have radical and socialistic ideas; that the student body as a whole pays very little attention to their activities and surely would not co-operate with them in case of a disturbance at Saturday's game."[81]

The Pinkerton detective returned to Ann Arbor the following day and met with William Fisch whom he described as "decidedly Jewish."[82] Fisch claimed that the Ward United Front Committee's campaign was over and that it was now up to the students to take whatever actions they deemed necessary. Far from being a mere publicity stunt that some of the students claimed was the primary

78. I.F.H. report dated October 18, 1934, BCIA, box 20, folder 1, BHL. It is unclear if I.F.H. refers to the detective's initials or some other designation.

79. I.F.H. report dated October 18, 1934, BCIA, box 20, folder 1, BHL.

80. I.F.H. report dated October 18, 1934, BCIA, box 20, folder 1, BHL.

81. I.F.H. report dated October 18, 1934, BCIA, box 20, folder 1, BHL.

82. I.F.H. report dated October 19, 1934, BCIA, box 20, folder 1, BHL.

motivation for the agitation, Fisch contended that Willis Ward was truly grateful for all the efforts that occurred on his behalf. Fisch claimed that Yost was hostile to the students' assistance of Ward because he was a southerner and that Yost "should never have signed this game while he knew Ward was on the team."[83] Nonetheless, Fisch attempted to convince the detective that the Ward United Front Committee had not planned any action during the game and "that they could not afford to start any action as they are known and it would jeopardize their standing and no doubt force them out of the University." When asked about the committee's meeting scheduled for that night, Fisch answered that it was meant to gauge student sentiment in advance of the game, "to see how the students accepted their campaign; that if anything happens tomorrow, it will be put over by the majority of the students who might be so angered by the fact that Ward cannot play, that they will forget themselves."[84]

That afternoon, the Pinkerton agent provided Yost with a brief verbal report of his investigation. The athletic director reminded the Pinkerton man to go to the Ward United Front Committee's meeting that evening. That night, the Natural Science Auditorium was nearly filled to capacity. The detective claimed that "a large percentage of those present were observed to be people of other than the white race, such as Jewish, Orientals, etc."[85] He claimed that the meeting was disorderly and that many of the speakers were shouted down. Later, it was reported that hecklers from the secret society, Michigamua, whom Yost had also asked to go to this event, disrupted the speakers by booing and tossing coins at them. The rally soon degenerated into a verbal shouting match between the pro- and anti-Willis Ward factions "while invective was hurled back and forth across the auditorium with undimin-

83. I.F.H. report dated October 19, 1934, BCIA, box 20, folder 1, BHL.

84. I.F.H. report dated October 19, 1934, BCIA, box 20, folder 1, BHL.

85. I.F.H. report dated October 19, 1934, BCIA, box 20, folder 1, BHL.

ished bitterness."[86] The Pinkerton detective heard nothing in the way of plans for a demonstration or disturbance at the game itself, although "a resolution was passed to the effect that the majority at the meeting were in favor of having Ward in the game tomorrow."[87]

For all its efforts, however, the Ward United Front Committee achieved little except being subjected to yet another invective from the *Michigan Daily* and incurring President Ruthven's increasing hostility. It was one thing for NSL members to participate in a May Day parade, quite another to present the university in an unfavorable light on the national stage. As to the event itself: Yost did not budge from his decision. Ward did not appear anywhere in the stadium, and the game was played without him. The Georgia State game was Michigan's only win in what was to become an abysmal season (Ward scored all of the points that the team accrued for the remainder of the season). Yet the Pinkerton investigation produced one item, albeit secretly, that had a later consequence: a list of the active members of the Ward United Front Committee who attended the game, their campus residences and hometowns, and even where these students sat in the stadium during the game [Figure 4.7]. Tellingly, the hometowns of all but one of the students were in the New York or New Jersey area. Moreover, the first three names on the list—Joseph D. Feldman, William L. Fisch, and Danny Cohen—were three of the four students later dismissed from the university by President Ruthven in July 1935.[88] Thus, by the time of the Willis Ward controversy, Jewish students from the East Coast were being increasingly identified with political radicalism.

86. "Wolverines Ready for Game; Ward Rally Is Wild Session; Athletic Officials Stay Silent," *MD*, October 20, 1934, Clippings, box 27, folder Football 1931–35, BHL. See also Steward, "In the Shadow," 141–44.

87. I.F.H. report dated October 19, 1934, BCIA, box 20, folder 1, BHL.

88. The other three students on this were Emanuel Levine (Jersey City, NJ), Pauline Cohen (New York, NY), and William Samborski (Pinckney, MI). Charles Orr and Kendall Wood were listed as advisors. BCIA, box, 1, folder 1, BHL.

ACTIVE MEMBERS

UNITED FRONT COMMITTEE ON WARD

Joseph D. Feldman 421 S. Fifth Ave.	'37 Lit. New York City	Sec. 43	Row 27	Seat 15
William L. Fisch 427 S. Fifth Ave.	'37 Lit. Newark, N. J.	Sec. 43	Row 68	Seat 6
Danny Cohen 408 Hamilton	'37 Eng. Trenton, N. J.	Sec. 24	Row 49	Seat 9
Emanuel Levine 321 S. Division	'37 Lit. Jersey City, N. J.	Sec. 43	Row 18	Seat 21
Pauline Cohen 1029 Vaughn	'37 Lit. New York City	Sec. 25	Row 53	Seat 4
William Samborski 506 S. Fifth Ave.	'36 Lit. Pinckney, Michigan	Sec. 43	Row 68	Seat 24

Advisors

Charles Orr   Sec. 22   Row 29   Seat 21

Kendall Wood   (No order)

Figure 4.7 [Active Members of United Front Committee on Ward], Board of Control of Intercollegiate Athletics box 20, folder 1, Bentley Historical Library, University of Michigan.

The embarrassment that the Ward United Front Committee caused the university by agitating on Ward's behalf deeply antagonized members of the student body and the administration as well. If the earlier May Day incident in Detroit appeared to the university leadership and its official authorities almost as a kind of college prank, this time the radical students of the NSL and the Vanguard Club generated serious acrimony. Clearly some threshold had been crossed and the activities of the NSL, the Vanguard Club, and other radical organizations were not taken lightly. Moreover, thanks to Yost, the university had identified certain students as the main instigators, and these were mainly Jewish students from the East Coast. The day after the game, the *Michi-*

gan Daily's editorial singled out the Michigan NSL for using "the affair as a means of causing as much embarrassment and gaining as much publicity as possible, achieved neither its professed purpose of putting Ward in the game nor the greater purpose of lessening discrimination against Negroes—both in the North and the South."[89] In a private letter, Ruthven concurred with the Michigan NSL's critics claiming that the actions of the organization and its sympathizers had done more harm than good: "it was obvious to members of the Board that the people who were insisting that he [Ward] should play were doing a great deal of damage to our reputation as a democratic institution."[90] Yost put the matter more bluntly: "The agitation was developed by a committee of five Jewish sophomore students, four of them from New York City and vicinity and one from Michigan. They did it in the name of 'the United Front Committee on Ward.'"[91] In a private letter that Yost sent a few days after the game, the athletic director complained about the agitation produced by the Ward United Front Committee: "You cannot realize the effort that was made by the colored organizations and local radical students to create trouble. Their slogan was, 'WARD PLAYS OR THE GAME MUST BE CANCELLED.' The colored race must be in a bad situation judging from the number of national organizations that are organized to insure racial equality or no racial discrimination."[92] For Yost, Ruthven, and the administration, the Ward United Front Committee, composed of the Communist-dominated and heavily Jewish NSL members as well as members of the Vanguard Club,

89. They did, however, support the position, if not the tactics, of the "Tory group" that disrupted the rally at the Natural Science Auditorium, arguing that its methods "did not convince one single person, despite the soundness of its arguments." "Willis Ward Summary . . . ," *MD*, October 21, 1934, Clippings, box 27, folder Football 1931–35, BHL.

90. Ruthven to A. Richard Frank, letter dated October 31, 1934, Ruthven, box 11, folder 18, BHL.

91. Behee, *Hail to the Victors!* 26–27; quoted in Steward, "In the Shadow," 162.

92. Yost to McGugin, letter dated October 23, 1934, BCIA, box 1, folder 2, BHL.

was testing the boundaries of the university's vaunted pluralism in ways that members of the administration were coming to see as unacceptable.

Nonetheless, the Willis Ward controversy constituted a sort of moral victory for the Michigan NSL if for no other reason than that it raised the chapter's visibility. From that moment, "the campus and the general public, too, began to speculate interestedly on the aims and methods of the group."[93] Whatever hostility they had generated among the administration and the conservative elements of the student body, both the NSL and the Vanguard Club continued to plan events and activities undauntedly. These events included speeches by newspaper editor Michael Gold and Angelo Herndon, an African American escaped convict sentenced to eighteen to twenty years on a Georgia chain gang for violating a Civil War–era anti-slave insurrectionary law.[94] More pointedly, especially in light of later events, the chapter held a discussion forum about, and published an editorial against, CCNY President Frederick Robinson's November 1934 expulsion of over twenty students for protesting a delegation of visiting students from Fascist Italy, an action that received the hearty endorsement of the Hearst-owned *Detroit Times*.[95] Denouncing Robinson's actions as fascist, the Michigan NSL editorial disavowed any relation to the Communist Party and claimed to be open to all students who supported its platform of demanding free educational facilities, academic freedom, anti-discrimination, abolition of the R.O.T.C., and "improved student conditions more generally."[96] Yet, as

93. Whipple, "What Is the National Student League?" *MD*, March 31, 1935, Clippings, box 44, folder Political Clubs—NSL, BHL.

94. For Gold, see "Michael Gold Will Deliver Talk Tonight," *MD*, December 2, 1934. For Herndon, see "Negro Convict to Speak on Labor Cases," *MD*, February 21, 1935. Herndon was introduced at this event by Willis Ward.

95. The incident is described in Cohen, *When the Old Left Was Young*, 115–16. See "Punish Student Reds," *Detroit Times*, November 21, 1934; "Student Activity Attack Discussed in Meeting," *MD*, November 29, 1934; both in Clippings, box 44, folder Political Clubs—NSL, BHL.

96. "NSL: Students' Champion," *MD*, December 1, 1934, Clippings, box 44, folder Political Clubs—NSL, BHL.

the aforementioned March 1935 *Michigan Daily* article by Guy Whipple—the reporter who accompanied the May Day excursion from campus to Detroit—attests, campus conservatives considered the chapter's members as "a narrow sect of Eastern Semites, a band of Communists, a group of alien agitators." Moreover, Whipple himself averred that "there are many Communists, with a capital 'C' or a small 'c', in the organization. Some of these are 'from the East,' some are not. There are Socialists in the organization. There are dissident radicals of all types in the NSL."[97] The sentiments that students had expressed during the Willis Ward controversy—that the NSL and the Vanguard Club were composed of Jewish aliens and that these groups held little appeal to broader student body—evidently persisted. Arthur Miller's memoir recalls that "with all the radical turmoil on the campus in the thirties, it was a myth that the student body, let alone the faculty, was predominantly leftist. Most students by far, and almost all the faculty, were mainly interested in their careers, just as they always are. I might editorialize in the *Daily* against the university's refusal to allow John Strachey to speak on his famous book *The Coming Struggle for Power*, but I had no illusions that I was in anything other than the tiny minority that was even aware of his book or point of view."[98]

Michigan NSL's plans for the winter 1935 term brought it into open conflict with the Ruthven administration. Not only had the May Day incident in Detroit and the Willis Ward controversy widened the chapter's visibility beyond the confines of Ann Arbor, but these events had also emboldened NSL to expand its activities. As Miller's aforementioned quote shows, the Michigan NSL invited the British Communist economist, and former Labour member of Parliament, John Strachey, whose recent book *The Coming Struggle for Power* (1933) was a critical history of capitalism, to speak at Hill Auditorium in March as part of a lecture tour

97. Whipple, "What Is the National Student League?" *MD*, March 31, 1935, Clippings, box 44, folder Political Clubs—NSL, BHL.
98. Miller, *Timebends*, 97.

that Strachey was doing on American campuses. Additionally, the Michigan NSL and the Vanguard Club also sought to coordinate a one-day walkout from classes in support of the national NSL's planned second annual anti-war strike on campuses nationwide scheduled for April 4.[99]

The Michigan NSL's plans, however, came at a particularly sensitive moment for President Ruthven and the university. Still reeling from the budget cuts of the previous years; angered by the bad publicity generated by the Willis Ward controversy; and facing a conservative state legislature and a Republican governor in Lansing both of whom were growing restive against the radicalism they perceived was spreading into the state's colleges; Ruthven was at pains to demonstrate that the university was not becoming a hotbed of political radicalism. Addressing the State Senate in mid-February, he reassured the senators that, unlike other campuses such as CCNY, the University of Michigan was a "center of conservative thought." "You need not lose one hour's sleep fearing that your boys and girls are taught a brand of radicalism," he averred.[100] In essence, Ruthven sought to control the "optics" of the situation by minimizing the presence of radical activity in the likely hope that he would not have to act against it. Unlike other college presidents, who had started to crack down on left-wing agitation in 1934, Ruthven still took a restrained attitude, though with growing animosity, toward Michigan NSL's activities well into 1935. But it was clear that the NSL's political activities overshadowed the president's efforts to foster a pluralist campus community through the networks of on-campus religious organizations affiliated with the university. Despite the president's care-

99. This would be the NSL's second such annual nationwide student strike, held on the anniversary of the United States' entry into the First World War. See Cohen, *When the Old Left Was Young*, 93–94. For an outline of the Michigan NSL's plans for the winter 1935 term, see "National Student League Outlines Plans for Future," *MD*, January 17, 1935, Clippings, box 44, folder Political Clubs—NSL, BHL.

100. "Fitzgerald Will Support University Finance Plan; 'Radical' Charges Denied," *MD*, February 15, 1935.

ful assurances to conservative audiences, it was also clear that the prolonged Depression had had an impact on the University of Michigan students' political attitudes. A survey of two hundred students published in the *Michigan Daily* in early March showed that ninety-five identified as "liberal" and thirty as radical, while seventy-two identified as conservative and ten as reactionary.[101] Although the campus was hardly a radical tinderbox in the spring of 1935, Ruthven was clearly exaggerating by describing the University of Michigan as a "center of conservative thought" in the hopes of placating Republicans in Lansing.[102]

The pressure exerted by Republican state senators may help to explain why the Ruthven administration did an about-face on its initial decision to allow the Michigan NSL to use Hill Auditorium for Strachey's lecture. The talk was announced on February 12, two days before Ruthven's address to the State Senate. NSL chapter president William Fisch and member Ascher W. Opler duly applied to the University Committee on Lecture Policy, a faculty group that authorized the use of university premises for guest lectures, for permission to host Strachey's lecture at Hill Auditorium. NSL obtained the university's official permission on February 16 with the explicit proviso that Strachey "would give

101. "University Changes Student Political Philosophy, Senior Survey Reveals," *MD*, March 6, 1935. An editorial written later that month by a member of the Michigan NSL claims that the University of Michigan "showed the second largest anti-war sentiment in the Literary Digest poll." See "Amazing Experience," *MD*, March 29, 1935.

102. The state elections of 1934 saw a Republican resurgence following their historic defeat in 1932. Facing persistent unemployment and a popular backlash over a tax increase, the Democratic governor William Comstock lost his seat to the Republican Frank D. Fitzgerald. Most other Republicans won their races for legislative seats. Beginning in early 1935, Ruthven faced a far more conservative legislature than he had for the previous two years. In the 1936 elections, Roosevelt's landslide reelection carried many Democrats into state office, including the liberal Democratic governor, Frank Murphy. From 1937 to 1939, Ruthven had a more liberal administration and legislature in Lansing with whom to work. See Dunbar and May, *Michigan: A History of the Wolverine State*, 524–25.

no instructions on what to do in case of war."[103] However, in early March, after the NSL chapter had made all the arrangements with Strachey, the Lecture Policy committee revoked its original authorization for the use of Hill Auditorium, claiming that the chapter had misrepresented the nature of Strachey's talk, which, instead of being on the prospects for international peace, was about "the coming struggle for power" that, Vice President Shirley Wheeler Smith claimed, "did not sound like a peaceful subject."[104] The chapter protested the university's rescinding its original authorization, especially since NSL had, by that time, already made all the necessary arrangements for Strachey's visit. After submitting an appeal, the chapter received a different, more sweeping, rationale from the Lecture Policy committee: "The committee is not convinced of the responsibility of this organization to sponsor public lectures in University buildings and therefore refuses to approve its request."[105] The Michigan NSL, in other words, was no longer merely guilty of misrepresenting the nature of Strachey's talk; the chapter was now deemed to have been an irresponsible organization that could no longer hold its events on campus.[106]

The Lecture Policy committee's decision to bar Strachey from campus sparked a wave of protest activity and a small flurry of editorials in the *Michigan Daily*. Signed petitions from the Liberal Students Union, a Unitarian group, and the Lawyers Club requested that the Administration reverse its stance in the name of free speech.[107] Michigan NSL president Fisch submitted a long

---

103. "Fisch's Statement," *MD*, March 12, 1935. See also Van de Water's account of the Strachey incident in *Alexander Grant Ruthven*, 141.

104. "Lecture Policy Committee Verifies Decision Refusing Strachey Hill Auditorium," *MD*, March 9, 1935.

105. "Lecture Policy Committee Verifies Decision Refusing Strachey Hill Auditorium," *MD*, March 9, 1935.

106. Wechsler claims that Strachey had been barred because "his opinions did not coincide with those of the solid citizens of the community." See *Revolt on the Campus*, 190–91.

107. Located in Ruthven, box 58, folder 8, BHL. Future Michigan Governor G. Mennen Williams's signature can be found on one of the Lawyer's Guild's petitions.

statement to the *Michigan Daily*, detailing how the chapter had meticulously followed university policy in making the arrangements for Strachey's visit.[108] Even the *Daily*, which as evident from previously mentioned incidents, was clearly no friend of the Michigan NSL, argued that Strachey should be allowed to speak in Hill Auditorium as a matter of free speech.[109] In response to the university's charge that the NSL chapter was an "irresponsible organization," a committee of faculty members, including the renowned sociologist Robert Angell, local citizens, students, and NSL members, emerged. This group denounced the administration's actions as a derogation of free speech and proposed to take responsibility for the lecture itself.[110] The Lecture Policy committee's secretary, Carl Brandt, refused to consider the petition, and the university demanded that this "Strachey committee" drop its student representatives—including Michigan NSL chapter president Fisch—before the Lecture Policy committee reconsidered the proposal.[111] Having duly done so, the "Strachey committee" resubmitted its proposal, which was promptly turned down by the Lecture Policy committee, a decision communicated by Brandt.[112]

The event was at risk of unraveling anyway. At the moment when the Lecture Policy committee vetoed the faculty proposal for the second time, Strachey was arrested in Chicago "for entering the United States on false and misleading pretenses."[113] Although

108. "Fisch's Statement," *MD*, March 12, 1935.

109. "John Strachey and Free Speech," *MD*, March 13, 1935.

110. "New Group Created to Back Strachey Lecture; Committee Gives Report," *MD*, March 10, 1935.

111. "Strachey Arrested in Chicago on Charge of False Entry into U.S.; Deny Lecture Permission Again," *MD*, March 13, 1935, Clippings, box 44, folder Political Clubs—NSL, BHL.

112. "Strachey Arrested in Chicago," *MD*, March 13, 1935.

113. Strachey had previously entered the United States during Christmas 1934. Since then he had declared himself a Communist, and US immigration officials claimed that this declaration meant that he had previously entered the country under false pretenses, having not declared his Communist affiliations before. See "Strachey Arrested in Chicago," *MD*, March 13, 1935.

Strachey managed to convince immigration officials to allow him back into the country, he faced deportation charges throughout his lecture tour.[114] Arriving late to his Ann Arbor talk courtesy of his detainment in Chicago, Strachey spoke to a packed house of over 1,000 at an off-campus venue, Granger's Ballroom, on March 14 about the difficulties of achieving reform within the capitalist system.[115] Although the Ruthven administration had succeeded in preventing Strachey from speaking on campus, it also handed the Michigan NSL another moral victory by allowing it to claim that it was merely defending Strachey's rights to free speech. The university's refusal to let Strachey speak at Hill Auditorium as had been planned originally turned into a *cause célèbre* that brought out more spectators than would have likely attended a lecture by a British economist.

Yet, if the Strachey affair showed that the Ruthven administration took a rather ham-fisted approach to campus radicalism, it also demonstrated that its patience was running out. To wit, the Michigan NSL chapter, branded as an "irresponsible organization," was effectively barred from using university facilities for guest lectures. Indeed, the chapter's planned one-day student strike on April 4 proved to be the tipping point. The walkout was part of a broad-based series of actions scheduled for that day that was to be coordinated by the NSL and other religious and pacifist groups.[116] The strike was the second annual national strike coordinated by the national NSL. It occurred on the anniversary of the United States' entry into the First World War. Although the *Michigan Daily* did not report very much on the strike's preparations, it did publish an unsigned editorial by a Michigan NSL member at the end of March claiming that the strike would have

114. Deportation charges were finally dropped against him at the end of March. See "Strachey Case Is Dropped by United States," *MD*, March 30, 1935.

115. Bernard Weissman, "Strachey Asserts 'Dilemma' Facing Capitalist System," *MD*, March 15, 1935.

116. "NSL Plans for Walk-Out from Classes," *MD*, February 28, 1935.

the support of a majority of the student body.[117] Stoking the fires, this same editorialist asserted his radicalism and belief in the necessity of political mobilization to stop the advent of war. "We believe that the militant **organization** of youth and of labor in all nations against war," it closed, "offers the last hope of avoiding legal butchery. The students of the world are eagerly looking to American students to demonstrate their opposition to war. We must not fail them."[118] After the event, the *Michigan Daily* did not report on the effectiveness of the strike, although it did report on an anti-war meeting where more than 1,000 students turned out, 450 of whom took the Oxford Pledge, a vow to refuse to fight in any future conflict, even if a draft were called.[119] Yet, if the account in the *Washtenaw Post-Tribune* is accurate, over 800 students and some faculty members walked out of classes at 11:00 a.m. in support of the NSL strike.[120] More conservative elements on campus organized an anti-war convocation in Hill Auditorium that was attended by several thousand students and faculty from the university and local high schools and whose intention was, seemingly, to divert support away from the NSL's strike: the chapter itself ultimately did not endorse the convocation.

The April 4 strike, and specifically, the administering of the Oxford Pledge to 450 students, provoked Ruthven into clamping down on the Michigan NSL and its activities. On April 16, the

117. "Amazing Experience," *MD*, March 29, 1935.

118. "Amazing Experience," *MD*, March 29, 1935. The boldface is in the original editorial.

119. "1,000 Turn Out for Anti-War Meeting," *MD*, April 5, 1935. Van de Water claims that the anti-war strike attracted between 1,000 to 1,200 students. See *Alexander Grant Ruthven*, 144–45. On the Oxford Pledge, see Cohen, *When the Old Left Was Young*, 79–82. Seemingly unconnected with the Michigan NSL action, a group of law students hung an effigy of the publishing magnate William Randolph Hearst that evening on the steps of the Library. This effigy was not carried out by the NSL but was lumped into press accounts of the anti-war strike. See "Hearst Is Hanged in Effigy by Merry Group of 350 Students," *MD*, April 5, 1935. See "Students in War 'Strike,'" *Washtenaw Post-Tribune*, April 5, 1935.

120. "Students in War 'Strike,'" *Washtenaw Post-Tribune*, April 5, 1935.

president issued a public statement, declaring that "perversive activities," as he deemed them, had interfered with university work and would no longer be tolerated.[121] Ruthven's resolution also stated that "students who are known to have interfered with the proper conduct of university affairs and with the work of their fellows are being investigated." The *Michigan Daily* hypothesized that the president was directly responding to "criticisms leveled at the University, the recent lecture by John Strachey, English Communist, sponsored by radical students, and the strike against war and fascism."[122] But it was also clear that Ruthven was facing considerable outside pressure as well. Already in March, Republican State Senator Miller Dunckel had introduced an anti-Communist bill into the state legislature.[123] On the same day that Ruthven denounced the "perversive activities," the Republican governor of Michigan, Frank D. Fitzgerald, announced his support for any administrative actions against radical activities on the state's campuses and specifically denounced the efforts of "non-patriotic" groups to organize pacifist movements. "We should slam the doors on any students who wish to take advan-

121. "Ruthven Bans 'Perversive Activities' in Ultimatum; Governors Scorns Pacifists," *MD*, April 16, 1935. A carbon copy of Ruthven's statement is in Ruthven, box 58, folder 13, BHL.

122. "Ruthven Bans 'Perversive Activities,'" *MD*, April 16, 1935.

123. Guy M. Whipple Jr., "Smash the 'Sedition' Bill," *MD*, March 22, 1935. The Baldwin-Dunckel Bill (Senate Bill 292), as it came to be called because it was co-sponsored by State Sen. Joseph A. Baldwin (R-Albion) and Sen. Miller Dunckel (R-Three Rivers), made it a felony to advocate or to work toward the overthrow of the American government. It required teachers and college students to swear an oath of allegiance to the national and state constitutions, and withheld state funds to those higher education institutions that did not comply. A full text of the bill is printed in the article, "Text of Proposed Senate Bill Making Communism a Felony," *MD*, April 20, 1935. After passing the Senate in late April, the bill occasioned numerous editorials in the *Michigan Daily* as well as campus meetings in opposition to it. Returned to the Senate following changes by a House subcommittee, the revised bill was passed by the Senate in late May 1935 and later signed into law by Governor Fitzgerald. Dunckel, for his part, attempted to introduce a bill outlawing the Communist Party, which later withdrawn. "Dunckel to Withhold His Anti-Red Bill," *MD*, April 26, 1935.

tage of [the] higher education offered by their government and then refuse to support the government in time of war."[124]

By this time, conservative administrators on other campuses in the state of Michigan and prominent businessmen were, like the Republicans in the legislature, reacting forcefully against the perceived surge of radical activity both within the state and nationally. On April 12, a peace strike at Michigan State College (now Michigan State University) was disrupted when a mob, with the tacit approval of the college's president, heckled and jeered the speakers and ended up throwing five participants into the Red Cedar River.[125] Moreover, conservative watchdog groups like the American Vigilant Intelligence Federation sought to disrupt the NSL's national strike day and reported on the "red" activities in the universities to prominent businessmen like retired chairman of Packard Motors, Henry B. Joy. "We are doing everything that is humanely possible," the general manager of this federation wrote, "to offset the program of the reds, pinks and yellows in the universities and institutions of higher learning."[126]

Ruthven's denunciation of "perversive activities" thus occurred at a moment of considerable conservative reaction both against the NSL's activities and against what the university leadership saw as a growing threat of communism on campus. The president's actions prompted both ardent support and strong condemnation.[127] At an Ann Arbor community forum, Rabbi Heller

124. "Ruthven Bans 'Perversive Activities,'" *MD*, April 16, 1935. Fitzgerald was not simply responding to events at the University of Michigan. On April 12, a pacifist demonstration at Michigan State College (now Michigan State University) was broken up when five pacifist leaders and a Unitarian minister were thrown into the Red Cedar river by students. See "Ruthven Bans 'Perversive Activities.'" Moreover, there were red scare-like reports that the Michigan NSL was seeking to organize students at Ann Arbor High School. See "NSL Unit Is Denied in High School," *Washtenaw Post-Tribune*, April 19, 1935.

125. Fermaglich, "Social Problems Club Riot," 93–115.

126. Harry A. Jung to Henry B. Joy, letter dated April 2, 1935, Henry B. Joy Papers (hereafter cited as Joy), box 6, folder April–July 9, 1935, BHL.

127. See the letter in Ruthven, box 58, folder 8, BHL.

of Hillel defended the president's stance by questioning whether "youngsters who have no responsibilities . . . shall be allowed to endanger the economic status of one thousand members of the faculty and the reputation of the University."[128] The consequences for the Michigan NSL were immediate. The Lecture Policy committee refused point-blank to provide any university resources for the committee's events, including an upcoming debate between history professor Preston Slosson and the secretary of the Michigan Communist Party.[129] The administration, through Joseph A. Bursley, the dean of students, asked the NSL chapter to provide it with an updated membership list, which, in order to demonstrate that NSL was a responsible organization, it promptly did. The list, dated May 8, 1935, was sent on the "understanding that the names of the members will not be used in discriminating against any member in the obtaining of positions, scholarships, etc.," in the words of NSL organizational secretary Leo Luskin. The list identified not only the organization's overall membership but also the members of the executive board.[130] It appears that, underneath its assertive rhetoric, the chapter was nervous about Ruthven's ultimatum and what it portended. Joseph Feldman,[131] the editor

128. "Divers Views Expressed on Freedom of Speech at Forum," fragment of article, likely from April 30, 1935, in Ruthven, box 58, folder 8, BHL.

129. See the carbon of the letter from the Lecture Policy committee to the NSL, dated May 8, 1935, in Ruthven, box 58, folder 8, BHL. The debate was ultimately held in the Ann Arbor Unitarian Church, see "NSL Debate Packs Church," *Student News* 1.2 (May 23, 1935), VPSS, box 5, folder NSL, BHL.

130. Luskin to Bursley, letter dated May 8, 1935, VPSS, box 5, folder NSL, BHL.

131. In Arthur Miller's memoir, *Timebends*, he recalls Feldman as "one of the most intelligent people I have ever known" and "the symbolic Marxist for me." Feldman almost never attended class because he could "devour texts at incredible speed, preparing in a day or two for any exam." Yet Miller's memory of Feldman appears to be faulty, as he also recalled that the *Michigan Daily*'s attempts at objectivity "drove [Feldman] wild, especially in regard to Spain." Feldman was dismissed from the university in July 1935, a full year before the beginning of the Spanish Civil War. A Hathi Trust search of the *Michiganensian* yearbooks for 1936–38 does not reveal any mention of a Joseph Feldman. As we discuss later in this chapter, Feldman actually transferred to the University of North Carolina following his dismissal from

of *Student News*, the Michigan NSL chapter's newspaper, interviewed Ruthven in May to verify a rumor that "certain students would be barred from reregistering because of their active interest in social and economic questions."[132] Ruthven averred that certain students indeed were to be so barred but not because of their political beliefs but because they engaged in "certain activity." When pressed by Feldman as to what kind of "activity" he meant, the president demurred and showed the editor the door, saying as the young man left, "you and I don't speak the same language." Feldman was soon to discover for himself the message within Ruthven's cryptic remark.

"Four boys . . . of one particular persuasion": President Ruthven and the Dismissals of 1935

It is worth pausing our story here to note that it was at this very moment, in mid-May 1935, when President Ruthven confirmed to Joseph Feldman that certain students were to be barred from reregistering. It was also at this time that Leo Luskin provided an NSL membership list to Dean of Students Joseph Bursley and that Elisabeth Lawrie from the Admissions Office first proposed that East Coast applicants—a disproportionate number of them Jewish—be subjected to interviews so that university officials obtain "personal impressions" of each candidate. Although the Michigan NSL had numerous Gentile, as well as Jewish, members, many conservatives on campus had identified the chapter as Jewish since the Cheyfitz era. Following the controversy over the Strachey visit, a group of conservative students, who called themselves the Hundred Michigan Men, distributed a circular warning the Michigan NSL against further radical agitation and identifying

Michigan. Interestingly, Miller never discusses the dismissals or the fact that his friend, Feldman, was one of those who were removed from the university. See Miller, *Timebends*, 97–98.

132. This and the following are from Joseph Feldman, "'Certain' Students Face Expulsion," *Student News* 1.2 (May 23, 1935).

seven members by name—five Jewish, two Gentile.[133] This group, whose flyers were unsigned, comprised, according to an article in the *Detroit Free Press*, members of a Junior Class honor society called the Sphinx and included two night editors on the *Michigan Daily*, Thomas Groehn and Thomas H. Kleene.[134] The Jewish students identified on the "Warning!" flyer were William Fisch, the NSL chapter's executive secretary; Joseph Feldman, editor of Michigan NSL's paper *Student News*; Daniel Cohen, and Leon Ovsiew. Claiming to speak for the majority of Michigan students, the Hundred Michigan Men submitted that the seven NSL members whom it identified by name had "overstepped the bounds of propriety and good breeding" and that the "methods employed by such groups are damaging to the best interests of the University; and, in many cases, treasonable to the government of the country and of the state which furnish them with the opportunity for an education."[135]

Four of these five names—Fisch, Feldman, Ovsiew, and Cohen—appeared subsequently in a private letter to Ruthven, dated May 20, written by the secretary of the Lecture Policy committee, Carl G. Brandt.[136] Recall that three of them had been listed as active members of the Ward United Front Committee during the Willis Ward controversy the previous fall. Brandt informed the president "I have had some disagreeable contacts with certain

---

133. The flyer, titled "Warning!" appears in Ruthven, box 58, folder 13, BHL. It is likely from late April 1935; see "U. of M. Reds Hear Vigilante Rumble," *Detroit Free Press*, April 27, 1935, BHL, Clippings box 44, PC-NSL. For a brief description of the Hundred Michigan Men, see "Pamphlet-Distributors Irk Loyal Students," *Michigan Alumnus* 41 (May 11, 1935): 368. The Hundred Michigan Men passed out seemingly several flyers against the NSL that spring, see "'Michigan Men' File Answer to Radical University Group," *Ann Arbor [Daily?] News*, May 1, 1935, Clippings, box 44, folder Political Clubs—NSL, BHL.

134. "U. of M. Reds Hear Vigilante Rumble," *Detroit Free Press*, April 27, 1935, BHL, Clippings box 44, PC-NSL.

135. "Warning!" Ruthven, box 58, folder 13, BHL.

136. All the citations in this paragraph are from Brandt to Ruthven, letter dated May 20, 1935, Ruthven, box 58, folder 13, BHL.

members of the National Student League. It is my feeling that a number of these individuals are a bad influence to the University." Brandt then identified five students as "undesirable" and listed their names and respective hometowns—Daniel Cohen, Trenton, New Jersey; William Fisch, Newark, New Jersey; Joseph Feldman, New York City; Leon Ovsiew, Elizabeth, New Jersey; and the fifth, whose name was crossed out in pencil, Leo Luskin, Buffalo, New York. As if anticipating a future charge of political persecution against him or the university, Brandt added that "this statement is made, not because of their political views, but rather because of the methods which they employ." Ruthven likely followed up on Brandt's suggestion and conferred with the Board of Regents and the Discipline Committee sometime in late May or early June after which he concluded that Cohen, Feldman, Fisch, and Ovsiew "be asked not to return to the University because they cannot be persuaded to refrain from interfering with the work of the University and with the work of other students."[137] Having concluded that these four Jewish students from the New York–New Jersey area were henceforth inadmissible, Ruthven waited until well into the summer—July 9—to send them letters informing them of his decision.[138]

Despite the earlier intimations that Feldman, writing in the *Student News*, had picked up in his May conference with President Ruthven, the four students and their parents were understandably shocked by this apparently arbitrary decision on Ruthven's part. In an angry letter to the president, Feldman asked why he had

137. Ruthven to Dean E. H. Kraus, letter dated June 21, 1935. This letter lists Fisch, Feldman, and Ovsiew as they were liberal arts students. The letter identifying Cohen was sent to the Dean of the College of Engineering, H. C. Sadler. See Ruthven to Sadler, letter dated June 21, 1935; both letters are in Ruthven, box 58, folder 13, BHL.

138. Carbon copies of the letters, all dated July 9, 1935, appear in Ruthven, box 58, folder 13, BHL. Van de Water's account of the dismissals does not mention the fact that the four students were Jewish, nor that their dismissals coincided with the administration's introduction of the interview process. See Van de Water, *Alexander Grant Ruthven*, 142–44. Peckham, Steneck, and Steneck's account of the dismissal cases are in *Making*, 216–17.

not been accorded the right to any disciplinary hearing, what the specific nature of his interference had been, and whether or not his political activities constituted this "interference." Unwisely, Feldman's letter also drew implicit parallels between Ruthven's actions and Mussolini's Italy and instructed the president to "carefully consider the questions I have raised," believing that "you will discover that it is far better for both the University and for the students that I be permitted to reenter the University."[139] While such a hectoring tone was unlikely to persuade the president to change his mind, Ruthven endured ongoing charges that the students had not undergone any formal disciplinary hearings and that they were dismissed due to their political beliefs.

The *Michigan Daily* announced the dismissals on the front page of its August 1, 1935, edition in an article ironically written by Guy Whipple who, as we have seen, had been involved in radical activities the year before. Although the article did not mention that these students were all Jews, it did provide each of the students' hometowns in the East. Despite the article's subheading that all four students were members of the NSL, it quoted Ruthven's argument that his decision to dismiss these students had nothing to do with their political affiliations. Ruthven is quoted as saying that "the action has nothing whatsoever to do with the National Student League." In Ruthven's view, it was more a matter of character instead: "We do not consider that they are the type of student wanted on the University campus."[140] Nonetheless, Whipple's article implicitly criticized Ruthven's justifications by recounting the NSL's activities during the 1934–35 academic year,

139. Letter from Feldman to Ruthven, dated July 16, 1935, Ruthven, box 58, folder 13, BHL. Even letters from the students' parents failed to move Ruthven. See Philip Feldman's letters to Ruthven, dated August 12 and August 26, 1935, respectively, and Ruthven's responses dated August 14 and August 29, 1935, respectively, in Ruthven, box 58, folder 13, BHL.

140. "Four Students Asked Not to Re-Enter This Fall by University Administration," *MD*, August 1, 1935.

including the campaign on behalf of Willis Ward, its sponsorship of the Strachey lecture, and its organizing the anti-war strike in April during which the Oxford Pledge was administered. The article concluded by reprinting Ruthven's public statement from mid-April in which he blamed "a few professional agitators" and "certain other misguided persons not connected with the University" as well as a "small group of immature students."[141]

If the lead article was somewhat ambiguous on the dismissals, the *Michigan Daily* also printed on its front page for August 1 an editorial that wholeheartedly endorsed the president and his actions. Titled "Good Riddance of Bad Rubbish," the editorial praised the administration's courage in risking public opprobrium by getting rid of students who had been nothing but "publicity-hounds, agitators, and black marks on the name of the University, invariably placing their personal advantage above any end they might, at first glance, be seeking."[142] The editorial cited such actions as the May Day incident, "storming of the meeting of the Board of Regents a year before to present a series of 'demands,' the hanging of William Randolph Hearst in effigy on the Library steps, and the attempted strike against war to include a walk-out from classes."[143]

The dismissals also attracted the regional and national news outlets and provoked outraged responses from left-wing groups like the National Methodist Youth Federation and the Student League for Industrial Democracy. In his classic survey of mid-thirties campus radicalism, *Revolt on the Campus* (1935), American Student Union (ASU) member and future *New York Post* editor James Wechsler put the dismissals right on the first page: "Even as I write, four students prominent in the espousal of anti-war doctrines at the University of Michigan are 'denied readmission'

141. "Four Students Asked Not to Re-Enter," *MD*, August 1, 1935.
142. "Good Riddance of Bad Rubbish," *MD*, August 1, 1935.
143. "Good Riddance of Bad Rubbish," *MD*, August 1, 1935.

to the institution. Although they were unmistakably proficient in their studies, President Ruthven explains that they are 'not the type of students wanted on a university campus.'"[144]

Ruthven's office received angry letters from individuals and organizations for months. As early as August, the *Daily Worker* charged that the students had been asked not to return "because of their activities in such organizations as the National Student League."[145] A Brooklyn-based alumnus wrote to Ruthven, protesting the students' removal and that "such stifling of student activity at a University which likes to think that it is a center of culture in the Mid-West is most discouraging."[146] Like Brandt, Ruthven was continually at pains to explain that the students were not dismissed because of their political beliefs but because they were "undesirables" whose activities interfered with the work of the university. As Ruthven wrote to another correspondent, "these young men on several occasions told untruths to administrative officers and faculty committees . . . they were told very plainly that they were asked not to come back because we felt that to tell an untruth to an official of the University is just as reprehensible as cheating in an examination."[147] Following an hour's interview with Ruthven, the attorney, Nicholas Olds, who represented three of the young men, came away with the view that "these students were particularly disliked by the President because of their active participation in the Strachey affair involving the rental of Hill Auditorium."[148]

However much the four students' behavior and political con-

144. Wechsler, *Revolt on the Campus*, 3.

145. Alex Ross to Ruthven, letter dated August 4, 1935, Ruthven, box 58, folder 13, BHL.

146. Victor Rabinowitz to Ruthven, letter dated August 1, 1935, Ruthven, box 58, folder 13, BHL.

147. Ruthven to George Calingaert, letter dated October 18, 1935, Ruthven, box 58, folder 13, BHL.

148. Olds to Hemans, letter dated October 11, 1935, Ruthven, box 58, folder 13, BHL.

victions contributed to their dismissals, the fact that they were Jews from the New York–New Jersey region proved to be a factor too. The NSL distributed a circular, whose language was reproduced in its paper *Student News*, that flatly underlined the ethnic and geographic dimension of Ruthven's actions: "While a majority of the membership of the NSL resides in the state of Michigan, each of the four students was Jewish and from the East. Only one of those asked not to return was a member of the executive committee of the NSL, which was composed of three Gentiles and two Jews. One of the students, Ovsiew, had been a normally active member of the organization for only a few months."[149] Against the NSL's insinuation of racial or religious prejudice, other writers attempted to paint the NSL as a Jewish redoubt. An article in the *Ann Arbor Daily News* chimed in claiming that the National Student League was the "'red spot' of the Michigan campus . . . The membership is believed to number about 100 at Michigan, and a large percentage are Hebrews, as are Messrs. Fisch, Cohen, Feldham [*sic*] and Ovsiew."[150] However, "the vast majority of Michigan's Hebrew students decline to have anything to do with the league."[151] Reverend J. H. Bollens from the Conference for the Protection of Civil Rights, a federation of different left-wing religious and civic groups, wrote to Ruthven likely citing this *Ann Arbor Daily News* editorial that "the (National Student League) membership is believed to number about 100 at Michigan, and a

149. National Student League, "Four University of Michigan Students Requested Not to Reenter," Civil Rights Congress Collection (hereafter cited as CRC), series 8, box 76, folder "U. of M. student cases–1935," Walter Reuther Library, Wayne State University (hereafter cited as WRL).

150. R. Ray Baker, "Radicals Agitate to Make Public Issue of Episode at University," *Ann Arbor Daily News* [n.d. likely October 1935], Hillel scrapbook 1935-36, Hillel, box 2, BHL.

151. Baker, "Radicals Agitate to Make Public Issue," *Ann Arbor Daily News* [n.d. likely October 1935], Hillel scrapbook 1935-36, Hillel, box 2, BHL.

large percentage are Hebrews."[152] Despite claiming that most Jews on campus ignored the NSL, Bollens charged that this editorial was "likely to promote race hatreds."

Racial antagonism was certainly one feature of the feedback that Ruthven's office received. One correspondent sent in a clipping from the *Trenton (NJ) Evening Times* with a front-page picture of Daniel Cohen, who was suing the university for re-admittance, and had scrawled on the paper's masthead, "typical kike no doubt—good luck to you to keep them all out."[153] William Babcock, an NSL member and '35 graduate, testily wrote the president that "it is clear to me, as it must be to any thinking individual that their expulsion was the result of political and racial discrimination."[154] Ruthven's private correspondence reveals that, while the four young men's Jewishness was not *the* primary factor in his decision to dismiss them, he did regard them as representatives of the kind of radical East Coast Jews that he did not feel belonged at the university. In other words, his very language validates the suspicions aired in the *Student News*: that these four young men were singled out in part because they were East Coast Jews and because they were associated with political activities that had become beyond the bounds of acceptable student action. That is, East Coast Jews, by their very association with radical, even Communist, political agitation, became increasingly identified as a group that was beyond the bounds of pluralism. In a letter to the Detroit and Wayne County Federation of Labor, Ruthven noted that "last year there were four boys on the campus from New York and New Jersey who made a great deal of unnec-

152. This and the following quote appear in Bollens to Ruthven, letter dated October 21, 1935, Ruthven, box 58, folder 13, BHL.

153. Clipping from the *Trenton Evening Times*, November 8, 1935, Ruthven, box 58, folder 13, BHL.

154. Babock to Ruthven, letter dated September 26, 1935, Ruthven, box 58, folder 13, BHL. Babock's name is on the membership list that Luskin provided to Dean Bursley in May 1935 as well as the undated list that was compiled by Bursley's office. Both are located in VPSS, box 5, folder NSL, BHL.

essary disturbance and interfered with the regular routine of the University."[155] He was even more specific in a letter to university counsel George J. Burke, "the four boys, is it necessary to say, were from New York and New Jersey and they all belong to one particular persuasion."[156]

Yet the dismissal controversy also underscored Ruthven's ambivalence toward Jewish students from the East Coast. To be sure, the president did not single out these four students by dint of their being Jewish—in other words as Jews *qua* Jews—but because they were a specific *type* of Jewish student who, Ruthven had come to believe, had no place at the University of Michigan. The days of indulging the NSL's political activities, such as those led by Edward Cheyfitz, were over. Making this position clear was the fact that the president was especially appreciative to receive letters of support for his actions from Jews. That October, a George Levey wrote to the president expressing his support for dismissing the four students. Levey continued to say that "in as much as I am of the Jewish faith myself, I feel that it is just too bad that these boys being Jewish have to be guilty of such activities. They are not representatives of the rank and file of American jewry."[157] Ruthven thanked Levey, claiming that he [Ruthven] was more pleased with Levey's letter than with any other communication on this matter. However, Ruthven also emphasized his view that small groups of troublemakers on campus were a serious matter and that "when any of the students disciplined are Jews,

155. Ruthven to Dwight Erskine, letter dated September 24, 1935, Ruthven, box 58, folder 13, BHL.

156. Ruthven to Burke, letter dated September 21, 1935, Ruthven, box 58, folder 13, BHL. Van de Water also uses this quotation in his account of the dismissals suggesting that Ruthven meant the four NSL students' *political* persuasions. At best, Ruthven's sentence is ambiguous: the fact that he also invoked their New York–New Jersey origins, and that he had recently approved of the interview plan to filter out potentially radical Jewish applicants from this region, suggests that Ruthven's use of the term *persuasion* had a double meaning. See Van de Water, *Alexander Grant Ruthven*, 143.

157. Levey to Ruthven, letter dated October 8, 1935, Ruthven, box 58, folder 13, BHL.

they give out the information that the University is discriminating against their race."[158]

Moreover, Hillel's Rabbi Heller stated that he did not believe that "religious or racial considerations entered into Dr. Ruthven's decision. Furthermore, the young men studiously avoided identification or affiliation with the Hillel Foundation. I can't recall their ever participating in any of the religious or cultural activities sponsored by the foundation. It is not unlikely that their aloofness was prompted by the belief, current in radical circles, that their only valid associations must be based on class consciousness and issues."[159] In seeking to shield Hillel from any association with the four dismissed East Coast Jewish students, Heller was actively enforcing the boundaries that Ruthven had established on what was acceptable behavior and, more so, who was an acceptable Jew on campus. In Heller's pointing out that the four dismissed students' primary identification was with their radical politics, and not with their Jewish heritage, the Hillel director effectively sanctioned their removal from campus by dint of these students' acting outside the boundaries of Michigan's accepted religious and political pluralism.

For its part, the *Detroit Jewish Chronicle* sided with the administration and its Jewish allies. Even before the dismissals occurred, the paper printed an interview with Heller in which he rebuffed the contention that Jews were responsible for radical activities on college campuses.[160] Heller claimed that he had made an inquiry into the participation of Jewish students in the NSL and was told "that Jews do not constitute a majority of its members or governing body. Even if their membership was greater in that organization than their percentage of the student population, it would not

158. Ruthven to Levey, letter dated October 11, 1935, Ruthven, box 58, folder 13, BHL.

159. Baker, "Radicals Agitate to Make Public Issue," *Ann Arbor Daily News* [n.d. likely October 1935], Hillel scrapbook 1935–36, Hillel, box 2, BHL.

160. "Denies Jews Lead Campus Radicalism," *Detroit Jewish Chronicle*, June 7, 1935.

indicate that the radical convictions or tendencies of the Jewish students are greater than of the Gentile students."[161]

Other prominent Jews sought to distance themselves from the NSL, and political radicalism more generally, by claiming that Jewish NSL members were a minority within their community. They also accused these Jewish NSL members of acting in bad faith by characterizing Ruthven's actions as antisemitic. Writing to Philip Slomovitz, editor of the *Detroit Jewish Chronicle*, George Levey of the Financial Service Company of Detroit, complained that "the sooner that American Jewry expresses a strong desire to make a serious attempt to purge themselves of the obnoxious individual who deliberately and willfully creates misunderstanding on the part of the public as against the American Jewry, the sooner our people will receive the respect and consideration in public mind that we are entitled to."[162] Ruthven himself claimed publicly, and in most of his private correspondence, that his decision was based on the students' actions and not their identities. By his dismissal of the students, the president saw himself as upholding the standards of "good character, sound scholarship, and orderly conduct." Indeed, the *Detroit Jewish Chronicle*'s only article on the dismissals was a reprint of a letter from October 8 from Ruthven to Levey assuring him that he [Ruthven] did not dismiss the students on account of their race. "When any of the students disciplined are Jews," Ruthven wrote, "they give out the information that the University is discriminating against their race. The University of Michigan, as you know, never has and never will discriminate between students on the grounds of race, creed, or color."[163] Despite this disavowal, though, it is undeniable that the only students punished for the Michigan NSL's radical

161. "Denies Jews Lead Campus Radicalism."

162. Levey to Slomovitz, letter dated October 12, 1935. Philip Slomovitz collection, box 110, accession 1494. Reuther Library, WSU.

163. "Statement by President Ruthven Comments on U. of M. Expulsions," *Detroit Jewish Chronicle*, October 18, 1935.

activities during the busy 1934–35 academic year were four Jewish students from the East Coast and not any of the NSL's Gentile members.

In addition, Jewish fraternities like ZBT were also attempting to distance their membership from Jewish radicals. In their October-November 1932 issue, the national *Zeta Beta Tau Quarterly* published an article that dismissed the growing belief that college students' minds were being poisoned by radicalism.[164] By the March 1935 issue, however, the *Zeta Beta Tau Quarterly* was much more vigorously attempting to distance the majority of Jews from left-wing radicalism, as one article clearly contended: "It was said that one of the pretexts of the Nazis in Germany to persecute the Jews was that they were communists. Less than one half of one per cent were, but they made a lot of noise. The onus of the few, as is always unfortunately the case when Jews are considered, was attributed to all of the Jews and the party was on."[165] The article then called on its Jewish readers to disavow any association with campus radicalism: "With the Silver Shirts and other emotional organizations springing up in this country ostensibly to combat communism here, might it not be well for well minded Jews to disavow, openly, any connection with that insignificant minority of them who rant red! Could not these few campus reds ignite a flame that might sear all Jews and cause them, in their innocence to suffer the horrors of a rampant race prejudice!"

While organizations like Hillel and ZBT thus sought to shield themselves, and the majority of Jewish students, from any association with Jewish student radicals, the four dismissed students pursued different strategies for redress. One of them, Leon Ovsiew, sent Ruthven a letter fully recanting his earlier radical activities, claiming that he "allowed a subsidiary interest to destroy the only real interest in my life—that opportunity given me by my parents

164. Jerome N. Michell, "The Radicals Are Coming—Oh Yeah?" *Zeta Beta Tau Quarterly*, October–November 1932, 26–27.

165. Philip Spira, "Campus Reds," *Zeta Beta Tau Quarterly*, March 1935, 15.

and the state of Michigan—to receive an education."[166] Ruthven responded with a handwritten letter, commending Ovsiew for taking personal responsibility and reaffirming that "there is no desire on the part of University officials to dictate the political views of students or to censor discussion."[167] Having conformed to Ruthven's reasons, Ovsiew promised not to engage in any further political activity should he be readmitted to the university. Although Ruthven told Ovsiew that he could only return to the University in the winter 1936 term, Ovsiew was ultimately readmitted on probation for the fall 1935 semester. He was fully reinstated in February 1936.[168]

Cohen, Fisch, and Feldman collectively sought legal redress through their joint attorney, Nicholas Olds. In letters using identical language, the three young men formally requested to reenroll at Michigan promising to abide by university policy. They were apparently each given a brief audience with Ruthven, after which their requests were rejected.[169] Although Ruthven had accepted Ovsiew's contrite letter, he still bristled against Feldman's more strident reaction: Feldman "has continued to make trouble and complains that the men were asked to leave because of their political views."[170] Olds then wrote to Ruthven arguing that the students could not be expelled from the university as they were all in good academic standing and had not been brought before the Disciplinary Committee before their removal, as was required by university policy.[171] Ruthven instructed university counsel,

166. Ovsiew to Ruthven, letter dated August 14, 1935, Ruthven, box 58, folder 13, BHL.

167. Ruthven to Ovsiew, letter dated August 19, 1935, Ruthven, box 58, folder 13, BHL.

168. See Ruthven to Daniel Rich, letter dated October 10, 1935; and Ruthven to Ovsiew, letter dated February 20, 1936; both in Ruthven, box 58, folder 13, BHL.

169. See Ruthven to Feldman, letter dated October 4, 1935, Ruthven, box 58, folder 13, BHL.

170. Ruthven to Burke, letter dated September 21, 1935, Ruthven, box 58, folder 13, BHL.

171. The specific rule cited by Olds was Section 3, Chapter VI, C, which states that "a student may be suspended, dismissed, or expelled by a two-thirds vote of a dis-

George J. Burke, to respond by affirming that while a Disciplinary Committee hearing was indeed required prior to expulsion, in this case the three students had not been *expelled*. Rather, they had merely been told that they could not reenroll. Ruthven made this distinction-without-a-difference because, had he taken the expulsion route, he would have had to present specific charges against the students in a Disciplinary Committee hearing, which he simply did not have. Instead, he framed his decision as one of benevolence. "As you know," he told Burke, "expulsion means that they could not enter any reputable school in the United States. The University chose to deal with the boys more leniently in the hope that they would see the error of their ways."[172]

Faced with Ruthven's reluctance, Feldman opted to go elsewhere. Ruthven sent a letter endorsing his acceptance at the University of North Carolina at Chapel Hill. Fisch followed suit a year later.[173] Cohen, however, decided to sue in federal court, petitioning for a writ of mandamus that would force Ruthven to readmit him on the grounds that the University of Michigan had not followed its own disciplinary policies.[174] However, the court decided that it had no jurisdiction over state of Michigan public officials and discarded the suit.[175] Cohen then sued in Michigan State Supreme Court in January 1936 on the same grounds.[176] Yet

ciplinary committee appointed by the faculty of the school or college in which he is registered after a full and impartial hearing before said committee and with the approval of the proper Dean." See Olds to Ruthven, letter dated October 18, 1935, Ruthven, box 58, folder 13, BHL.

172. Ruthven to Burke, letter dated October 19, 1935, Ruthven, box 58, folder 13, BHL.

173. Ruthven to Dean Thomas J. Wilson, letter dated November 3, 1936; and Olds to Burke, letter dated February 20, 1936; both Ruthven, box 58, folder 13, BHL.

174. "University Ban Fought in Suit," *Trenton Evening Times*, November 8, 1935, clipping in Ruthven, box 58, folder 13, BHL. A brief account of Cohen's suit can also be found in Hollingsworth, *Unfettered Expression*, 123–24.

175. See the sheet "Dictated on phone by Mr. Burke to R.A. Rouse," attached to Watkins to Burke, letter dated March 2, 1936, Ruthven, box 58, folder 13, BHL.

176. *State of Michigan: Cohen vs. the Regents of the University of Michigan*, copy of peti-

Cohen's attorneys, Nicholas Olds and Patrick O'Brien, appear to have recognized the deficiencies of their case: Ruthven held *in loco parentis* authority over the university, and the courts were not likely to overturn that. In a communication with the Board of Regents, the two attorneys offered to withdraw the case if the university permitted Cohen to reenroll. The board, however, instructed university counsel, Burke, "to make no compromise with these plaintiffs and no suggestion of any compromise."[177] Indeed, the State Supreme Court fully supported the administration's decision and action, denying Cohen's petition without comment in early March 1936.[178] Wherever Cohen completed his education, if in fact he did, it was certainly not in Ann Arbor; a search of the *Michiganensian* yearbooks for 1937 through 1939 revealed no mention of him.[179]

Ruthven's autobiography, of course, and the sole book-length study of his presidency, Peter Van der Water's *Alexander Grant Ruthven: Biography of a University President*, supports the president's rationale that the students were dismissed for being mere troublemakers and not as a result of their political beliefs or their ethnicity/religious affiliation coupled with their geographic origin in the New York City metropolitan region. Indeed, Ruthven later used this defense for the dismissal of students in both 1935 and 1940: that it was the students' behavior and not their politics or ethnicity that was being punished. Yet the existence of the data and interview sheets, the fact that the interview process was established for East Coast applicants at the very moment when Ruthven moved against the four Jewish members of the Michigan NSL, and that the number of Jewish interviewees were being

tion in Ruthven, box 58, folder 13, BHL.

177. Watkins to Burke, letter dated March 2, 1936, Ruthven, box 58, folder 13, BHL.

178. "Refuse to Hear Student's Case," *Ludington Daily News*, March 12, 1936.

179. Peter Van de Water's research notes also indicate that he was unable to track Cohen down in 1970.

compared to Gentiles belie this claim. Once again, we need to emphasize that none of these items show that Ruthven was in any meaningful manner an antisemite. Clearly, he was not!

In fact, one could argue that the 1935 dismissal case shows the relative *leniency* in Ruthven's handling of radical, and Jewish radical, students. Compared to Frederick Robinson at CCNY, the number of students dismissed from Michigan was quite low and one of them, Leon Ovsiew, was readily readmitted when he opted for contrition rather than challenging the university's charges against him. Ruthven, however, confronted a conservative state legislature and a Republican governor who held the university's purse strings with both institutions baying against any form of radicalism as well as passing bills like the Dunckel-Baldwin law to suppress the perceived threat of growing radicalism in the state's educational institutions. Ruthven was compelled to do something, especially in the wake of the negative publicity surrounding the Strachey affair and the one-day class strike in early April.

But by moving against four Jewish young men from the New York and New Jersey area, and approving the interview process for East Coast Jewish students, Ruthven was also tacitly admitting to associating Jews from the New York metropolitan region with political radicalism. The interviews functioned as a mechanism to identify them and to filter a disproportionate number of them out of the admissions process. Ruthven's correspondence with George Burke and Dwight Erskine from the Detroit and Wayne County Federation of Labor shows that these sentiments were widely shared and that Ruthven felt sufficiently comfortable to express them in written correspondence. In this view of "acceptable" antisemitism, Jews who were apolitical or who were involved with "acceptable" associations like Hillel or ZBT would not suffer much more than a polite "social" discrimination. But radicalized Jews—unlike their radical Gentile colleagues—put themselves at a much greater risk for reprisals.

Indeed, even non-radical Jews acknowledged the way that radical Jews could create a problem in terms of fostering a negative way in which Gentiles perceived all Jews on campus. A November 1934 editorial in the *Hillel News* cautioned that "every Jew is judged by the action of his fellow coreligionists. . . . We must remember that we are in a peculiar position and should at all times act in such a manner that will reflect only glory on our race."[180] Rabbi Heller, penning his "Director's Column" piece in April 1935 at the height of the NSL's radical activities, was even more direct in spelling out the implications that radical Jewish activities possessed for the broader Jewish student community at the University of Michigan. **"What distresses me,"** he wrote, **"is the tendency of these Jewish students to protrude themselves to the leadership or forefront of such groups.** . . . When Jews are at the helm, the inevitable consequence of such zeal is an increase in anti-Semitism. **The possible retort of the Jewish radical that his demeanor is his own affair is not exactly true, for Jews do suffer by each other's actions."**[181]

This tension within the administration—singling out East Coast Jews for punitive treatment but seeking to be lenient at the same time—also appeared in a relatively minor controversy that followed in the wake of the dismissals. In October 1935, two Jewish members of the Michigan NSL—Ascher W. Opler, from Westbrook, Connecticut, and the native New Yorker Edith Folkoff—were suspended for passing out leaflets in the middle of the University of Michigan campus, the Diag, which was against university policy. According to the Disciplinary Committee's summary report, University Secretary Shirley Smith advised Opler and Folkoff not to engage in such an activity on the Diag. Instead, the university official asked the students to post such fliers on the designated billboards to prevent the accumulation of paper in such an open-air public space.[182] Defying this, the two passed out

180. "Jews on Campus," *HN*, November 3, 1934.

181. Bernard Heller, "Director's Column," *HN*, April 15, 1935; original boldface as emphasis.

182. This quote and the following account as based upon "Cases of Ascher Opler and Edith Folkoff" [October 1938], Ruthven, box 58, folder 13, BHL.

leaflets on October 8 and, following a second warning by Smith, Opler alone did so again on the following day. Opler's brash assertion to Secretary Smith that he would continue to distribute NSL leaflets despite the university rules, and Folkoff's reluctance to disavow any future actions, led to both of these students' suspension by the Disciplinary Committee from the university as "undesirable students" on October 17, 1935.

The Discipline Committee's decision to suspend, rather than dismiss, Opler and Folkoff was clearly influenced by the dismissals of the four men earlier that summer. In a sense, Opler's and Folkoff's intransigence on distributing leaflets put the university in an awkward position: having recently received criticism for Ruthven's dismissals of the four students, the university did not want to attract more negative publicity. Yet its leadership wanted to make an example by punishing Opler and Folkoff in some manner. In the discussion following Opler's and Folkoff's questioning, Disciplinary Committee member Lloyd said "I don't want to make martyrs of them and yet I don't think they should be allowed to put a University official [presumably Smith] in such an embarrassing position."[183] Joseph Bursley, dean of students, did, however, see this as an opportunity to bring the Michigan NSL into line. "Of course," he said, "we have to consider these two in connection with all of the rest of them . . . my idea is to have a meeting with the organization and make it clear to the National Student League that, unless they are willing to submit to us in writing a statement that they will observe all rules in the future, official recognition will be withdrawn." In the end, the committee decided that a suspension, which was to be immediately withdrawn upon a written promise of good behavior, was the best way to deal with a potentially unpalatable situation. Although we do not have Folkoff's letter, Opler—the more strident of the two—

---

183. This and the following quotation are from Meeting of Sub-Committee on Discipline notes, dated October 14, 1935, Student Discipline Committee Records, University of Michigan, box 1: 87112 Bimu C15 2, BHL.

sent such a promise of good behavior on October 21 and was reinstated two days later.

Conclusion

These October suspensions, and the dismissals of June 1935, show that the Ruthven administration, in its efforts to crack down on the radical activities of the NSL, singled out this organization's Jewish members for disciplinary actions up to and including dismissal. In so doing, the administration was also defining the boundaries of its pluralist policies. That the Ruthven administration associated Jewish students from the New York–New Jersey area with radical leftism is clear given how Ruthven moved against four Jewish members of the NSL (to the complete exclusion of its many Gentile members). Ruthven also approved a policy of conducting interviews of East Coast Jewish applicants to screen out potential subversives before they ever arrived in Ann Arbor. Thus, although the University of Michigan did not target or exclude Jews as Jews per se—except in the well-established case of the university's Medical School—a specific type of radical East Coast Jewish student became a clear object for the university's disciplinary actions and exclusion. In this way, the University of Michigan's vaunted pluralism—while still admirable given the more rigid quota systems of the East Coast's elite universities at the time—had its clear limits.

CHAPTER FIVE

AMBIGUITIES AND ANXIETIES, 1935–38

P resident Ruthven's July 1935 dismissal of four Jewish members of the National Student League (NSL) demonstrated to
social and political conservatives that, despite his pluralist rhetoric, the president was prepared to act brusquely against those
who traduced the appropriate boundaries. To those who had previously charged him with being "soft" on communism on campus,
the dismissals served as a rejoinder; to those who supported his
pluralist initiatives like the Spring Parleys, they appeared to be
hypocritical. Yet, seen as a form of boundary marking, especially
against a small number of students "of a particular persuasion,"
Ruthven's actions made sense: the dismissals were sufficiently
satisfactory to mollify conservatives (for the moment) while not
being so numerous or draconic as to compromise his pluralist
agenda. After all, for all of Ruthven's obvious hostility toward the
NSL, he did not suspend the group from campus, and the Spring
Parleys and interfaith dialogues continued apace. Indeed, when
the national NSL merged with the Socialist-led Student League of
Industrial Democracy over the 1935 Christmas holiday to form the
American Student Union (ASU), the university gave prompt and
full recognition on this new group.[1]

---

1. See Cohen, *When the Old Left Was Young*, 137–45. See "NSL Is Out of Existence as
an Individual Unit," *MD*, January 12, 1936.

Yet the tumultuous events of the spring of 1935 never quite abated. Ruthven's liberal reputation had been marred. In October 1935, the left-wing American Youth Congress organized a meeting with representatives from the National Association for the Advancement of Colored People (NAACP), the League of Industrial Democracy, the Detroit Jewish Community Center, and other groups to prepare "some common action in regard to the outrageous violation of academic freedom by the University of Michigan administration."[2] For its part, the ASU published a scathing portrait of Ruthven in its national journal, the *Student Advocate*, in February 1936.[3] Portraying the president as a rather dull-witted time-server, the journal claimed that Ruthven's vaunted liberal pluralist sentiments were due more to convenience than to any genuine conviction: "Dr. Ruthven was, he said, a liberal. The early years of his regime did nothing to damage that claim. . . . Two factors unquestionably served to make Dr. Ruthven's early reign comparatively harmonious; no considerable number of students did anything sufficiently unorthodox to merit reprisal; issues in the outside world had not developed to the point where cautious, 'practical' liberals must make a stand."[4]

However, the growth of radical student activity, as witnessed by the 1934 May Day event and the incidents surrounding Willis Ward and John Strachey, as well as the election of Republicans to a majority in the Michigan state legislature, compelled Ruthven to temper his apparent liberal views. And with the April 1935 antiwar strike, in which the Michigan NSL administered the Oxford

2. Arthur Clifford to Marie Hempel, letter dated October 5, 1935, CRC, series 8, box 76, folder "U of M. Student Cases—1935," WRL. A search of the *Michigan Daily* for the 1935–36 academic year (October 1, 1935–June 30, 1936) did not turn up any action by the American Youth Congress on behalf of the dismissed students.

3. This issue is available online at the University of Pittsburgh's digital collection, https://digital.library.pitt.edu/islandora/object/pitt%3A31735059397426/viewer#page/1/mode/2up.

4. Clifford McVeagh. "Academic Napoleons No. 1: Ruthven of Michigan," *Student Advocate*, February 1936, 13.

Pledge on the steps of the library, Ruthven shifted to what one could rightfully characterize as a reactionary stance by dismissing the four (and ultimately three) NSL students. Remarkably, the *Student Advocate* not only reasserts the NSL's old charge that Jewish students were singled out but also connects this fact to the creation of the in-person interviews for prospective East Coast Jewish students: "The fact that all [the dismissed students] were Jewish and resided in states outside of Michigan seemed designed to win public support for the ousters. Several non-Jewish students— some from the state—were equally prominent in these activities; they were not expelled. (The president's strategy may prove a political *faux-pas*. I know that Joseph Bursley, dean of men, was sent on a novel summer errand to New Jersey, New York City, and Long Island to interview prospective students, particularly Jewish ones, and to explore their interests and activities.)"[5] The article then continues to overstate the degree to which Ruthven imposed "political repression" on campus, although it concludes by returning to the president's vaunted liberalism to underscore his hypocrisy: "He still delivers addresses resounding with the credo of independent expression. He is capable of threatening outspoken students one week and reciting the glories of uncensored thought the next. It may be that he neither determines his own policies nor writes his own speeches; he has mastered the amiable essential to a college presidency—inconsistency."[6]

While the radical students of the ASU scorned Ruthven's "inconsistency," the controversy over the three dismissed students faded. There were no further dismissals of radical students and, for campus organizations like Hillel, activities and initiatives continued apace. A scrapbook preserved from the 1936–37 academic year reveals a very active Hillel organization sponsoring talks on many intellectually challenging subjects, Nazism among them; offering concerts and discussing music (including

5. McVeagh, "Academic Napoleons," *Student Advocate*, February 1936, 14.
6. McVeagh, "Academic Napoleons," *Student Advocate*, February 1936, 15.

Richard Wagner's); and featuring the theatrical troupe, the Hillel Players. The scrapbook also shows that Hillel participated in four Inter-Faith Symposia at the Michigan League chaired by Reverend Edward Blakeman. The symposia sought to promote the interfaith pluralism that President Ruthven had long championed. They featured such intellectually sophisticated topics as "Blueprints for Utopia," "Truth—Relative or Absolute?" and "Does the Cosmos Reveal Intelligence?"[7]

Although the 1935 dismissals did not derail Ruthven's vision of the pluralist campus, the charge of contradiction between his liberal views and his actions persisted. Indeed, the accusation of Ruthven's inconsistency received further confirmation in the next crisis that Ruthven faced, which also affected Jews: Ruthven's and the University of Michigan's endorsed official participation by the physical presence of Michigan faculty at the 550th anniversary celebrations of Heidelberg University. One of Germany's oldest and most pedigreed institutions of higher learning that had garnered a stellar reputation for its innovative research and first-rate scholarship, it had become thoroughly Nazified since Hitler's accession to power evicting its Jewish faculty and students and changing its entire agenda to espouse the Nazis' worldview. Beyond Ruthven's eagerness to have the University of Michigan participate in Heidelberg's festivities, Michigan students were concerned over the portent of Ruthven's actions that contradicted his liberal speeches. Michigan students expressed their continued reservations about the president's and the university's actions in the parleys and other venues on campus with the dismissal of the Jewish students still assuming pride of place. At least among left-wing and politically engaged students, the 1935 dismissals produced reverberations that were still felt years later. Finally, by 1938–39, the escalation of Nazi conquest and violence in Europe led to a growing perception of antisemitism both abroad and at home. Antisemitism then became a real issue on

7. See the Hillel scrapbook 1936–37, Hillel, box 1, BHL.

the Michigan campus as well: it was studied, and initiatives were launched to combat, or at least understand, this pervasive prejudice. This chapter, then, discusses a murky moment for Jews on campus. To be sure, the University of Michigan retained its pluralist orientation, and even acted on it repeatedly. But at the same time its leadership harbored an ambivalence toward Jews because of the Ruthven administration's continued contradictory behavior on matters related to Jews. Not only did Ruthven demonstrate a surprising tone deafness to the impact on Jews concerning the university's decision to send a delegation to Heidelberg; but the East Coast interviews continued apace with students on campus commenting on them. Thus, this was an era of ambiguities and anxieties both about Jews' place on campus (and in the world) and the true degree of commitment that Ruthven exhibited of his pluralist vision.

Ruthven, Jews, and the Heidelberg Affair, 1936

The agitation concerning the student dismissals had barely abated when Ruthven became embroiled in another controversy with, arguably, an even more direct bearing on Jews both inside and outside the university. Heidelberg University, the third-oldest university in the German-speaking world after Prague and Vienna, invited American university presidents (as well as those of other advanced industrial countries, Great Britain among them) to send delegations to celebrate its 550th anniversary in June 1936.[8] There was only one major problem: by 1936, Heidelberg had become thoroughly Nazified by Hitler's regime. Sending a faculty delegation to honor this event appeared to many as being tantamount to an endorsement of the Third Reich and its hideous policies and actions.

8. "All English Universities Reject Heidelberg Bid While U.S. Schools Accept Invitation," *Detroit Jewish Chronicle*, March 13, 1936. For Harvard President James Conant's experience with the Heidelberg controversy, see Tuttle, "American Higher Education," 49–70.

Ruthven's office received the invitation from Heidelberg early in 1936, and unlike all British universities, Ruthven responded positively and had the University of Michigan accept the invitation. In his reply to Heidelberg's rector, Ruthven nominated two faculty to be Michigan's representatives—DeWitt Parker from the philosophy department and Aloysius Gaines, from Germanic Languages and Literatures.[9] A week later, Ruthven extended the offer to a third faculty member, John W. Eaton, former department head of Germanic Languages and Literatures, who was spending early 1936 on a sabbatical leave at the Goethe-Haus Museum in Frankfurt am Main.[10] Later in February, a *New York Times* piece about the university's positive response to the Heidelberg invitation occasioned a flurry of angry letters to Ruthven's office.[11] The article described how Heidelberg's official student league, the *Studentenschaft*, protested the decision by all British universities not to send delegations to Heidelberg whereas many American universities such as Columbia, Cornell, Vassar, Western Reserve, and Michigan had accepted. "The sending of a delegate from Michigan at such a time and under such hideous and unholy circumstances as the Nazi regime in Germany," wrote one irate Michigan alumna, "represents before a world aghast at such cruelty, such a crushing of human rights and freedom of citizenry as daily characterize this government can mean only one thing to liberty-loving Americans

9. Ruthven's Assistant to Heidelberg, letter dated February 5, 1936, Ruthven, box 53, folder 18, BHL.

10. Ruthven's Assistant to Eaton, letter dated February 13, 1936, Ruthven, box 53, folder 18, BHL.

11. "Heidelberg Scores Student Boycotts," *New York Times*, February 29, 1936, Ruthven, box 53, folder 18, BHL. A collection of letters and articles explaining the British universities' decision to boycott the Heidelberg festivities appear in Charles Culp Burlingham, *Heidelberg and the Universities of America* (New York: Viking, 1936). For the British universities, the concern wasn't only that Heidelberg had been Nazified but also that the celebration fell on the second anniversary of the Roehm purges and thus "there is widespread suspicion here that the anniversary is intended not to honor Heidelberg but to glorify the Nazi Reich." See "Ban on Heidelberg Extends in Britain," *New York Times*, February 28, 1936, Ruthven, box 58, folder 13, BHL.

and Englishmen: The University of Michigan approves of a Fascist State! The University of Michigan would clasp academic hands with Hitlerian Dictatorships."[12]

The Michigan president also received letters and news clippings from prominent rabbis and members of anti-Nazi leagues, seeking to make him aware of the importance of his decision. Rabbi Leon Fram from the Congregation Beth El in Detroit wrote to President Ruthven in early March informing him not only of the British universities' refusal to participate in the Heidelberg celebrations but also the impact of Nazi racial policies on the German educational system. Participating in the Heidelberg celebration would mean giving Michigan's endorsement to the "ruthless suppression of academic freedom, the prohibiting of the teaching of any scientific works written by people of non-Aryan blood, and the cruel and sudden dismissal of more than one hundred faculty members whose scholarship and ability was unquestioned and whose sole guilt was that they had non-Aryan parents or grandparents."[13] The *Detroit Jewish Chronicle*, however, offered relatively muted criticism, choosing to print a letter from an anti-Nazi organization to Ruthven's assistant, Frank Robbins, that the university's presence at the event, to be held on the second anniversary of the "blood purge" of June 1934 no less, would provide the Nazi regime with valuable propaganda. "We feel," the letter stated, "that such a university as yours, standing for all that is finest in American culture, for freedom of thought, conscience and teaching, cannot under any circumstances allow itself to be used as an instrument of propaganda through the presence of an official representative at the Heidelberg celebration."[14] In addition to the publication of this document, the *Chronicle* only printed one angry letter to the editor before the event; the paper ran no

12. Helen I. Davis to Ruthven, letter dated February 29, 1936, Ruthven, box 58, folder 13, BHL. Davis's letter also makes reference to the *New York Times* article about the Michigan delegation.

13. Fram to Ruthven, letter dated March 3, 1936, Ruthven, box 5, folder 18, BHL.

14. "U. of M. Criticized," *Detroit Jewish Chronicle*, March 20, 1936.

official editorial against President Ruthven's decision to allow a faculty delegation to attend the Heidelberg festivities.[15]

Ruthven's response was almost willfully naïve. "The invitation was accepted," he replied to Fram, "simply as one of the customary transactions with another educational institution. This action has no political significance and certainly is no indication of sympathy with recent German policies."[16] Ruthven reminded the rabbi that the United States still maintained diplomatic relations with the Third Reich as well as with Italy, Russia, and Japan "despite the fact that all of these countries are doing things which are contrary to our democratic ideals." Fram replied in mid-April by including a clipping from a reprint in the *New Republic* published in the Congregation Beth El newsletter that described the conditions of German universities and especially some of their more notorious recent antisemitic incidents, including the fight launched by German scientists against the "Jewish physics" of Albert Einstein.[17] Fram's accompanying letter took a much more forceful tone with the Michigan president, flatly asking him, "do you not think you ought to re-consider the question of lending yourself to the Nazi program of the subordination of science to political and racial propaganda, and the utilization of the universities for the spread of hatred against Jews, Catholics and the institutions of democracy and civil liberty?"[18]

This time, Ruthven was more forthright, both expressing his exasperation that he was yet again misunderstood and remaining adamant in his view that sending faculty representatives to the Heidelberg celebrations did not indicate any endorsement of Nazi policies by the University of Michigan. "No one deplores

15. "Criticize U. of M. Acceptance of Heidelberg Bid," *Detroit Jewish Chronicle*, May 8, 1936.

16. Ruthven to Fram, letter dated March 10, 1936, Ruthven, box 53, folder 18, BHL.

17. "The Heidelberg Celebration," enclosure with Fram to Ruthven, letter dated April 16, 1936, Ruthven, box 53, folder 18, BHL.

18. "The Heidelberg Celebration," enclosure with Fram to Ruthven, letter dated April 16, 1936, Ruthven, box 53, folder 18, BHL.

the activities of the Nazi government more than I do," Ruthven averred. "In fact, there is very little sympathy expressed among the members of the university faculty with the policies and methods of the German government."[19] Nonetheless, Ruthven refused to draw any connection between the university's actions and the potential message that it sent to the broader academic community. As he explained, "we are allowing our men to go to Germany to study, using the facilities of the German universities, and we do not feel that we are either contaminating our men or placing the stamp of our approval on the German government when we continue these relations with the German institutions." Indeed, so the president argued, these continuing programs made it possible for Michigan faculty to observe the changing conditions in Germany up close. Pushing his view further, Ruthven compared the voluminous negative feedback he had obtained concerning the Heidelberg celebration to the muted response the university received when it sent a legation to Mussolini's Italy the previous year. "When we sent representatives from the University to Rome last year, no one accused us of commending the Italian government even though the educational exercises were dominated not only by the Fascist educators but also by Mussolini himself. Certainly what the Germans have done to the Jews and the Catholics pales into insignificance when we view the wholesale murder in Ethiopia."[20]

This explanation begs a response on at least three levels. First, by invoking the Italo-Abyssinian War, Ruthven effectively admitted that he was fine with sending the university's delegates to a fascist regime. Second, the comparison was inexact: if the Michi-

19. Ruthven to Fram, letter dated April 25, 1936, Ruthven, box 53, folder 18, BHL.

20. Ruthven to Fram, letter dated April 25, 1936, Ruthven, box 53, folder 18, BHL. This was not the first time that Ruthven made this comparison, having done so in a March 24, 1936, letter to mathematics professor, Louis Karpinski. Yet the timing of this comparison's appearance in the *New York Times* one week later suggests that Ruthven's letter to Fram served as the basis for the ensuing controversy discussed below. Also, in October 1934, twenty students at the City College of New York were expelled for protesting a delegation of Italian Fascist students who had been invited by President Frederick Robinson. See Cohen, *When the Old Left Was Young*, 115–16.

gan legation to Rome occurred before October 1935, Fascist Italy was a member of the Stresa Front, whose mission was to curb the territorial ambitions of Germany. Until the Ethiopian conflict, many Americans saw Mussolini's Italy as a potential bulwark against Nazism. "One measure of Mussolini's success in separating himself and his regime from Hitler and Nazism may be seen in the fact that in 1933 American Jewish publishers selected him as one of the world's twelve 'greatest Christian champions of the Jews.' Ultimately, the growing menace of Nazism, far from discrediting Mussolini, enabled the Italian Premier to parade as the enlightened statesman who could counter Hitler's aggressive designs."[21] Third, of course, was the fact that Mussolini had not promulgated anything like the Nuremberg Laws, which had come into effect in Germany in 1935. Mussolini's conquest of Ethiopia, as horrible as it was, could be regarded either as revenge for Italy's humiliation at Adwa in 1896 or as an example of empire building. Although Hitler had successfully annexed the Rhineland in March 1936 at a far lower loss of life than Mussolini's conquest of Ethiopia, the German leader was, in contrast to Mussolini, actively creating a "racial state" that required the persecution and exclusion of all Jews from all aspects of civic life.[22]

Ruthven's comparison of the different responses to the two Michigan faculty legations occluded the specific contexts in which they occurred and appeared as appallingly insensitive to Jewish sympathies. Fram's reply expressed both resignation and a muted disgust at Ruthven's obduracy. "Just because the relations of international life are so organized that democratic governments are compelled to recognize even the vilest despotism," he asserted, "all the greater is the duty of the private citizens of a democracy, and of the heads of democratic institutions, to resist the Nazi horror with every resource at their command. It is hopeless to think of stemming the tide of Nazism if men like you who are the chief objects of its venom can be inveigled into giving it aid

21. See Diggins's classic, *Mussolini and Fascism*, 40.
22. The term *racial state* comes from Burleigh and Wipperman.

and comfort."[23] Finally, Fram stated that he did not desire a reply unless the president changed his mind.

Somehow, Ruthven's comparison of Hitler's treatment of Jews to Mussolini's treatment of Ethiopians as being equivalent per his letter to Rabbi Fram became a news item in the May 1, 1936, edition of the *New York Times*, initiating a new round of angry letters to the president that caused him great consternation.[24] Robert Engel, a 1935 graduate of Michigan and then a first-year student at Harvard Law School, threw Ruthven's comparison back in his face in a heated letter. "Whether Italy is right or wrong in its quarrel with Ethiopia is certainly immaterial in deciding whether or not the University of Michigan should send its representatives to help the Nazis commemorate the founding of the University of Heidelberg," Engel declared. "But I do know that the Nazi government has seen fit to discharge and pauperize all of its Jewish professors and many of its Catholics scholars for no other reason than fate has been fit that they be born into the religion. I know that some of the most eminent pedagogues of the Michigan faculty are members of the Jewish and the Catholic religions. I wonder if the University of Michigan would ask them to represent it abroad."[25] Another correspondent, William Fondiller, submitted that "one of your [Ruthven's] outlook can hold such a view [about the equivalence between Mussolini and Hitler] only because of lack of adequate knowledge."[26] For his part, Ruthven expressed no small irritation at having his private correspondence appear in America's newspaper of record, writing to Fondiller that "I suppose everyone should become reconciled to being misquoted, but this publicity is particularly irritating to me."[27]

23. Fram to Ruthven, letter dated May 7, 1936, Ruthven, box 53, folder 18, BHL.

24. The clipping appears attached to letters to Ruthven from William Fondiller and Robert Engel, respectively. Given that Ruthven's letter was dated on April 25 and that the *New York Times* item was dated on April 30, Fram must have passed on the comparison to the newspaper. Ruthven, box 53, folder 18, BHL.

25. Engel to Ruthven, letter dated May 1, 1936, Ruthven, box 53, folder 18, BHL.

26. Fondiller to Ruthven, letter dated May 5, 1938, Ruthven, box 53, folder 18, BHL.

27. Fondiller to Ruthven, letter dated May 12, 1936, Ruthven, box 53, folder 18, BHL.

Ruthven's comparison of Hitler's treatment of the Jews to Mussolini's of Ethiopians also provoked responses that hit a bit closer to home. One Michigan alumnus, Robert Gessner, then of the Department of English at New York University, curtly opined that "you apparently justify violence in one Fascist country because it is the practice of another Fascist country."[28] Twisting the knife, Gessner then added: "There seems to be a dangerous inference that persecutions of Catholics, Jews, and Negroes are justifiable. This inference is borne out by your action of last year when you expelled four students with Jewish names from the East because of their social and political beliefs. Your apparent approval of Hitler's policies seems a substantiation of your own curtailment of academic freedom." Ruthven, equally curtly, slammed Gessner for being blinded by prejudice and not getting his facts straight.[29]

Yet Ruthven's actions also evoked a response among Jewish members of Michigan's faculty and, uncharacteristically, Hillel itself. Both, however, were quite muted. In late March, the *B'nai B'rith Hillel News* published a critical editorial calling for a boycott of the Heidelberg celebration that carefully avoided singling out Michigan or naming Ruthven. "All these deeds of the Hitler regime are well known. They are presumably abhorrent to American educational institutions. Will American universities now join in the Heidelberg festivities—to commemorate the death of German learning?"[30] Jewish professors like I. L. Sharfman, long chair of the economics department and as evident from our presentations in previous chapters a towering figure in the University of Michigan's Jewish community, wrote diplomatically to Ruthven, validating the president's claim that his Hitler and Mussolini comparisons were misconstrued. Nonetheless, Sharfman added, "the difficulty arises, not from what we do, but from the inter-

28. Gessner to Ruthven, letter dated May 4, 1936, Ruthven, box 53, folder 18, BHL.

29. Ruthven to Gessner, letter dated May 12, 1936, Ruthven, box 53, folder 18, BHL.

30. "Boycott Heidelberg," *BBHN*, March 31, 1936, Ruthven, box 53, folder 18, BHL.

pretation placed upon our action in Germany and from the use made of this action in bolstering up the repressive tactics of the Government." Sharfman then elucidated his point further: "Since Heidelberg, despite its great past, is one of the outstanding examples of the current academic breakdown in Germany, the recognition accorded its celebration is bound to be construed, at the least, as indifference to the ruthless destruction of the true spirit of universities."[31] Ruthven respectfully insisted to Sharfman of his regret to being misquoted about the comparative equivalence of Hitler and Mussolini's crimes, although Ruthven almost immediately effaced this by reasserting that "I think we will all agree that, dreadful as are the conditions in Germany, certainly Mussolini's performance in Ethiopia is also very deplorable."[32]

In addition, mathematics professor Louis Karpinski wrote, "the ancient University of Heidelberg is dead, and in its place there is a Nazi institution recognizing only so-called Aryans."[33] Ruthven was generally congenial and even appreciative of these comparatively restrained criticisms from his faculty. Karpinski even went so far as to ask Ruthven's permission to publish his own letter protesting the sending of a delegation from Michigan. Ruthven allowed the protest to be published but also stressed that "I think it is a stretch of the imagination to interpret the naming of the delegates to the celebration as approval of the Hitler regime."[34] While Karpinski thanked his president in a subsequent letter, he also reminded him that the University of Göttingen, home to arguably the world's greatest mathematics department at the time and Heidelberg's equal in prestige and reputation, had dismissed all of its Jewish and many other

31. Sharfman to Ruthven, letter dated May 7, 1936, Ruthven, box 53, folder 18, BHL.

32. Ruthven to Sharfman, letter dated May 5, 1936, Ruthven, box 53, folder 18, BHL.

33. Karpinski to Ruthven, letter dated March 23, 1936, Ruthven, box 53, folder 18, BHL.

34. Ruthven to Karpinski, letter dated March 24, 1936, Ruthven, box 53, folder 18, BHL. This letter is the first extant one in which Ruthven makes the Hitler-Mussolini comparison.

prominent faculty. Karpinski added "in sending representatives officially we enable the Nazis to further delude their people in thinking that our universities recognize this new brand of national scholarship."[35]

Yet, by the middle of May 1936, Ruthven's patience with the whole controversy was clearly wearing thin. Replying to a letter from Bernard Heller, Hillel's director, Ruthven wrote that "someone, and I do not want to know who it was, evidently told this [the Hitler-Mussolini comparison] to the paper or to some reporter with the statement that I was using this as a justification for certifying staff members to the Heidelberg celebration. This is, of course, ridiculous and a rather disheartening experience. I refuse to comment any more on the whole matter."[36] Ruthven appears to have stuck to his guns in this case. A *Michigan Daily* article from June 5 announces the departure of Professor Gaiss, of the German department, "to represent the University at the 550th anniversary of the founding of the University of Heidelberg."[37] No mention of the controversy appeared in this short announcement.

Although it is difficult to assess with certainty what the Heidelberg controversy reveals about the possibly shifting place of Jews within Ruthven's pluralist vision, a few key points emerge. Despite enormous public pressure, and polite but unmistakable criticisms emanating even from allies like Sharfman, Karpinski, and Heller, Ruthven curiously persisted on nominating and sending a faculty delegation to Heidelberg to represent the University of Michigan. Moreover, although Ruthven claimed that his comparison between Hitler's treatment of Germany's Jews and Mussolini's of Ethiopians was misconstrued, his letter to Sharfman shows that Ruthven actually did indeed consider this to represent a fundamentally sound equivalence. By authorizing a faculty del-

---

35. Karpinski to Ruthven, letter dated March 30, 1936, Ruthven, box 53, folder 18, BHL. The underlined text is in the original letter.

36. Ruthven to Heller, letter dated May 19, 1936, Ruthven, box 53, folder 18, BHL.

37. "Gaiss Departs for New York and Germany," *MD*, June 5, 1936.

egation to Heidelberg despite all the evidence presented to him, Ruthven, at best, appeared to be merely insensitive to his Jewish constituency on campus. But one could also read this as Ruthven's potential indifference to the Nazi persecution of Jews.

We actually see a third factor as the most plausible explanation for Ruthven's sudden edginess concerning Jewish matters. Ruthven seems to have lost at least part of his previously ample good will toward Jews quite possibly due to the events of 1934 and 1935. Ruthven's angry response to Gessner's letter, which invoked the president's dismissal of the NSL students the year before, hints that Ruthven's willingness to respond to Jewish concerns had soured based on his experiences with the NSL and the nature of the dismissal's ensuing controversy.

Quite evidently, Ruthven developed an edge in his tone concerning Jewish matters that simply did not exist previously. The only extant supportive letter for Ruthven's Heidelberg decision came from a Mr. H. L. Smith of Philadelphia who wrote on May 5, "I am glad to see that you are going to send delegates to the 550th anniversary of Heidelberg University in June. It is most encouraging to see an American university run by the President and not the Jew students."[38] Ruthven's response neither admonished nor refuted Smith's blatantly antisemitic remark. Instead, the president simply stated that "the University certainly did not feel that it committed itself as in accord with German political and social views when it gave to two or three members of the staff . . . certificates which would allow them to attend the meetings at the time of the Heidelberg celebration."[39] Subsequently, in an unusual bit of coyness, Ruthven averred that "perhaps we are wrong, but, up to this time, I cannot believe it. If so, we are innocent offenders." This most certainly constituted a noteworthy tonal shift from Ruthven's earlier advocacy of Hillel's solvency in the dark days of early 1933.

38. Smith to Ruthven, letter dated May 5, 1936, Ruthven, box 53, folder 18, BHL.
39. Ruthven to Smith, letter dated May 8, 1936, Ruthven, box 53, folder 18, BHL.

Finding Venues for Criticism, 1936–39

Even if the Heidelberg controversy ultimately proved to be a tempest in a teapot, it did indicate the extent to which the worldwide political situation began seeping into the University of Michigan's campus community. Whereas the NSL had focused its energies in 1933–35 on the domestic problems of impoverished students and the promotion of communism on campus, by the fall of 1936 the focus of the student Left was shifting to the international scene and specifically toward anti-fascism.[40] Increasingly, student discontent on campus appeared in the language of anti-fascism, and Ruthven's actions against the dismissed four persisted in students' memories as an expression of political intolerance. They expressed these views at the Spring Parleys, an annual event organized largely through the Office of Religious Education and its head, Reverend Edward Blakeman, whom the university hired in 1932.[41] A student-faculty committee developed a general theme and various subtopics related to this theme. Moreover, during the parley itself, any student could ask faculty members questions pertaining to the parley's themes. One could reasonably interpret the creation of this forum as a means by Ruthven to try to channel students' politics into a "safe" venue and contain it there in a relatively confined space officially created for this purpose. The university thus appeared to offer the students a space to voice their views and opinions but under the institution's aegis and watchful

40. See Horowitz, "Peace, Protests, and Parties."

41. The university held its first spring parley in March 1931, roughly a year before Blakeman joined the university. This first parley, called a "Human Relations Parley," was sponsored by the Student Christian Association. The purpose of the parley was to analyze "religious values, in their application to individual and group living." Ruthven provided the opening speech while the guests included Rabbi Leo Franklin of Temple Beth El, Everett Clinchy, the director of the National Conference of Jews and Christians and "15 University faculty members and Ann Arbor religious leaders." See "Ruthven to Open Session of Human Relations Parley," MD, March 28, 1931. Blakeman preserved a copy of the program in his files. See the folder "The Spring Parley—University of Michigan 1930-31 and 1931-32 in Edward Blakeman Papers (hereafter cited as Blakeman), box 3, BHL.

eye. Although the number of students who attended these parleys seems to have been quite small, these parleys attained an important standing on campus and were given full press attention in the *Michigan Daily.*[42]

By the mid-1930s, the discussions at these parleys became increasingly politicized. With the resurgent labor movement, epitomized by the Flint sit-down strike of 1936–37, and the growth of anti-fascist politics following the start of the Spanish Civil War in July 1936, the parleys became a lively venue for political discussion. The students who attended the 1936 Spring Parley had certainly heard rumors about the interviews of East Coast applicants. These clearly added to a general concern about academic freedom on campus. At the parley's opening session in late April, one student asked, "Does the administration examine students for their beliefs in regard to religion, home, state, politics?" The faculty respondent, Howard Mumford Jones of the English department, replied "political beliefs—don't know. Religion—don't know. If they are, true situation is damnable."[43] Jones fielded another question about the three dismissed students, to which he replied, with a mixture of obfuscation and incorrectness, "relations of student-faculty involved and complicated. In refusal of admission University is a judge—no student shall be kept out until his case been heard by faculty body and a regular trial before refusals of admission goes through." This was patently erroneous because no university disciplinary procedures had been followed in the dismissal cases. In the Saturday afternoon session the next day, stu-

42. That this was an important forum for progressive students is best indicated by the fact that the student chairman of the 1936 parley was future Democratic governor of Michigan, G. Mennen Williams, and that Arthur Miller was recommended by English professor Erich Walter for participation in that year's parley (Miller does not appear to have played any executive or organizing role, however). Interestingly, in *Timebends*, Miller claims that Williams was head of the campus peace movement although, if this were the case, Williams did not do so under the auspices of the NSL or ASU. See Miller, *Timebends*, 94.

43. This and the following quote are from "Friday Evening General Session," 1935–36 Spring Parley notebook, Blakeman, box 3, BHL.

dent participants pressed Jones on the issue of Jewish admits to the Medical School, one student claiming, "it is marked very carefully whether a student is Jewish or not."[44] While Jones deflected this question dismissively by stating that such assignation was merely a matter of determining internships, the student pressed him further on the issue of the rumored interviews of East Coast–based undergraduate applicants and why the university had instituted such a procedure:

> Student: We were told last night by Jones that it was denied that students from other states were interviewed, and asked "Do you belong to the NSL?" This business was brought up at a faculty committee meeting. Is there ture(?) that there is such a committee?
>
> Jones: Ira Smith was called to answer this question in faculty meeting
>
> Shepherd: It is not denied that students were interviewed. It is said no questions concerning political leanings were asked. There is no evidence of this but an oral report now and then.
>
> . . .
>
> Student: I have known three students who have been interviewed.
>
> Shepherd: We have tried to collect evidence in the form of affidavit.

The *Michigan Daily*, still largely a conservative bastion at this time, rather dramatized the students' critical questioning of the Ruthven administration's actions in its headline, "Spring Parley Hits Expulsion of 3 Students."[45] The article noted that the dis-

---

44. This and the following quote are from "Saturday Afternoon," 1935–36 Spring Parley notebook, Blakeman, box 3, BHL.

45. "Spring Parley Hits Expulsion of 3 Students," *MD*, April 24, 1936. The political orientation of the *Michigan Daily* would soon change in part by the hiring of Elliott Maraniss (1918–2004) as a writer and later editor from 1937 to 1940. Maraniss's family were Sephardic Jews who originated from Spain, as did so many Sephardic Jews. Typically, many Jews who were expelled from Spain by the Inquisition eventually ended up in various parts of Eastern Europe, as did Elliott's family, who lived in Odessa, Russia, before coming to America. As David Maraniss writes about his father's years at the *Michigan Daily*, "Anyone who read the *Daily* between 1937 and

missals of Fisch (misspelled as Fish), Feldman, and Cohen were discussed at the opening session and that the faculty was opposed to Ruthven's actions. When the question of "prospective students [being] interviewed to find their views on the National Student League and related questions" was posed to the faculty, the *Daily* dutifully reported Professor Howard Mumford Jones's demurral.

Subsequent parleys showed that the issues raised by Ruthven's actions refused to disappear completely. During the 1937 Spring Parley, for example, students asked about quotas on black and Jewish students at the Medical School and whether Jews composed a dominant share of members in radical student organizations.[46] It was during the 1938 Spring Parley, however, that questions concerning Ruthven's actions, and the discrimination against East Coast Jewish students, emerged more thoroughly and forcefully. The parley's theme that year was the University of Michigan itself, featuring topics such as student opinion and leisure time, among others. On the opinion panel, Joseph Mattes, a student member of the parley's executive council, drafted a "Spring Parley Indictment," to which another student had to respond in a rebuttal. The topic at hand was the Strachey affair and the 1935 dismissals. Mattes averred "these instances . . . were what I considered definite curtailment, if not outright censorship, of the expression of student opinion."[47] The defender Alfred Lovell Jr. argued that the university was already reasonably tolerant, having allowed the socialist Norman Thomas to speak on campus several times. Lovell compared Strachey to a public rabble-rouser, stating flatly

1940 became familiar with Ace Maraniss's rhetorical style . . . Distraught over the injustices and horrors of the twentieth-century world, he reached for a systematic explanation of what happened and the best way to create something better. He wrote with confidence, in a voice ranging from sardonic to scholarly to didactic, his approach alternating between a newspaperman's keen realism and a romantic idealist's yearning for perfection." See Maraniss, *Good American Family*, 129.

46. See the "Our Government" section, questions 21 and 42, 1936–37 Spring Parley notebook, Blakeman, box 3, BHL.

47. Joseph S. Mattes, "Spring Parley Indictment," 1937–38 Spring Parley notebook, Blakeman, box 3, BHL.

that "the University does not feel that a Union Square orator has much to offer an Ann Arbor audience."[48]

In the subsequent discussions, which occurred during both an afternoon and evening session and largely focused on the issue of control over student publications, considerable attention was given to the right of radical groups to express their opinions on campus. A debate also emerged whether the University of Michigan was an institution of higher learning or a business enterprise. One student, however, raised the East Coast interviews in this context: "Interviews were held in a N.Y. hotel one summer for students wanting to apply—especially Jewish students." This student indicated that the University of Michigan representatives sought to discourage these East Coast Jewish students from applying and questioned their political views: "Told how far A.A. is . . . told how expensive it is to live here . . . asked what changes should be made in society. Brought up at last Parley . . . administration categorically denied these conferences."[49] The parley made a move to condemn this procedure and "advise some other criteria. Urge U. to judge merits of each incoming student on matters other than political, social, and economic beliefs." The resolution also included an amendment that the university "shouldn't restrict interviews to Jewish students."[50] The leisure time panel took up the issue of racial prejudice and discussed, among other topics, the difficulty that Jewish and African American women students encountered regularly in their attempts to find accommodations in Ann Arbor.[51]

48. Alfred Lovell Jr.'s response, 1937–38 Spring Parley notebook, Blakeman, box 3, BHL. Lovell was the son of U-M Engineering Professor Alfred Lovell and brother of future Medical School Dean Robert G. Lovell. See http://faculty-history.dc.umich.edu/faculty/robert-gibson-lovell.

49. Evening session, opinion section, 1937–38 Spring Parley notebook, Blakeman, box 3, BHL.

50. Evening session, opinion section, 1937–38 Spring Parley notebook, Blakeman, box 3, BHL.

51. "Leisure Time Panel," outline dated April 21, 1938, 1937–38 Spring Parley notebook, Blakeman, box 3, BHL.

The parley's resolutions were, of course, non-binding on the administration, and, as we have seen, interviews of East Coast, largely Jewish, applicants continued into 1939. Yet, as these parleys show, in the eyes of the politically interested and engaged students the Ruthven administration's position oscillated between a rhetoric of (relative) tolerance, as defended by Alfred Lovell Jr., and a reputation as selectively tolerant at best. Indeed, in these years, it is increasingly clear that the administration's relationship with its left-leaning students—Jewish or otherwise—remained fraught long after the events of the spring of 1935.

One student, the Brooklyn-born son of a Polish Jewish family, sought to place Ruthven's dismissal decisions within a broader political-economic context. He chose to do so in the form of a drama. Arthur Miller came from Brooklyn to Michigan in 1934 and had just finished his freshman year when the dismissals occurred. Although Miller himself was not a member of the NSL—his name does not appear on the organization's membership lists—he wrote articles for the *Michigan Daily* on such politically charged issues as the Willis Ward controversy, which the *Daily* refused to publish; the opposition to the anti-radical Dunckel-Baldwin Bill; and the university's refusal to provide a venue for Strachey in the spring of 1935. All of these issues were very salient to the left on campus and beyond. During Miller's sophomore year, his interest switched from journalism to drama. Having worked arduously during his freshman and sophomore years at two different campus jobs while maintaining a full class schedule, he decided to try his hand at a drama that addressed social conflicts of the time: "My first attempt at a play, rather inevitably, had been about an industrial conflict and a father and his two sons, the most autobiographical dramatic work I would ever write. I was gunning for a Hopwood Award, which at Michigan was the student equivalent of the Nobel."[52] Miller's play, *They Too Arise*, did earn him his first Hopwood in 1936 and was staged subsequently by the Hillel

52. Miller, *Timebends*, 209.

Players in the Lydia Mendelssohn Theater in March 1937 [Figure 5.1].[53] The play received plaudits from the English faculty, one of whom said that the play "is excellent theatre . . . It is fortunate for Mr. Miller that there is such a group as the Hillel Players that will undertake a presentation of a play written by a Michigan student."[54]

If Miller's first play was autobiographical, Ruthven's dismissals of the four NSL students were one of the inspirations for his second play, *Honors at Dawn*, which he finished later in 1937.[55] Winning Miller his second Hopwood Award, the work—never staged—was an ambitious effort to merge a caustic, if somewhat puerile, critique of university politics. The play featured a university president's obsequiousness to the demands of a prominent industrialist modeled after Henry Ford. Miller also painted a portrait of the struggles of impoverished students and of striking workers whom he clearly modeled after the Flint sit-down strike participants of December 1936 to February 1937. *Honors at Dawn*, then, ambitiously attempts to depict the complex nexus of social conflict within the capitalist system stretching from struggling students and workers all the way to college presidents and their superiors, industrial capitalists.

The main protagonists are the two Zibriski brothers, Harry, a dilettantish university student, and Max, his proletarian brother who loses his job at the automobile parts plant, Castle Parts, when he is caught distributing union literature. Convinced by Harry to enroll at the university, Max finds himself embroiled in political controversy there. The university president—here named President Burns—fires a left-wing history professor, Dr. Dickinson (possibly modeled after the left-leaning history professor Pres-

53. For clippings about this play, see Hillel scrapbook 1936–37, Hillel, box 1, BHL.

54. "Richness of Miller's Play Is Lauded," *MD*, March 10, 1937.

55. He did, however, receive a faculty nomination to the executive committee of the 1936 parley. See 1935–36 Spring Parley notebook, Blakeman, box 3, BHL. *Honors at Dawn* is discussed in Enoch Butler, "Early Days, Early Works," 9–10. Miller himself never mentions the play in his memoirs, *Timebends*, although he recalls winning "two successive Avery Hopwood Awards at Michigan." See Miller, *Timebends*, 91.

Figure 5.1 [Playbill for Arthur Miller's *They Too Arise*], Hillel Scrapbooks, box 1, scrapbook 1936-37, Bentley Historical Library, University of Michigan

ton Slosson), for encouraging Castle's workers to demand their rights. Max, fearing additional persecution, refuses to have anything to do with the efforts to demand Dickinson's reinstatement. Two students active in the campaign, Stan and Saul, receive letters in which they are unilaterally dismissed from the university in language similar to Ruthven's: "By your efforts to discredit the integrity of the administration of this university, you have given ample proof of your unwillingness to accept the responsibilities of a university student."[56] Concluding that he does not fit within a university environment, Max goes back to the Castle Parts plant to support his former colleagues during a sit-down strike. The police kill him after he encourages the strikers to resist all efforts by the authorities to break the strike. For Max, such martyrdom represents his true matriculation and his dying words are "I ran away once, but I'm back and I graduated. I did, didn't I, Barney?"[57]

Miller's depiction of the arbitrary dismissals of Stan and Saul, or even of Dickinson's firing, were not the most pointed reference to Ruthven of *Honors at Dawn*. The play includes a fascinating, early scene where President Burns receives a visit from Castle, the parts plant manufacturer seemingly modeled after Henry Ford. Castle, we learn, agreed to donate two new buildings to the university but is clearly displeased with Professor Dickinson's political activities and the general left-wing tone prevalent on campus:

Castle: ... I'd like you to consider this, though. The buildings and the research equipment I've decided to give the university are costing me a sizable fortune. You can't expect me to invest money in an institution which turns out enemies of our government. I don't think it's fair to ask me to pay for the education of men who will eventually turn around and organize against me. A strike costs a lot of money, President Burns.

President: I realize that. What do you suggest?

56. Miller. *Honors at Dawn*, 77. Special Collections Library, Univ. of Michigan
57. Miller, *Honors at Dawn*, 97.

> Castle: Get somebody inside of these Red organizations around here. Get the names of the leaders at least, and force them out of school. Before you admit new students, see that they're the right kind and once they're in, keep them that way. That's the whole story in a nutshell.[58]

Miller's *Honors at Dawn*, thus, explicitly connects both the dismissals and the interviews ("before you admit new students") to a single directive—to keep out left-wing students—and, above all, one that powerful business interests promulgated. That Castle appears to be a clear stand-in for Ford is best substantiated by the fact that Castle has a right-hand man named Gunliffe who is known for his ruthless strike-breaking tactics and general brutality. There is little doubt that Miller's Gunliffe stood for Harry Bennett, director of Ford's notorious Service Department who, in the spring of 1937, orchestrated the infamous Battle of the Overpass, in which Bennett's men savagely beat Walter Reuther and other organizers for the United Automobile Workers outside of Ford's Rouge Plant.

Along with the parleys, Miller's play showed that Ruthven's dismissals of the four Jewish students affected some among the student body—largely left-leaning Jews and their Gentile colleagues—long after the events had occurred. At least for this subset of students on the Michigan campus, the parleys and Miller's play clearly called into question the extent to which Ruthven's efforts to build a truly diverse and pluralist campus extended to them. The number of Ruthven's "victims" in 1935 may have been small—ultimately only three dismissals—but it established a precedent that the president was more than willing to use his *in loco parentis* authority to get rid of "undesirable" students. Some students also voiced suspicion that the president's interview process, which the university administration had quietly implemented, filtered out applicants whom the university found unde-

58. Miller, *Honors at Dawn*, 43.

sirable. Increasingly, these mainly left-wing students also argued that Ruthven was effectively doing the bidding of other, more powerful men, who, through antisemitism and anti-communism (which, in this case, amounted to effectively the same thing) sought to stifle pluralism on the Ann Arbor campus.

The Haunting Specter of Antisemitism

Given Ruthven's handling of the Heidelberg issue, his seeming tolerance of privately expressed antisemitic sentiment, and the complaints among parley participants about the dismissals over the ensuing three years, two questions then must be posed: How much did antisemitism pervade the University of Michigan? And to what extent did Jewish students feel or experience any sense of increased hostility toward them? Importantly and perhaps tellingly, no dismissals occurred after 1935 (we discuss matters in 1940 later) and no organization or person appears to have suffered from opposing Ruthven's decision on Heidelberg. Aside from its relatively restrained protests of Ruthven's Heidelberg decision, the Michigan Hillel chapter spent the winter 1936 term actively fundraising for the Joint Distribution Committee (JDC) to aid Jewish refugees. Hillel also engaged in activities geared to enhance its own membership. Little appears in the extant issues of the *B'nai B'rith Hillel News* concerning the foundation's stance on the Michigan delegation to Heidelberg, although it is important to note that only one further issue of the paper survives of this year following the copy that featured Hillel's anti-Heidelberg editorial.

Two articles in the paper mentioned the JDC explicitly. The May 27, 1936, issue also included a coupon for donations offering *prima facie* evidence that the troubling currents of the outside world began to emerge within the confines of Hillel.[59] Although

---

59. "Hillel Foundation to Raise $3,000" and "European Problems Alleviated by Joint Distribution Committee," *BBHN*, both May 27, 1936. The Hillel scrapbook 1935–36

blurbs and articles discussing Nazism and antisemitism had appeared in the pages of *Hillel News* before, this is the first extant instance of the paper's active solicitation of funds on behalf of Europe's Jews.[60] Awareness of the increasingly dangerous predicament of Europe's Jews spread beyond Hillel, spurred by faculty members like history professor Preston Slosson, while "collection plates at strategic points on the campus and in the dormitories was [*sic*] accepted. Faculty speakers have been invited to many of the fraternity and sorority houses to discuss reasons for the campaign."[61] Rabbi Heller, Hillel's director, chaired the campaign, and the paper's editorial exhorted that "it is the duty of every Jewish student to do everything in his power to help raise urgently needed funds for this work."[62]

If Hillel's efforts on behalf of the JDC reminded Jewish students of the rising incidence of antisemitism overseas, editorials in the *Michigan Daily* during the 1936–37 academic year showed both that Jewish organizations on campus were becoming increasingly concerned about Nazi Germany and that there was a growing feeling that antisemitism was alive on the Michigan campus. In addition to showing Hillel's participating in the Inter-Faith Symposia and staging plays and concerts, the Hillel scrapbook for 1936–37 also reveals that many invited speakers addressed the issue of Nazism and that Rabbi Heller spoke on the conditions of Jews in Poland and Germany.[63] While acknowledging the growing concern among American Jews for their European brethren, Professor Herbert Blumer of the University of Chicago asserted in a November 1936

includes an unsourced article from April 3 [1936?] titled "Wineman Is Selected as Chairman of Pre-Campaign Efforts for Allied Jewish Drive to be Held May 12-22." The source appears to be a Petoskey, Michigan, newspaper. See Hillel scrapbook 1935–36, Hillel, box 2, BHL.

60. For one example, see the articles "Pollack Explains Situation Existing in Nazi Germany" and "Shades of Hitler!"; both in *BBHN*, March 10, 1935.

61. "Hillel Foundation to Raise $3,000," *BBHN*, May 27, 1936.

62. "Support the Drive!" *BBHN*, May 27, 1935.

63. Hillel scrapbook 1936–37, Hillel, box 1, BHL.

lecture at Hillel that American culture was not fertile ground for such European-style antisemitic sentiments.[64] Moreover, in January 1937, an emeritus University of Michigan professor of French language and literature, Moritz Levi, had reprinted in the *Daily* a list of twenty-three facts about the Nazi regime that had originally appeared in an essay by the Reverend John Haynes Holmes in an edited volume called *Nazism: An Assault on Civilization* (1934).[65] Along with such facts as the Nazis' inaugurating "a persecution of the Jews more terrible in its rigor than anything known since the Middle Ages" and characterizing it as a "'dry' pogrom of political disenfranchisement, social outlawry and economic ruin which dooms Israel to extinction or ghetto," Holmes also listed Nazi outrages on Catholic and Protestant churches, the Nazis' subordination of women, and their destruction of democratic government.[66]

Levi's reprint of this list prompted an angry response in the *Michigan Daily* by a senior named Willis Player. Player blasted Levi for what the author claimed to be Levi's intolerant and inane attacks on Nazi Germany. Hitler's regime "is vigorous, militant, and unafraid. No wonder Jews object to it. It is relentless in coping with its enemies, true and loyal to its friends. Of course, Communists and Jews endeavor to see that it has as few friends as possible." To Holmes's and Levi's charges that the Nazis had destroyed intellectual and cultural life in Germany, Willis Player retorted that "the National Socialists have found living, vital substitutes

---

64. "American Jew Will Not Become Crisis Scapegoat, Blumer Says," *MD*, November 10, 1936.

65. Van Paassen and Wise, eds., *Nazism*.

66. "A Pastor's Indictment," *MD*, January 10, 1937. Levi published numerous entries in the *Michigan Daily* over the previous three years outlining the Nazi regime's barbarism, usually through quotes from *Mein Kampf* or German newspapers. See Charles N. Staubach, "Mr. Player's Letter," *MD*, January 9, 1937. Other Levi editorials include "Nazism: Self Revealed," *MD*, April 24, 1936; and "Mein Kampf," *MD*, March 11, 1936. Clippings are located in Hillel scrapbook 1935–36, Hillel, box 2, BHL. Preston Slosson wrote a rejoinder to Player's argument in "Mysterious Nazi Culture," *MD*, January 9, 1937.

for the contamination of decayed Jew-intellectualism." Player's editorial ends on a predictably isolationist note by arguing that America should leave Germany well enough alone to manage its own affairs adding facetiously that "I cannot go on record as anti-Jew or entirely pro-Nazi. But please list me as anti-Levi."[67]

Player's tirade occasioned a range of responses. Some, like Moritz's colleague Charles N. Staubach, pointed out Player's puerility and "eloquent infantility."[68] Others either agreed with Player or sought to find some middle ground between the two positions. One correspondent, named R. M., chided Levi, arguing: "I am not sure that his [Levi's] facts give us a complete and impartial picture of the situation."[69] More disconcerting was an editorial published under the name of "Dickell" in the January 13, 1937 edition of the *Michigan Daily*. After declaring him (or her-)self "equally appreciative of the German and Jewish races," Dickell goes on to state that the Nazis "have adopted the notion (evolved by the Jews long before the 'Aryans' became self-conscious) that a race has a unique contribution to make to world-culture and that to make this contribution, a race must maintain its purity."[70] Equating Nazi racial policies with Jews' very complex belief in their status as God's chosen people, Dickell argues that Nazi persecution

67. A. Willis Player was an occasional letter writer to the *Michigan Daily*, although most of his letters were in reference to Levi. His graduating class is indicated in a *Daily* article announcing his election to treasurer of Le Cercle Français ("Officers Elected to Le Cercle Francais," May 29, 1936). After graduating in 1937, he became a columnist for the *Ann Arbor News*. See Stan Swinton's "Town & Gown" column, *MD*, June 30, 1939. The quotations in this paragraph are from "A Word Coined by Communists . . . ," *MD*, January 8, 1937. See also Hillel scrapbook 1936–37, Hillel, box 1, BHL.

68. Staubach, "Mr. Player's Letter," *MD*, January 9, 1937. The article is also located in Hillel scrapbook 1936–37, Hillel, box 1, BHL.

69. R. M., "What Mr. Player Might Have Meant," *MD*, January 12, 1937; and Hillel scrapbook 1936–37, Hillel, box 1, BHL. Levi responded to R. M's criticism in "Holmes, Not Levi," *MD*, January 15, 1937; and Hillel scrapbook 1936–37, Hillel, box 1, BHL.

70. Dickell, "The Race Problem," *MD*, January 13, 1937, Hillel scrapbook 1936–37, Hillel, box 1, BHL.

was an outcome of mutual intolerance and was fundamentally no different to Jews' intolerance of Arabs in Palestine. "There is probably as much anti-Nazi propaganda from Jewish sources," Dickell concludes, "as there is anti-Jewish propaganda from Nazi sources."[71] Heller took pains to discredit Dickell's equating Nazi racial doctrine to traditional Jewish belief. For Heller, Jews' status as the "chosen people" was, if anything, a religious concept based on scriptural literature, not a racial doctrine grounded on biological difference.[72] As for Dickell's claim that Nazi persecution was a product of mutual intolerance between Germans and Jews, Heller retorted: "I know no Jewry which was as eager to identify itself with the national and cultural life of the people amongst whom they dwelt as were the German Jews in pre-Hitler days."[73]

The Levi-Player flap seemed to have abated after this brief flurry of articles in early 1937. Yet it was indicative of the ways in which awareness of the Nazis' persecution of Jews was slowly seeping into the Michigan campus community. It also demonstrated the ambivalence that this frightening news provoked regarding the Jews themselves. For starters, Jews at the University of Michigan were subjected to an increasingly loud articulation of antisemitism that largely emanated from sources outside the university. Indeed, by the late 1930s, the State of Michigan was home to three of the most vocal and virulent antisemites in the United States: Henry Ford, of course, who, despite the discontinuation of the *Dearborn Independent* in 1928, was still vocal in his antisemitism and in 1938 received the Grand Cross of the Supreme Order of the German Eagle from Nazi Germany; Father Charles Coughlin, whose radio broadcasts had increasingly grown antisemitic and reactionary due to his hatred of Roosevelt's New Deal; and Gerald L. K. Smith, an evangelist minister who moved

71. Dickell, "The Race Problem," *MD*, January 13, 1937, Hillel scrapbook 1936–37, Hillel, box 1, BHL.

72. Fred Warner Neal, "Nazi Doctrine Unlike Jewish, Heller Asserts," *MD*, January 22, 1937; and Hillel scrapbook 1936–37, Hillel, box 1, BHL.

73. Neal, "Nazi Doctrine Unlike Jewish, Heller Asserts," *MD*, January 22, 1937.

to Detroit in 1939 and solicited support from Ford.[74] Moreover, the state had endured in 1936 and 1937 a campaign of terror led by the Black Legion, a KKK splinter organization with a marked enmity toward Jews.[75]

Even if Ann Arbor was, in many ways, a haven, Jews on campus could hardly be unaware of both the deteriorating situation of European Jews and the increasing virulent rhetoric directed against them at home, be it in the state of Michigan or indeed the United States as a whole. While the University of Michigan remained committed to its pluralist ethos, especially in its continued efforts to build interfaith dialogues among Jews, Christians, and other denominations, nonetheless Jews seemed to have felt an increasing vulnerability due in no small part to the political environment around them. Thus, antisemitism may have felt more palpable simply because it was "in the air" (literally in Coughlin's case), even if most Jewish students at the university rarely experienced anything more than mild occasions of it. Still, there were some troubling incidents that could stoke fear more directly. In the main, however, antisemitism appears to have been a specter in Ann Arbor—articulated by bigots like Coughlin and Willis Player—but one that rarely touched Jewish students directly, at least based on the limited evidence we could find pertaining to this matter. To clarify: By specter, we do not mean that antisemitism was imaginary. Indeed, our next chapter will show that there were active antisemites on the Michigan campus who sought to effect political change at the university in the 1939–40 academic year. Instead, we see the specter of antisemitism as a phenomenon in which the presence of antisemitism was increasingly *felt* even if not directly *experienced*. Paradoxically, and even

74. For Ford, see Baldwin, *Henry Ford and the Jews*, and Wallace, *American Axis*. For a good survey of Coughlin's career, see Warren, *Radio Priest*. In *Right in Michigan's Grassroots*, Vinyard examines Coughlin's influence in Michigan politics (99–171) and his embarrassing antisemitism (168–69). See also Alan Brinkley's classic *Voices of Protest*. For Smith, see Jeansonne, *Gerald L. K. Smith*.

75. On the Black Legion, see Amann, "Vigilante Fascism."

encouragingly, this growing specter of antisemitism prompted efforts among Jews and non-Jews in the university community to understand, and hopefully, combat it.

With the *Anschluss* of Austria to and by Nazi Germany in March and the Sudeten crisis of September 1938, both Hillel and the broader Michigan campus community became increasingly aware of Hitler's ultimate ambitions and the vicious attacks on the Jews that accompanied them. The *B'nai B'rith Hillel News*, in its (now monthly) November 1938 issue, informed readers that the fate of Europe's Jews rested on the survival of the newly autonomous Ruthenian rump state that was carved out of Czechoslovakia pursuant to the decisions reached at that fateful Munich gathering.[76] That same month, Hitler's persecution reached an early crescendo with the *Kristallnacht* pogrom of November 9–10, 1938. In Ann Arbor, the Student Senate passed a resolution condemning the vicious attacks on Jewish lives and property and encouraged the Roosevelt administration to admit Jewish refugees.[77] The Faculty Senate also requested that 11 o'clock classes on the morning of November 18 be canceled to allow students to participate in a demonstration against racial and religious discrimination. It seems, however, that the administration did not approve this. Ruthven asked the faculty to postpone the walkout to Tuesday, November 22, which the faculty respected and with which it complied.[78] A larger Committee on Human Rights, composed of the leaders of many campus organizations, secured Hill Auditorium for the demonstration and hoped—unsuccessfully as it turned out—to get Democratic governor Frank Murphy to attend the event.[79] Ultimately, the anti-Nazi rally scheduled for November

76. Leonard Schleider, "Fate of Eight Million Jews Depends on Ruthenia's Future," *BBHN*, November 1938.

77. "Student Senate Condemns New Nazi Outrages," *MD*, November 16, 1938.

78. "Anti-Nazi Meeting Slated for Today Moved to Tuesday," *MD*, November 18, 1938.

79. "Nazi Envoy Called Home; Campus Groups Protest Persecution of Minorities," *MD*, November 19, 1938; and "Murphy Unable to be Present at Rally Today," *MD*, November 22, 1938.

22 was postponed as well only to be totally canceled. Reaction to the cancellation was mixed; one letter to the editor in the *Daily*'s November 23 issue complained that if President Roosevelt could request prayers for martyred Jews, "there is no reason conceivable as to why the usual procedure of the University cannot be withdrawn in favor of a matter of such paramount importance to all of us."[80] Others took the occasion of the rally's cancellation to remind readers that the United States had acquiesced in Japan's brutal war in China or to draw comparisons with the persecution of blacks in the United States.[81] Ultimately, it appears that the planned rally was quietly dropped for reasons that we do not know. No further mention of such a rally appears in the *Daily* after November 24.[82]

Even though the anti-Nazi rally was shelved, *Kristallnacht* did appear to bring increasing awareness to the Michigan campus of the plight of Jews in Europe and to the specter of antisemitism more broadly. Articles appeared in the *Daily* with such titles as "History Shows Jews Always Oppressed, Prof. Long States" and "Jews Look to President to Furnish Western Outlet."[83] The Nazi pogrom also heightened Jews' increasingly palpable sense of antisemitism both in Germany and at home. A January 1939 article in the *Hillel News* reported "Anti-Semitism Is Widespread Survey Shows."[84] Summarizing a survey at sixty-three institutions of higher education asking their students how they gauged the presence of Jews on their respective campuses, the author claimed that these students' responses led to the conclusion that there indeed existed "a major increase in anti-Jewish feeling since the rise of Hitlerism in Germany." Many who participated in the sur-

---

80. Donald Simon, "Why No Demonstration?" *MD*, November 23, 1938.

81. "We're Doing It Too," *MD*, November 23, 1938; and John S. Lash, "Persecution—Home and Abroad," *MD*, November 24, 1938.

82. Based on a search of *Michigan Daily* through the end of December 1938.

83. Both are on page 1 of the *Michigan Daily*, November 29, 1938.

84. This and the quotations in the paragraph are from Leonard Schleider, "Anti-Semitism Is Widespread Survey Shows," *HN*, January 1939.

vey blamed Jews themselves for the existence of antisemitism: some cited the Jews' allegedly clannish behavior while "others, chiefly Midwesterners, condemned 'New York Jews' and 'campus radicals' as trouble-makers." A small minority was of the opinion that Jews should segregate themselves "in all-Jewish universities and, especially, in separate professional schools."[85]

Participants in this multi-university survey classified their institutions based on the degree of anti-Jewish feeling. First, of those institutions classified with "none or little anti-Jewish feeling," as would be expected, a highly disproportionate number were schools based in New York City and New York State, such as Brooklyn College, Bucknell University, CCNY, New York University (Washington Square division), Lehigh University, Union College, Rensselaer Polytechnic Institute, and Hunter College. Some East Coast institutions not based in New York were also in this category, such as the University of Vermont, Amherst College, Connecticut State College, Bates College, as were two non–East Coast schools, the University of Arizona and Vanderbilt University. The next category comprised schools in which there was "some anti-Jewish feeling." Here we find, among others, schools such as the Massachusetts Institute of Technology, the University of Alabama, the University of California, the University of Chicago, the University of Pennsylvania, Syracuse University, and the University of Nebraska.

The next category, institutions in which there were "strong anti-Jewish feelings," included schools such as New York University (University Heights division), Dartmouth College, Duke University, Harvard University, Indiana University, Princeton University, Stanford University, the University of Wyoming, and also the University of Michigan. The last category features schools in which respondents experienced "severe anti-Jewish feelings," such as Carnegie Tech, Columbia University, Colgate University, Cornell University, Johns Hopkins University, University of Minnesota, University of Missouri, the Ohio State Univer-

85. Schleider, "Anti-Semitism Is Widespread Survey Shows," *HN*, January 1939.

sity, Northwestern University, the University of Illinois, and Yale University.[86] Although we have no idea how robust this survey's methodology was, it does provide at least a rough indication of the degree of antisemitism at these institutions of higher learning in the United States in the late 1930s. Justified or not, realistic or not, clearly Jews at the University of Michigan expressed experiencing "strong anti-Jewish feelings" at the time. This was quite a departure from four years previous, when a November 1934 editorial in the *B'nai B'rith Hillel News* claimed that "Anti-Semitism has not been particularly rife on this Campus. True, there are numerous discriminations; but the anti-Semitism displayed is of the passive and not the active type."[87]

The perception that antisemitism was growing on campus received unsettling confirmation in February 1939 when two men, who were never identified, painted swastikas on the doors of three Jewish fraternities.[88] Members of one of the fraternities suspected that this was part of an organized effort since they had been "annoyed recently by taxis and dinners, which they had not ordered, being sent to their house. The house president suspected a possible connection between the two." Others believed that the defacement of the house was a by-product of the "German-American Bund meeting in New York Monday night, but a Daily investigation failed to substantiate this suspicion."[89] In addition, the *Detroit Jewish Chronicle* published an article that April on "Prejudice in Universities" that claimed that petitions were being

86. Schleider, "Anti-Semitism Is Widespread Survey Shows," *HN*, January 1939.

87. "Jews on Campus," *BBHN*, November 3, 1934.

88. See the report titled "College Prank?" in Civil Rights Congress (CRC) files at the Walter Reuther Library, Wayne State University (WRL). The folder includes a clipping from an article in the *Washtenaw Progressive*, dated March 1, 1939, about a swastika painted on the door of one house in "Ann Arbor where Jewish students reside." However, the *Michigan Daily* report from February 24, 1939, confirms that these reports are about the same event. See CRC, series 8, box 76, folder Ann Arbor Incident—1940," WRL; and "Two Men Paint Jewish Houses with Swastikas," *MD*, February 24, 1939.

89. "Two Men Paint Jewish Houses with Swastikas," *MD*, February 24, 1939.

circulated in state universities, including the University of Michigan, "with the intention of forcing further restrictions upon the number of Jews admitted to colleges."[90] Ruthven sent a letter to the *Chronicle*'s editor, Philip Slomovitz, expressing his doubt that any such petition was circulating on campus and suggesting that the newspaper get its facts straight.[91] Slomovitz, respectfully yet firmly, insisted that he had checked out the facts, stating that a University of Michigan student, who was half-Jewish, and whose Jewishness was thus not apparent, provided him with a statement that he was approached twice to sign such a petition. "We have had numerous reports of anti-Jewish activities in other state schools, and more recently at Wayne," Slomovitz informed the president. "Invariably, Jewish students are afraid to report such incidents. It is only when we have investigated and have statements and affidavits to corroborate verbal reports that we make references to unfortunate happenings."[92]

Kristallnacht and the increasing specter of antisemitism on campus also left Jews themselves in a quandary as to how to respond. Some argued that Jews needed to moderate their supposedly "loud, aggressive, and radical" behavior and that the "Jew curb his activities in fields where he is not wanted, that he consider himself always to be on 'dress parade,' as an example to his people and that he conform to the customs of the non-Jewish community in which he lives."[93] Others, however, bristled against this quiescence and advocated a more forceful response. One letter writer to the *Hillel News* argued that "proper" comportment was a naïve strategy against the Nazi menace and that "the only way to alleviate and to finally remove such persecution is to fight reaction wherever it occurs and to fight it not only as Jews but in

90. "Prejudice in Universities," *Detroit Jewish Chronicle*, April 14, 1939.

91. Ruthven to Slomovitz, letter dated May 15, 1939. Philip Slomovitz Collection, box 110, accession 1494. Reuther Library, WSU.

92. Slomovitz to Ruthven, letter dated May 18, 1939. Philip Slomovitz Collection, box 110, accession 1494. Reuther Library, WSU.

93. "Sokolsky on Jews," *HN*, November 1938.

unity with every other progressive force."[94] *Hillel News*'s editorial for January 1939 agreed, arguing for a more assertive approach to the growing menace of antisemitism: "this is no time for palsied shrinking in the corner. This is the time to display some of the stuff from which the prophets were made."[95] Even Rabbi Heller, who had denounced the political activities of Jewish students in 1935, was becoming increasingly vocal about the rise of antisemitism; during services at Hillel in early December 1938, he denounced a speech by the right-wing Catholic priest Father Charles Coughlin as being un-American, antisemitic, and pro-Nazi.[96] Despite Heller's comments on this occasion, Hillel was not about to turn toward radical political agitation meaning some version of socialism; or Jewish separatism meaning open Zionism. Instead, most of its activities during the war years were to be consumed by raising monies for Jewish refugees.

Concerns about antisemitism not only manifested themselves on the pages of the *Hillel News*. Both Hillel and the Student Religious Association (SRA), the latter working in conjunction with the Office of Religious Education, took positive steps to assess the extent to which antisemitism existed on campus and how Jewish students were coping with the increasingly tense climate. In January 1939, Hillel sponsored a class, taught by its incoming director, Dr. Isaac Rabinowitz, on Current Jewish Problems.[97] Many of the students praised the course for showing "a need for Jewish education on campus" and held that "the discussion of antisemitism was surprisingly fruitful."[98]

94. Letter of Bernard Friedman to *HN*, January 1939.

95. "Don't Hush Me!" *HN*, January 1939.

96. "Heller Labels Coughlin Talk 'Un-American,'" *MD*, December 3, 1938.

97. Lucille Flaum, "Classes Considering Jewish Problems Are Applauded by Students in Survey," *BBHN*, January 1939. Heller stepped down as director of Hillel at the end of February 1939 and was replaced by Isaac Rabinowitz. "Dr. Heller Resigns After 9 Years as Director," *BBHN*, January 1939. See also Markovits and Garner, *Hillel at Michigan*, 127–28.

98. Elaum, "Classes Considering Jewish Problems," *BBHN*, January 1939.

In keeping with the broader Ruthven-inspired pluralist vision, as well as its particular ecumenical philosophy, the SRA, under its director Kenneth W. Morgan, appears to have pursued its own initiatives, although the evidence for them is not particularly abundant.[99] In late 1938, the SRA formed a Seminar in Social Minorities, whose purpose, described in a retrospective letter from 1941, was to study "the problem of anti-Semitism at the University of Michigan." This group was likely the "Semitic Study Group," whose December 9, 1938, attendance list appears in the same archival folder as documents from the Social Minorities Seminar.[100] The group, which seems to have comprised predominantly students, developed "Areas to Be Explored" lists including attitudes toward Jews, opinions as to the causes of antisemitism, and the effects of European antisemitism and of the Detroit-based Catholic "radio priest" Father Charles Coughlin on attitudes on campus.[101]

One undertaking that this Semitic Study Group commenced occurred in conjunction with the SRA. It featured a survey of Jewish-Gentile relations, which was administered by the SRA's Bureau of Student Opinion, during the winter 1939 term. This was a survey specific to the University of Michigan, and is distinct from the multi-university survey featured in the *Hillel News*. In the words of the bureau's director James Vicary, a junior, the student-run bureau chose this topic because "interest in this problem was very apparent on the campus during the first of the [1938–39] school year."[102] Yet Vicary's presence on the Semitic

99. See Morgan's letter dated March 15, 1939, SRA, box 8, folder Jewish Student Problems, BHL.

100. Form letter by Doyle Soldenright, dated March 3, 1941, SRA, box 8, folder Jewish Student Problems, BHL. That the Semitic Study Group may be the same as the Seminar in Social Minorities is hinted by the participation of James Vicary, a member of the SRA and founder of its Bureau of Student Opinion in 1937. Vicary would develop the 1939 survey of Jewish-Gentile relations for the seminar and the Semitic Survey Group's to-do list included in this folder mentioned, "Areas to be Explored: Attitude toward Jews."

101. See Semitic Study Group membership list and the "Areas to Be Explored" sheet in SRA, box 8, folder Jewish Student Problems, BHL.

102. Vicary, "Survey." Antisemitism was also the focus of studies by the American

Study Group membership list suggests that the survey was part of the Semitic Study Group's effort to assess the degree of anti-semitism on campus. Without specifically naming the Semitic Study Group, Vicary's introduction to the report noted that the impetus for the report had been "a group of thirty-five students, representing varied religious and political views" who, "after two meetings at the Student Religious Association," had decided "that a survey of the problem should be undertaken. The chief <u>sources of information</u> were from the original student group, faculty and clergymen who were invited to talk with them."[103] After a lengthy discussion of the survey method and the denotation of "Jews" from "non-Jews," Vicary's report showed that at 10%, Michigan had a lower percentage of Jews than the average enrollment of Jews at US and Canadian institutions of higher education with 5,000 or more students, where the figure on average was 21% of the student population.[104] Moreover, the report also reaffirmed that Jews were still not allowed to join Gentile fraternities and that the Jews' numbers in Michigan's elite Literary College were higher than that of Gentile students.

Without specifying the Medical School, Vicary's report also confirmed that "it is well known that there is a Jewish quota in at least one of the professional schools."[105] The survey revealed that while Jewish students tended to be more secular than their Gentile peers, it was surprising, still, that there were few places of worship for any of the religion's three branches. "The three divi-

Institute of Public Opinion and *Fortune* magazine. The *Fortune* quarterly survey is in *Fortune*, April 1939, 104. James Vicary (1915–77), who graduated in 1940, became famous, or notorious, for pioneering the concept of "subliminal advertising" but was discredited when he falsified an experiment to demonstrate the effectiveness of this technique. See Kelly B. Crandall, "Invisible Commercials and Hidden Persuaders: James M. Vicary and the Subliminal Advertising Controversy of 1957" (undergraduate honors thesis, University of Florida, 2006), http://plaza.ufl.edu/cyllek/docs/KCrandall_Thesis2006.pdf.

103. Vicary, "Survey," 1. The underlining is in the original quotation.

104. Vicary, "Survey," 3.

105. Vicary, "Survey," 3. See also Borst, "Choosing the Student Body."

sions of the Jewish Faith, Orthodox, Conservative, and Reform have little or no facilities in Ann Arbor; the only Synagogue is a made over home, and the Hillel Foundation chapel seats thirty or thirty-five persons."[106] Along with the paucity of sites for worship for Jews, the survey hinted at some of the prejudices that Jewish students faced that encouraged many to downplay their ethnicity or religious affiliation. The report also cited the Counselor of Religious Education, Edward Blakeman, "during the past several years there has been an increasing number of requests coming to him from prospective employers asking if University graduates have been listed as Jews. Students have come to the office and have asked to have such affiliations removed from the records."[107]

The report then moved into the more imprecise and thorny area of student attitudes. In the main, the text described the relationship between Jewish and Gentile students as collegial, if not particularly close. "For the non-Jewish student," Vicary writes, "proportionally the greatest frequency of contact with Jews is in social gatherings and in living in the same house or dormitory with Jews, where about three quarters of these students have had such contacts. On the other hand, about three quarters of the non-Jewish students have never dated a Jew (74%), lived in the same neighborhood (78%), or roomed with a Jew (86%)."[108] Interestingly, roughly the same percentage—one-third—of Jewish and Gentile students accepted as true many of the stereotypes associated with Jews, including their alleged clannishness and their purportedly aggressive, industrious, radical, and excitable nature: "Many of the Jewish students are affected by the same stereotypes as the non-Jewish students, except in matters of honesty and trustworthiness, where more Jewish students say he is more honest and more non-Jews say the Jew is less honest."[109] Where

106. Vicary, "Survey," 4.
107. Vicary, "Survey," 5.
108. Vicary, "Survey," 7.
109. Vicary, "Survey," 10.

Jewish and Gentile students split, however, was on their beliefs about the causes of antisemitism, with a majority of Gentile students claiming that its existence was due to the personal characteristics of Jews, whereas Jewish students either attributed it to Gentiles or to social and economic factors.

Vicary concluded by sketching the "typical" University of Michigan Jewish student in contrast to his "typical" Gentile counterpart: more urbane, more literate, more involved in campus organizations, more interested in theaters and concerts than beer gardens and bars, and predominantly non-Michigan in origin. Vicary encouragingly noted that non-Jewish students who had interactions with Jews reported them as pleasant and that "more of these students . . . are willing to continue such relations in the future."[110] Yet Vicary also mentioned that many more Jews than non-Jews were concerned with antisemitism and that "about half of the student body suggests assimilation or toleration, with proportionally more Jews favoring these methods of avoiding anti-Jewish feeling."[111] The report concluded that only a small number of non-Jewish students had any antisemitic feelings: "roughly five to ten percent of the total student body report that they have some real predisposition to act in opposition to the Jews."[112]

Vicary's report appeared to be at odds with findings mentioned in the January 1939 issue of *Hillel News* that characterized Michigan as a campus with "strong antisemitism." Instead, the Vicary study painted a portrait of a relatively benign campus atmosphere where traditional stereotypes of Jews, while widely shared among both Jews and non-Jews, did not foster antisemitic sentiment beyond the, at that time, generally accepted "polite" antisemitism of restricting Jews from joining Gentile fraternities. Yet, even if the University of Michigan was generally tolerant toward Jews within its bounds, this does not mean that Jewish students' per-

110. Vicary, "Survey," Conclusions.
111. Vicary, "Survey," Conclusions.
112. Vicary, "Survey," Conclusions.

ceptions about rising antisemitism on campus were incorrect. As already suggested, antisemitism had developed a specter-like quality, especially in the immediate political context around Ann Arbor. That is, although Vicary's report portrayed the university as generally tolerant, there was a growing perception on campus by mid-1939 that antisemitism at the University of Michigan was on the rise. A *Daily* editorial from mid-July noted, "Even on the University campus an increase in stupid race prejudice is noticeable. A poll taken last year, the results of which were never publicly released, showed anti-semitism to be prevalent to an amazing degree. It was not many months ago that someone . . . smeared a Nazi swastika on the walk in front of a Jewish fraternity. This in a University community where the universality of humanity, the vital importance of maintenance of human dignity; the clear thinking which alone can prove the salvation of democracy at a time when it is so bitterly challenged, should possess vital life.[113]

Much of the antisemitic rhetoric of the late 1930s combined the standard accusation that Jews were importing disruptive political radicalism onto peaceful, quaint college campuses with a newer, isolationist argument that Jews were actively trying to push the United States into a war against the fascist powers. On one level, these right-wing isolationists were correct: By the latter 1930s, much (though certainly not all) of the student Left had abandoned its previously held anti-war pacifism, which, of course, was virtually identical with the Right's isolationism. Instead, the Left adopted a more militant anti-fascism as its new mantra.[114] Moreover, it was the Communist students within the American Student Union (ASU)—the successor organization to the NSL—that had successfully defeated their socialist and pacifist colleagues' efforts to retain the pacifist Oxford Pledge on the organization's platform. The Communist ASU students were, of course, follow-

---

113. Stan Swinton, "Prejudice in a Democracy . . . ," *MD*, July 11, 1939. Although his article appears to discuss Vicary's report, if so, he misinterprets its findings.

114. See Cohen, *When the Old Left Was Young*, chap. 6.

ing the line decreed by the Young Communist League (of which many were members), the youth arm of the CPUSA, and, ultimately, by Moscow itself, which, under Stalin, adopted a policy of building an anti-fascist coalition among the Left—the so-called United Front—as the best means of saving the Soviet Union from Hitler. Although organizations like the ASU took a strong anti-fascist, de facto interventionist line, especially after the onset of the Spanish Civil War in the summer of 1936, the right-wing isolationists were incorrect in asserting that Jews, in the main, were trying to push the United States into war.

Conclusion

Although the Bureau of Student Opinion's 1939 Jewish-Gentile survey and its 1940–41 surveys on war attitudes indicate that Jews were hardly out of the mainstream in their attitudes on campus, the old associations of Jews as radicals, combined with the new aggressive isolationist rhetoric on the Right, led to another set of student dismissals on Ruthven's part in the summer of 1940. Jews were not the only students targeted, but their presence among the dismissed was once again disproportionate to their representation within the NSL's successor group, the ASU. This chapter highlighted with examples the precarious standing of Ruthven's pluralism as well as the Jews' shaky position in it during the turbulent 1930s. Things were not going to improve for either constituent in the years to come. As shown in the ensuing chapter, some of the main instigators behind Ruthven's actions were both anti-left and antisemitic. Ruthven's decision to dismiss seventeen students in June 1940—most of whom were in good academic standing—appears capricious unless one understands the particularly toxic climate in which he was operating at that moment.

CHAPTER SIX

THE RIGHTWARD DRIFT, 1938–40

I n June of 1940, President Ruthven opened his annual commencement address with a warning that was completely at odds with the pluralistic philosophy and the political tolerance that characterized most of his first decade as Michigan's president. "Michigan does not welcome students who are not convinced that democracy is the ideal form of government for a civilized people. She will not be confused by sophistries built around meaningful but ill-defined phrases, such as 'freedom of the press' and 'freedom of speech,' but will deal firmly, without fear or favor, with subversive, or so-called 'fifth column' activities."[1] Almost as if he were fulfilling a campaign pledge, in the days following the speech, Ruthven sent letters to seventeen students informing them that they had been dismissed from the university and were not invited to reenroll for the fall term. More than half of the students were Jews. All of these students were members of the American Student Union (ASU), a successor to the National Student League (NSL), which had formed when the national NSL merged with the Students League of Industrial Democracy over the Christmas holiday of 1935–36.[2]

1. Ruthven, commencement address, 1940, https://bentley.umich.edu/legacy-support/commence/.

2. For the creation of the ASU, see Cohen, *When the Old Left Was Young*, 139–54.

Like the NSL, the ASU ultimately served as a front for the Young Communist League despite its pretensions of being a voice for a unified student Left. Following the onset of the Spanish Civil War in July 1936, the ASU led the shift away from anti-war pacifism, which had been the NSL's main plank, toward articulating an assertive anti-fascism, with its implicit recognition of military intervention to stop the spread of fascism. Yet, the move away from pacifism toward anti-fascism rendered the ASU in no ways more palatable to the Ruthven administration, or to conservatives, than the earlier NSL had been. If the NSL's earlier pacifism could be construed as unpatriotic and its actions in favor of the poor and disadvantaged viewed as strident criticisms of capitalism, the ASU's anti-fascism derived from Stalin's decision to have the national communist parties and their auxiliary organization build popular front coalitions to oppose Hitler. Thus, the ASU appeared to embody two largely unpopular positions: first, as a front for the Communist Party and second, as a proponent for encouraging American entry into another European war.

Nonetheless, Ruthven's initial decision to oust seventeen members of the group (some of whom were reinstated rather quickly) proved surprising and garnered national media attention. Articles with titles like "Michigan Wants No Ism Students" appeared in the *New York Sun*, while another article from the *Pathfinder* declared "last week Michigan's prexy implemented his words with deeds. To seven students, all living in the east, went curt letters informing them that they would not be readmitted to class when school opens next fall. . . . The common denominator of the chastised undergraduates was their membership in the American Student Union, a loose-knit campus organization originally founded by Communists, swelled by a merger with a Socialist group, and now composed mainly of youths affiliated with neither party."[3] The issue did not abate during the summer

---

3. "Michigan Wants No Ism Students," *New York Sun*, June 27, 1940; "Michigan Stir," *Pathfinder* [n.d.]; both are clippings attached to letters in Ruthven, box 58, folder 2,

recess: a Michigan Committee of Academic Freedom emerged to defend the students and demand their reinstatement.[4] The committee held a mock trial of Ruthven in November 1940 while the Michigan chapter of the ASU vigorously protested the dismissals. As in 1935, Ruthven's office received numerous letters both in support and in bitter denunciation of his actions. On campus, the speculation for Ruthven's motives circulated ever more vigorously. Ruthven's strident commencement speech and the dismissals that followed almost immediately seemed to have emanated as a bolt from the blue.

Historians have had a difficult time accounting for Ruthven's strident tone and his seemingly unprovoked decision to dismiss a far higher number of students than he did five years earlier. The official university history fails to provide a clear reason for the president's actions, essentially accepting Ruthven's claim that the students were dismissed because they were "disruptive of the good order of the University."[5] Ruthven's biographer, Peter Van de Water, admits that the president's papers "do not shed much light on the reasons for dismissal" but avers that it was largely due to the students' active participation in the ASU.[6] This argument appears to have received some substantiation in a *Michigan Today* article on the dismissals which argued that Ruthven cracked down on the ASU for its neutrality stance.[7] Kristine LaLonde's senior thesis from 1991 suggests that the president's actions against the ASU had more to do with the president's protracted fight over

BHL. *Prexy* is an old colloquialism for president. The quoted total of seven students suggests that news outlets were unable to obtain a confirmed number of dismissed students. Other sources reported nine and thirteen, respectively.

4. On this committee, see Johnson, *Maurice Sugar*, 232.

5. Peckham, Steneck, and Steneck, *Making*, states on page 222 that nine students were dismissed. Van de Water, *Alexander Grant Ruthven*, states seventeen. In truth, both are correct: seventeen being the initial number of students dismissed, or warned, nine being the eventual number of students who were not reinstated.

6. Van de Water, *Alexander Grant Ruthven*, 145.

7. Tobin, "Doves of 1940."

control of the *Michigan Daily* and its governing Board in Control of Student Publications as well as the "pressures for national conformity" due to the increasingly impending war waging across the seas.[8] An online exhibition of photos by the Ann Arbor District Library shows an October 1940 walkout in support of the dismissed students and also attributes Ruthven's decision to the ASU's "radical and fifth column activities."[9]

Although all these explanations contain elements of truth, each falls short of providing a satisfactory account of Ruthven's decision to launch a wider crackdown than he had in 1935. Van de Water and LaLonde suggest that the ASU's policy of neutrality played a decisive role in the president's action. However, neither author had the benefit of Robert Cohen's *When the Old Left Was Young*, which observed that by the spring of 1940, the broader volte-face of Communist politics had fatally weakened the ASU. Following the Molotov-Ribbentrop pact of August 1939, the ASU lost considerable credibility on the nation's campuses after it abandoned its anti-fascist activism in order to hew the new Stalinist line of appeasing the Nazis and furthering the Soviet Union's own expansionist ambitions. "The ASU," Cohen writes, "could not long endure once student disillusionment with the communists' flip-flops on foreign policy, their abandonment of anti-fascism, and their defense of Soviet aggression [against Finland], had set in."[10] James Tobin, who cites Cohen's work in his article, does not mention the declining fortunes of the ASU during the 1939–40 academic year. On the face of it, it makes little sense that the president would likely have invited a barrage of public and private criticism by repressing a campus organization that historians claim was beginning to decline especially following its dramatic

8. LaLonde, "Student Activism," 39.

9. Ann Arbor District Library, "Hugo Reichard and the Campus Radicals of 1940," https://aadl.org/node/347740. [Accessed March 1, 2020].

10. Cohen, *When the Old Left Was Young*, 306.

turn to neutrality in August 1939 after many years of advocating anti-fascist intervention.

Indeed, the justifications that Ruthven ultimately used for his decision to bar individual students were non-political, deliberately vague, and seemingly padded. They featured items such as the misrepresentation of a residence "as a result of which the State of Michigan was cheated out of non-resident tuition"; falsification of applications for use of Michigan facilities; attempts to interfere with residence hall operations; interference with the work of freshmen; jamming locks on university buildings; attempts to incite racial antagonisms; and dishonesty in conference with university officials.[11] In their public pronouncements, and even in much of their private correspondence, Ruthven and members of his administration claimed that the students had not been dismissed due to their political affiliations and activities.

What is surprising is that historians have failed to account for the fact that many Michigan students at the time had their own ideas about what lay behind Ruthven's 1940 dismissals. Indeed, it appears that the University of Michigan students of the time proved a lot more incisive about these events than later accounts by historians. Moreover, almost as a reenactment of Miller's *Honors at Dawn*, the story involves the influence of big business and, in a departure from Miller's argument, flagrant efforts by antisemites and people on the extreme Right to force Ruthven to curtail political pluralism on campus. Indeed, one Michigan student, a sophomore named Robert Copp, published an especially popular theory in the pages of the *New Republic*:

> It is possible that an unfair share of the blame for fascist conditions at Michigan has been put on President Ruthven. . . . Numerous people on the campus are anxious to take the blame from his shoulders and place it where it belongs: on the legislature and

11. Van de Water, *Alexander Grant Ruthven*, 147–48.

on the interests that control the legislature. That the Ford Motor Company is one of these is a commonplace. It is said here that Regent Harry Kipke, who was practically elected by Harry Bennett, the Ford "personnel" director, presented Mr. Ruthven with an astounding list of one hundred persons he wanted expelled from the university last spring.[12]

Copp was hardly alone in surmising that Ruthven had been pressured by the Ford Motor Company acting through the recently elected University of Michigan regent and former Michigan football coach Harry Kipke to crack down on the ASU. Notes from a floor discussion during the 1941 Winter Parley recount the following observation: "on academic freedom—missed something centering on 13 expelled students. Money behind school does not like the A S U or radical groups. Is that the cause of the cut in the budget, or merely an excuse."[13] Indeed, a continuous theme that runs through the discourse of the dismissal controversy—at least among some students—was the extent to which it occurred by virtue of outside factors such as Harry Bennett and his close friendship with the recently installed regent and former football coach.

In this chapter, we trace this "Kipke connection" and determine to what extent Ruthven's final crackdown on the student

12. Robert Copp, "Michigan, Ford's Football," *New Republic*, January 6, 1941, 23–24. In a December 2015 interview with the authors, the ninety-five-year-old Copp could not recall from whom he had heard about the existence of this list. However, Copp generously recalled many stories about the University of Michigan at that time for which we are grateful. The papers in Ruthven's archives contain a typed transcript of Copp's *New Republic* article with a handwritten note inquiring into Copp's residence in Ann Arbor. Copp recalled that he was given a warning by his supervisor at the library where he had a job, but to Ruthven's credit suffered no other sanction. The transcript to Copp's letter is located in Ruthven, box 58, folder 3, BHL.

13. "The Future and the Student's Relation to It," Winter Parley, January 1941, 2, Blakeman, box 3, BHL. In 1940, the parley was apparently moved back to the end of the fall term, rather than the spring, in order to encourage more student participation.

Left in June 1940, which involved the dismissal of a disproportionate number of Jewish students relative to the composition of
the ASU as a whole, happened due to outside pressure coming
from Ford through his surrogates. The evidence strongly suggests
that both Ford operatives like Harry Bennett and Kipke as well
as antisemites like Elizabeth Dilling believed the campus to be a
hotbed of communism that was largely, though not solely, instigated by Jewish students. Given the context of Kipke's accession
to the Board of Regents in 1940 and the active student hostility to
this, the return of the state government to Republican control in
1939, and the increasing demands for isolationism, it is likely that
Ruthven responded to outside pressure when he moved against
the ASU in the summer of 1940. Following the summer crackdown, the university suspended the ASU in December of 1940.
Additionally, the legacy of East Coast Jewish radicalism abated
considerably. The political agency of Jewish students diminished
within the much tighter boundaries in which it now operated
compared to previous years concentrating largely on relief work
sponsored by Hillel that fitted more comfortably into Ruthven's
view of campus pluralism. In order to understand how outside
antisemitism played a role in this final assault on the ASU, we
must carefully trace the often-murky relationships that led to the
instalment of Harry Kipke to the position of regent of the University of Michigan.

"Unsavory Connections": Ford, Bennett, and Kipke

It is not surprising to discover that prominent business leaders
frequently complained about the presence of left-wing radicals on
college campuses in the 1930s. Roger Magnuson's 1963 dissertation shows that, even before the First World War, Michigan businesses were blaming immigrants for the presence of socialism
in the state's classrooms.[14] As retired Packard chairman, Henry

14. Magnuson, "Concern of Organized Business," 111.

B. Joy, curtly wrote, in response to an inquiry, "I am at a loss how to answer your inquiry as to how best to combat the Red activities at the University of Michigan, which have been quite obvious for years."[15] Indeed, we already suggested that one motivation for Ruthven's dismissals in 1935 was his concern to appear "soft" on communism in the face of the Republican governor and legislature.

From describing communism as an unwanted European import, it was but a short step to equating Jews with Communists. Kristen Fermaglich's article on the April 1935 conservative suppression of the Social Problem Club's peace march at Michigan State College in East Lansing shows that mobs taunted a Jewish speaker with cries of "Comrade" and "Back to Russia."[16] The Reverend William Howe, a pastor at St. Paul's Evangelical Church in Ann Arbor, made the same point more explicitly in a letter to Joy. "As you know," he averred in the midst of defending Hitler's elimination of the German Communist Party, "the leaders of the Communists are Jews."[17] By the late 1930s, of course, another Detroit-area preacher had built a large public following in part by propagating this very premise. By 1938, Father Charles Coughlin, priest of the National Shrine of the Little Flower church in Royal Oak, Michigan, who had gained fame for his weekly radio program, had veered from his earlier support of Roosevelt and the New Deal toward an open embrace of the most egregious forms of antisemitism. His late 1930s broadcasts endorsed the *Protocols of the Elders of Zion* and this screed's long-discredited argument

---

15. Joy to Linton B. Dimond, letter dated March 13, 1935, Joy, box 6, folder April–July 9, 1935, BHL. This is also quoted in Magnuson, "Concern of Organized Business," 123.

16. Fermaglich, "Social Problems Club Riot," 107.

17. Rather confusingly, Howe goes on to state that the Jews' "flag—as a Jew told me some time ago—is the dollar bill," thereby combining in one paragraph the far Right's dual condemnation of Jews as both fomenting worldwide communist conspiracies and simultaneously controlling the levers of capitalist financial power. See Howe to Joy, letter dated August 5, 1936, Joy, box 7, folder Aug 4–13, 1936, BHL.

about a secret Jewish conspiracy to attain worldwide financial and political domination. Coughlin also claimed that Jews propagated, led and financed the Bolshevik Revolution. As Coughlin claimed during one broadcast, "the achievement, the Russian Jewish Revolution destined to figure in history as the overshadowing result of the World War, was largely the outcome of Jewish thinking and Jewish discontent, of Jewish effort to reconstruct."[18]

One of Coughlin's supporters was Henry Ford. The great automobile industrialist had long harbored, and expressed, deeply ingrained prejudices against Jews both because he saw them as propagating worldwide communism and because of their presumed control over international finance.[19] While the origins of Ford's antisemitism remain contentious with historians continuing their debates on this topic, his early experiences in financing his initial ventures led him to distrust bankers whom he viewed as predatory and associated with Jews. Consequently, following the founding of his third, and lasting, company, the Ford Motor Company, in 1903, Ford refused to accept capitalization from Wall Street firms. Ford's antisemitism seems also to have emerged from a frustrated idealism. After all, he was a pacifist who believed that the United States should have stayed out of the European War of 1914. Yet Ford's pacifist initiatives, including a "Peace Ship" voyage to Europe in late 1915 to try to broker peace, met with failure and derision. It was clear that, by the end of the First World War, Ford had, in the words of Neil Baldwin, "metamorphosed from

18. Quoted in Warren, *Radio Priest,* 157.

19. Warren, *Radio Priest,* 146. The origins of Ford's antisemitism have been the source of scholarly debate. Baldwin's *Henry Ford and the Jews* argues that Ford's antisemitism grew out of the negative representation of Jews that he saw in the *McGuffey's Eclectic Readers* that he read in school. Others have taken Baldwin to task for rooting Ford's lifelong virulence to Jews in the school textbooks of his distant past: "Other influences within the culture at the time almost certainly did more to create and sustain prejudice against Jews . . . one can hardly explain Ford's unusually virulent prejudice by referring to a few scattered passages in textbooks also read by many millions of other American children." See Stockton, "McGuffey, Ford, Baldwin, and the Jews," 85–96; quote is on 95.

ignorant idealist to embittered anti-Semite."[20] Following the war, and the high tide of labor activism that immediately followed in its wake, Ford decided to air his beliefs concerning the Jews' role in controlling both international finance and in fostering communism and labor activism by acquiring his own newspaper, the *Dearborn Independent.*

Under the guidance of Ford's private secretary, Ernest G. Liebold, who became the *Independent*'s general manager, the newspaper very quickly took a viciously antisemitic stance soon after Ford purchased it in 1919. From May 1920 through May 1921, the *Independent* ran a series of articles, instigated by Liebold and the paper's editor, William Cameron, under the title "The International Jew". This series purported to be an extended exposé on the "Jewish Question" in the United States; the "question" being that Jews were unable to integrate fully into American culture given their "rootless cosmopolitanism" and their drive for worldwide control of finance. Liebold also saw to it that the *Independent* serialized the *Protocols of the Elders of Zion*, a forged account written by the Tsarist secret police alleging that a secret meeting among Jews occurred with the purpose of attaining world domination. This text had recently been translated into English by the White Russian émigré Boris Brasol.

Prominent Jews themselves were appalled by the *Independent*'s virulent antisemitism but also cautious in responding to the outrages perpetuated by such a powerful figure as Ford. Some of the most anguished were those Jewish individuals who knew Ford personally. Among them were the founder of Temple Beth El and one of Ford's Dearborn neighbors Rabbi Leo Franklin, and Ford's architect, Albert Kahn. Less reluctant was Aaron Sapiro, a young lawyer and activist in the farm cooperative movement in the 1920s. Sapiro's efforts to organize farmers' cooperatives incurred the ire of Henry Ford, himself a former farmer, which spurred a renewed series of antisemitic articles in the *Dearborn Independent*

20. Baldwin, *Henry Ford and the Jews*, 327.

beginning in 1924.[21] After failing to convince Ford to retract the articles written against him and the Jewish people, more broadly, Sapiro filed a suit against Ford for $1 million on the grounds of defamation of character.[22] Although Ford's lawyers deftly prolonged the process for nearly two years, the trial itself—which finally got underway in late 1926—produced a flurry of bad press for Ford. At the same moment, Ford's son, Edsel, was desperate to convince his father to change his business model from producing the same durable, but unchanging, Model T year after production year to a more updated vehicle that offered more options to consumers. By 1926, Ford's sales were in steep decline, and only the abandonment of the Model T was to ensure the company's future. As Baldwin and others have attested, Ford ultimately realized that he needed to improve his public relations "optics" if the company was to change course successfully. Ford ultimately issued an apology to Sapiro and to the Jewish people more broadly in July 1927 and shuttered the *Dearborn Independent* by the end of that year.

Despite Ford's closing of the *Independent*, and his public disavowals of antisemitism, Ford seemed to have never significantly altered his views about Jews and, indeed, grew even more stubborn in his prejudices against them, spurred especially by the rise of labor militancy in the 1930s. Despite the *Dearborn Independent*'s closure, Ford kept its former editor, and author of the "International Jew" articles, William Cameron, employed as a kind of press secretary, while Liebold retained his position as Ford's personal secretary. Indeed, it was Liebold who introduced Ford to Coughlin because of the latter's radio broadcasts that had, in Liebold's words, "talked about Wall Street money interests controlled by Jews. He touched upon the currency issues. . . . They were all matters that Mr. Ford was more or less interested in."[23]

---

21. For more on Sapiro, see Larsen and Erdman, "Aaron Sapiro: Genius of Farm Cooperative Promotion."

22. See Woeste, *Henry Ford's War on Jews*.

23. Liebold quoted in Warren, *Radio Priest*, 146.

Although no hard proof exists, scholars like Donald Warren have argued that Ford probably provided patronage to Coughlin, subsidizing his journal, *Social Justice*, which became increasingly antisemitic in the latter 1930s, often parroting Ford's obsessions with "international Jews" and republishing sections of the *Protocols* in 1938.[24] Indeed, by the late 1930s, Coughlin was far from the only antisemite and reactionary who sought Ford's largesse.

If Ford's name was synonymous with antisemitism in the 1930s, his right-hand man, Harry Bennett, head of Ford's Service Department, was infamous for his ruthless shop floor discipline, his union breaking activities, and the vast patronage and spy network that he developed under Ford's umbrella. The name "Harry Bennett" was one with which many Michiganders were familiar in the 1930s and whom still many recognize as a nefarious character with a violent history. The character of Gunliffe in Miller's *Honors at Dawn* (1937) is a reasonably accurate depiction of him: pugnacious, stubborn, and ready to employ violence as a first response to the sit-down strikers whose actions open the play. For nearly twenty years, Bennett had worked for the Ford Motor Company, reporting directly to Henry Ford himself.[25] Hired by Henry Ford personally while he was furloughed from the Navy in 1916, Bennett became the automaker's brutal right-hand man, enforcing labor discipline on the shop floor, breaking unionization efforts, and implementing whatever other tasks his boss wanted done. Under his reign, Bennett built up Ford's Service Department, which was essentially a "collection of street fighters, ex-convicts, underworld figures, and athletes [that] numbered about three thousand by the early 1930s [and who] . . . dominated daily life at the company."[26]

Bennett became notorious not only for creating an enormous

24. Warren, *Radio Priest*, 149–50.

25. For Bennett, see his autobiography, *We Never Called Him Henry*. Bennett's relationship with Ford is discussed in Brinkley, *Wheels for the World*, 426–32, 469–78, 496–501; Watts, *People's Tycoon*, 446–53. Stefanick's senior honors thesis provides an excellent biography of Bennett, see "Personality and Power in the Ford Motor Company Hierarchy."

26. Watts, *People's Tycoon*, 447.

spy ring that first detected and then punished recalcitrant workers or those who seemed interested in establishing a union at the company but also for the brutally coercive ways with which he broke strikes and demonstrations. In March 1932, Bennett was responsible for repressing the Ford Hunger Strike that saw 3,000 workers march on Ford's Employment Office at the River Rouge plant in Dearborn. Bennett's Service Department worked with the Dearborn police and fire departments to break the strike using both water hoses and gunfire, ultimately costing four strikers their lives. Five years later, Bennett and his men from the Ford Service Department launched the famous Battle of the Overpass when they attacked Walter Reuther and other members of the United Automobile Workers (UAW) who were passing out unionization literature just outside the Rouge plant.

Ford rewarded Bennett's ruthless and successful suppression of every effort to unionize his plants by making him effectively second-in-command of the company by the late 1930s; even top administrative and managerial brass at the company feared Bennett. With his network of undercover spies who populated every shop floor but also the managerial ranks, Bennett knew everything that happened in the company. In turn, Bennett developed a vast patronage network that rewarded loyal friends with jobs for them and their acquaintances. "With control over every job at Ford and most of the local dealerships," Brinkley recounts, "he [Bennett] developed a network of cooperative judges and other politicians in Dearborn and Detroit, and throughout the state of Michigan."[27] Bennett ruled over the Ford Motor Company through fear and intimidation. Thus, for example, he fired over 4,000 Ford workers for their suspected affiliations or even sympathies with the UAW.

Bennett's patronage extended well beyond Dearborn and Detroit and included the college town Ann Arbor. He loved football, and especially the Michigan Wolverines, and took an active interest in some of the players' welfare. Willis Ward, who served as the team's right end from 1932 to 1934 and was—as noted earlier—

27. Brinkley, *Wheels for the World*, 427.

notoriously benched during the Georgia Tech game in October 1934, recalls how Bennett's interest in Michigan football led him to cultivate relationships with the team's players and coaching staff. "Mr. Ford," he recalled, "as I understand it, saw several of those games as well as Mr. Harry Bennett. He became very interested in Michigan football during that period. I think as a result of seeing me out there playing football, some discussion arose as to what I planned and sought as a career. As a result I was given the opportunity of coming into Ford Motor Company on vacations and during weekends while getting my A.B."[28] As Ward attests, Bennett's patronage extended to other team players as well:

> . . . at the same time that I went into Ford Motor Company to work during vacations and on weekends several other boys on the football squad were given the same opportunity. Bill Heston, who was on the team up there, is still with the Ford Motor Company, I understand. Stan Faye was to ultimately become the secretary to Mr. Harry Bennett, and at one time Charles Bernard was head of Plant Production. We had a crackerjack ball club and I came to the plant with the team. I think this was Harry Bennett's way of economically helping out the men who were playing football to get a little extra funds to help them continue on.[29]

Another player who received patronage from Bennett was the team's former star quarterback Harry Newman, who, although never denying his Judaism, did not participate in any Jewish events or belong to any Jewish organizations on the University of Michigan campus. In Bennett's papers, a note from April 1943 reads that Newman "was doing special work for us that termi-

28. Willis F. Ward, "Reminiscences," May 1955, 4, Owen W. Bombard Interviews Series, 1951–1961, accession 65, Benson Ford Research Center (hereafter cited as BFRC). Ward's career with the Ford Motor Company is described in detail in Steward, "In the Shadow," 235–76.

29. Ward, "Reminiscences," 4–5, Owen W. Bombard Interviews Series, 1951–1961, accession 65, BFRC.

nated in 1940 and we were asked by Mr. Bennett to assist Newman in obtaining an account. We lined up Raybestos and Newman, himself, obtained Bishop & Babock."[30] Although the note does not describe the "special work" that Newman did for Ford and Bennett, Baldwin in his *Henry Ford and the Jews* (2002) describes Newman as a "right-hand aide" to Bennett who, in the wake of *Kristallnacht*, accompanied Bennett and Ford to Rabbi Leo Franklin's office in late November 1938 to draft a statement wherein Ford claimed to support Jewish immigration to the United States (this being a mere four months after Ford had received the Grand Cross of the German Eagle from Hitler).[31]

Why did Ford accept Newman, a Jew, not only as an employee but as a trusted associate to his own right-hand man, Bennett? Bennett's memoirs shed some light on this aspect of his boss's antisemitic feelings when it came to individual Jews. "Mr. Ford did, of course," Bennett recalled, "like many Jews and Catholics. But he always had an out. When he liked a Jew—as he did Harry Newman and Hank Greenberg and Judge Harry Keyden and others—he'd say to me, 'Oh, he's mixed, he's not all Jewish.'"[32] Newman's championship winning career at Michigan and, all too briefly, although equally successfully, with the New York Giants and the fact that he did not emphasize or foreground his Jewishness likely helped with his integration into the Ford Motor Company. Newman ultimately became an executive at Ford Motor Company and owned Ford dealerships in Detroit and Denver.

However, Newman was not Bennett's most important connection to the University of Michigan football team. Back in 1933 and 1934, when both Ford and Bennett were beginning to cultivate their interest in the team, Willis Ward recalled that "at the time we had this good ball club Mr. Bennett also met Mr. Harry

30. Note on Harry Newman, dated April 2, 1943, Henry and Clara Ford Estate Records, accession 587, Campsall Files, BFRC.

31. Baldwin, *Henry Ford and the Jews*, 300.

32. Bennett, *We Never Called Him Henry*, 47.

Kipke."[33] In 1934, Kipke was only thirty-five and, as Ward recalled, "was one of the youngest coaches in the business."[34] Kipke first came to Michigan to play under legendary coach, Fielding Yost, for whom he played as a halfback and a punter, proving so successful that he attained the coveted status of All-American in 1922 and became the team captain in 1923.[35] Following graduation, Kipke served as an assistant coach at the University of Missouri for four seasons before becoming head coach for Michigan State College in 1928. He held that position for a single year before Ann Arbor came calling: Yost, his mentor, retired from coaching to become Michigan's athletic director and Kipke was hired as his replacement. Although the 1929 season, Kipke's first at Michigan as its head coach, proved to be rocky, Kipke then hit his stride with an amazing winning streak between 1930 and 1933, when he won four conference championships and two national titles, due in no small part to Harry Newman's brilliance as a quarterback. Ward's account suggests that it was Michigan's winning streak in 1933 that sparked Ford and Bennett's interest in the team. "I went up to Michigan," he recalled, "and being the first colored fellow and being on a team that was a national championship team, and inasmuch as Mr. Bennett was interested in Harry Kipke too as our fortunes rose, he got interested in me particularly. At the same time Mr. Ford [got] interested in me too."[36]

While Newman and Ward parlayed Bennett's interest in them into successful careers at Ford Motor Company, Coach Kipke cultivated a close friendship with Ford's enforcer that proved to be especially lucrative to Kipke but problematic for the University of Michigan. With the wealth stemming from his role as Ford's

33. Ward, "Reminiscences," 5, Owen W. Bombard Interviews Series, 1951–1961, accession 65, BFRC.

34. Ward, "Reminiscences," 6, Owen W. Bombard Interviews Series, 1951–1961, accession 65, BFRC.

35. http://bentley.umich.edu/athdept/football/coaches/hkipke.htm.

36. Ward, "Reminiscences," 6, Owen W. Bombard Interviews Series, 1951–1961, accession 65, BFRC.

right-hand man, Bennett built a luxurious residence, nicknamed the Castle, in Ann Arbor where he and Kipke were neighbors.[37] According to Bennett, Kipke also sought Bennett's help with improving the quality of the football team. "During the early and middle 1930's I tried to help Kipke build better football teams," Bennett recalled. "He told me that he was having trouble building first-rate teams because of a lack of good material, and I did what I could to help him attract more promising men."[38] Kipke had good reason to reach out to his powerful friend: despite winning two national championships in 1932 and 1933, the Wolverines skidded to a tenth-place finish in the 1934 season and struggled to make a 4-4 showing in 1935. Kipke's downward spiral continued into 1936 with a catastrophic 1-7 showing, and, in his final year as coach in 1937, Kipke mustered only another measly 4-4 record.

Along with the Wolverines' stunning reversal of fortune, the nature of Bennett's friendship with Kipke provoked consternation. A circular likely from late 1936 addressed to the "Men of Michigan" complained about Kipke's friendship with Bennett: "Who is this Harry Bennett that shadows Kipke's footsteps or does Kipke shadow Bennett's footsteps?" it asked. It then continued to state sardonically, "We are not presidents of big Alumni Clubs and do not manufacture anything that Ford uses, so Bennett can't say support my pal Kipke or get your contracts cancelled. The worst of it for Michigan is that we believe Bennett has power to do that. Do Michigan men want that kind of power about

37. Culver, "Harry Bennett."

38. Bennett, *We Never Called Him Henry*, 106. Bennett and Kipke's friendship was also detailed in a profile in *Forum* magazine in February 1938: "A fellow trickster is his [Bennett's] good friend, Harry Kipke, until recently head football coach at the U. of M. Benett [*sic*] has always been liberal with summer employment for Michigan athletes; the Ford system, is sprinkled with Michigan's graduated heroes; and a former Michigan football captain is Bennett's personal secretary." See John H. O'Brien, "Henry Ford's Commander in Chief: Harry Bennett and His Private Army," *Forum*, February 1938. A typed transcript of the article is located in Maurice Sugar Collection (hereafter cited as Sugar), accession 232, box 53, folder 53.3: Harry Bennett, WRL.

the campus even for winning teams?"[39] This relationship also increased friction between Kipke and the chairman of the Board in Control of Intercollegiate Athletics, Ralph W. Aigler. "What I did to help Kipke," Bennett recalled, "was to give summer jobs to boys he brought to me. We'd hire them as gate guards or something like that, and then we'd give them an hour off each day to practice in Dearborn."[40] Once Aigler and the board learned that Michigan football players were holding practice on Ford-owned property, an investigation ensued. Moreover, rumors spread that Kipke, who had begun to appeal to Chicago-area alumni to preserve his position after the disastrous 1936 season, was receiving financial assistance from Chicago- and Cleveland-area alumni to support many of the football players.[41]

Despite pressure from Michigan alumni groups from all over the country to retain Kipke, Aigler and the Board in Control of Intercollegiate Athletics fired him in December 1937.[42] The board presented five reasons for its decision, including Kipke's subsidizing of athletes, his incompetence as a coach, his failure to organize his coaching staff, and, two especially important rea-

---

39. "To the Men of Michigan" circular, late 1936 (November 1936 is written in pencil on the typed document). Arthur Stace Papers (hereafter cited as Stace), box 2, folder Papers Concerning Harry Kipke, 1936–1937, BHL. Stace (1875–1950) was a career journalist and was from 1935 editor of the Ann Arbor News. See "Death Takes Arthur Stace, Editor of Ann Arbor News," MD, January 11, 1950.

40. Bennett, We Never Called Him Henry, 106.

41. "Kipke Presents Rocky Road of a Losing Coach," Chicago Daily Tribune, February 2, 1937; and "Michigan Probes 'Salaried Athletes,'" Chicago Daily Tribune, November 10, 1937. Our thanks to Greg Dooley for providing PDF copies of these and other articles about Kipke's firing in late 1937.

42. Ruthven's archives contain numerous letters and petitions from alumni protesting Kipke's firing. See Ruthven, box 18, folder 34, BHL. Kipke's scrapbooks include articles on his firing, but generally those that were sympathetic to him, one of which attributed his firing to "enemies" who were "instrumental in spreading rumors of alumni subsidization of athletes, which prompted the board in control of physical education to announce that it was conducting an investigation." See "Michigan Ousts Kipke as Football Coach," Harry Kipke Papers (Kipke), box 2 scrapbooks, BHL.

sons: "the board objected to his private associates," and Kipke had "tolerated summer practice."[43] Specifically, "the board was informed that Kipke allowed fifteen Michigan football players to practice three and four times a week throughout the last summer while employed at the Ford Motor Company. The players were said to have worked in the service department under Harry Bennett, Ford's personnel director. On practice afternoons, it was reported, they were driven in a truck from their posts about the plant to a remote place on Ford property along the Detroit river shore for practice." Although the article, and none of the sources surveyed, identified Kipke's "private associates" to whom the board objected, it seems quite likely that the board members were referring to Bennett.

For his part, Bennett himself wrote directly to Aigler for an explanation for Kipke's firing. If Aigler's reply is accurate, Bennett chastised the university for criticizing Ford's and his generosity in giving summer employment to the team. Aigler assured Bennett that the board did not object to Ford's employment of the team as such but rather that "the thing that caused us distress about the boys who worked at your plant during the summer was the fact that they indulged in practice that would have to be considered 'organized' and when we learned not so very long ago that they had been provided with pretty full sets of equipment, we could not ignore the incident." Nonetheless, "no one could attach any responsibility for such violations to your Company."[44] Bennett, however, was not buying what he saw as Aigler's mincing explanation. In his reply, Bennett charged that "there has been a long series of indirect communications winding up with your own over the radio in which it is not difficult for anyone to read that the Ford Motor Company's interest in assisting college athletes by employment was due, possibly, to my friendship with Mr. Kipke

43. "Charges Leading to Kipke Ouster Revealed at Michigan," *Chicago Tribune*, December 12, 1937.

44. Aigler to Bennett, letter dated February 28, 1938, Ruthven, box 18, folder 34, BHL.

and may now be changed by the appearance of a new coach."[45] Accusing the administration of showing no interest in its football players' welfare during the summer, Bennett also claimed that the Kipke controversy was the product of an anti-Ford sentiment in Ann Arbor: "The Ford Motor Company has been criticized, unfairly and severely, by you people at Ann Arbor, when it is obvious that the Company is not interested in training football squads." Bennett ended his letter on a threatening note: "the criticism of the Company, originating at Ann Arbor, is not settled and it is my purpose to have it settled in fairness to the Company, if fairness is possible."[46]

Taking umbrage at Bennett's muscling tone, and yet seeking not to make undue accusations against the Ford Motor Company, Aigler responded by angrily averring that "I should not deny your statement that in the minds of a considerable number of people it has been thought that the interest of the Ford Company in assisting college athletes by employment has been due, in a considerable part at least, to your friendship for Harry Kipke."[47] Nonetheless, Aigler insisted that he did not believe that Ford was paying players to practice but that "a boy working for the Ford Company was giving honest service for the compensation he was receiving." Nonetheless, Aigler stated that he had no control over newspaper and popular speculation, that "I have no idea on what basis you refer to 'faculty inspired paragraphs in the Michigan Daily.' I suspect that the Staff of the Daily would resent any suggestion that the faculty could inspire anything therein," and that "no responsible person connected with this University, so far as I know, has ever criticized the Ford Company, for such practice or such issuance of equipment."[48]

Whatever else Kipke's firing accomplished, it clearly exposed

45. Bennett to Aigler, undated [early March 1938], Ruthven, box 18, folder 34, BHL.

46. Bennett to Aigler, undated [early March 1938], Ruthven, box 18, folder 34, BHL.

47. Bennett to Aigler, undated [early March 1938], Ruthven, box 18, folder 34, BHL.

48. Bennett to Aigler, undated [early March 1938], Ruthven, box 18, folder 34, BHL.

a rift between Harry Bennett, and through him, the Ford Motor Company, with the university. Bennett's surviving letter to Aigler indicates that he, at least, perceived an anti-Ford bias among the university community and particularly the faculty. Bennett attributed Kipke's ouster to the Michigan faculty's envy over Kipke's remuneration: "the coaches at the university had been getting salary raises and the teachers had not. This made the professors jealous and bitter against Kipke. Also, they felt that under his regime too much of the university's attentions was going into athletics and too little into education."[49] For its part, the university stuck to its guns and hired Princeton football coach Fritz Crisler to replace Kipke for the 1938 season.

However, Kipke did not remain unemployed for very long. Ford offered Kipke a job as a plant supervisor, but the former coach preferred to go into sales work. As an internal Ford document later noted, "Mr. Harry Bennett asked if we could find something for Kipke. Collins-Aikman were linked up with a promise of an increase in business. The Colonial Woolen Mills were also handled on the same basis. Believe that the Sparks-Withington and Eagle-Ottawa Leather were obtained as accounts by Kipke himself."[50] Kipke served as the middleman between Ford and these suppliers, extracting a healthy sales commission; Bennett's autobiography was unabashed in admitting the extent to which he and Ford had assisted Kipke: "we built Kipke a house near Ann Arbor. We gave him two boats, a sailboat and a cruiser, one of which he later paid for. . . . The two accounts we gave Kipke, and the one he got himself, proved much more lucrative than I had anticipated—and more than Kipke admitted."[51]

Yet Bennett's largesse had another purpose. With Kipke set up as a well-compensated Ford loyalist "at my suggestion and at

49. Bennett, *We Never Called Him Henry*, 106.

50. Internal memo titled "Harry Kipke" and dated April 2, 1943, Office of Henry Ford and Clara Ford, accession 587, Campsall Files, BFRC.

51. Bennett, *We Never Called Him Henry*, 107.

my expense," Bennett encouraged Kipke to run for an open seat on the University of Michigan's Board of Regents in early 1939. If victorious, Bennett and Ford would have their company man on Michigan's Board of Regents.

Kipke, Dilling, and the Rightward Drift

Kipke's candidacy for a seat on the Board of Regents was unprecedented. Members of the Board of Regents had usually come from the academic, legal, or business professions and were men of high standing within their respective domains. Kipke, by contrast, was a former football player and a recently fired football coach who had only worked in the private sector for a single year. Moreover, as his relationship with Bennett was well known in Ann Arbor, many people in the university community saw his nomination as a political machination on the part of Ford and the Michigan Republican Party to gain influence over the University of Michigan. Indeed, Kipke's nomination for the position on the Board of Regents of the University of Michigan occurred at a Republican Party convention in Flint in February 1939 when the powerful Wayne County (Detroit) and Kent County (Grand Rapids) party leaders backed him over a challenger.[52]

Many within the university community were skeptical of, if not downright hostile to, Kipke's candidacy. One female student survey respondent said, "whether he will be out to even up the score [over his firing] we cannot say. Certainly he will be in a position to cause no small amount of uneasiness to the central figures in last year's l'affaire Kipke."[53] The Student Senate approved a resolution calling on Michigan's voters to "unconditionally repudiate" Kipke's candidacy claiming that "Mr. Kipke's background as discharged football coach does not indicate the

52. San M. Swinton, "Harry Kipke Gets GOP Nomination for Regents Post," *MD*, February 24, 1939.

53. Morton L. Linder, "God, Dorms, and Anti-Semitism Seen Major Campus Questions," *MD*, February 26, 1939.

necessary qualifications for a Regent of the University" and that his candidacy "is detrimental to the best interest of the general student body, faculty, and administration of the University of Michigan."[54] A Student Non-Partisan Committee on the Election of Regents sponsored a writing contest on "Why I Object to the Election of Kipke on the Board of Regents."[55] Ironically some alumni groups, who had supported Kipke after his termination as football coach, also opposed his candidacy on the grounds that it was "'engineered' by Edward N. Barnard, Wayne County political boss; Frank D. McKay, Grand Rapids political power broker, and Harry Bennett, personnel director of the Ford Motor Co."[56] A group of retired deans also opposed Kipke's nomination due to his perceived unfitness for such a high-level academic position. Moreover, an Alumni Committee urged Michigan's 15,000 public school teachers to vote against Kipke.[57] The Student Senate ultimately proposed that Kipke's nomination be subjected to a campus referendum all the while asking the campus to repudiate the nominee "because of his affiliations, his connection with machine politics, and his lack of training for the position."[58]

Letters to the *Daily* editor fretted that Kipke's election would be a catastrophe for the university's integrity. As one letter writer put it:

> In defense of Kipke, it is only fair to recognize that he is an average man, with no unusual ability, but, also with no flagrant faults. Further, because of the very nature of the Board of Regents, Kipke personally could do nothing villainous or destructive, even should he so desire.

54. "Student Senate Demands State Defeat Kipke for Regency," *MD*, March 22, 1939.
55. "Prize Winner Rejects Kipke Contest Award," *MD*, March 31, 1939.
56. "Kipke Defeat Urged by Alumni Group," *MD*, March 24, 1939.
57. "Retired Deans Rebuke Kipke for Candidacy," *MD*, March 31, 1939.
58. "Student Senate Will Consider Poll on Kipke," *MD*, March 28, 1939.

However, the forces responsible for his nomination can do the Board, and, through them, the University, great and lasting harm. Kipke's nomination was a coalition forced by his influential friends in the Republican party. Since many Republican leaders have openly voiced their opposition to the nomination, it is evident that a minority group has employed old unscrupulous political intrigue in this instance . . . **It is this possibility for political exploitation which threatens the very structure of our institution.** As has been the case in certain other State Universities, such an occurrence would result in discord and decadence, and Michigan would soon lose its high position in American education.[59]

For his part, Kipke remained rather sheepish toward this vocal opposition. He regarded the Student Senate's motion against him as a "thoughtless, not to say indiscreet student action" and averred "I am quite sure that if given the opportunity of talking with the boys, I could quickly change their minds."[60] Nevertheless, he declined an invitation to speak to the Student Senate.[61]

Despite the hostile reaction on campus, Kipke was swept onto the Board of Regents in April 1939 in the second wave of Republican victories that solidified the party's re-conquest of power in the state.[62] Come January 1940, when Kipke was to be sworn in, President Ruthven would have to contend with a regent who was a disgraced ex-coach, a loyalist of Bennett and Ford, and who had the backing of the resurgent Republican Party in Lansing.[63] Ben-

59. William Gram and Stanley Duffendack, "Kipke and Political Deeds," *MD*, March 25, 1939. The boldfaced text is in the original source.

60. "Student Senate Demands State Defeat Kipke for Regency," *MD*, March 22, 1939.

61. "Kipke Declines Senate Request to Speak Here," *MD*, March 30, 1939.

62. The first wave occurred the previous November when the Republican Frank Fitzgerald replaced Democrat Frank Murphy as Governor. See "Kipke, Herbert Sweep Regency Vote; Republicans Gain Heavily; Ann Arbor Supports Dr. Myers," *MD*, April 4, 1939.

63. That Kipke and Bennett were active in supporting conservatives is shown in a

nett's autobiography effectively admits that Kipke's installation was due to Republican machinations: "There was considerable opposition to Kipke's candidacy, but thanks to the help of Frank McKay, Republican boss of Michigan, Kipke was elected, to the chagrin of all his enemies within that seat of learning."[64]

Whereas Kipke's election was undoubtedly a major victory for Bennett, the ex-coach was not the only person whom Bennett used to 'get back' at the university. Around the time that he was helping to advance Kipke's election, Bennett received a visit from Elizabeth Dilling, a vehemently antisemitic author who had made a reputation for herself in right-wing circles by penning anti-Communist tracts like *The Red Network: A Who's Who Handbook of Radicalism for Patriots* (1934). Dilling, the wealthy wife of a Chicago lawyer, had developed her anti-Communist politics after a series of trips to Europe in the 1920s. A journey to the Soviet Union in 1931 convinced her that communism was a threat to Christianity.[65] She began speaking about the horrors she claimed to have witnessed in the Soviet Union, and her popularity increased throughout the Midwest and East Coast. Dilling began to catalog what she perceived as every Communist and pro-Communist organization in the United States, which ultimately evolved into *The Red Network*. Dilling's investigation into Communist Party activity also led her to become a strident antisemite. "Dilling claimed she had not set out to slander Jews," the historian Glen Jeansonne, writes, "but once she began investigating communism, she inevitably traced Marxism to its source. 'Sound Jews deplore the fact that no one with open eyes can observe a Red parade, a communist, anar-

letter written by Miller Dunckel, state treasurer under Republican Governor Frank Fitzgerald in 1940, and co-author of the anti-Communist Dunckel-Baldwin Bill in 1935. In the letter, dated July 18, 1940, he writes "Harry Kipke, Harry Toy and Harry Bennett are all back of me 1000%, and are doing wonderful work down in Wayne Country in my behalf." Dunckel to Herbert, letter dated July 18, 1940, Joseph Herbert Papers (Herbert), box 1, folder Correspondence 1940–1941, BHL.

64. Bennett, *We Never Called Him Henry*, 107.

65. On Dilling, see Jeansonne, *Women of the Far Right*, 10–28, 73–86, and *passim*.

chist, socialist, or radical meeting anywhere in the world without noting the prominence of Jewry.'"[66] Dilling, like Henry Ford,
was a bitter opponent of Franklin Roosevelt.[67] She claimed that
Roosevelt's "Jew Deal" was "implementing Marx's measures for
communizing a nation, such as the abolition of private property, a
progressive income tax, restriction of inheritances and the confis-
cation of dissidents' property."[68] Although Dilling never attained
the kind of national popularity enjoyed by Father Coughlin or the
antisemitic Christian Nationalist preacher Gerald L. K. Smith,
who established himself in Michigan in 1939 and would run for
the U.S. Senate in 1942, Dilling managed to attract some wealthy
business-based backers including the former Packard chairman
Henry Joy. She also founded her own (very modest) organization,
the Patriotic Research Bureau.

Hoping to find another patron in Henry Ford—"the inspira-
tion and financial godfather to dozens of antisemitic propagan-
dists," as Jeansonne describes him—Dilling soon came knocking
on Bennett's door.[69] Bennett's autobiography paints this encounter rather dismissively, as though he had been asked by Ford to
deal with this importunate woman who was becoming a nuisance:
"This was just about the time when Kipke was running for a place
on the University of Michigan's Board of Regents. To give Liz
something to do, I sent her to Ann Arbor to get some dope on
Communists there, thinking she might provide some ammuni-
tion for Kipke to use against the faculty. Actually, she did a pretty
good job, although probably not much better than any compe-
tent newspaperman might have done."[70] However much Bennett
wished later to minimize the importance of his dispatching Dill-

66. Jeansonne, *Women of the Far Right*, 26.

67. Bennett claims that one reason why Ford accepted the Grand Cross of the
German Eagle from Nazi Germany in July 1938 was that it would anger Roosevelt
because "Mr. Ford hated Roosevelt." See *We Never Called Him Henry*, 120.

68. Jeansonne, *Women of the Far Right*, 23.

69. Jeansonne, *Women of the Far Right*, 32.

70. Bennett, *We Never Called Him Henry*, 127.

ing to the University of Michigan, it seemed sufficiently concerning to some people that Ruthven received an anonymous letter in July 1939 [Figure 6.1] informing him of Dilling's Ann Arbor forays:

> Kipke and Harry Bennett have been paying Mrs. Elizabeth Dilling of "Red Network" fame. See July Mercury for details—to spy on you and the faculty of the University. She boasts that Harry Bennett has paid her $5,000 for this work and also says that Henry Ford is backing her.
>
> She has spent much time recently spying on different professors. She says the University [is] reeking with communism. I have her entire connection and will come to see you when time permits. Mrs. Dilling is working connection with the Germand [sic] Bund.
>
> She was carried to and from the University by a "Captain Parkney" [Pokorny] who is working under Bennett and Kipke. You make investigation and you will find this information correct.[71]

Dilling presented her "dope" to Bennett in the form of a typed ninety-six-page report that claimed that there was widespread communist influence and activities at the University of Michigan.[72] "The University of Michigan," she claims in her overture, "supported by the taxpaying 'fathers' of Michigan, is typical of those American colleges which have permitted Marxist-bitten, professional theorists to inoculate wholesome American youths with their collectivist propaganda.[73] No stone remained unturned

71. Anonymous [Yours for Fair Play] to Ruthven, letter dated July 24, 1939, Ruthven, box 25, folder 8, BHL.

72. The report, "Radicalism in the University of Michigan" [undated but likely spring 1939], is located in the files of Bennett's assistant, John E. Pokorny Papers (hereafter cited as Pokorny), box 2, Labadie Collection, Harlan A. Hatcher Library, University of Michigan (hereafter cited as HHL). Pokorny was an assistant to Harry Bennett and active in veterans and patriotic organizations during the 1930s.

73. Dilling, "Radicalism," 2.

C O P Y   Mrs. Dilling

July 24, 1939

Dr. Alexander G. Ruthven,
President University of Michigan,
Ann Arbor, Michigan.

Dear Sir:

There is a matter that you should know that
is soon to break. Kipke and Harry Bennett have
been paying Mrs. Elizabeth Dilling of "Red Network"
fame. See July Mercury for details - to spy on
you and the faculty of the University. She boasts
that Harry Bennett has paid her $5,000 for this
work and also says that Henry Ford is backing her.

She has spent much time recently spying on
different professors. She says the University if
reeking with communism. I have her entire connection
and will come to see you when time permits. Mrs.
Dilling is working connection with the Germand Bund.

She was carried to and from the University by
a "Captain Parkney" who is working under Bennett
and Kipke. You make investigation and you will
find this information correct.

I am withholding name until I see you this fall.

Yours for Fair Play.

Figure 6.1 [Anonymous letter to President Ruthven], Ruthven box 25, folder 8, Bentley Historical Library, University of Michigan

in Dilling's encyclopedic exposé. Thus, she portrayed the *Michigan Daily* as a communist redoubt that had lambasted Henry Ford in a July 1938 editorial. She claimed that the student literary magazine *Perspectives* featured radical items on the International Brigades. She wrote that communist and pacifist films like *Grand Illusion* ran on campus. Lastly, among other similar alarmist items, she warned that Communist Party–backed sex education and Freudianism were breaking down inhibitions and fostering immorality among students.[74] Dilling even found space to take up Kipke's cause in the concluding pages of her report: "a constant harangue has been carried on against . . . Harry Kipke, in the radically-controlled Michigan Daily. The most 'serious' charge made against him while he was running as candidate for Regent of the University was that he was favored for the post by Henry Ford's personnel director, Harry Bennett."[75] Finally, Dilling predicted that "Mr. Kipke's position as Regent will be a most difficult and unenviable one if he fights in behalf of Americanism with the courage he exhibited on the football field. He will receive the most bitter attacks from militant, well-organized, minority radical forces, if he attempts to curb Red teachings at the University of Michigan."[76]

More telling were Dilling's efforts to repaint Ruthven's own brand of religious pluralism with a red brush. She smeared Edward Blakeman, Ruthven's Counselor in Religious Education, "in connection with his activities in the very red Methodist Federation of Social Services, the Fellowship of Reconciliation, and the Christian, and the Christian Social Action Movement."[77] She also accused the latter group of "putting over Red propaganda under the guise of Christian 'pacifism.'"[78] Dilling's report tarred Hillel as much by dint of its Jewish character as by its association with Blakeman, as well as because of the putatively communist politics of its national leader, Abram L. Sachar, and the roster of "red" speakers that the foundation hosted during her brief time on the Michigan campus. Moreover, Dilling's report denounced B'nai B'rith, Hillel's national patron, as a "world-wide, pro-Communist,

74. For the reference to the July 17, 1938, editorial against Henry Ford, see Dilling, "Radicalism," 93.

75. Dilling, "Radicalism," 94.

76. Dilling, "Radicalism," 95.

77. Dilling, "Radicalism," 37.

78. Dilling, "Radicalism," 39.

anti-Christian organization [that] is narrowly Jewish in its inner literature" and an organization that fosters immoral tracts like the French socialist and prime minister Leon Blum's book about free love, *Du Mariage*.[79] Dilling then cast Ruthven's pluralism policy as a means for preventing the Christianization of young people. Referring to Ruthven's attendance at a dinner for outgoing Hillel director Rabbi Heller, Dilling characterized this gesture as "thus was a man [Heller], employed by a Red-defending B'nai B'rith saving Jewish students from being Christianized, praised by the University's President and its 'Christian' Religious Counselor."[80]

If castigating Ruthven's own religious pluralist initiatives was not enough, Dilling's report goes so far as to accuse Ruthven himself of endorsing the ASU's political program. Citing articles from the *Michigan Daily* from late April 1939, Dilling argued that the president's support of the Human Rights Roll Call, which she claimed was formulated by the ASU, was at best a case of woeful naïveté on Ruthven's part. "Anyone informed, as President Ruthven should be, knows very well that Communist organizations are not working for democratic principles but for Red dictatorship."[81] Overall, however, Dilling's report gives the strong impression that Ruthven was allowing the campus to be overrun by leftist speakers, groups, and activities. Speakers from the national ASU like Molly Yard and Joseph Lash were sponsored by the Student Religious Association (SRA), the ASU, and the American League for Peace and Democracy; students ran for Student Senate election on liberal and progressive platforms; Communist books lurked in the library stacks; and increasing numbers of students were taking up such left-wing causes as Spain, Negro liberation, anti-fascism, and sex education. Indeed, "long before President Ruthven endorsed the communist American Student Union program, American Student Union meetings were held on University

79. Dilling, "Radicalism," 42–43.
80. Dilling, "Radicalism," 47–48.
81. Dilling, "Radicalism," 4.

premises, announced on University bulletin boards, and in the Michigan Daily."[82] So permissive, according to Dilling, was Ruthven's administration to all things communist and leftist, that it had even allowed an Anti-Fascist Rally on April 20 "as part of the nation-wide Red program in schools for that day. . . . The rally was managed by the Young Communist League members, one of whose 'mass' vehicles is the American Student Union."[83] Ultimately, Dilling's report pours scorn on practically every aspect of Ruthven's leadership, especially in characterizing his own efforts at creating a religious pluralism and interfaith atmosphere as both undermining "good" Christian morality and as permitting radical groups to infiltrate the campus.

Nonetheless, it is difficult to know what exactly to make of Dilling's report. That Bennett received it and read it is certain, not only because it appears in his assistant's papers but also because he complimented her in his autobiography for having done a "good job." Yet we have not found any specific and actual *use* that either Bennett or Ford (assuming that he knew of this report) made of this document. Bennett seemed to be eager to get rid of the pestering, insistent Dilling: when she asked for additional funds to go to Europe to conduct more research on communism, Bennett quickly arranged to give her five thousand dollars to get her out of town.[84] Yet Dilling's material also provided a series of concrete attacks on Ruthven's pluralistic policy and its, in her view, naïve coddling or active collaboration with the radical Left, backed up by "proof" (mainly excerpts from the *Michigan Daily*), should anyone wish to use it as such.[85]

82. Dilling, "Radicalism," 81.

83. Dilling, "Radicalism," 49.

84. Bennett, *We Never Called Him Henry*, 127. One product of her further research was her most explicitly antisemitic tract, *The Octopus* (1940), which accused the Anti-Defamation League of seeking to engineer a Communist Party coup in the United States.

85. Philip Slomovitz, former president of Michigan Menorah and editor of the *Detroit Jewish Chronicle,* told an interesting story to his interviewer Robert Rockaway. He

Another brief report in John E. Pokorny's files suggests that Bennett had more than one person spying in Ann Arbor. There is a brief one-page account of the informant's attendance of a Young Communist League-supported course on Soviet history at the Ann Arbor Unitarian Church in April 1939. This person also observed a majority of the attendees of this course "on the occasion of the 'Peace Strike' which was supposed to be sponsored by a campus committee but in reality by the radical American Student Union and the Young Communist League."[86] Finally, the Pokorny files show that Bennett created, or received, lists of known Communists residing in the Detroit area. Although an Ann Arbor list is not among these papers, the existence of these lists provides further proof that Bennett's spy network gathered information on likely Communists and that he reported these individuals to the authorities.

Bennett's and Dilling's activities were just two efforts among many that sought to intimidate and expose Communists, Jews,

---

recalled being invited by Bennett to meet with him in Henry Ford's private dining room. Slomovitz went, accompanied by Harry Newman, the former All-American player from Michigan. At the meeting Bennett insisted to Slomovitz that Ford was not an antisemite and furthermore that paying $5,000 to Dilling was no big deal. Based on the advice of his lawyer, Slomovitz opted not to publish an editorial about the meeting. "'Harry Bennett,' Slomovitz's lawyer told him, "said that Rabbi Franklin [Rabbi Leo Franklin, of Temple Beth El] was a liar after they had met a short time ago, in an effort by Rabbi Franklin to get Ford to denounce Nazism. Ford consented and then he reneged. Just as Harry Bennett called Leo Franklin a liar,' he says, 'he'll call you a liar.'" Slomovitz also penned an essay about this encounter, and about Harry Bennett more generally, upon the latter's publication of his autobiography, *We Never Called Him Henry*. He rebuked Bennett for humiliating Franklin by denying the veracity of Ford's published disavowal of his antisemitism. Slomovitz's essay contended that "Bennett sat in on the Franklin-Ford meeting when the anti-Nazi statement was penned. He could have affirmed the truth of the statement without giving courage to Coughlin's anti-Semitism." See Rockaway, "To Speak Out Without Malice: An Interview With Philip Slomovitz, Jewish Journalist," 10. Slomovitz's essay is located in Philip P. Slomovitz collection, box 17, accession 1494, Reuther Library, WSU.

86. Untitled, undated report [likely spring 1939], Pokorny, box 1, Labadie Collection, HHL.

and members of the Left. In May 1938, the United States Congress established the House Un-American Activities Committee (HUAC) chaired by Martin Dies, a conservative Democrat from Texas who had broken with President Roosevelt and the New Deal over the president's tacit support of the sit-down strike of 1936–37.[87] The Dies Committee, as it came to be called, actively investigated political radicals on college campuses focusing especially on faculty members and left-wing political groups like the ASU. In October 1938, eight Michigan professors were summoned to appear before the Dies Committee by the chairman of the Michigan committee for un-American activities. The professors were investigated for providing aid to the Spanish republic.[88] Michigan's Democratic governor, Frank Murphy in turn accused the committee of being a tool for the Republican Party.[89] In response, conservatives accused Roosevelt and Murphy for shirking their responsibilities to end the Flint sit-down strike of December 1936 to February 1937.[90] In the end, Murphy lost re-election in the gubernatorial race of November 1938 to conservative Republican Frank Fitzgerald for a second, non-consecutive term.[91]

Thus, following the setbacks they experienced after the 1936 election, when Roosevelt was re-elected, the Right was resurgent

87. For the creation of the Dies Committee, see Schrecker, *Many Are the Crimes*, 90–94.

88. "Faculty Members Ridicule Charges of Dies Committee," *MD*, October 14, 1938.

89. "Governor Attacks Dies Probe; Pledges State Reorganization," *MD*, October 25, 1938.

90. "Mr. Lawrence and Governor Murphy . . . ," *MD*, October 30, 1938.

91. Schrecker claims that the HUAC hearings in Detroit caused Murphy ultimately to lose his re-election bid. See *Many Are the Crimes*, 92. Murphy's support of labor, especially during the Flint Sit Down Strike of December 1936-Feburary 1937, alienated conservatives while many left-wing groups felt that the governor had not advanced an ambitious enough reform program to alleviate the ongoing misery of the Depression. Unable to ride Roosevelt's coattails into re-election in November 1938, he lost to Fitzgerald and the state government returned to Republican control. Fitzgerald died early in his term and was replaced by the lieutenant governor, Luren Dickinson. Consequently, Ruthven faced another conservative governor and legislature beginning in early 1939. Dunbar and May, *Michigan: History of the Wolverine State*, 530-31.

in Michigan by early 1939: not only did a conservative Republican replace a liberal Democratic governor but, in addition, the Dies Committee's hearings in Detroit were starting to target educators. The committee had publicized charges that ten Detroit public school teachers were Communists. It then proceeded to conduct a three-month investigation of these charges.[92] Campus radicals like the ASU members and other students registered alarm over the Dies Committee's growing reach. Claiming that there was a "vast undercurrent that is carrying American public opinion to the extreme right," one student editorialist, Hervie Haufler, who later served as editor at the *Michigan Daily*, wrote that "it remained for the House of Representatives to climax this trend when, by a vote of 344 to 35, it granted $100,000 to the Dies committee so that progressives can be ferreted out as 'Reds' on a more grandiose scale than ever."[93] Students perceived the Dies Committee's action as a growing threat to their academic careers. "Whether the majority of students at Michigan imagine themselves to be in sympathy with activities of the Dies Committee or whether they are simply ignorant of them," one member of the ASU named Richard Bennett [no relation to Harry Bennett, we presume] wrote in an editorial in November 1939, "one thing is certain: each student . . . will be affected by any such investigation, if not directly, then indirectly by witnessing the general suspension of his friends, or (if he be friendless) by the obfuscation and final obliteration of cultural progress here at the university."[94]

The *Daily* editorial also delineated in prescient detail how investigations by the Dies Committee on college campuses was leading to purges of left-wing students and an abrogation of their civil liberties: "The first step is to weed out the communists. These are then identified with 'radicals' and 'left-wingers.' But

---

92. Schrecker, *No Ivory Tower*, 71. The ten teachers were ultimately cleared of all charges.

93. Hervie Haufler, "Burn the Witch . . . ," *MD*, February 14, 1939.

94. Richard Bennett, "Progressive Movements on Campus Are Menaced by New Dies Demand," *MD*, November 21, 1939.

the term 'left-wingers' is so broad that it comes to mean anyone advocating a single liberal or progressive view. . . . The progressive college paper, which had been working in the interest of the student body as a whole, is 'purged' or silenced at once—naturally. All organizations active for the maintenance of democratic rights are suppressed." Bennett's editorial then connects the suppression of civil liberties specifically to the Jews: "It is found that the Jew has been active in the preservation of those rights, since he is constantly reminded that it is the 'alien' who bears the brunt of the first anti-democratic attack: so the Jew is identified with communism (if you doubt it, talk with supposed 'liberals' on the campus and mark their statements anent the 'racial' problem) and his loss of educational privilege becomes effective."[95] As for Jews themselves, the *B'nai B'rith Hillel News* for the Michigan chapter opposed the ways in which Jews were being targeted for persecution, even though Hillel itself remained, as always, distant to the radical Left: "Criticism of them should NEVER take the form of Dies persecution, or F.B.I. raids; criticism of their position must come from an appreciation of their work in labor and politics, and from an understanding of the profound motivations that impel many of them."[96]

In this increasingly conservative—even reactionary—environment, activities that the ASU either sponsored or merely contributed to could only further the accusations of right-wingers like Dilling and Bennett that the university was excessively tolerant of political radicalism and radical Jews. One such event was a rally in February 1940 in defense of progressive groups whose members had been arrested in a series of FBI raids.[97] The ASU also helped to organize both an all-campus rally for peace and a roll-

95. Bennett goes on to say, "For different but obvious reasons the Negro follows suit. And concomitant with all this the faculty is 'investigated,' the curriculum is altered, and the students are regimented and drilled in a scholastic desert." Bennett, "Progress Movements on Campus Are Menaced by New Dies Demand."
96. "Ours Is to Ask and Reasons Why," *BBHN*, March 1940.
97. "Campus Civil Liberties Rally to Hear Knox," *MD*, February 15, 1940.

call for peace "to give concrete expression to the desire for peace evidenced by 3,000 students who attended the All-Campus Peace Rally on April 19."[98]

Ruthven's growing frustration over his awkward position between left-wing student agitation and right-wing pressure appears evident in his speech at the Hillel Annual Banquet held in April 1940 in which he forcefully reasserted his vision of a *religiously* motivated pluralism: "Concisely, I am disappointed with our Jewish students. If it is any comfort to you, I am also disappointed with our Christian students, Mohammedan students, and with those of other faiths on the campus. Education must have a religious foundation or it is not education in the best sense of the term, and yet observe the number of students who go on departmentalizing their activities and thinking, over-emphasizing the superficial things of life, and neglecting the faiths to which they give lip service."[99] Instead, Ruthven admonished his audience of Jewish students to remember that the essence of Judaism was to build a moral order of existence "leading necessarily to the spiritual union of all" inasmuch as the Jewish religion "is above all universal, not national or racial. If this work is faithfully performed, then the Foundation will be serving not only the Jewish student but also the University, because it will be assisting all students." For Ruthven, building a religiously plural campus remained fundamental to his vision and, as in his earlier efforts to save Hillel during the depths of the Depression, he envisioned Judaism as playing a pivotal and integrative role in this process. Not coincidentally, this religious pluralism was far more palatable to the university's rightwing critics—except, perhaps, antisemites like Elizabeth Dilling—than Ruthven's toleration of the ASU and its radical activities such as the April 1940 peace rally.

Thus, Ruthven's decision to dismiss over a dozen students from the university in mid-June 1940, just after the end of the

98. "ASU Will Take United Roll Call Against Wars," *MD*, April 30, 1940.
99. "Pres. Ruthven's April Address," *BBHN*, November 1940.

academic year, was in keeping with his pluralist vision. His form of pluralism extended to religiously defined student populations, but those who were outside of this framework, especially if they were Jews, placed themselves at risk. And as his commencement speech in June noted, Ruthven defined the boundaries of his pluralism not in terms of ethnicity but political ideology: "The University of Michigan is an institution of the people, and its staff must continue to insist that Americans who prefer to live under other forms of government are at heart *unfriendly aliens who have no right to the benefits provided by our schools.*"[100]

The connection between having an anti-democratic position in politics and possessing alien status was a particularly salient one in this view: the one assumed the other. Aliens introduced anti-democratic politics to the university, and those who were anti-democratic, or even critical of democracy, were aliens. Dismissing a disproportionate number of Jewish students followed entirely from Ruthven's perspective. But it is important to remember that this credo emerged at a time when the political environment surrounding the university was growing more difficult due to the ascendancy of Republicans in Lansing and the actions of right-wingers bent on demonstrating the pervasive presence of anti-Americanism on college campuses.

Conclusion

The boundaries of Ruthven's pluralism became ever harder during the last two years of the 1930s and in 1940. The president and his vision of a great university became the victims of two antagonistic forces that weaponized politics on the Michigan campus at this time. On the one hand, there emerged a massively powerful rightward drift that derived much of its power from sources beyond the walls of the university and resided in the nervous

100. Alexander Ruthven, commencement address, 1940, https://bentley.umich.edu/legacy-support/commence/; emphasis added.

capitalism of nearby Detroit, aided by an increasingly reactionary state government and much more threateningly by gangster-like strong-arm methods that always hinted at violence. On the other hand, there continued a palpable presence of left-wing actors on campus who still represented an irritant to the president's vision and policies at the university. It is clear that Ruthven had to heed the powerful conservative elements in the state—the state government and large industrialists like Ford—more than he had to tolerate the behavior of a relatively small band of left-wing students on his campus.

Working within an increasingly conservative environment in which the Dies Committee was actively investigating alleged Communists on American campuses, the president also had to face Harry Kipke, an ex-coach and Ford loyalist and good friend of Harry Bennett, as a regent. Moreover, Dilling's report, which was in Bennett's possession and which smeared Ruthven's beloved pluralistic program with Communist associations, provided potential fodder for the Dies Committee to justify looking into subversion at the state's flagship university. And, just as in 1935, Ruthven singled out a particular body of East Coast students—over half of them Jews—for dismissal as a means of appeasing the forces arrayed against the university. Unlike in 1935, Ruthven evidently felt that this time dismissing a mere four students was not enough. Whether Copp's assertion that Kipke gave Ruthven a list of one hundred students whom Bennett wanted to see dismissed was true or not, we have no way of telling. What we do know, however, with some certainty is that the president clearly decided that the time had come to end the ASU's influence on campus. His commencement speech set the tone and provided a rationale for what was to follow.

CHAPTER SEVEN

THE LIMITS OF PLURALISM, 1940–41

O n June 18, 1940, three days after Ruthven gave his commencement speech, letters went out from President Ruthven's office to over a dozen students stating curtly, "It is the decision of the authorities of the University of Michigan that you cannot be readmitted to the University."[1] That day, some other students received a slightly modified version from the president's office that stated that they could not be readmitted without the president's approval, which he would grant only upon having conducted a personal interview with the student. The president "will return to Ann Arbor about the middle of September and, if you care to have an interview with me between that time and the opening of the regular session, you may call my office." This in effect left these students' statuses in limbo over the long summer months, their continued education at the University of Michigan uncertain until the start of the new academic year.[2]

Ruthven's letters provided the dismissed students with no

1. Mimeographed copies of these letters are located in Ruthven, box 58, folder 11, BHL.

2. See Ruthven to Morris Gleicher, mimeographed letter dated June 18, 1940, Ruthven, box 58, folder 11, BHL.

explanations for his action. Many of the students and their parents, understandably confused and upset, wrote the president to demand an explanation. Many of the responses that the president received expressed a sense of trauma and the negative impact that the dismissals threatened to have on the students' aspirations. David Rinzberg, a dental surgeon in Brooklyn and father of Nathaniel, a graduate student in psychology, implored the president to reconsider his decision. "I earned my education through bitter struggle," he wrote. "I am at present living very meagerly from hand to mouth without any reserves for a rainy day. I am looking forward to assistance from my children as I have already passed my fifty-seventh birthday. If my son is punished, I am sentenced to despair."[3] Louis Forman, the brother of another dismissed student, Yale Forman, also wrote to Ruthven to explain the impact that Yale's dismissal would have on the family. "First it would be seriously detrimental to my father's health if Yale were not enrolled in some University next semester and," he continued, "secondly, Yale is very young, only 19, and we are convinced that his entire future lies in the benefits of a complete education."[4]

The dismissed students themselves wrote letters of protest to Ruthven and the administration and in certain cases tried to use their family or personal connections to change the president's mind. Howard Moss had just finished his freshman year when he was dismissed by Ruthven because he "affected the lives of first year men in the University," according to the president.[5] The son of a prominent New York businessman who had shown in his first year at Michigan "considerable ability in the field of creative

3. David Rinzberg to Ruthven, letter dated September 25, 1940, Ruthven, box 58, folder 11, BHL.

4. Louis Forman to Ruthven, letter dated August 29, 1940, Ruthven, box 58, folder 11, BHL.

5. Ruthven to David L. Moss, letter dated July 5, 1940, Ruthven, box 58, folder 11, BHL. Howard Moss' name appears in Ira Smith's interview schedule for June 7, 1939, with a handwritten circled 'J' by his name. See the interview sheet titled "Wednesday Morning - June 7" in Smith, box 4, folder 43, BHL.

writing," Moss enlisted the assistance of the poet Louis Unter-meyer for his cause.[6] Although Untermeyer could not speak to the actual accusations that the administration made against Moss, "I think the boy appealed to me for help because I showed an inter-est in his work and thought he showed promise as a poet—the more so, since his poetry was both experimental and mature for a freshman."[7] Hilda Rosenbaum's cousin, Eugene Rostow of Yale Law School, challenged the arbitrariness of the university's actions: "I feel sure that it is not your purpose to deny students, against whom such serious administrative action has been taken, the essentials of a fair hearing—an opportunity to be heard in their own behalf, to confront hostile witnesses and to controvert if possible the evidence against them."[8]

Yet for many of these students, though not all, President Ruthven and his administration remained stonily resistant to any reconsideration request, even as the initial charges issued in Ruthven's letter failed to specify what concrete behavior had led to the students' removal. In August 1940, Yale For-man wrote to the president, "I have just received your letter of August 10th and I notice that you make no mention of any of the questions which I have put to you. Thus far I have written

6. The assessment of Moss's creative ability is in a letter from W. B. Rea, assistant dean of students, to C. A. Smith of the University of Wisconsin, where Moss would be transferred to, along with two other dismissed students, and where he would finish his undergraduate studies before embarking on a notable career as a poet and editor at the *New Yorker*. See Rea to Smith, letter dated July 27, 1940, Ruthven, box 58, folder 11, BHL.

7. Untermeyer to Ruthven, letter dated June 26, 1940, Ruthven, box 58, folder 11, BHL.

8. Rostow to Ruthven, letter dated July 23, 1940, Ruthven, box 58, folder 11, BHL. Rostow would serve as Under Secretary of State for Political Affairs under President Lyndon Johnson from 1966 to 1969. Hilda Rosenbaum's name appears in Ira Smith's interview sheets. While there is no circled "J" by her name, the later ASU Draft Report confirms that she is Jewish. See the interview sheet titled "Tuesday Morning - June 6" in Smith, box 4, folder 43, BHL. For the ASU Draft Report, see CRC, series 8, box 76, folder Letters and Information from Dismissed Students, Walter Reuther Library (WRL), Wayne State University.

to you thrice—twice from Detroit on July 5th and July 23rd, and once on August 7th from Staten Island, N.Y., and as yet I have received no answer to any of my questions."[9] Nathaniel Rinzberg addressed a letter to Ruthven, complaining that the president had initiated this action without any warning and that "in the letter neither the authorities nor the facts involved are stated."[10] In another letter, he asked if he could sit for the exams for his master's degree that August, as he had already completed all the required coursework. Ruthven's response came nearly three weeks later: "it is our conclusion that you should not be allowed to complete the requirements for the Master's degree at the University of Michigan."[11] Howard Moss appealed to his relative youth and naïveté about the radical group, the American Student Union (ASU), with which he had begun associating in his second semester on campus. "The status of this organization on the campus was not clearly defined to my knowledge at that time," he explained. "I can truthfully say that I did not know how objectionable these activities were to the administration at that time."[12] This carried no weight with the president, as he told Howard's father, "several parents are saddened by the discipline which we have had to mete out to their sons, and they could not feel satisfied if the boy who had influenced theirs should be allowed to return on the mere promise to cease his activities."[13]

In certain cases, the university inflated fairly mild behavior into justifications for dismissal. Hilda Rosenbaum's mother, Sarah, wrote to Provost Frank Robbins on behalf of Hilda when she failed to hear back from Ruthven. Her letter was referred to the dean of women, Alice C. Lloyd, who proffered an explanation

9. Forman to Ruthven, letter dated August 20, 1940, Ruthven, box 58, folder 11, BHL.
10. N. Rinzberg to Ruthven, letter dated June 20, 1940, Ruthven, box 58, folder 11, BHL.
11. Ruthven to N. Rinzberg, letter dated July 15, 1940, Ruthven, box 58, folder 11, BHL.
12. Moss to Ruthven, letter dated June 26, 1940, Ruthven, box 58, folder 11, BHL.
13. Ruthven to David Moss, letter July 5, 1940, Ruthven, box 58, folder 11, BHL.

to Mrs. Rosenbaum for her daughter's dismissal: "I think if Hilda will be quite frank with you, you will understand why it seems better that she should not return to the University of Michigan. She organized the distribution of pamphlets at the dormitory in which she lived the second semester and she herself took part on several occasions in placing such literature in the lockers of the dormitory staff. This was not done openly or honestly, but in the middle of the night, as she knew very well that interference with the staff by the students would not be tolerated."[14] For good measure, Dean Lloyd also stated that Hilda and several other students used one of the university buildings on a Sunday afternoon, "when the building was supposed to be closed, for a meeting. This is very definitely against the regulations of the University."

Hugo Reichard, a graduate student in the English department, wrote President Ruthven to inquire as to the reason for his "exclusion from the University."[15] In his reply, Ruthven formulated an explanation that he later used whenever he was accused of unfairly expelling these students without providing any form of due process: "If your expulsion from the University were being considered, charges would be preferred and you would have a trial. May I call your attention to the fact that you are only being asked not to return. It is sufficient to say that the proper University officers would prefer to have you complete your work elsewhere."[16] After receiving this curt response, Reichard wrote the president again, more testily, asking, "May I call attention to the fact that you have completely ignored my repeated requests for an explanation of why I am being barred from the University. You have ignored my request for a statement on any possible relationship between your commencement remarks against 'subversive activities' and

14. Lloyd to S. Rosenbaum, mimeographed letter dated July 5, 1940, Ruthven, box 58, folder 11, BHL.

15. H. Reichard to Ruthven, letter dated June 21, 1940, Ruthven, box 58, folder 11, BHL.

16. Ruthven to H. Reichard, mimeographed letter dated July 2, 1940, Ruthven, box 58, folder 11, BHL.

my exclusion. You have ignored my request for an open, explicit statement of the charges which have been regarded by the University authorities as grounds for exclusion."[17] President Ruthven simply ignored Reichard's demands for a statement explaining his dismissal, and his request for an open hearing of his case. When Reichard's brother wrote a letter imploring Ruthven to reconsider, given the sacrifices that the family had made on Hugo's behalf, Ruthven replied, "you will understand, of course, that this is not expulsion. He is quite free to enter any other university." The president continued to offer his rationale for Reichard's dismissal: "In regard to his activities, I can only say that he belongs to a group of students, the members of which were by their activities and propaganda seriously interfering with the work of the other students. We have no desire to change Hugo's way of thinking, although we may not agree with his ideas. We must insist, however, that, if he intends to work on his fellow students, it must be in some other institution."[18] All of the students whose letters, and those by their families and supporters, we quoted were in good academic standing and had not suffered serious—or any—disciplinary measures in the past. None of the cited students, unlike some others who received letters in June 1940, were let off with a warning, and all of them were Jewish.

As the dismissals erupted into a public controversy that exceeded the outcry over the parallel events in 1935, Ruthven and his administration adhered to their two overriding contentions: (1) that the students were not *expelled*, which would have hindered their efforts to complete their education at another university, but merely *dismissed*, which gave them the chance to complete their education at other institutions, and (2) that the students were not dismissed on account of their political convictions but because their (unspecified) behavior was disruptive to the university community. Ruthven's administration consistently

17. Reichard to Ruthven, letter dated July 17, 1940, Ruthven, box 58, folder 11, BHL.

18. Ruthven to A. Reichard, mimeographed letter dated July 15, 1940, Ruthven, box 58, folder 11, BHL.

sought to avoid making the dismissals into an issue of academic freedom and free speech and rather sought to frame the university's actions as the application of appropriate disciplinary measures against unruly students.

In June of 1940, seventeen students received letters of dismissal or warnings that they needed to receive President Ruthven's approval to enroll in the fall term. There was some confusion in the press accounts of the exact number—some accounts mentioned nine, others thirteen. This was due to the fact that some students were dismissed outright and some were warned that they faced dismissal unless they met with the president or a university official. Ultimately, nine students were formally dismissed from the university. The names and hometowns of all seventeen affected students are listed beginning on page 350 (the hometowns are derived either from the address to which the university sent its correspondence or from which the student, or her or his parents, sent their letters to the university). In addition, an early draft pamphlet on the case written primarily by former *Michigan Daily* editor, ASU member, and recent graduate, Elliott Maraniss, called "First Draft OF: Brief of the Case," [Figure 7.1] and which would later be distributed by the Michigan Committee for Academic Freedom with the title *Without Fear or Favor: The Case of the Michigan Students*, is located in the Civil Rights Congress records at Wayne State University's Walter Reuther Library. This draft report provides brief biographies of thirteen of the dismissed students as well as short summaries of their cases. Handwritten notes adjacent to each biography identifies each student's name while the typed bio and summary indicates whether they were Jewish or African American (listed as "Negro" in the report).[19]

The Ruthven administration's own typed list clearly divides those students whom officials intended to dismiss ("not to return") from those whom the university administration intended

---

19. The published pamphlet, *Without Fear or Favor: The Case of the Michigan Students*, that came out in September 1940 omits any mention of the students' racial or ethnic identities. Folder ASU Bimu F24, BHL.

3.

No information as to the number or identity of the students who received letters or as to what action will be taken with regard to them has been issued by the authorities. The following list is based on the statements of the individuals themselves and their acquaintances:

A. Male, Jewish. [*Hugo*] Home - New Jersey. Graduate student in English, did last two years of undergraduate work at Michigan. Excellent scholastic record throughout -- grades of one A and two B's last semester; member of Phi Kappa Phi honorary society, Vice-president of the Student Senate and member of the Spring Parley Committee. He was vice-president of the ASU and was one of the leaders in organizing the Peace Rally at Michigan in April. He also took part in a debate on the ASU program in which he supported the national ASU decision to defeat a resolution condemning the U.SSS.R. for its action in Finland. To his own knowledge or the knowledge of his friends he was guilty of no infraction of disciplinary regulations. President Ruthven refused in a personal interview with this student to reveal what were the charges against him.

B. Male, Jewish. [*Nat*] Home- New York. Graduate student in psychology, did undergraduate work at Michigan. Good student -- held assistantship in his department; all A'S and B's for last two years; three incompletes at the end of last semester, but these are admissable and do not affect a student's scholastic record. Was a member of the ASU and formerly its president; active in many ASU projects. Participated actively in many campus discussions such as the Spring Parley, and was generally considered to have radical opinions. Knows of no infraction of discipline which would justify dismissal. Wrote to authorities on receipt of notice of dismissal and received reply substantially as follows: Surely it is not necessary for me to tell you why it would be better for you to

Figure 7.1: Civil Rights Congress of Michigan Records, box 76, folder "Letters of information from dismissed students - 1940." *First Draft of Brief of the Case*. Walter P. Reuther Library, Archives of Labor and Urban Affairs, Wayne State University. Please note that this initial draft provides the dismissed students' ethnicities. In subsequent drafts, and the resulting publication, *Without Fear or Favor*, this information is omitted.

to warn and then reinstate pending an interview with a university official ("warned") [Figures 7.2 and 7.3]. We took this university list and compared it to the ASU pamphlet draft mentioned above using it as corroborating evidence to denote the ethnicities of the students in the "not to return" category. In the university list below, students confirmed as Jewish are marked with a (J), and those confirmed as African American are marked with (AA)[20]:

[The list of Dismissed (Not to Return) Students and Warned Students are on the following pages, 350, 351, 352.]

20. The typed list of the seventeen dismissed or warned students, along with the university's original action as either "warned" or "not to return," is in Ruthven, box 58, folder 11, BHL. The draft report that confirms the ethnic identities of seven Jewish students and two African Americans, titled "First Draft OF: Brief of the Case," appears in CRC, series 8, box 76, folder Letters and Information from dismissed students—1940, WRL. A second biographical report appears in this folder that provides details on Roger Lawn, Robert Chapman, and Joseph Boyd but not their racial/ethnic identities. However, it is noted that Roger Lawn's family first settled in America in 1630 and that Robert Campbell's family first settled in 1720, which, if true, was well before the era of Jewish migration.

Dismissed (Not To Return)

Roy V. Cooley (AA)	Pontiac, Michigan
Margaret S. Cotton[21]	Cleveland, Ohio
Kenneth G. DeHaney (AA)[22]	Jamaica
Yale Forman (J)	Bayonne, New Jersey
Joan Geiger (likely J)[23]	Woodmere, New York
Holden Hayden[24]	Bedford, Massachusetts

21. In the ASU draft report, Cotton's ethnicity is not specified, unlike that of the Jewish students. Ruthven's files contain a letter written by a lecturer at the university in support of Cotton that averred "Her family background—three generations of which I am acquainted—is of the best." While neither document provides conclusive evidence of her ethnic identity, the fact that she was not identified as Jewish in the draft report, and the fact that she came from a very prominent Midwestern family, indicates that it is highly probable that she was not Jewish. The letter that references her family background: James Marshall Plumer to Ruthven, letter dated August 17, 1940, box 58, folder 11, BHL.

22. While his correspondence features his Ann Arbor address in a June 1940 letter to Ruthven, DeHaney refers to himself as a "foreign student." See DeHaney to Ruthven, letter dated June 28, 1940. On a mimeographed copy of Ruthven's list of the seventeen dismissed students, a handwritten note next to DeHaney's name reads "Jamaica—British citizen." For both see Ruthven, box 58, folder 11, BHL.

23. Although Geiger does not appear in the ASU draft report, we surmise that she is likely Jewish by dint of her surname and her home in the Borough of Queens in New York City. However, the lack of evidence makes it impossible to ascertain this with complete certainty.

24. Ruthven's files contain nothing pertaining to Hayden except his dismissal notice. In the ASU draft report, he is noted as "Joe Hayden" and described as originally from Massachusetts. The draft report does not indicate that he is Jewish. In fact, the Haydens were a prominent family in Bedford, Massachusetts. One Arthur Holden Hayden was a graduate of Harvard University in 1918 and, with his wife Virginia, had a son Arthur Holden Hayden, 2nd, in October 1920. There are several indications that Arthur 2nd was indeed the Holden Hayden on the dismissal list. First, his hometown on the university's dismissal list is Bedford; second, his birthdate of October 21, 1920, would have made him a sophomore in the 1939-40 academic year. In August 1953, Hayden was interrogated by the California Senate Fact-Finding Committee on Un-American Activities in San Francisco where the report gave his birthdate as October 21, 1920, and that he "resided in Michigan during 1939 and possibly a part of 1942." There is no evidence that the university reinstated him after

John Cresswell Keats[25]   East Orange, New Jersey
Howard L. Moss (J)   New York, New York
Hugo M. Reichard (J)   South Plainfield, New Jersey
Nathaniel Rinzberg (J)   Brooklyn, New York
Hilda Rosenbaum (J)   Brookfield, Connecticut
Abraham B. Stavitsky (J)[26]   Newark, New Jersey

his dismissal. Moreover, given the prominence of the Hayden family in Bedford, which went back at least to the 1860s, we are confident that Holden Hayden was not Jewish. Hayden's birth announcement is in the *Harvard Alumni Bulletin,* volume 23 (1921), 375: For information about the Haydens in Bedford, see Julia McCay Turner, "A Slice of History: Bedford Springs, the New York Pharmaceutical Company, and the Hayden House," *The Bedford Citizen* (July 6, 2018). For Hayden's testimony to the Un-American Activities committee, see *Eighth Report of the Senate Fact-Finding Committee on Un-American Activities 1955.* (Sacramento: California State Senate, 1955), 403–04.

25. There is no mention of Keats in the ASU draft report and the correspondence about him in Ruthven's files provides no indication of his ethnicity. His *New York Times* obituary states that he was born in Moultrie, Georgia, but does not provide any family history. No further information is provided in his *Wikipedia* entry. Yet, we deem it highly likely that he was not Jewish based on his family surname. Keats' *New York Times* obituary is accessible at https://www.nytimes.com/2000/11/24/arts/john-keats-79-a-writer-who-noted-american-foibles-and-obsessions.html. Like Margaret Cotton, Ruthven's files indicate that Keats was reinstated in August 1940 but had decided instead to enter the University of Pennsylvania. See Rea to Keats, letter dated August 30, 1940, for the university's notice of his reinstatement and Harold Keats (John's father) to Rea, letter dated September 9, 1940, informing the dean that John had already started at Penn. Both letters are in Ruthven, box 58, folder 11, BHL.

26. In a letter to Ruthven's biographer, Peter Van de Water, Stavitsky stated that he had already completed his master of science degree at Michigan before Ruthven's dismissal letters went out: "I had completed my education at Michigan, had no intention of returning there." Stavitsky to Van de Water, letter dated April 19, 1970, Van de Water, box 519-I, BHL. The authors wish to thank Michelle McClellan for providing us with copies of Van de Water's correspondence with the dismissed students.

Warned

Joseph F. Boyd, Jr. (AA)	Saint Louis, Missouri
Robert L. Chapman	Detroit, Michigan
Philip D. Cummins[27]	Ann Arbor, Michigan
Morris Gleicher (J)	Detroit, Michigan
Roger Lawn	New York, New York

Immediately striking is how all but one of the students known to be Jewish were on the administration's "not to return" list and that only one Jewish student, Gleicher, was placed on the "warned" list. Indeed, the list also shows the far greater number of East Coast students who were denoted as "not to return," compared with students from other regions. The results become even more striking considering that two of the "not to return" students— Roy V. Cooley and Kenneth G. DeHaney, both of whom were not from the East Coast—were African American students whose sit-

27. According to Assistant Dean Rea's handwritten report, Cummins withdrew from the university on June 6, 1940, "upon recommendation of Health Service (nervous breakdown)," although a dismissal notice was sent to his address at 1402 Henry St. in Ann Arbor on June 18. He was hospitalized soon thereafter and would suffer from mental health issues for the remainder of his life. For obvious reasons, Ruthven's files contain no other documentation on his case. Assistant Dean Rea's notes state that Cummins was "very active in radical groups—distributed literature to leaders who met at League (History Club). He and his sister, Mary, have been outstanding in several such groups." According to David Maraniss, Cummins had been active, with his older brother, Bob, on the Michigan campus "in the cause of establishing worker rights for Michigan students who were employed by restaurants and other establishments in town or who had found jobs through the New Deal's National Youth Administration." Phil would suffer a mental breakdown during the war and was diagnosed with schizophrenic disorder. His sister, Mary Cummins, married Elliott Maraniss, member of the ASU and writer and editorial director for the *Michigan Daily* from 1937 to 1940, while they were at Michigan. Based on internal correspondence in the Civil Rights Congress files, Maraniss was the principal writer of the *Without Fear or Favor* on behalf of the dismissed students. For the Maraniss and Cummins families, see Maraniss, *Good American Family*, quote is on page 82. For Maraniss's authorship of the pamphlet, see Ed Magdol to Bernard Goodman, letter dated August 20, 1940, CRC, series 8, box 76, folder ASU, WRL.

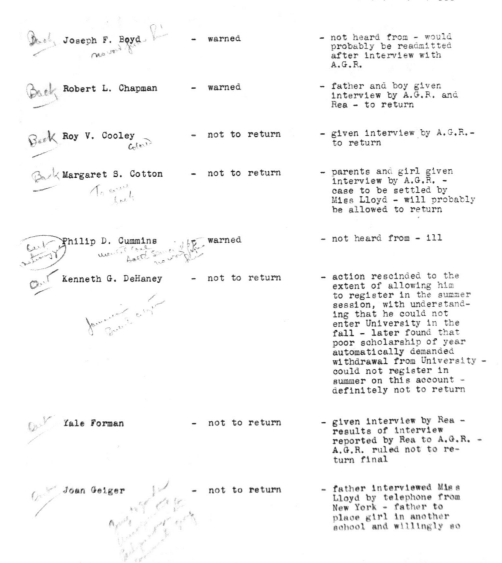

Joseph F. Boyd	– warned	– not heard from – would probably be readmitted after interview with A.G.R.
Robert L. Chapman	– warned	– father and boy given interview by A.G.R. and Rea – to return
Roy V. Cooley	– not to return	– given interview by A.G.R.– to return
Margaret S. Cotton	– not to return	– parents and girl given interview by A.G.R. – case to be settled by Miss Lloyd – will probably be allowed to return
Philip D. Cummins	– warned	– not heard from – ill
Kenneth G. DeHaney	– not to return	– action rescinded to the extent of allowing him to register in the summer session, with understanding that he could not enter University in the fall – later found that poor scholarship of year automatically demanded withdrawal from University – could not register in summer on this account – definitely not to return
Yale Forman	– not to return	– given interview by Rea – results of interview reported by Rea to A.G.R. – A.G.R. ruled not to return final
Joan Geiger	– not to return	– father interviewed Miss Lloyd by telephone from New York – father to place girl in another school and willingly so

Figure 7.2: [List of dismissed and warned students, page 1], Ruthven box 58, folder 11, Bentley Historical Library, University of Michigan

-2-

Morris Gleicher	- warned	-	given interview by AG.R. and Rea - may seek readmission in fall - if so, undoubtedly will be allowed to return
Holden Hayden	- not to return	-	not heard from
John C. Keats	- not to return	-	reinstated by A.G.R. for purposes of clear record for admission elsewhere - not to return to University
Roger Lawn	- warned	-	correspondence with father - allowed by A.G.R. to return
David L. Moss	- not to return	-	interviewed by Rea - results of interview reported to A.G.R. - not to return action stands
Hugo M. Reichard	- not to return	-	given interviews by A.G.R. and Rea - not to return action stands
Nathaniel Rinzberg (now Brooke)	- not to return	-	correspondence with A.G.R. - did not ask for interview - not to return action stands
Hilda Rosenbaum	- not to return	-	correspondence between Miss Lloyd, mother and girl - girl granted interview with Miss Lloyd on Lloyd's return in September - interview not yet held - Miss Lloyd indicates that girl cannot be readmitted if she (Miss Lloyd) is to rule in the case
Abraham B. Stavitsky	- not to return	-	given interview by A.G.R. and Rea - to be readmitted in fall

Figure 7.3: [List of dismissed and warned students, page 2], Ruthven box 58, folder 11, Bentley Historical Library, University of Michigan

uations were somewhat unique. Cooley wrote an appeal letter to President Ruthven in which he admitted to having once been an ASU member but having become disabused of the group's tenuous commitment to democracy "at the time of the vote regarding the Russo-Finnish question, and have not attended a meeting since." Cooley also disavowed any membership in the Civil Rights Federation "or with the Communist Party or any organization that advocates the overthrow of the American government by the use of armed force or is even passively opposed to the democratic form of government."[28] Following additional appeals on Cooley's behalf, Ruthven decided to reinstate him, telling one of Cooley's defenders, "Frankly, I consider that he [Cooley] was more sinned against than sinning. . . . I want to point out to him that he has, by his activities, not only caused himself harm but, what is important, in the opinion of the other colored students, he has brought considerable embarrassment upon them. I think he will see the point and be more careful in the future."

Kenneth DeHaney's dismissal was justified partly due to what the university termed his "poor scholarship" as well as his political activities, especially in connection with an incident that occurred at a popular Ann Arbor restaurant called the Pretzel Bell. In an April 1970 letter to Ruthven's biographer, Peter Van de Water, the now Dr. Roy Cooley recalled that "in the year 1940, there was an attempt by black and white students to alleviate some of the racial discrimination on the university campus, particularly in the areas of restaurants and housing."[29] Cooley claimed that he initiated a lawsuit against one on-campus eatery for discrimination that was quashed by the university authorities but that a second lawsuit was filed against the Pretzel Bell, which was not on campus. The incident that led to the lawsuit against the Pretzel Bell is rather murky. It occurred sometime in the spring of 1940, but there is no account of it in the *Michigan Daily*.[30] According to an ASU mem-

28. Cooley to Ruthven, letter dated July 15, 1940, Ruthven, box 58, folder 11, BHL.
29. Cooley to Van de Water, letter dated April 20, 1970, Van de Water, box 519-I, BHL.
30. The incident is discussed in a paragraph in Smith and Woodman, *Vanishing Ann*

ber, Donald Slaiman, DeHaney and he went into the Pretzel Bell one evening.[31] When they tried to order food, two white employees told DeHaney that they refused to serve him. DeHaney then went to the police station to register a complaint and, according to Slaiman's account, the police agreed to speak with the servers at the Pretzel Bell. DeHaney and Slaiman returned and were served.[32] However, DeHaney told another story about the incident that involved five African Americans. In his own letter to Ruthven, DeHaney explained that "I was alone in the previous Pretzel-Bell issue; that is, I was only active in the incident in which I was

Arbor, 35: "In 1940, students filed a lawsuit against the Pretzel Bell over its refusal to serve customers who were African American. According to the *Michigan Daily*, the suit went nowhere, and some of the students involved were asked not to return to campus for the 1940 fall term." The *Michigan Daily* article is not sourced, however.

31. Donald Slaiman was listed as one of the dismissed students in a draft script for the open hearing on the students' case held in November 1940. However, his name does not appear in any extant university documents or lists as one of the dismissed. While the draft script claims he received the same dismissal notice as the others, no such copy of this notice appears in Ruthven's archives. The draft script also states "it is our impression that his scholarship was poor, but dismissals on that basis are not made in this manner usually." Whatever disciplinary action the university took against Slaiman, it was not part of Ruthven's purge of June 1940, although the organizers of the open hearing lumped it in as such. The draft script for the open hearing is located in CRC, series 8, box 77, folder Hearing—1940, WRL. A native of New York, Slaiman (1919–2000) went on to lead the Detroit office of the Jewish Labor Committee and the Michigan Labor Committee for Human Rights. As assistant director and then director of the civil rights department of the AFL-CIO during the fifties and sixties, he worked to achieve passage of the Civil Rights Act of 1964 and labored for the acceptance of minority members as full and equal union members. In his later life, he was president of the Jewish Labor Committee and chairman of the Social Democrats USA. His October 2000 obituary in the *New York Times* states that he did graduate work in political science at Michigan but does not indicate if he obtained a degree. See https://www.nytimes.com/2000/10/26/us/d-s-slaiman-81-union-official-active-in-civil-rights-movement.html.

32. Donald Slaiman to Rea, undated letter, Ruthven, box 58, folder 11, BHL. Interestingly, Slaiman, who was an ASU member himself, sought in his letter to distance himself from DeHaney: "Since that day our association has really been over. We are acquaintances and little more." Slaiman is described as an ASU member in Dean Rea's handwritten notes located in Ruthven, box 58, folder 11, BHL.

involved. . . . I had nothing to do with the case involving Joseph F. Boyd Jr. [also one of the dismissed seventeen] and the other three colored boys at the Pretzel-Bell."[33] Joseph Boyd himself wrote to Ruthven in June 1940 claiming that he was the instigator of the incident and the litigation at the Pretzel Bell and that none of the others were involved.[34] Only one thing became certain in these contradictory accounts: the Pretzel Bell ended up in court. According to Abram Stavitsky, writing to Van de Water many years later, the Pretzel Bell faced a trial for discrimination. Stavitsky recalled this as "one of the most disillusioning experiences of my life. I was vilified repeatedly, as were others testifying, as 'Eastern, radical, Jews.'"[35] Stavitsky said that the Pretzel Bell was cleared of all charges.[36]

As for DeHaney, Ruthven permitted him to apply to the Administrative Board of the Literary College for permission to enroll for the summer 1940 session only. When the board refused him permission, DeHaney was automatically withdrawn from the uni-

33. DeHaney to Ruthven, letter dated June 24, 1940, Ruthven, box 58, folder 11, BHL. Assistant Dean of Students W. B. Rea, in his handwritten summary of the radical activities of the dismissed students, largely followed Slaiman's account. Under the heading "Kenneth G. DeHaney," he wrote, "Active in promotion of rights of colored people. Created disturbance in Pretzel Bell, in company with Donald Slaiman of A.S.U. by demanding that he be served. Also claimed discrimination by Little Sandwich Shop on State St. Although he has associated with members of A.S.U., DeHaney denies that he is a member of the organization, and contends that he is not a radical." Ruthven, box 58, folder 11, BHL.

34. Boyd to Ruthven, letter dated June 24, 1940, Ruthven, box 58, folder 11, BHL.

35. Stavitsky to Van de Water, letter dated April 19, 1970, Van de Water, box 519-I, BHL.

36. Indeed, in his appeal letter to Ruthven, Stavitsky claimed that it was his appearance at this trial that led to his being associated with the ASU: "the only link between myself and subversive activities on the campus was my testifying at the trial and the allegations of certain individuals, whom I do not know and whom I am willing to face at any time. . . . My record for four and one-half years is absolutely clear of any affiliations with any radical organizations." Stavitsky to Ruthven, letter dated July 27, 1940, Ruthven, box 58, folder 11, BHL.

versity due to his poor academic standing.[37] DeHaney ended up graduating from Howard University two years later.[38]

Along with these two African-American students, there were three other non-Jewish students on the "dismissed (not to return)" list: Margaret Cotton, Holden Hayden, and John Cresswell Keats. Of these three, Cotton was readmitted upon the promise that she would "settle down" and Keats was reinstated although he chose to enter the University of Pennsylvania instead. Only Hayden was not reinstated. Thus, of the five non-Jewish dismissed students, only two (DeHaney and Hayden) were truly dismissed. Of the seven Jewish students who were on the "dismissed (not to return)" list: only one—Stavistky –was reinstated. The favoritism shown by the administration to the non-Jewish students is also indicated by the fact that there was only one Jewish student—Gleicher—on the "warned" list while the four remaining students were either African-American (Boyd) or white (Chapman, Cummins, Lawn). Thus, Jewish students were both over-represented on the "dismissed (not to return) list" and under-represented on the "warned list." Moreover, the Jewish students were more likely than non-Jewish students not to be reinstated. Only one Jewish student of seven on the "dismissed" list was reinstated, while three of the five non-Jews on the same list were allowed back into the university.

Following the pattern that Ruthven established when he approved the creation of interviews for East Coast–based undergraduate applicants, and then with the dismissals of 1935, the president appeared to single out a particular demographic, East Coast Jewish students, for the most severe disciplinary action. Within that geographical subset, the disproportionate number of dismissed students in this group was Jewish. Yet several ques-

37. See Ruthven to DeHaney, mimeographed letter dated November 7, 1940, Ruthven, box 58, folder 11, BHL.

38. A commencement announcement is preserved in Ruthven, box 58, folder 11, BHL.

tions remain about Ruthven's actions of June 1940. First, what indication do we have that Ruthven acted against the students on account of their political beliefs rather than for disciplinary reasons as stated in his administration's official justification for its actions? Second, how did the students, and the broader university community, understand and react to Ruthven's actions? Third, do we have any indication that Ruthven's action may have been shaped by actors such as Kipke and, by extension, Bennett and Ford? And, fourth, to what extent were the students' ethnic identity a factor in their dismissals?

At first blush, the fourth question seems the easiest to answer. Of the twelve dismissed students (that is, those on the "dismissed" and not the "warned" list), we have shown that seven of them were confirmed as Jewish based on the ASU draft report or other sources. Of the remaining five students, we reveal that two were African-American and three were Gentiles based on our analysis of the extant available information of their backgrounds. Jews thus composed over half of the "dismissed" (and not merely "warned") students and were less likely to be reinstated: of the seven "dismissed" Jews, only Stavitsky was reinstated, while of the five "dismissed" non-Jews, three (Cooley, Cotton, and Keats) were reinstated with Keats deciding to go elsewhere. Moreover, as we have shown, only one Jewish student made the "warned" list while four non-Jews did. Thus, while non-Jews were certainly affected, Jewish students—and specifically *East Coast* Jewish students—disproportionately faced arbitrary dismissal and were not given the same opportunity to be reinstated to the same extent as their non-Jewish colleagues.

Thus, as in 1935, a particular subset of student was singled out for dismissal, although perhaps not as blatantly as before. And as Stavitsky's recounting of the Pretzel Bell trial indicated, the coding of "Eastern" and "radical" with "Jew" was well established by the spring of 1940. Moreover, this very type of student stood the least chance of reinstatement following the administration's initial decision to dismiss her or him. Keeping this in mind, there are other indications that the students' ethnicity was likely a factor in their dismissals. However, to answer fully the questions listed above, it is now necessary to explain what happened in the wake of Ruthven's dismissals.

Competing Narratives between the Students and the Ruthven Administration

After the administration issued the dismissals or warning notices in mid-June, the university's initial concern was how to manage the inevitable reaction among the students, their parents and family members, the press, and the broader public. Given that the university sent notices exclusively to members of the ASU or those deemed sympathetic to its ideological orientation, it was clear that the ASU planned to generate publicity against Ruthven very quickly. The administration, then, sought to control the narrative: it treated the dismissals solely as a disciplinary matter by claiming that the students had disrupted the university community. Having heard about the dismissals from their fellow students, members of the *Michigan Daily* staff contacted the president's office on June 24 for a comment. The administration ordered the *Daily*'s reporters to withhold publishing any articles about the dismissals, and the *Daily* did not report on the event until June 29. Tellingly, the *Daily*'s first piece on this issue appeared in the form of a lengthy editorial by a conservative undergraduate supporting the administration's decision.[39]

39. For the charge that the administration ordered the *Daily* not to print anything about the dismissals, see the pamphlet later produced by MCAF, *Without Fear or Favor*, September 1940, folder ASU Bimu F24, BHL. The first article in the *Daily* was an editorial hostile to the ASU and in particular to Hugo Reichard, written by Bill Gram, then a sophomore. Interestingly, Gram uses the same language about the importance of "character" that many eastern colleges had deployed as early as the 1920s to limit the enrollment of Jewish students. While Gram acknowledges Reichard's high scholarly standing, he argues, "The University of Michigan is a cultural institution, and scholarship is only one manifestation of culture. The character and

Ruthven's correspondence also makes it clear that his administration sought to control the flow of information and to shape the narrative. On June 25, W. B. Rea, assistant dean of students, sent a letter to Ruthven at the president's summer residence in Frankfort on the Lake Michigan shoreline.[40] Rea was anxious to inform the president of the ASU's response to the dismissal notes: "Yesterday afternoon twelve members of the ASU met to decide upon a plan of action with regard to some of their members who have been 'expelled.' I cannot name these students, but I have information that they plan to distribute handbills on the Campus this noon, and I will endeavor to secure a sample of the sheet which they will hand out. They are likewise organizing a faculty-student committee to protest this so-called encroachment on academic liberty as an invasion of fascism on the Campus, and the denial of the rights of free speech." Rea proceeded to describe other actions that the ASU was rumored to be considering, which included enlisting the support of the Congress of Industrial Organizations (CIO), initiating a letter writing campaign to demand the dismissed students' reinstatement, and bringing the ASU's national president, Bert Witt, to Ann Arbor for a potential rally or mass meeting. The assistant dean also concluded that the ASU planned to attract the attention of the Detroit papers and that the university had to issue a statement on the dismissals that "might possibly react to our benefit in the minds of many of our good taxpayers and others who have been inclined to criticize the University for the activities of some of our students."[41]

Ruthven then authorized his assistant, Frank E. Robbins, to provide an official statement that was distributed to the press on June 27. The statement, which was published in the *Detroit Free*

personality of the student is equally important. The University, a cultural institution, is right in expecting its representatives to conduct themselves in gentlemanly fashion. The actions of ASU members have, on more than one occasion, been anything but gentlemanly." See Gram, "Expulsions Approved," *MD*, June 29, 1940.

40. Rea to Ruthven, letter dated June 25, 1940, Ruthven, box 58, folder 11, BHL.

41. Rea to Ruthven, June 25, 1940, Ruthven, box 58, folder 11, BHL.

Press the following day, read, "It is a fact that a small number of students have been notified that they may not reregister in the University and that a few others have received warnings. Because the exact disposition of these cases is not yet determined, President Ruthven is not ready to make any further statement now. The University, however, is not concerned about frank discussion leading to a clear understanding of issues, but is concerned with activities likely to prove detrimental either to the work of other University students or to the public interest."[42] In the ambiguity of this statement's language, we see the Ruthven administration walking a fine line while it developed its justifications. The university did not want to appear to be punishing the students for their exercise of free speech or even their political affiliations. Instead, the administration argued that the students' activities—left undefined in the statement—were disruptive to the campus community to the extent that they affected the ability of other students to get their education without disruption. Although almost all the dismissed students were either members of the ASU, or harbored views that were sympathetic with this organization's political orientation, the university justified its actions on the basis of the students' behavior rather than their politics, even though officials, including Ruthven himself, refused to specify what behavioral infractions these students had actually committed.

Accounts by the dismissed students themselves support this interpretation. Following his dismissal and his failure to get into another college, Yale Forman and his mother traveled from New York to Ann Arbor to meet with Ruthven. "There we were told by Ruthven that I had not been dismissed for political activities or beliefs, but because of some question as to the validity of my registration as a Michigan student."[43] Hilda Rosenbaum also recounted

42. Robbins to Ruthven, letter dated June 27, 1940, Ruthven, box 58, folder 12, BHL.

43. Forman to Beatrice Kahn, letter dated October 14, 1940, CRC, series 8, box 76, folder Letters and Information on Dismissed Students, WRL. In a subsequent letter, dated November 6, 1940, Forman claims that at that meeting, Ruthven "denied that he even knew my political opinions." In fact, Forman credited Assistant Dean Rea

her meeting with Assistant Dean Rea who explained to her that "all of this was to break up certain undesirable activities and not against the ASU in particular. But he refused to discuss my case with me and referred me to [Dean of Women, Alice] Lloyd. . . . she evaded every question very shrewdly—(that really isn't the word, but will have to do for present)."[44] Much later, Abram Stavitsky, who ultimately became a Professor of Microbiology at Case Western Reserve University, told Ruthven's biographer Peter Van de Water that "no clear-cut reasons were ever given me for my dismissal." Having already left Ann Arbor with his master's degree in hand, Stavitsky returned to meet with Ruthven after receiving the dismissal notes. The president, Stavitsky recalled, "made many vague remarks about my membership in the Communist party, subversive activities, etc. I never belonged to the Communist Party, but have assumed that I was dismissed because I was involved in a situation at the Pretzel Bell . . . I do not feel that the action was justified—particularly since no reasons ever were given, let alone documented."[45]

While behavioral shortcomings by the students may have been the official line justifying their dismissals, the Ruthven administration's actions were widely recognized as a crackdown on "Red" activity at Michigan. A *Detroit Free Press* article on July 1, titled "'M' Red Ouster Spurs Action" referred to how the "recent expulsion of seven to 10 students for left-wing political activities" had prompted both rebukes by the ASU against Ruthven and more conservative students against the ASU in the pages of the *Michi-*

for his acceptance into Wisconsin. "Rea," he claimed, "it seems, felt pretty much ashamed of Ruthven's hypocrisy, especially after he (Rea) had committed himself to me. He has been very fair to me, and I can frankly say that he has been a friend." Forman to Knox, letter dated November 6, 1940, CRC, series 8, box 76, folder Letters and Information on Dismissed Students, WRL.

44. Rosenbaum to Kahn, letter dated October 12, 1940, CRC, series 8, box 76, folder Letters and Information on Dismissed Students, WRL.

45. Stavitsky to Van de Water, letter dated April 19, 1970, Van de Water, box 519-I, BHL.

gan Daily.[46] A *Detroit Free Press* editorial, published on June 28, warmly endorsed Ruthven's actions and encouraged measures to make it more difficult for non-Michigan-homed students to enroll at the university:

> Clearly the purge is on. And it is a highly timely one. This is no time to provide such young people with a first class, liberal education at expense to Michigan taxpayers. Most of these radical students are reported to come from outside the State, largely from the East. They repay hospitality with ill-manners, ingratitude, and treacherous conduct. It has been suggested that the Board of Regents recently raised materially the tuition to be charged students not residents of Michigan, in part because it was tired of seeing the University treated as an easy mark by young people of this sort. The stand the University authorities are taking against radicalism and subversive infiltrations reveals a watchfulness and sense of responsibility which the people of Michigan cannot fail to appreciate and approve.[47]

A brief column in the *New York Sun* mentioned that the university had barred "7 Undergraduates from Eastern Cities" and reprinted Ruthven's insistence, made in his 1940 commencement address, that Michigan would only admit democratically minded students.[48]

Reactions to the dismissals fell along political lines. Left-wing organizations, faculty and students from different universities, and unions were highly critical of Michigan's actions, whereas conservative groups and alumni applauded Ruthven's measures. In the months following the news of the dismissals, locals from

46. "'M' Red Ouster Spurs Action," *Detroit Free Press*, July 1, 1940, folder ASU Bimu F24, BHL.

47. "Purge at Ann Arbor," *Detroit Free Press*, June 28, 1940, Ruthven, box 58, folder 2, BHL.

48. "Michigan Wants No Ism Students," *New York Sun*, June 28, 1940, Ruthven, box 58, folder 2, BHL.

the United Automobile Workers (UAW) and the CIO sent Ruthven resolutions demanding that the students receive an open hearing, while students and faculty from the University of Wisconsin, Sarah Lawrence, Brooklyn College, Harvard, and Purdue sent telegrams to the president's office asking for the dismissed students' reinstatement or—at a minimum—their being given an opportunity to defend themselves openly.[49] On the other side, Ruthven received many compliments from individuals and groups who were happy to see the president crack down on radical activity. One Dr. W. C. Woolgar from Flint, Michigan, wrote to the president immediately after the *Free Press*'s initial article to exclaim, "if one is to believe what they read in this morning's Free Press, it is with many thanks that they relize [*sic*] that at last there is some one that still sees the light, and is to awaken the rest of the people to the necessity of ridding our schools, as well as country of people that are set to upset [our] Democracy."[50] Woolgar helpfully added "while you and the board are planning on cleaning house, it would be well to look over your Faculty. For no doubt you will find many Radicles [*sic*] there also. For I am firmly convinced that if a man wants his children to be a first class Radical as well as an athetist [*sic*] all they have to do is to send their children to a University."[51] The president of the Second National Bank and Trust Company in Saginaw, Michigan, congratulated Ruthven on his splendid stand "in taking such action as is necessary to rid the University student classes of these damnable raidcals [*sic*] and 'ismites.' I think that old-fashioned Simon-pure patriotism is the big issue today—and Lord knows there is too little of it."[52]

In his responses to both his critics and reporters, as well as to the bewildered parents of the dismissed students, Ruthven insisted that his decision was not based on the students' political

49. These petitions and telegrams are in Ruthven, box 58, folder 2, BHL.
50. Woolgar to Ruthven, letter dated June 28, 1940, Ruthven, box 58, folder 2, BHL.
51. Woolgar to Ruthven, letter dated June 28, 1940, Ruthven, box 58, folder 2, BHL.
52. Shorts to Ruthven, letter dated June 28, 1940, Ruthven, box 58, folder 2, BHL.

affiliations or sympathies but rather that their activities proved disruptive to the campus community. Responding to one correspondent, Ruthven averred, "I can tell you frankly that the students whom we asked not to return to the University were guilty of serious infractions of University rules and regulations. In no case were they asked to leave because of any political ideas they had." In fact, the president argued that "in claiming that they were asked not to return because they are radicals, they are simply putting up a smoke screen to conceal the real reasons for their dismissal."[53] In some correspondence, the president even denied all knowledge of the dismissed students' political activities or leanings: "We were not concerned with the political ideas of these young people, in spite of what they have said. We did not know that they belong to the American Student Union or any other organization. They were asked to stay away because they were guilty of breaking University rules and regulations." And, again, he characterized the students' argument that they were dismissed for political reasons as a smoke screen.[54]

Yet the incongruity between the administration's official line and the way that the dismissals were interpreted in the press and among the campus community leads us to our first question: What indication do we have that Ruthven acted against the students for their political beliefs rather than the stated official reason? Here the evidence is quite compelling: despite the consistency of Ruthven's messaging, members of his administration made it clear behind the scenes that the students were dismissed due to their political convictions and affiliations. In some of the president's responses to his sympathetic correspondents, Ruthven hinted that the cause of the dismissals was not for disciplinary infractions. "It seems to us," he wrote to a Los Angeles-based

53. Ruthven to Weaver, letter dated November 27, 1940, Ruthven, box 58, folder 2, BHL.

54. Ruthven to Robinson, later dated November 27, 1940, Ruthven, box 58, folder 2, BHL.

attorney, "that we should refuse admittance to the students who have, through one influence or another, come to the firm conclusion that our democracy should give way to some other form of government."[55] Assistant Dean Rea's letter of June 29, 1940, to Ruthven reports that the ASU's initial reaction to the dismissals was beginning to cool down, and, he remarked, "I notice that M.S.C. [Michigan State College, the forerunner to Michigan State University] is following our example and is investigating radical activities on the campus."[56]

Second, and as Robert Cohen has shown for other campuses, the administration actively cooperated with the Federal Bureau of Investigation by providing it with a list of the dismissed students, which would not have been the case had the dismissals been based on behavioral infractions as the administration had claimed.[57] In January 1941, Rea wrote to John S. Bugas, head of the FBI's Detroit office, reiterating that the university had agreed to provide "Mr. [George] Hymers [Special Agent in the Detroit FBI office] and your department with information regarding the activities of the local chapter of the American Student Union." Whereas the administration wanted to demonstrate its cooperation, Rea also sought to place some limits on the materials the administration provided the FBI. "Mr. Hymers likewise asked me for a list of the names and addresses of the students who were requested not to return to the University last fall. We have carefully avoided giving out the names of the students involved in these and other University discipline cases and *while we will gladly provide information as to their contacts*

55. Ruthven to Sinclair, letter dated July 15, 1940, Ruthven, box 58, folder 2, BHL.

56. Rea to Ruthven, letter dated June 29, 1940, Ruthven, box 58, folder 11, BHL.

57. In an appendix to *When the Old Left Was Young,* Cohen provides a list of universities who cooperated with student radicals in the 1930s. On pages 328–29, he indicates that a Professor More provided the FBI with ASU pamphlets; Eleanor H. Scanlan, secretary to the dean of students, provided a list of ASU officers for 1939–41; and Ruthven gave the FBI an account of his conflicts with the ASU and agreed to notify the bureau "of any future agitation by ASU 'troublemakers.'"

Robert L. Chapman - '43 Lit. - (Alumni scholar)
Friend of Hayden, Moss, and others. Held meetings
in their rooms, attempted to influence other boys
in dormitories, and displayed radical attitude.
Did quite a bit of drinking during second semester.

Margaret Cotton - '4x Lit.
Active in Mosher Hall, and was source of
trouble there (Miss Lloyd.)

Philip D. Cummins - '40 Lit.
Withdrew 6/6/40 upon recommendation of Health
Service (nervous breakdown). Very active in radical
groups, — distributed literature to leaders who met
at League (History Club.) He and his sister, Mary,
have been outstanding in several such groups.

Kenneth G. DeHaney - '41 Lit. (Colored).
Active in promotion of rights of colored people.
Created disturbance in Pretzel Bell, in company
with Donald Sloiman of A.S.U., by demanding
that he be served. Also claimed discrimination
by Little Sandwich Shop, on State St. Although he
has associated with members of A.S.U., DeHaney
denies that he is a member of the organization,
and contends that he is not a radical.

Yale Forman - '4x Lit.
Active in A.S.U. and C.I.O. meetings. Apparently
satisfied J.W.Smith that his enrollment as a Mich.
student was bona fide.

Morris Gleicher — '4x Ed.
Promoted cause of negro students; member of
A.S.U. and Civil Rights Committee. (DeHaney said
- 6/19/40 - that he had warned Gleicher to discontinue
his efforts to exploit colored student and that he,
DeHaney, felt that Gleicher was stirring up trouble).

Figure 7.4: [Report on dismissed and warned students from Dean Rea, page 1], Ruthven box 58, folder 11, Bentley Historical Library, University of Michigan

Holden Hayden – '43 Lit.
Organized meetings in his room, distributed handbills in dorms, and was a recognized leader in radical activities.

John C. Keats – '43 Lit.
Conspicuous in his support of Communist party, met with Hayden, Moss and others.

Howard I. Moss – '43 Lit.
Like Keats, Hayden, and Chapman, Moss was very voluble on the subject of Communism. All four of these boys were conspicuous in their Houses for their radical inclinations.

Hilda Rosenbaum, – '43 Lit.
Assisted Hayden in distribution of literature in Stockwell Hall. Attended group meetings in Nat. Science Bldg. (probably led by Ringberg).

Howard Moss – '43 Lit.
Rates with Moss, Hayden & Chapman.

Hugo M. Reichard – Grad.
He and Ringberg apparently were leaders of movement, conducting meetings to instruct members of various groups.

Nathaniel I. Ringberg – Grad.
Acted as chairman of discussion groups, held meetings in his office in Nat. Science Bldg., – rooms same address as Reichard.

Abraham B. Stavitsky – Grad.
Attended C.I.O. and A.S.U. meetings. Was instrumental in promoting the charges of discrimination placed against Ralph Bell.

Figure 7.5: [Report on dismissed and warned students from Dean Rea, page 2], Ruthven box 58, folder 11, Bentley Historical Library, University of Michigan

and activities, we do not feel that we should expose these individuals to the possibility of increased or prolonged punishment."[58]

Finally, Ruthven's archives hold an intriguing two-page document, written in the hand of Assistant Dean Rea.[59] [Figures 7.4 and 7.5] The document includes the names of fourteen of the seventeen dismissed students and provides brief summations of their political activities. Hilda Rosenbaum "assisted [Holden] Hayden in distribution of literature in Stockwell Hall. Attended group meetings in Nat. Science Bldg. (probably led by [Nathaniel] Rinzberg)." Rinzberg himself "acted as chairman of discussion groups, held meetings in his office in Nat. Science Bldg.—rooms same address as [Hugo] Reichard." Rea also noted that Reichard "and Rinzberg apparently were leaders of movement, conducting meetings to instruct members of various groups." Abraham Stavitsky "attended CIO and ASU meetings—was instrumental in promoting the charges of discrimination place against Pretzel Bell."[60] Although the list was compiled *after* Ruthven's dismissal notices had been issued on June 18—there is a reference to a meeting with DeHaney on June 19—it is clear that the ASU students were fundamentally correct in their view that the University of Michigan had chosen to dismiss them because of their political activities, and not because of any rule-breaking on their part.

Organizing against Ruthven: The Michigan Committee for Academic Freedom

While Ruthven extended an offer to meet with the students to discuss their dismissals, the administration had already decided

---

58. Rea to Bugas, letter dated January 21, 1941, Ruthven, box 58, folder 11, BHL; emphasis added.

59. According to the index card affixed to the document by Ruthven's biographer Peter Van de Water. The document and index card are in Ruthven, box 58, folder 11, BHL.

60. With respect to the Pretzel Bell incident, Rea notes that Kenneth DeHaney was "active in promotion of rights of colored people. Created disturbance in Pretzel Bell, in company with Donald Slaiman of ASU by demanding he be served." Ruthven, box 58, folder 11, BHL.

which students were to be considered for readmission as indicated by the university list in figures 7.2 and 7.3. An index card preserved in Ruthven's archives listed DeHaney, Forman, Geiger, Hayden, Keats, Moss, Reichard, Rinzberg, and Rosenbaum as "definitely not to return."[61] The seemingly arbitrary nature of the president's decisions and his inflexibility provoked dismay and consternation both from the students' parents and families and from outside organizations such as labor unions.

Reverend Owen A. Knox, minister of the Bethlehem Methodist Church and the recently elected president of the Michigan Civil Rights Federation, became one of the most active opponents of Ruthven's dismissal decision. Founded in 1935 as the Conference for the Protection of Civil Rights, the Michigan Civil Rights Federation's purpose was to "provide a Left alternative to such liberal organizations as the American Civil Liberties Union (ACLU), the Jewish Community Council, and the NAACP."[62] Knox was an adherent of Methodist social action that Elizabeth Dilling castigated in her report. As part of his commitment to social action, Knox pursued left-wing objectives such as combating poverty and advocating for civil rights.[63] The Michigan ASU had already invited Knox to campus in February of 1940 to speak at the all-campus rally in protest of the FBI's recent attacks on progressive groups.[64] Following the dismissals that June, Knox agreed to appear at an ASU-sponsored public meeting on campus scheduled for June 28 that, however, was canceled when the university refused to provide the ASU use of its facilities. [65]

61. Ruthven, box 58, folder 11, BHL.

62. Dillard, *Faith in the City*, 16.

63. Founded in 1907, the Methodist Federation for Social Action (MFSA) continues to work as a national progressive social justice organization to this day.

64. "Campus Civil Liberties Rally to Hear Knox," *MD*, February 15, 1940. Knox had helped to found a Defense Committee on behalf of the progressives arrested by the FBI in February 1940. The Defense Committee produced a statement of facts on the case claiming that the twelve people were arrested for recruiting volunteers to defend the loyalist government in Spain. See "Statement of Facts on the Detroit Arrests," Stace, box 2, BHL.

65. According to the pamphlet later distributed by the Michigan Committee for Aca-

With Ruthven summering in Frankfort, the controversy appeared to abate after the initial flurry of press reports. The only action reported in the *Michigan Daily* was a mid-July speech by Hugo Reichard and the national ASU's executive secretary, Herbert Witt, on the dismissal case.[66] Nonetheless, a more organized response to the dismissals was in progress. Knox and the Civil Rights Federation met with members of the University of Michigan's chapter of the ASU at the federation's offices on Saturday, July 13, during which it was decided to hold a meeting in Ann Arbor on Thursday, July 18, with representatives from the federation, the National Association for the Advancement of Colored People (NAACP), the Wayne State and Michigan chapters of the ASU, and "members of the faculty and prominent individuals."[67] The purpose was to establish a group, called the Michigan Committee for Academic Freedom (MCAF) that was to mobilize awareness on a national scale with the aim of pressuring Ruthven to rescind the dismissals.[68] The group aimed to attract prominent names such as the famous anthropologist Franz Boas, the president of the American Federation of Teachers George Counts, the writer Dashiell Hammett, the artist Rockwell Kent, and leading religious and labor figures.[69] In order to generate this national awareness, MCAF encouraged the Michigan chapter of the ASU to draft and massively distribute a pamphlet outlining the facts of the students' case and arguing that the university administration provided only the vaguest explanation for its decision. MCAF also

demic Freedom (MCAF). See MCAF, *Without Fear or Favor*, September 1940, folder ASU Bimu F24, BHL.

66. "Reichard to Speak at ASU Gathering," *MD*, July 19, 1940.

67. Kemnitz to Kemnitz, letter dated July 15, 1940, CRC, series 8, box 76, folder Correspondence July–Sept. 1940, WRL.

68. For the group's aspirations to generate nationwide awareness in the case, see the letter from Ed Magdol to Ernest Goodman, Chairman of the MCAF, dated July 29, 1940, CRC, series 8, box 76, folder Correspondence July–Sept. 1940, WRL.

69. See the open hearing notice, dated November 9, 1940, folder ASU Bimu F24, BHL.

wanted to get a delegation to Ruthven demanding open hearings for all the dismissed students.

Unsurprisingly, MCAF's efforts to gain an audience with Ruthven came up short. Ruthven refused to interrupt his summering in Frankfort, and he claimed further that the Board of Regents had ordered him not to speak of the dismissals before its first meeting of the fall semester.[70] MCAF's other early initiative—producing a pamphlet that presented the case of the dismissed students— also revealed the new group's lack of coordination. Both MCAF and the national chapter of the ASU had produced their own pamphlets, the latter written by the recent University of Michigan graduate and former *Michigan Daily* editor and writer, Elliott Maraniss.[71] This led to confusion over which pamphlet should be printed and circulated, especially given the limited available financial resources. The national ASU office finally persuaded MCAF to accept its draft with both groups splitting the printing costs.[72]

Printed in early September 1940 in time for a major peace mobilization in Chicago and just before the start of the fall semester, MCAF's pamphlet, *Without Fear or Favor: The Case of the Michigan Students*, provided an account of the dismissals and stressed how they had disrupted the lives of students in good standing.[73] [Figure 7.6] While the published pamphlet, unlike the draft report, did not reference any of the students' ethnic identities, all of the people specifically profiled in the pamphlet were Jewish students

70. Goodman to Edmonds, letter dated August 6, 1940, CRC, series 8, box 76, folder Correspondence July–Sept. 1940, WRL.

71. Maraniss' career at Michigan and the *Michigan Daily* is chronicled by his son in Maraniss, *Good American Family*, 124–48.

72. Magdol to Goodman ("Bernie"), letter dated August 20, 1940, CRC, series 8, box 76, folder American Student Union, WRL.

73. Several copies of this pamphlet exist in the Bentley archives including in the folder ASU Bimu F24, BHL; Ruthven, box 58, folder 12, BHL; Stace, box 2, BHL; and VPSS, box 4, folder ASU, BHL. Reference to the Chicago Peace Mobilization during which the ASU sought to distribute copies of the pamphlet appears in Magdol to Goodman ("Bernie"), letter dated August 20, 1940, CRC, series 8, box 76, folder American Student Union, BHL.

"WITHOUT FEAR OR FAVOR"

The spring of 1940 will be remembered by some thirteen students of the University of Michigan as a crucial moment in their lives and their careers. To the student body and faculty members it will represent a challenge to the reputation of the University as a free and socially responsible institution of higher learning. And to the American people it will be recalled as a period during which the question of academic freedom became a serious problem, vitally linked with the struggle to defend civil liberties and the rights of labor.

During the week of June 18, 1940, some thirteen University of Michigan students, residing in Ann Arbor, Detroit, Cleveland, New Jersey, New York, Massachusetts, and other places in the Mid-West and East, received from University President Alexander Grant Ruthven a letter consisting of one sentence:

"It is the decision of the authorities of the University of Michigan that you cannot be readmitted to the University."

The news came as a complete surprise and a shock to the recipients of the letter. There had been no previous warning. The letter did not state what authorities had made the decision, nor did it cite the facts on which the decision was based.

The Students in the Case

Among the students who received letters from President Ruthven was Nathaniel Rinzberg, twenty-two year old graduate student. Nathaniel, a graduate from the University in 1939, had just completed his course requirements for a Master's degree in psychology. He planned to return for the summer session to take his oral and written examinations. He had already made application to several institutions that require trained psychologists. .There was not the slightest possibility of getting a position if he did not acquire his degree.

For nineteen-year-old Hilda Rosenbaum the news was equally unexpected and disconcerting. Hilda had finished her first year at Ann Arbor and her college career was the most important thing in her life. She too was interested in psychology and had worked hard all year in her studies and at the NYA job which enabled her to attend college. The girls in Stockwell dormitory knew Hilda as an earnest, friendly, freckle-faced girl. She was one of the few in the huge dormitory who had achieved the distinction of being chosen for Alpha Lambda Delta, the women's freshman honorary society.

Figure 7.6 [*Without Fear or Favor*], Vice President of Student Services box 4, folder American Students Union (ASU), Bentley Historical Library, University of Michigan. Please note that all references to the students' ethnicities were removed before the pamphlet's publication.

from the East Coast: Rinzberg, Rosenbaum, Reichard, and Forman. After the pamphlet criticized the administration for its hol-
low justifications, it leveled a charge of political persecution: "for
while the students differ in race, in religion, in state of residence,
and in interests, one characteristic is common to all: they have all
engaged in progressive political activity—in particular, activity in
favor of peace, against Negro discrimination, and for the rights of
labor."[74] The pamphlet explained that the ASU was responsible
for organizing the mid-April 1940 peace rally, for leading a union
organization drive among the university's employees, and for
ASU members' involvement in the Pretzel Bell incident. In the
latter case, the trial of the restaurant owner "was characterized
by the baiting of Negroes, Jews, and aliens—for some of the witnesses were Jewish and one of the Negro complainants an alien.
Four of the students who received letters of dismissal, including
two Negroes, were involved in these cases."[75]

Without Fear or Favor then described the mounting opposition to Ruthven's actions including the unanimous resolution
passed at the UAW annual convention as well as a similar resolution passed by several locals of the State, County, and Municipal
Workers of America. For good measure, MCAF included lengthy
condemnations from Edward A. Ross, professor of sociology at
the University of Wisconsin and president of the ACLU; George
Axtelle of Northwestern University; and Knox himself. The pamphlet concluded by reiterating the ASU students' demands for an
open hearing. "If President Ruthven has, as he says, information
that would warrant the dismissal of the students, then he should
have nothing to fear from an airing of that information. If he
refuses to grant such a hearing, the inescapable conclusion is that
thirteen students of an American University have been summarily
dismissed because of their political beliefs and activities."[76]

74. MCAF, *Without Fear or Favor*, 4, September 1940, folder ASU Bimu F24, BHL.
75. MCAF, *Without Fear or Favor*, 6, September 1940, folder ASU Bimu F24, BHL.
76. MCAF, *Without Fear or Favor*, 8, September 1940, folder ASU Bimu F24, BHL.

In mid-September, just before the start of the fall term, Reverend Knox sent the pamphlet, with an accompanying letter on MCAF letterhead, to each member of the Board of Regents.[77] In the letter, Knox argued that the administration's explanation for the dismissals was incorrect and accused the University of Michigan of violating the students' academic freedom: "These students have been engaged during the previous year in activities on the campus on behalf of peace, the civil rights of Negroes, labor unions, and student organization. It is the conviction of our committee as well as of numerous organizations and individuals who have interested themselves in this case that these activities constituted the real motive for the action taken. If this is true, we believe you will agree that the action constitutes a serious blow to a once high reputation held by the University for academic and intellectual freedom."[78] Five days after sending the board this request, Knox wrote to Ruthven asking whether he stood with the committee's request for an open hearing "in view of the national importance which the case of the Michigan students has assumed, and the wide interest it has attracted as a test case of academic freedom and democratic procedure in a state university."[79]

Neither the Board of Regents nor Ruthven saw fit to comply with the committee's request: Ruthven sent Knox a response on October 3—well after the board meeting—claiming that the reverend was misinformed about the facts of the case.[80] After none of the regents responded to Knox's letter, the reverend led a group from MCAF to the Board of Regents meeting on September 20. There, the group was roundly rebuffed as the regents affirmed their full support for Ruthven's actions.[81] MCAF drafted a press

77. Knox to the Board of Regents, letter dated September 18, 1940, Ruthven, box 58, folder 12, BHL.

78. Knox to Board, letter dated September 18, 1940, Ruthven, box 58, folder 12, BHL.

79. Knox to Ruthven, letter dated September 24, 1940, Ruthven, box 58, folder 12, BHL.

80. Ruthven to Knox, letter dated October 3, 1940, Ruthven, box 58, folder 12, BHL.

81. "Expulsion Cases Reviewed," *MD*, October 3, 1940.

release following the board's refusal stating that "since they [the Board of Regents] are unwilling to recognize that it is only fairness and decency to tell the students what is charged against them, and to hear their replies, we will continue to fight for justice for these students if we have to take it to the people's representatives in the State legislature, or even to the voters themselves."[82]

Although Ruthven and the board were successful in stonewalling Knox's ragtag committee, they were less so in containing and controlling the narrative. The *Nation* magazine, a prominent left-wing periodical, published a provocative article, "Ann Arbor Hysteria," in its September 14, 1940, issue.[83] The piece claimed that some of the students were dismissed for helping the CIO to organize the university's 3,000 non-faculty employees. Two students were dismissed over the Pretzel Bell incident while others were dismissed for their participation in a campus-wide peace demonstration or for supporting pacifist and pro-Soviet politics. The article's author, S. R. Kaye, also noted that "four were residents of Michigan; eight were from outside the state. Six were Jewish." Yet Kaye's article goes much further than a simple recounting of these facts. It argues that Ruthven's administration was tolerating "a group of reactionary aides who devote half their time to harassing students with unorthodox views. These administrative assistants have set up boards to question applicants for admission about their political beliefs. They have interfered again and again with free expression in student publications. They have denied the use of lecture halls to a wide variety of speakers."[84]

The *Nation* article painted Ruthven as craven and timid by its assertion that "Regents, legislators, politicians, and wealthy alumni call many of his signals. The purse-strings of the institution are controlled in large part by the state legislature, made up

82. MCAF press release, dated September 20, 1940, Stace, box 2, BHL.

83. S. R. Kaye, "Ann Arbor Hysteria," *Nation*, September 14, 1940, 214–15. The authors consulted a copy found in CRC, series 8, box 77, folder U. of M. Regents—1940, WRL.

84. S. R. Kaye, "Ann Arbor Hysteria," *Nation*, September 14, 1940, 214–15. The authors consulted a copy found in CRC, series 8, box 77, folder U. of M. Regents—1940, WRL.

of up-state farmers and down-state representatives of the automobile companies." And, in its most controversial assertion, Kaye went after the corporate character of the board itself: "The university's Board of Regents, which is directly elected by the voters of the state, contains, among its eight members, Michigan's former head football coach, Harry Kipke, who as a candidate for his post received the aid of Ford's anti-union personnel director, Harry Bennett. Since his election Kipke has been given the luncheon concession at the River Rouge plant."[85] Kaye also mentioned that five regents were corporation lawyers, one a Democratic national committeeman, one a retired banker, and one the wife of a retired GM executive. Kipke, however, was the only one named in Kaye's article. "This being the structure of the university," Kaye concluded, "it is hardly strange that freedom is curtailed."[86] While the local Detroit and Ann Arbor press had reported on Kipke's connections with Bennett at the time of Kipke's nomination, Kaye's article effectively introduced it in a nationally distributed magazine. Published almost concurrently with the *Without Fear or Favor* pamphlet, and around the same time that Knox demanded an audience with the Board of Regents, this article likely served only to harden the president's and the board's determination not to let outside groups interfere with what they saw as university business. The *Nation* piece does, however, provoke the question as to what extent Ruthven may have been subject to outside pressure—especially by Kipke, Bennett, or Ford—to purge a number of East Coast student radicals, a disproportionate number of whom were Jewish. For this, we must turn away from the MCAF and its efforts to galvanize national attention to consider the implications about Kipke's (and, through him, Bennett and Ford's) influence.

85. S. R. Kaye, "Ann Arbor Hysteria," *Nation*, September 14, 1940, 214–15. The authors consulted a copy found in CRC, series 8, box 77, folder U. of M. Regents—1940, WRL.

86. S. R. Kaye, "Ann Arbor Hysteria," *Nation*, September 14, 1940, 214–15. The authors consulted a copy found in CRC, series 8, box 77, folder U. of M. Regents—1940, WRL.

Harry Kipke's Secret Reports and the Case of George Stein

Kipke's close relationship with Harry Bennett, the head of Ford's Service Department, Ford's de facto head of security, and the director of his own private spy network, was public knowledge at the time. Moreover, documentation exists that shows Bennet's offering Kipke lucrative concessions as a middleman for some of Ford's vendor accounts (Collins-Aikman of New York and Colonial Woolen Mills of Cleveland, Ohio). Based on existing independent documentation, this, however, was not the case pertaining to the lunch commission at the Rouge plant.[87] Everybody knew about the close friendship between Bennett and Kipke. What is less certain, though, is whether Bennett acted through Kipke to put pressure on the university, especially in the matter of the dismissed students. More important for our purposes remains the issue as to whether the close relationship between Bennett and Kipke was a factor in some of these students' dismissals from the university by dint of their Jewish identity.

Robert Copp's accusation in the January 1941 *New Republic* that Kipke handed Ruthven a list of one hundred students to have dismissed from the university seems not to be borne out by the existing evidence. Indeed, Copp, then a student at Michigan, was hardly in a position to have firsthand knowledge of this sensitive issue. Rather, it seems more probable that he was recounting rumors that likely circulated among the more politically engaged students on campus at this time. That is to say, there is no "smoking gun" that indicates that Kipke specifically ordered Ruthven, at Bennett's behest, to rid the campus of radical students, especially those of Jewish background hailing from the East Coast. However, some evidence does exist that Bennett's network was spying on student radicals, that the reports generated by this network reached Kipke, and that Kipke forwarded them to Ruthven's office.

87. Office of Henry and Clara Ford Estate Records, accession 587, Campsall Files—folder Harry H. Bennett 1929–1945, BFRC.

In August of 1940, Kipke received a report about three individuals whom the Detroit Police Department questioned.[88] They were all University of Michigan students: "Two of them are Jews and the third a negro" who were in Detroit to meet Reverend Owen Knox's secretary. The report claimed—inaccurately—that "[t]hey had a letter from Knox to this work and stated that they came to Detroit to register protests against President Ruthven's order banning members of the Young Communist League from continuing their classes."[89] The three students were Horace Kamm, Irving M. Copilowish, whom we will discuss below, and Kenneth DeHaney, one of the three dismissed African American students who had been involved with the Pretzel Bell incident. The report repeated that "the first two are Jews, the other, a negro" and that they were the "'contact at the University of Michigan for the Civil Rights Federation and should be either excluded or watched."

88. Although the report does not have any attribution, given that Bennett maintained a vast and well-trained network of spies and informants that he used to suppress union organizing efforts on behalf of Ford, that Bennett and Kipke were close friends, and that the report references an incident in Detroit rather than Ann Arbor, it seems highly likely that Bennett was the source for this report. Moreover, the *Forum* article from February 1938, referenced earlier, describes the extent of Bennett's private network: "Bennett's organization has no parallel in the modern world. It is the largest, most efficient, most ubiquitous army of private police employed anywhere. The men who form it are undeniably low in caliber when compared with similar type in industry in Michigan. Ninety percent of them are prize fighters or wrestlers, ex-convicts, former policemen discharged by trial boards, or simply husky gentlemen handy in a rough-and-ready tumble with no holds barred." The article also claimed that Bennett's private force was "reliably estimated to number 3,000. 'Official' figures, however, range only up to 400." See John H. O'Brien, "Henry Ford's Commander in Chief: Harry Bennett and His Private Army," *Forum*, February 1938, Sugar, accession 232, box 53, folder 53.3: Harry Bennett, WRL.

89. Report attached to Kipke to Ruthven, letter dated August 14, 1940, Ruthven, box 28, folder 20, WRL. A second copy is in Ruthven, box 58, folder 12, BHL. That the notes and the report appear to be an internal university investigation is borne out by the fact that both Stein's and Copilowish's transcripts are stapled to them and that the investigator's to-do list on the last page strongly suggests a university administrator based on such tasks as "Answer Arthur Reichard's letter in re brother"; "Answer Rinzberg's question concerning the master's degree"; "Answer unfavorable letters," etc.

HARRY G. KIPKE
12821 DIX AVENUE
DEARBORN, MICHIGAN

C O P Y

August 8, 1940

The following three individuals were questioned
by the Detroit Police Department while standing
on a corner at W. Warren and Thirds.

Two of them are Jews and the third a negro.
Investigation disclosed that they are University
of Michigan Students and they were in Detroit
to go to 938 W. Forest Avenue and see a Miss
Lillian DuBarr, reportedly a secretary to Rev.
Owen Knox of the Civil Rights Federation.

They had a letter from Knox to this woman and stated
that they came to Detroit to register protests against
President Ruthven's order banning members of the
Young Communist League from continuing their classes.

Irving M. Copilovish, 1325 N. University, Ann Arbor, Mich.
Horace Komm, 1452 Washington, Ann Arbor, Michigan
Kenneth DeHaney, negro, 841 E. University, Ann Arbor, Mich

The first two are Jews, the other, a negro. These men
are "contact" at the University of Michigan for the
Civil Rights Federation and should be either excluded
or watched. Harry Kipke should be advised of the above.

Figure 7.7 [Report on student activities forwarded from Regent Kipke to
President Ruthven, August 8, 1940], Ruthven box 28, folder 20, Bentley
Historical Library, University of Michigan. The original report was sent
to Kipke's office August 8. A copy was put on Kipke's letterhead and sent
to President Ruthven a few days later while retaining the report's original
date.

George Stein and wife - graduate student

Copilowish, Irving M. - teaching fellow, Mathematics and Philosophy

Is Stein on N.Y.A. list?
Is Copilowish?

Live in same house, 1324 or 1326 N. University, or at
        least next door neighbors

Meetings, quiet, held from 1-4 about three times a week,
        1-4 AM

Many students attend meetings

Students come for advice and guidance on Communistic program

Copilowish receives a great deal of mail, much of it from
        the other side of the Mexican border

People come from out of town and as transients are housed
        by these people, or are recommended to owner of
        apartment as desirable transient renters.

Noticeable that radical students major in Mathematics and
        Logic. This combination of subjects will
        identify a radical student.

Person who reported this wishes to become unknown.

Mostly Jewish students under hand of Stein and Copilowish.

Figure 7.8: [Investigation notes on radical students, summer 1940, page 1],
Ruthven box 58, folder 12, Bentley Historical Library, University of Michigan. Given these notes' presence in Ruthven's files, and that the investigator also had a "to-do" list that including responding to inquiries from the
dismissed students or their family members (see Figure 7.9), we conclude
that these are notes from an internal University of Michigan investigation.

Maraniss   Rontal

Reichard   Lamken

Rinzberg

Mr. and Mrs. Stein (Agnes Hippen)

Copilowish

Munz

————

Is Mrs. Maraniss a sister of Philip Cummins?

Answer Arthur Reichard's letter in re brother.

Answer Rinzberg's question concerning the master's degree.

Talk to C.S.Y. in re

Answer Heavenrich letter.

Answer unfavorable letters.

Write O'Donnell.

Write Bloomfield.

How about Stavitsky?

Figure 7.9: [Investigation notes on radical students, summer 1940, page 2], Ruthven box 58, folder 12, Bentley Historical Library, University of Michigan.

The report closed with the directive that "Harry Kipke should be advised of the above." [90]The document, dated August 8, 1940, was copied onto Kipke's personal stationary and was sent with an accompanying letter to Ruthven on August 14. [Figure 7.7]

This report appears to have spurred the Ruthven administration to investigate Copilowish, a graduate student in mathematics. Ruthven's archives contain a typed list of notes and a report on Copilowish and his former roommate (or neighbor, the records are not clear), George Stein, a graduate student in philosophy.[91] The notes include a brief summary of an interview of their former landlady, who considered "both men as dangerous in that they made every effort to influence other students with whom they came in contact."[92] To her interviewer, the landlady claimed that she had several talks with Stein that displayed his "Communistic attitude," one in which he advocated the overthrow of the government by force, and that, after attending several of the meetings he held with other students, she had "no doubt as to Stein's radical and Communistic inclinations and activities." The landlady also claimed to have read Copilowish's correspondence—especially with respect to his defecting from the Stalinist camp to the Trotskyist—and that many of the letters that he received "were written in a mathematical code and much subversive litera-

90. Report attached to Kipke to Ruthven, letter dated August 14, 1940, Ruthven, box 28, folder 20, BHL.

91. The notes express uncertainty as to whether Copilowish and Stein had been roommates or next-door neighbors, 1324 or 1326 North University. Ruthven, box 58, folder 12, BHL. In a later discussion with Jerome Davis of the New School of Social Research, Ruthven claimed that the police had given him Stein's name. Davis recounted this in his speech during the "open hearing" in November 1940. It is possible that the interview with the landlady was a police interview that the university managed to obtain a copy of and followed up on accordingly. However, nothing in the report itself indicates precisely whether it was a police report or an internal university report. See R. H. Hamilton's handwritten transcription of the open hearing in CRC, series 8, box 77, folder Hearing—Nov. 9, 1940, WRL.

92. "Notes on interview with Mrs. Florence Rowen Flook Danby" [undated but likely August–September 1940], Ruthven, box 58, folder 12, BHL.

ture came to him from Mexico."[93] The list of notes was typed after the interview and contained such statements as, "Many students attend meetings" and "students come for advice and guidance on Communistic program" and that "Copilowish receives a great deal of mail, much of it from the other side of the Mexican border." [Figure 7.8] The notes also draw some interesting observations: "Noticeable that radical students major in Mathematics and Logic. This combination of subjects will identify a radical student. Mostly Jewish students under hand of Stein and Copilowish."[94]

On an affixed piece of paper, the names of some students appear: Maraniss, Reichard, Rinzberg, Mr. and Mrs. Stein (Agnes Hippen), Copilowish, Munz, Rontal, and Lamken. [Figure 7.9] Both Stein's and Copilowish's graduate transcripts are stapled to these notes. Although this investigation appears to have occurred in the late summer, after Ruthven's initial dismissal order in mid-June, it appears that the administration pursued matters raised by the secret report that Kipke had forwarded to the president. A university administration official was tasked with finding such information as to whether, for example, Mrs. Maraniss was a sister of one of the dismissed students, Philip Cummins (she was his sister) and to answer letters from the dismissed students' relatives. Undoubtedly, this provided Ruthven with more confirmation that his decision to dismiss the students had been correct and justified. Moreover, this new documentation formed the basis for effectively terminating Stein from the university by revoking his fellowship.[95]

93. "Notes on interview with Mrs. Florence Rowen Flook Danby" [undated but likely August–September 1940], Ruthven, box 58, folder 12, BHL.

94. See the investigation notes in Ruthven, box 58, folder 12, BHL.

95. Materials on the Stein case are located in CRC, series 8, box 77, folder "George P. Stein—1940," WRL. While it is not known if the University of Michigan took any specific actions against Copilowish, he completed his PhD there in the philosophy of logic in 1948. Copilowish was born in Duluth, Minnesota, not the East Coast, and had been at Michigan since 1934, when he began his undergraduate education. As Irving Copi, he became a significant figure, publishing *Introduction to Logic* (1953), long the standard textbook in the field and, as of this writing, in its thirteenth edi-

Just before the beginning of the fall term, on September 24, Dean Clarence S. Yoakum of the Graduate School and Vice-President in Charge of Educational Investigations summoned Stein to a meeting.[96] Yoakum questioned Stein as to whether he had received literature from Mexico, why he had moved out of his address on North University Street, what his relationship with Copilowish was, and whether he had been encouraged to study mathematics "because of its possible usefulness in the future."[97] Stein denied a close relationship with Copilowish, claimed that he had received no subversive literature from Mexico, had not been encouraged to study anything, and denied that there were any meetings in the house he and Copilowish rented. Yoakum warned Stein to stick to his studies and "bother with no activities which would interfere with his career in Philosophy."[98] Two days later Stein enrolled for the fall term and was given a graduate teaching fellowship soon thereafter. However, on October 10, the administration denied official confirmation of Stein's appointment, effectively barring him from teaching thus terminating his income. Stein's department head was unable to provide an explanation for the decision, and Stein secured an interview with Ruthven.

tion. His online biographies at the Bertrand Russell Society and ZenithCity.com do not mention any of his student radicalism; the Russell Society web page says only that "He dropped out of college during the Second World War to work in the auto factories of Detroit, where he became a UAW shop steward and organizer." Copi would hold professorships at the University of Michigan (1958-69) and the University the Hawaii (1969-90). He died in 2002. See https://users.drew.edu/jlenz/brs-obit-copi.html; http://zenithcity.com/archive/people-biography/irving-copi/.

96. For background on Yoakum, please see the entry from the *Michigan Alumnus* at http://faculty-history.dc.umich.edu/faculty/clarence-stone-yoakum/named-dean-graduate-school.

97. The following details of the case are from a leaflet, titled *Case of George Stein*, that was drafted in support of Stein's case. See CRC, series 8, box 77, folder George P. Stein—1940, WRL.

98. See CRC, series 8, box 77, folder George P. Stein—1940, WRL.

The president stated that Stein had used "poor judgment in political activity on the dismissals last summer ([Stein] had distributed the Michigan Committee for Academic Freedom leaflet, <u>Without Fear or Favor.</u>)."[99] Ruthven also claimed that Stein was biting the hand that fed him and that he had exercised poor judgment by not going to the administration to find out the true reasons for the students' dismissal. Following his now familiar argument, Ruthven submitted that the revocation of Stein's fellowship had nothing to do with his politics. Stein's subsequent meetings with Yoakum and Rea failed to provide him with any clarification of the matter. Finally, one of Stein's professors informed him that the philosophy department had been told that he had received subversive literature from Mexico, had political relationships with Copilowish, held radical meetings in his room, and had been asked to leave his North University Street address because his landlady had discovered "incendiary literature in his room."[100] Apparently, the faculty in the philosophy department did not believe the university's claims against Stein, "but they also could not see what could be done about it."

Stein then confronted Ruthven, Yoakum, and Rea about the charges of his radical activity but to no avail since each of them denied that Stein's political activities had anything to do with the revocation of his fellowship. Left with few options, Stein turned to the Civil Rights Federation and to MCAF who, from mid-October onward, bundled Stein's case with those of the thirteen dismissed students. MCAF distributed a statement declaring that "The action of the University of Michigan on October 10th in withdrawing a teaching fellowship from one of its graduate students, thus terminating his University career,

99. See CRC, series 8, box 77, folder George P. Stein—1940, WRL. The underlined text is the original source.

100. See CRC, series 8, box 77, folder George P. Stein—1940, WRL.

388 | THE BOUNDARIES OF PLURALISM

because he dared to protest the previous arbitrary dismissal of at least thirteen students, should fill all American educators with consternation."[101] Moreover, MCAF obtained the supportive signatures of the famous anthropologist Franz Boas, as well as those of Rockwell Kent and Lawrence Blythe of the Michigan Industrial Union Councils, and five others protesting Ruthven's actions against Stein. A press release from the "Federated Press" characterized Stein's de facto dismissal as an effort by the president "to Hitlerize the University of Michigan" and claimed that "No action by Pres. Alexander G. Ruthven and his administration could have emphasized more dramatically the need for a thorough airing of the current attacks on academic freedom."[102]

As the story of George Stein makes clear, Ruthven was prompted into this action courtesy of Harry Kipke, who had delivered a secret report about Copilowish and two other Michigan students to the president's office. This led to an investigation of these students, which ultimately resulted in Stein's effective dismissal from the university. Moreover, in Stein's case, too, Ruthven and his administration had used the same argument for their action as they had against the dismissed students: that it was ultimately Stein's "behavior" and not his politics that led to his removal from the university.

Was Stein's Jewish identity also a factor? On the surface, it appeared somewhat doubtful since his former roommate/neighbor, Irving Copilowish, who was also Jewish, did not appear to incur any disciplinary action. The leaflet addressing Stein's case does not make any mention of Copilowish, and we know that

101. "Statement on President Ruthven's Latest Action," CRC, series 8, box 77, folder George P. Stein—1940, WRL.

102. Federated Press, "Michigan University Head Accused in New Charges," November 7, 1940, CRC, series 8, box 76, folder "Letters and Information from Dismissed Students," WRL. A typed copy of the announcement, "An Announcement by Eight Prominent Americans of Extreme Importance to Each Michigan Student" is located in VPSS, box 4, folder ASU, BHL.

the latter received his doctorate from Michigan many years later. Yet the university investigator's typed notes state that Stein and Copilowish were radicalizing mainly Jewish students, which clearly was a point that served to reinforce the link between Jewishness and radicalism. Moreover, the August report secretly sent to Kipke twice referred to the students' ethnic/racial and religious identities.

Certainly, there were those at the time who believed that the students' Jewish identity was a factor in the university's dismissing them. Upon receiving a letter of solicitation from Knox, E. A. Ross of the University of Wisconsin's sociology department and chairman of the ACLU, replied to the reverend: "It would be helpful to me if you could pass on to me—in confidence—if you like, whatever inside information may have trickled into yours ears anent the thirteen expelled students. How many of them were Jews? How many are Negroes? Is there any possibility that they were eliminated for reasons of race rather than of activity?"[103] Some of the dismissed students themselves suspected the administration of an anti–East Coast and anti-Jewish biases. In a letter from late June 1940 to Robert Chapman, John Cresswell Keats— who transferred to the University of Pennsylvania—claimed that "The school is trying to get rid of as many out of state kids as it can, and has the idea that N.Y. Jews are sending out six-hundred kids a year to Midwestern schools to spread radicalism."[104] As it turns out, Keats's suspicions had some basis in fact. While Kipke may never have actually produced a list of a hundred students to dismiss, Kipke's sources produced reports that clearly emphasized student radicals' ethnic/racial (Jewish/African American) identity. Yet the August 1940 report that Kipke forwarded to Ruthven was

103. Ross to Knox, letter dated November 1, 1940, CRC, series 8, box 76, folder Correspondence November 1–10, 1940, WRL. Ross's position with the ACLU is mentioned in the *Michigan Daily*'s account of the open hearing, "Davis Speaks at Trial of 13 Students Told Not To Return," *MD*, November 10, 1940.

104. Keats to Chapman, an abridged version of a letter sent in late June 1940, CRC, series 8, box 76, folder Letters and Information from Dismissed Students—1940, WRL.

not the only one, as we will show below. The case of George Stein, however, provides proof that Stein's identity as Jewish was linked to his radicalism and that this linkage prompted the university to cancel his fellowship and, effectively, end his graduate career at the university.

Seeking a Public Forum: The Dismissed Students' Open Hearing—November 1940

Faced with the refusal by President Ruthven and the Board of Regents to reconsider the dismissals or even allow the effected students an audience, Reverend Knox and the MCAF decided to shift their strategy in late September. First, they had one of the dismissed students, Hugo Reichard, attempt to register for the fall 1940 term as a means to prompt a protest and a letter writing campaign when the university inevitably refused to enroll him.[105] Although the publicity generated from this action compelled Ruthven to meet with Reichard and to promise clarification of university policy with respect to the dismissals, Reichard was still not allowed to reenroll. Given the administration's unwillingness to provide more than vague explanations for the dismissals, and the board's refusal to accede to an open hearing, MCAF decided to organize a public hearing of the dismissed thirteen students for Saturday, November 9. As Knox explained,

105. Carbon copy of letter from Knox, no date [likely late October 1940], first page missing, CRC, series 8, box 76, folder Correspondence July–Sept. 1940, WRL. The Michigan chapter of the ASU also coordinated with its national office. See Ace to Beattie (Beatrice Kahn), undated letter, which states "The demonstration in Ann Arbor, and the plan to have Hugo try to register sound good. We will cooperate. All the districts of the ASU have been notified to organize a wide letter campaign to coincide with your action Friday." CRC, series 8, box 76, folder Correspondence October 1–19, 1940, WRL. Photos of Reichard and his supporters leaving Angell Hall after his failed attempt to register for fall classes can be found on the Ann Arbor District Library's website, "Hugo Reichard and the Campus Radicals of 1940," https://aadl.org/node/347740.

Because our experience in this case has shown that the University is unwilling to make clear the reasons for its action and equally unwilling to discuss the case with the students directly involved or with the faculty or with representatives of any interested organizations; because of the national importance which this case has assumed as a test of academic freedom; and because the individuals' and organizations' concerns in this case are completely convinced that open discussion of the facts involved is absolutely necessary, the Michigan Committee for Academic Freedom and the Michigan Civil Rights Federation will sponsor an open hearing on the U of M case in Ann Arbor on Saturday, November 9. [106]

The organizers planned to use the open hearing not only to provide the dismissed students with a chance to state their case in a public forum but also to highlight attention to curtailments of academic freedoms on other campuses. The organization committee hoped that "such action will tremendously arouse public feeling on issues of civil liberty within Michigan, and as regards academic freedom throughout the nation. . . . Involvement of labor in this event will help cement union of labor and liberal forces for an election campaign to elect a slate of liberal Regents next spring."[107] Moreover, the organizers hoped that the event would not only raise the profile of the Michigan Civil Rights Federation but at the same time also thoroughly shame Ruthven and the Board of Regents: "This action will 'blow the lid' off the Michigan case itself. If the administration at U of M remains silent in face of such damning evidence against it

106. Carbon copy of letter from Knox, no date [likely late October 1940], first page missing, CRC, series 8, box 76, folder Correspondence July–Sept. 1940, WRL.

107. "A Public Open Hearing on the Michigan Case," confidential memorandum dated October 12, 1940, CRC, series 8, box 76, folder Correspondence October 1–19, 1940, WRL. See also the MCAF's meeting minutes, especially the one for October 14, 1940, which are preserved in CRC, series 8, box 77, folder Michigan Committee for Academic Freedom—Minutes, WRL.

as can be compiled, the expelled students will at any rate have been vindicated in public eyes."[108]

MCAF's plan was to secure the participation of delegates from multiple organizations and groups as well as numerous national figures including Theodore Dreiser, Carl Sandburg, Rockwell Kent, Franz Boas, Langston Hughes, and Paul Robeson in addition to academics such as George Axtelle and Jerome Davis.[109] The ninth of November was chosen both because it was two days before Armistice Day, a "traditional day of national student action," and because there was no home football game that weekend. MCAF expected that the combination of nationally renowned speakers and the absence of a home game would attract at least one thousand students. To that end, MCAF secured the use of the Masonic Temple in Ann Arbor to accommodate this deeply anticipated massive turnout.[110]

By early October, MCAF had good reason to believe that it, along with the national ASU, was indeed generating broad awareness of the dismissed students' cause. The ASU's national office wrote to Beatrice Kahn, a member of MCAF and wife of Robert Kahn, a member of the Michigan ASU chapter, demanding copies of the *Without Fear or Favor* pamphlet: "We are being besieged with demands from our chapters, from college newspaper editors, from interested individuals of all sorts for copies of 'Without Fear or Favor.' A Harvard order for 1,000 copies lies on my desk. The West Coast wants 1,500 immediately, more later. Orders totaling well over 15,000 are already in, and less than half of our chapters

108. "A Public Open Hearing on the Michigan Case," confidential memorandum dated October 12, 1940, CRC, series 8, box 76, folder Correspondence October 1–19, 1940, WRL.

109. The details in the following paragraph, unless otherwise cited, are from "A Public Open Hearing on the Michigan Case," confidential memorandum dated October 12, 1940, CRC, series 8, box 76, folder Correspondence October 1–19, 1940, WRL.

110. Letter from Harper Poulson [a member of MCAF] to the National Office, American Student Union, dated October 12, 1940, CRC, series 8, box 76, folder Correspondence October 1–19, 1940, WRL.

have been heard from."[111] In addition, other civil rights organizations such as the National Federation for Constitutional Liberties and the American Committee for Democracy and Intellectual Freedom were offering their assistance by reaching out to prominent speakers.[112] In their efforts to recruit support for the open hearing, members of the ASU and MCAF met with many organizations. During these meetings, they not only described the dismissals but also alleged that Kipke was behind them. Another secret report sent to Ruthven from Kipke details a meeting on October 15, 1940, of a Detroit-based political campaign organization named the Stanley Nowak Federation [Figure 7.10].[113] The report

111. Bert Witt to Khan, letter dated September 27, 1940, CRC, series 8, box 76, folder Correspondence July–September 1940, WRL. Beatrice Kahn (née Goldstein) (1918–2012) had just married Robert Kahn in the summer of 1940 as the dismissal controversy was unfolding. A circular announcing a get together for "Michigan friends" on August 24, 1940, states "Toast Bob Khan and Beattie Goldstein who will be making their final public appearance before they get 'hitched' Sunday." Ruthven, box 58, folder 12, BHL. Beatrice does not appear to have been a member of Michigan ASU chapter herself as she does not appear on any of the extant lists that are preserved in VPSS, box 4, folder ASU, BHL. Nevertheless, she played an instrumental role in organizing the MCAF's activities during its short life and also maintained correspondence with many of the dismissed students, especially Yale Forman. Their correspondence survives in CRC, series 8, box 76, folders Correspondence November 11–30, 1940 and Letters and Information from Dismissed Students—1940, WRL. The Kahns were lifelong residents of Ann Arbor. Beatrice was a social worker and family therapist at the Child and Family Services and was an active volunteer with Legal Services of Southeast Michigan and then with the Osher Lifelong Learning Institute. Dr. Robert Kahn (1918–2019) earned his PhD at the University of Michigan, where he specialized in organization theory and survey research and was one of the founding members of the Institute for Social Research. He also directed the Survey Research Center. The Center for the Education of Women established a Beatrice Kahn Scholarship, which has awarded over $40,000 to students since 2013. For Beatrice Kahn, see https://obits.mlive.com/obituaries/annarbor/obituary.aspx?n=beatrice-kahn&pid=161139987. On Robert Kahn, see https://en.wikipedia.org/wiki/Robert_L._Kahn, http://www.cew.umich.edu/news-story/dr-robert-l-kahn/, and https://record.umich.edu/articles/obituary-robert-l-kahn.

112. See Kemnitz to Poulson, letter dated October 15, 1940, CRC, series 8, box 76, folder Correspondence October 1–19, 1940, WRL.

113. Stanley Nowak had been an international representative of the United Automo-

LINCOLNIERS BRANCH - STANLEY NOWAK FEDERATION, cont.

TUESDAY, OCTOBER 15, 1940

The Stanley Nowak Federation will hold a mass meeting,
which will be held at Martin Hall, located on Martin and
Linzee, Detroit. The purpose of this meeting is to organize
the Ford Motor Company. Michael F. Widman Jr., assistant
C.I.O. organization director, who at the present time is
here to direct the drive against the Ford Motor Company, will
be the principal speaker, along with R. J. Thomas, president
of the U.A.W.-C.I.O. Other important labor leaders will
also speak. He urged the members of the Lincolniers Branch
to be represented at this meeting. Nowak also stated that at
the present time U.A.W.-C.I.O. has about 46 paid organizers
and 700 voluntary organizers, working on the Ford organizational
drive.

ROBERT CONN:

Robert Conn, a Jew graduate of the University of Michigan,
who seemed very well acquainted with the majority of the comrades
who belonged to the Young Communist League, was the next speaker.
He stated that he had been at U. of M. for a period of 5 years,
and that he had taught the English Language for one scholastic
year. Stated that the purpose for his presence at this meeting
was to acquaint all the persons present with the U. of M. case,
which dealt with the dismissal of 13 students from the University.
He stated that the Ford Motor Company not only dominates labor,
but has extended its claws into the University of Michigan,
their main tool, being Harry Kipke, who at the present time
presides as one of the Regent at the University of Michigan.
He was given what they call a "gravy" job by the Ford Motor
Company, which gives him control of the majority of the
lunch-wagons which we laborers have to support.

Conn stated that specific cause for the expulsion of these
students is not known, and no statement was made by Dr. Ruthven,
president of the University, as to the reason of the dismissal of
these students. Stated that these students were accussed of trying
to organize the University employees into a C.I.O. Local, and
creating radical activities within the Campus.

Upon refusal of Dr. Ruthven to reinstate these students into
the University, the Michigan Committee for Academic Freedom, has
arranged a public trial which will be held at the Masonic Temple
Auditorium, November 9, 1940, about 1 p.m., in Ann Arbor. This
trial has been greatly approved and supported by the American
Students Union, Civil Rights Federation, U.A.W.-C.I.O. and
numerous other progressive organizations. They intend to give
this trial nation wide publicity, in order to focus attention
on any further attempts to oust students from Universities, on
account of their political beliefs.

See page #5.

Figure 7.10: [Investigation report of the Stanley Nowak Federation, October 1940], Ruthven box 28, folder 20, Bentley Historical Library, University of Michigan. This report profiles Robert Conn [Kahn], a "Jew graduate" who gave a speech to this organization implicating Harry Kipke and the Ford Motor Company in the dismissal of the thirteen students.

Page #5.

LINCOLNIERS BRANCH - STANLEY NOWAK FEDERATION, cont.

TUESDAY, OCTOBER 15, 1940

The following are scheduled to preside at the trial of the 13 expelled students at Ann Arbor:

JEROME DAVIS - Professor at Columbia University.

R. J. THOMAS - President of the U.A.W.-C.I.B.

GEORGE AXTELIE - Professor at Northwestern University.

REV. OWEN A. KNOX - Chairman of the National Civil Rights Federation.

Also numerous other important speakers.

Dr. Ruthven and members of the Board of Regents will be sent notices to attend this trial.

Upon conclusion of his speech, pamphlets were distributed among those present, regarding the case at Ann Arbor.

A motion was then made by Steve Kipcha to send a letter or telegram to President Ruthven, protesting the dismissal of these students. This was immediately followed by a suggestion from Stan Patchell, to mimeograph a few thousand leaflets to acquaint the neighborhood with the facts concerning the case and advertise the mass trial to be held at Ann Arbor. Motion was seconded by Billie Peters and greatly approved by Robert Conn.

Patchell, along with Leucthman, were elected as delegates to represent the Lincolniers Branch, at the Ann Arbor trial, and bring back a full report.

The Lincolniers Branch, under the guidance of the Stanley Nowak Federation will sponsor a dance to be held Sunday November 3, 1940, at Martin Hall, located at 4959 Martin and Linzee, Detroit. Tickets for the Dance were distributed among the members. An add amounting to $5.00 was given to the Branch by Congressman John Lesinski.

The printing of the tickets was paid for by S. Grubiak, proprietor of the New Warsaw Restaurant, located at 7511 Michigan Avenue.

And interesting thing to note at this dance is that liquor will be served without securing a license or permit from the Police Dept. It will be served undercover. They are just going to have a beer permit.

See page #6.

Figure 7.11 [Investigation report of the Stanley Nowak Federation, October 1940], Ruthven box 28, folder 20, Bentley Historical Library, University of Michigan. "This part of the report discussing the upcoming "open trial" of President Ruthven and indicates the Nowak Federation's offer to provide support and delegates to the trial.

details a speech made by "Robert Conn," as the name appears in the report, who was "a Jew graduate of the University of Michigan, who seemed very well acquainted with the majority of the comrades who belonged to the Young Communist League."[114] That this was undoubtedly Robert Kahn, a member of the Michigan ASU, is evident through the report's description of his educational background: "He stated that he had been at U. of M. for a period of 5 years, and that he had taught the English Language for one scholastic year."[115] Kahn was at the Stanley Nowak Federation to acquaint the group with the student dismissals and inform it that the university had not provided any sufficient explanation for its action.

bile Workers (UAW) since the union was founded in 1935 and was active in unionizing activities in Flint from 1935 to 1937. He was elected as a state senator in 1938, the first avowed Communist to be elected to the legislature. Early in 1940, he established a federation of clubs to assist with his reelection campaign. See Nowak, *Two Who Were There*. Nowak's efforts to organize Ford workers are detailed on pages 161–67. At the time this October 15 meeting was held, the UAW had just launched an intensified organizing drive among Ford's 90,000-strong labor force, and Nowak was instrumental in canvassing Ford's Polish workers. Thus, it is highly likely that the source for the secret report on the October 15 meeting was someone from Bennett's organization. The report is filed in Ruthven's archives under "Kipke," Ruthven, box 28, folder 20, BHL. Nowak had been warned during 1940 that Bennett's serviceman had threatened to assault him (see Nowak, *Two Who Were There*, 162–63). Nowak also later recalled Bennett's network of spies: "You see the Ford Motor Company had well-organized what they called security guards. . . . And they had stool pigeons everywhere. (They did it for the money.) You appeared at a union meeting, public meeting. . . . And the next day, you were fired." See Stepan-Norris and Zeitlin, *Talking Union*, 64. In addition, Nowak's role as a union organizer in the Polish community is also described in Johnson, *Maurice Sugar*, 186–87, 208–11. See also the lengthy interview of Stanley and Margaret Nowak, from 1979, on the website for the University of Michigan Flint: http://www.umflint.edu/archives/stanley-and-margaret-nowak. The claim that the October 15 meeting "is to organize the Ford Motor Company" appears on page 4 of the secret report, Ruthven, box 28, folder 20, BHL.

114. According to his biography on the University of Michigan's Institute for Social Research page, Kahn completed his bachelor's in English in 1939 and his master's in English in 1940: https://isr.umich.edu/news-events/news-releases/remembering-bob-kahn/.

115. "Lincolniers Branch—Stanley Nowak Federation: Tuesday, October 15, 1940," 4, Ruthven, box 28, folder 20, BHL.

In following the *Nation*'s article from the previous month, Kahn linked the dismissals to Kipke and Ford: "He stated that the Ford Motor Company not only dominates labor, but has extended its claws into the University of Michigan, their main tool, being Harry Kipke, who at the present time presides as one of the Regents at the University of Michigan. He was given what they call a 'gravy' job by the Ford Motor Company, which gives him control of the majority of the lunch-wagons which we laborers have to support."[116] Kahn then described MCAF's plans to hold an open hearing in November in which it hoped to generate national publicity for the students. The Stanley Nowak Federation agreed to send a protest letter to Ruthven and the Board of Regents to distribute leaflets "to acquaint the neighborhood with the facts concerning the case" and to send delegates to the open hearing. [Figure 7.11]

For his part, Reverend Knox also secured the support of the editor of the *Jewish Review*, a New York–based journal, who agreed to introduce the controversy on his weekly radio broadcast. The editor, Ed Morand, underlined the urgency of the matter by telling Knox, "We are up to our ears in a fight against antisemitism and discrimination against Negroes and Italians!"[117] Indeed, one can read a palpable excitement in the extant MCAF correspondence in early October, a heady sense that the committee was about to pull a major coup against Ruthven, the University of Michigan, and the forces of reaction. MCAF member Harper Paulson wrote, "Isn't it a lalapalooza! Remember, 'What happened to Ruthven . . . !'"[118]

Yet the MCAF's hasty decision to organize a major protest meeting in less than four weeks coupled with an apparent hostility to the event by the university began to undermine MCAF's efforts almost as soon as they had begun. While some of the

116. "Lincolniers Branch—Stanley Nowak Federation: Tuesday, October 15, 1940," 4, Ruthven, box 28, folder 20, BHL.

117. Ed Morand to Knox, letter dated October 22, 1940, CRC, series 8, box 76, folder Correspondence Oct. 20–31, 1940, WRL.

118. Paulson to ASU national office, letter dated October 12, 1940, CRC, series 8, box 76, folder Correspondence October 1–19, 1940, WRL.

prominent figures agreed to be named as supporters or sponsors in MCAF's literature, almost all of them were unavailable to come to Ann Arbor on such short notice.[119] George Axtelle, who served both as a professor at Northwestern and as a vice president for the American Federation of Teachers (AFT) was pressured by AFT members into canceling his appearance.[120] Others were skeptical of the actual intent of the open hearing. Though approving of the group's efforts to censure Ruthven, an English professor from the University of Chicago, deplored what he saw

119. The MCAF files in the Civil Rights Congress's archives contain a telegram of regret from Langston Hughes and from the famous civil liberties advocate, Charles Erskine Scott Wood, CRC, series 8, box 76, folder Correspondence Oct. 20–31, 1940, WRL. In a letter to Beatrice Knox, Yale Forman claimed that Paul Robeson visited the University of Wisconsin, where Forman had transferred, and "knew all about [the case], and very gladly offered to sponsor the committee and offer any other help within his power. He told me that whenever he will be in Detroit or Ann Arbor he will be very glad to make a statement on the case. What a guy!" Robeson appears on the list of sponsors for the open hearing, although he did not attend it. See Forman to Kahn ['Beatie'], [n.d. but likely October 1940], CRC, series 8, box 76, folder Letters and Information from Dismissed Students, WRL. The underlined text is in the original source. A list of sponsors for the open hearing appears in CRC, series 8, box 77, folder Hearing—Nov. 9, 1940, WRL.

120. Axtelle received a letter from Wesley H. Maurer, a professor of journalism at Michigan, on October 23 that advised him not to come to the meeting. Maurer argued that "it would be unfortunate to have a representative of the national office of The American Federation of Teachers at this meeting." He went on to question MCAF's presumptions that Ruthven was hiding the real reasons for the dismissals and that "if any representative of ours approaches this problem with the notion that the University is wrong and that the students are right he would do our membership great injustice and great harm." Maurer to Axtelle, letter dated October 23, 1940, Ruthven, box 58, folder 12, BHL. See also Harper Paulson to Hugo Reichard, letter dated October 25, 1940. Although the signature on the letter is indistinct, Reichard's reply to it indicates that Paulson was the correspondent. Paulson claimed that the head of the Michigan Teachers Federation and the former president of the Detroit Teachers union pressured Axtelle out of appearing, despite subsequent pleas by Knox to reconsider. The author recounts a recent AFT convention in which "the AFT officially is not really on record on the case it appears, altho there were numerous evidences of unanimous support for an open hearing." CRC, series 8, box 76, folder Correspondence Oct. 20–31, 1940, WRL. For Axtelle's position within the AFT, see http://reuther.wayne.edu/ward/aft/people.html.

as MCAF's pretense in characterizing the event as an actual open hearing. "It's perfectly obvious," he wrote, "that what is to happen on November 9 is not a trial of the students but a public rebuke to the university. . . . No trial is projected, nor could a fair trial be carried on before a prejudiced jury of two thousand people."[121] Constance Warren, the president of Sarah Lawrence College, was even blunter in her refusal to have anything to do with the open hearing. She calumniated the *Without Fear or Favor* pamphlet for soft-pedaling the dismissed students' political views as "progressive" when, in Warren's view, "they were undoubtedly very far to the left—I would suspect that at least some of them were probably communists."[122] Moreover, Warren also claimed that by calling it an open hearing, Knox and the MCAF were misrepresenting the actual purpose of the event: "You are going to make no effort at all to get at the facts but you are going to hold a public demonstration, which is a very different matter.[123]"

Prominent academics and speakers were not the only ones unwilling to attend. Several of the dismissed students themselves were reluctant to do so—some because they had been re-admitted and feared administrative reprisals and others who had left for other schools where they did not want to call attention to themselves on

121. Percy Boynton to Knox, letter dated October 22, 1940, CRC, series 8, box 76, folder Correspondence Oct. 20–31, 1940, WRL.

122. Warren to Knox, letter dated October 31, 1940, CRC, series 8, box 76, folder Correspondence Oct. 20–31, 1940, WRL.

123. Warren to Knox, letter dated October 31, 1940, CRC, series 8, box 76, folder Correspondence Oct. 20–31, 1940, WRL. Warren's letter does, however, provide some insight into the pressure that presidents of higher education institutions received as a result of student radical groups on campus. In her letter, she recounts receiving a letter from a distinguished businessman who had enrolled his daughter in Sarah Lawrence and "urged me to follow the very fine example of President Ruthven of the University of Michigan in dismissing student members [of the ASU]" and threatened to withdraw his daughter if the ASU chapter wasn't disbanded. Although no supporter of the ASU, Warren refused to accede to the businessman's request as she felt it "exceedingly important that the members of that group, who were generally very able and very much in earnest in their efforts to bring about justice and democracy, should have the best possible education."

their new campuses. Both the ASU and MCAF had solicited from the dismissed students accounts of their dismissals and had invited them to participate in the ASU's and MCAF's anti-Ruthven agitation. Margaret Cotton, who remained at Michigan, wanted no part of any response to Ruthven's actions.[124] Hugo Reichard, who had been actively working with MCAF on distributing pamphlets, was prevailed upon to recruit at least one of the reinstated students to appear at the open hearing with MCAF encouraging him especially to procure the presence of Robert Chapman and Roger Lawn in particular.[125] Reverend Knox, accompanied by Harper Paulson, also encouraged Chapman and Lawn to attend the open hearing although, given their recent reinstatements, they were reluctant to potentially offend the administration. Knox also wrote to Reichard expressing Chapman and Lawn's fears of potential administrative reprisals resulting from their involvement. "Roger [Lawn] is 100 per cent convinced already. Bob is scared—scholarship, family, and publicity."[126] (Chapman ultimately declined to participate in the open hearing).

Reichard also agreed to contact the three dismissed students who had transferred to the University of Wisconsin: Forman, Moss, and Rosenbaum.[127] From Madison, Hilda Rosenbaum wrote to Beatrice Kahn offering to provide information about her new life at the University of Wisconsin, but stopped short of attaching her name to any MCAF action. "'We are trying to keep our names out of the whole busi-

124. Cotton to "Gentlemen," letter dated July 24, 1940. A subsequent letter, dated October 30, 1940, informing her of the upcoming open hearing was addressed to Mosher-Jordan Hall on the Michigan campus. Both letters are located in CRC, series 8, box 76, folder Letters and Information on Dismissed Students, WRL.

125. Paulson to Reichard, letter dated October 25, 1940, CRC, series 8, box 76, folder Correspondence Oct. 20–31, 1940, WRL.

126. Paulson to Reichard, letter dated October 29, 1940, CRC, series 8, box 76, folder Correspondence Oct. 20–31, 1940, WRL.

127. Reichard to Paulson, letter dated October 26, 1940, CRC, series 8, box 76, folder Correspondence Oct. 20–31, 1940, WRL.

ness at W. [Wisconsin] and any literature with our names on would really mess things up." Rather, she advised "I think if you described me as a student from a small New England town—the daughter of a former University faculty member—the effect would be better."[128]

Echoing the concerns that Rosenbaum described to Beatrice Kahn, her fellow exile, Yale Forman provided more insight into Moss', Rosenbaum's, and his situation at the University of Wisconsin: "We are all in a fairly ticklish spot here. All of us are on probation and the attitude of the Administration can best be summed up by the statement made by C.A. Smith, Chairman of the Wisconsin Advanced Standing Committee, to Hilda: 'you are coming to Wisconsin for an education, not for agitation.'"[129] Moreover, while Forman also happily recounted how one of Wisconsin's student groups, the University League for Liberal Action [ULLA] had been conducting an extensive campaign to have the Michigan students reinstated, he was also afraid that Rosenbaum, Moss, and he would be "outed": "Finally the news broke that 3 of the Michigan 'Reds' were at Wisconsin. Immediately the Cardinal [the student newspaper] demanded that their names be divulged. The Administration and the ULLA refused to do this. The press there began to blast away, the Cardinal and the Milwaukee Journal leading the way. The latter had a prize headline, declaring that 'Reds find Refuge at U of W.'"[130] While Forman ultimately chose to come to the open hearing, it appears that he did not participate in the day's events beyond merely attending; Moss and Rosenbaum elected not to attend at all.[131] Ultimately, only four of the

128. Rosenbaum to Beatrice Kahn, letter dated, October 12, 1940, CRC, series 8, box 76, folder Letters and Information from Dismissed Students—1940, WRL.

129. Forman to Knox, letter dated October 14, 1940, CRC, series 8, box 76, folder Letters and Information from Dismissed Students, WRL.

130. Forman to Knox, letter dated October 14, 1940, CRC, series 8, box 76, folder Letters and Information from Dismissed Students, WRL.

131. Although a draft script shows that Forman was to be questioned by the attorney Maurice Sugar at the open hearing, neither Hamilton's notes nor the *Michigan Daily*

402 | THE BOUNDARIES OF PLURALISM

dismissed students appeared at the open hearing: Reichard, Rinzberg, Forman, and Lawn, the latter of whom had been reinstated.

If getting prominent individuals, and even the dismissed students themselves, to attend the open hearing was hard enough, MCAF's efforts became seriously jeopardized at the end of October when the Masonic Temple revoked its agreement to house the event.[132] The temple management claimed that it was canceling the contract due to "the non-participation of the University in the hearing."[133] While Reverend Knox wrote to Ruthven asking in vain for the use of a university auditorium in the name of free speech and free assembly, the temple management insinuated to MCAF "that it was 'pressure' which decided this move."[134] MCAF unsuccessfully attempted to obtain a court injunction to force the Masonic Temple to honor its contract, leaving the group scrambling to find another locale in the very last week before the hearing was to occur.[135] Efforts to obtain another hall in Ann Arbor proved fruitless, with Knox complaining in one letter that "we shall probably be forced to erect a tent in this 'company town' in

account mention him. The draft script and Hamilton's notes is in CRC, series 8, box 77, folder Hearing—Nov. 9, 1940, WRL. His name is also not mentioned in the Ann Arbor Police report on the meeting (see VPSS, box 4, folder ASU, BHL). Nonetheless, it does appear that Forman was in attendance: he wrote Beatrice Kahn to ask for reimbursement for his travel expenses to Ann Arbor. See his letters to her dated November 19 and November 30, 1940, CRC, series 8, box 76, folder Correspondence November 11–30, 1940, WRL.

132. The earliest mention of this is in Paulson's letter to Reichard, dated October 25, 1940: "Masonic Temple now bucking, say we can't have auditorium after all. Legal fight doubting coming up." CRC, series 8, box 76, folder Correspondence Oct. 20–31, 1940, WRL.

133. Knox to Ruthven, letter dated November 2, 1940, CRC, series 8, box 76, folder Correspondence Oct. 20–31, 1940, WRL.

134. This and the other details in the paragraph, unless otherwise cited, are from a letter to Yale Forman, dated November 5, 1940, CRC, series 8, box 76, folder Correspondence November 1–10, 1940, WRL. See also "Freedom Group Sues Temple," *MD*, November 1, 1940.

135. "Rev. Owen Knox Address Rights Committee Today," *MD*, November 4, 1940. As late as the day before the open hearing, a locale had not been found: "Admittance Hearing Will Be Tomorrow," *MD*, November 8, 1940.

order to have a roof over our heads."[136] Ultimately, MCAF was not even able to arrange a tent: the hearing was held in the open air on a baseball diamond in Island Park, a local park, on a bitterly cold November afternoon.

The lack of time to find a new location inevitably depressed turnout, with only six hundred of the projected one to two thousand attending.[137] Handbills were passed out that reflected the organizers' aspirations more than the event as it transpired: "Two Thousand Jurors will hear the evidence in the Case of the Michigan Students [Figures 7.12 and 7.13] ."[138]

Given the forty-degree weather and the smaller than anticipated turnout, MCAF decided to shorten the proceedings "to keep our audience from disappearing, in self-defense against the cold."[139] As a result, the open hearing, far from galvanizing greater interest in the case, proved to be anti-climactic. After introductions by Poulson and Knox, the chairman of the ACLU, E. A. Ross, delivered a speech chiding Ruthven for putting aside Michigan's vaunted liberal tradition of tolerance.[140] "I am afraid," he told the audience, "the University is not as tenacious of American

136. Knox to D. S. Gillmer, letter dated November 5, 1940, CRC, series 8, box 76, folder Correspondence November 1–10, 1940, WRL.

137. See the letter from Iva Nauta to the Civil Rights Federation, dated November 11, 1940, complaining that no notice had been posted or people placed at the Masonic Temple to re-direct attendees to the new location. The figure of six hundred is given both in the *MD*, November 10, 1940, and in a letter to W. K. Kelsey of the *Detroit News*, dated November 20. Both letters are in CRC, series 8, box 76, folder Correspondence November 11–30, 1940, WRL. The previous month, Kelsey had communicated to Knox his doubts on the strength of MCAF's case against Ruthven. See Kelsey to Knox, letter dated October 24, 1940, CRC, series 8, box 76, folder Correspondence Oct. 20–31, 1940, WRL.

138. The handbill is located in CRC, series 8, box 77, folder Hearing—Nov. 9, 1940, WRL.

139. Letter to Kelsey, dated November 20, 1940, CRC, series 8, box 76, folder Correspondence November 11–30, 1940, WRL.

140. According to the report from the Ann Arbor Police, Knox claimed in his speech that Ann Arbor was a "company town" and that he implicated university authorities putting pressure on organizations not to rent their venues for the event. See VPSS, box 4, folder ASU, BHL.

Two Thousand Jurors

Will hear the evidence in

THE CASE OF THE MICHIGAN STUDENTS

TWO THOUSAND Americans will gather in the Masonic Temple auditorium in the college city of Ann Arbor on November 9, to give to more than thirteen students the Open Hearing to which they are entitled, and which they have been denied.

The students were informed last June in curt one-sentence letters from President Alexander G. Ruthven that "IT IS THE DECISION OF THE AUTHORITIES OF THE UNIVERSITY OF MICHIGAN THAT YOU CANNOT BE READMITTED TO THE UNIVERSITY." The letters gave no *reason* for this "decision of the authorities".

The surprised students, many of them winners of academic honors, none of them aware of having committed any breach of discipline, have asked again and again for a statement of the charges against them. None has been given.

Their requests for an open hearing, backed by Michigan labor, student, professional, civil rights and other organizations, and prominent persons from every part of America, have been flatly denied.

What are the reasons which Dr. Ruthven refuses to make public? Dr. Ruthven's Commencement address of June 15 may provide a hint. In that address he said:

> "To those young people who are planning to enter or return to the University next year I issue this warning: Michigan welcomes only students who are convinced that democracy is the ideal form of government for a civilized people. She will not be confused by sophistries built around meaningful but ill-defined phrases such as 'freedom of the press' and 'freedom of speech', but will deal firmly, without fear or favor, with subversive or so-called 'fifth column' activities."

Examination of the records of the students provides an interpretation of this statement. For some of the students were active in the American Student Union; some fought against Negro discrimination in Ann Arbor; some helped organize an anti-war meeting in which 3,000 students took part; some assisted the SCMWA-CIO in passing out union leaflets to the low-paid University employees.

We know, too, that the University has made it difficult for its employees to organize; that the Regents refused to talk with the representatives of organized labor who came to them on September 20th to ask for an open hearing. Is it possible that Dr. Ruthven considers student activities in behalf of labor "subversive"? Does President Ruthven's action mean that the University of Michigan will henceforth deny an education to students whose views and actions are not in accordance with the wishes of a few administrators?

THE Administration of the University has been invited to the Open Hearing to present its side of the story . The students, teachers, representatives of labor, will present theirs. YOU, as one of the American people, concerned with the preservation of our democratic traditions, will be there too, to pass judgement on the guilt or innocence of the students—to decide whether academic freedom has been violated by the University of Michigan.

This Hearing will be a milestone in the history of America's traditional fight for free education.

Will hear

PROF. GEORGE E.
AXTELLE
Northwestern University

JEROME DAVIS

REV. OWEN A. KNOX
President, Civil Rights
Federation

PROF. E. A. ROSS
Chairman, American Civil
Liberties Union

HON. RUDOLPH G.
TENEROWICZ
Congressman from
Michigan

R. J. **THOMAS**
President, UAW-CIO

HERBERT WITT
Exec. Sec'y American
Student Union

MAURICE SUGAR
Labor Attorney
EXAMINING ATTORNEY

COME!

to the
OPEN HEARING
ANN ARBOR
MICHIGAN

MASONIC TEMPLE
Auditorium—1 p. m.

SATURDAY
November 9

Send Delegates
from your organization!

MICHIGAN COMMITTEE FOR ACADEMIC FREEDOM ★ CIVIL RIGHTS FEDERATION

Sponsors: FRANKLIN P. ADAMS — JOSEPHINE TRUSLOW ADAMS — WALTER H. ALLMENDINGER — JOHN T. BERNARD — PROF. FRANZ BOAS — PROF. EDWIN BERRY BURGUM — PROF. GEORGE S. COUNTS — DR. HENRY HITT CRANE — JOSEPH M. CURRAN — DR. NED DEARBORN — HON. CHARLES C. DIGGS — ERNEST GOODMAN — DASHIELL HAMMETT — REV. CHARLES A. HILL — ROCKWELL KENT — REV. OWEN A. KNOX — PROF. ROBERT S. LYND — DR. J. J. McCLENDON — C. L. MEADER — REV. JOHN M. MILES — HON. STANLEY NOWAK — JEROME SHORE — C. LeBRON SIMMONS — PROF. ROBERT K. SPEER — ALFRED K. STERN — MAXWELL S. STEWART — DR. HARRY F. WARD — MORRIS WATSON — LAWRENCE BLYTHE AND OTHERS.

(PLEASE ANNOUNCE AND POST)

Figure 7.12: [Michigan Committee for Academic Freedom handbill for the open hearing, November 1940], Vice President of Student Services box 4, folder American Students Union, Bentley Historical Library, University of Michigan.

Figure 7.13: [Michigan Committee for Academic Freedom handbill for the open hearing, November 1940], Vice President of Student Services box 4, folder American Students Union, Bentley Historical Library, University of Michigan.

Students Testify At Open 'Hearing'

Figure 7.14: Hugo Reichard and Maurice Sugar at the Open Hearing. *Michigan Daily*, November 10, 1940 (p. 1). Photo: Will Sapp/The Michigan Daily

rights as it used to be."[141] Three of the four dismissed students in attendance (Reichard, Rinzberg, and Lawn) were questioned by the prominent labor attorney, Maurice Sugar [Figure 7.14]. The fourth, Yale Forman, appears not to have participated in the hearing beyond making an appearance. Each presented their accounts of their dismissals and their audiences with Ruthven.[142] During his questioning, Reichard said that he had come all the way from Chicago, where he now lived, because he sought to achieve the affirmation of the entire campus that the dismissed students should have a fair and open hearing.[143] Rinzberg testified to the absurdity of Ruthven's distinction between *dismissing* him and *expelling* him.

Roger Lawn's testimony proved to be the most dramatic and requires some context as it shows that Ruthven was willing to show preferential consideration to certain of the dismissed students over the others. Ruthven informed Victor Lawn, a newspaper reporter and a Michigan alumnus (class of 1912), in June 1940 that his son, Roger, had received a dismissal warning both due to his political activity and to his poor grades. The elder Lawn responded in a letter thanking Ruthven for enlightening him as to his son's perilous standing. "I have already told him," Victor Lawn wrote to Ruthven, "that unless he gives up all extra-curricular activities until he has mastered his curricular duties, I will personally go to An Arbor and remove him bodily from college for all time. (That should save you some trouble.)"[144] Roger was permit-

---

141. The quote is from Hamilton's notes; it does not appear in the *Michigan Daily* account. CRC, series 8, box 77, folder Hearing—Nov. 9, 1940, WRL.

142. Although there are some differences in emphasis, the handwritten notes by an attendee, R. H. Hamilton, are in general agreement with the account printed in the *Michigan Daily* on November 10, 1940, under the heading, "Davis Speaks at Trial of 13 Students Told Not to Return." Hamilton's notes are located in CRC, series 8, box 77, folder Hearing—Nov. 9, 1940, WRL. The most significant differences are in the presentation of Roger Lawn's testimony. For a biography on Sugar, see Johnson, *Maurice Sugar*.

143. *MD*, November 10, 1940.

144. Victor Lawn to Ruthven, letter dated June 27, 1940. Ruthven box 58, folder 11, BHL. Victor (1892-1982) was an officer of the University of Michigan Club of New York and this letter was typed on its letterhead. In 1943, Lawn joined the *New York*

ted to enroll for the fall term. On Wednesday, November 6, he asked his father to be released from his promise not to engage in 'extra-curricular activities'—which referred to the open hearing—and the elder Lawn angrily sent a letter informing Ruthven of his decision to withdraw his son.[145]

Victor Lawn also came straight from New York to Ann Arbor to try to persuade Roger in person not to attend the open hearing but found little success. He also requested a meeting with the president declaring his intention to withdraw his son and thus avoid embarrassing his beloved alma mater.[146] The father's actions, and his willingness to withdraw Roger, put the administration in some quandary; few of the other dismissed or warned students were offered even a fraction of such forbearance. As the Office of the President noted, "will the action on Roger's part in participating in the hearing, and apparently in preparation for this meeting, prove sufficient to ask his father to remove him now, or will he be again talked to and warned and be out at end of semester if he does not attend to his business and who is going to know whether or not he is attending to his business."[147]

Roger's appearance at the hearing, then, was not merely a bold protest against the Ruthven administration, given that he had been permitted to enroll in fall classes, but was also an act of filial defiance. Roger claimed in his speech that he wanted to "go down fighting against the manifestations of fascism in America."[148] As

Times as a reporter, and remained at the paper until 1958. See Lawn's *New York Times* obituary, dated November 22, 1982: https://www.nytimes.com/1982/11/22/obituaries/victor-h-lawn.html

145. Victor Lawn to Ruthven, letter dated November 8, 1940. Ruthven's files also contain a report of events related to Roger Lawn and printed on Office of the President stationary. Both Lawn's letter and this timeline are in Ruthven box 58, folder 11, BHL.

146. See the Office of the President report on Roger Lawn in Ruthven box 58, folder 11, BHL.

147. Office of the President report on Roger Lawn in Ruthven box 58, folder 11, BHL.

148. See Hamilton's notes, CRC, series 8, box 77, folder Hearing—Nov. 9, 1940, WRL. Lawn's speech and the resulting altercation with his father are not in the *Michigan*

soon as Roger finished his speech, his father rushed to the stage and insisted on speaking himself. He not only told the assembled group that he was an alumnus but, while a student at Michigan himself, had participated in the Socialist Society and therefore "Mr. Lawn claimed to be as liberal as anyone present at the open hearing."[149] He claimed that Roger had only been re-admitted after promising Ruthven to refrain from 'extra-curricular activities' and to improve his scholarship. The elder Lawn claimed his son's moral fiber had been weakened by not fulfilling his promise and then that Roger had been "damned by inference to the organizations and individuals who had brought pressure on Rodger [sic] to take this step [i.e., participate in the open hearing]."[150] After demanding to speak again, Roger said that it was "intellectually impossible to abide by this promise." When his father still refused, Roger told the assembled that he thought testifying was still necessary.[151] Maurice Sugar praised Roger's moral tenacity: "If I were that father, I would be proud of that son!"[152]

The Lawns were, in fact, reconciled during a meeting with Ruthven held on Monday, November 11. During the meeting, Roger's father again expressed his intention to withdraw his son from the university. Ruthven "dissuaded the father and gained his permission for Roger to continue in school."[153] MCAF issued a press release that same day announcing both the Lawns' reconciliation and the lifting of any restrictions against Roger's 'extra-curricular activities.' Reverend Owen Knox was quoted in the news release as

Daily account of the open hearing.

149. Hamilton's notes, CRC, series 8, box 77, folder Hearing—Nov. 9, 1940, WRL.

150. Hamilton's notes, CRC, series 8, box 77, folder Hearing—Nov. 9, 1940, WRL.

151. See the MCAF press release, dated November 11, 1940, Ruthven, box 58, folder 12, BHL.

152. Hamilton's notes, CRC, series 8, box 77, folder Hearing—Nov. 9, 1940, WRL.

153. See Knox's letter to Jerome Davis, dated November 13, 1940, CRC, series 8, box 76, folder Correspondence November 11–30, 1940, WRL. The quote comes from an MCAF press release, dated November 11, 1940, CRC, series 8, box 77, folder Press Releases.

thanking Ruthven for his intercession and claiming that the lifting of the restrictions against Roger Lawn justified MCAF's existence. "If the University will reconsider its position in regard to each of the other students who were dismissed," Knox said, "and reach a similar decision, the primary objective of the Michigan Committee for Academic Freedom will have been achieved."[154]

Speaking during the open hearing, Victor Lawn claimed that Roger had not been shown favoritism despite being the son of an alumnus.[155] Yet, it is indisputable based on the surviving evidence that Roger was shown far more leniency by Ruthven and his administration than any of the other students and certainly more than any of those dismissed outright. He had one of the weakest academic records among all the dismissed students, his only grades were Cs and Ds.[156] Ultimately, Roger Lawn had a weaker case for reinstatement than did many of those dismissed outright: Yale Forman, for instance, had twenty-three credit hours of A grades, twenty-six of Bs, and 11 of Cs. Yet, Ruthven provided Lawn with multiple opportunities to 'shape up' while at the same time he was unyielding with those that he had concluded were to be dismissed. Although Lawn's ethnicity did not play a part in this decision, it is clear that had Ruthven so wanted, he could have offered all the dismissed students the same opportunity for reinstatement, as Knox had said in the MCAF press release. The considerable forbearance that Ruthven showed Roger Lawn belies Ruthven's claim that those students who were dismissed could not be reinstated at all.[157]

154. The quote comes from an MCAF press release, dated November 11, 1940, CRC, series 8, box 77, folder Press Releases.

155. MCAF press release, dated November 9, 1940. CRC, series 8, box 77, folder Press Releases.

156. Ruthven's files contain an undated grade report of all seventeen students. Lawn was on probation, having accumulated 26 credit hours of C grades and 4 credit hours of D grades. Only De Haney and Hayden had weaker showings. The grade report is in Ruthven box 58, folder 11, BHL.

157. Indeed, Lawn persisted both in his interest in radical activities and in failing to improve his scholarship. During a mid-November meeting with Carl Brandt, Director of Student-Alumni Relations, Roger indicated that "he would like to attend an

But to return to the open hearing: following the Lawns' separate testimonies, Jerome Davis, professor at the New School for Social Research recounted an interview that he had had with Ruthven and administration officials the previous day.[158] According to Davis, Ruthven told him that "there was no such thing as academic freedom," which Davis likened to Cornelius Vanderbilt's slogan, "the public be damned!" Davis continued to say that Ruthven refused to provide him with the reasons for the dismissals, told him that each student had been informed of the reasons, and that the Student Senate did not amount to much.

occasional meeting of the Michigan Student Union but that he did not want to take any active part to the extent of permitting his studies to suffer." Brandt attempted to dissuade him. Brandt also informed the elder Lawn about the MCAF press release of November 11 that detailed his reconciliation with his son. Brandt told Victor that "it seems to me that only one or two conclusions can be drawn from this story. Either Roger was guilty of extremely bad faith in telling about the conference that was held with President Ruthven on Sunday morning, or the Reverend Knox and his group are not going to permit Roger to follow the dictates of his own conscience." Combined with Roger's continuing poor academic performance, Brandt advised Victor Lawn to withdraw his son from the university. Brandt to Victor Lawn, letter dated November 16, 1940, Ruthven box 58, folder 11, BHL. In January 1941, Ruthven himself sent a letter to Victor Lawn expressing his regret in persuading him not to withdraw his son given the excessive absences he accrued in the fall 1940 term and that the Dean has asked Roger to withdraw. In reply, Victor thanked the university for all that they had done for Roger. "Roger has been treated with utmost consideration and fairness," he wrote to Ruthven, "and you, personally, came to his aid and urged me not to compel the University to accept my letter withdrawing Roger from attendance as long ago as November 8th or 9th. You literally pleaded with me that he be given another chance." The elder Lawn also attacked, though not by name, the ASU and MCAF for exploiting, as he saw it, his son's ordeal. "It may very well be that certain individuals or groups may try to make another cause celebre in Roger's case. That would be one of the most bitterly unjust things I could imagine. In such event I earnestly hope you will publish or make public in the responsible circles this letter." See Ruthven to Victor Lawn, letter dated January 15, 1941; and Victor Lawn to Ruthven, letter dated January 16, 1941. Both in Ruthven box 58, folder 11, BHL. The underlined text is in Mr. Lawn's letter. A separate note to Ruthven stated that Lawn intended to get a job in the "one of the war industries." In fact, Roger Lawn was killed in action during the Second World War, according to his friend, Robert Copp during an interview with the authors. See also: https://www.fairlawn.org/government/honor-roll-war-deceased.

158. The following details are from Hamilton's notes and almost completely accord with the *Michigan Daily* account.

According to Davis, Ruthven then boasted that he had helped Forman get into the University of Wisconsin, prompting Davis to ask if Wisconsin was good enough for Forman, why not Michigan? When Davis brought up the case of George Stein, Ruthven admitted that Stein's teaching fellowship had been revoked "because Stein had distributed circulars protesting the action of the University in the dismissal" and that Ruthven had gotten Stein's name from the police. When Davis reminded Ruthven that Stein had a constitutional right to distribute leaflets, the president replied "yes, but when a student who had received scholarship loans, isn't it most ungrateful from him to criticize the University?" Finally, Davis concluded his speech by recounting a conversation with a Michigan faculty member who told him that the four students dismissed in 1935 were all "brilliant and the whole action was regarded as 'unjustifiable.'"

Finally, current members of the ASU spoke starting with the organizing secretary, Margaret Campbell, who claimed that the university threatened to revoke her scholarship if she did not discontinue her activities with the ASU. The last speaker was Herbert Witt, executive secretary of the ASU's national organization, who spoke on the national significance of the dismissed students' cases and presented telegrams of protest against Ruthven from students and faculty at numerous colleges.

Despite Witt's insistence to the contrary, the open hearing proved to be the peak in the campaign on behalf of the dismissed students. The nearly impromptu event had succeeded at least in attracting the interest of the authorities with the Ann Arbor Police submitting a report to the FBI on the event.[159] The police report on the open hearing stated that the spectators totaled between 250 to 300 persons "noticeably Jewish and some Negroes." The police report also featured a different conclusion to the event than

159. Hamilton's notes claim that rumors went around that "several Ford Service men were in the crowd, noting the license plates of parked automobiles." However, it is more likely that these were undercover police. The Ann Arbor Police report, dated November 18, 1940, is in VPSS, box 4, folder ASU, BHL.

either Hamilton's notes or the *Michigan Daily*'s account, stating that Sugar gave a closing argument by asking "if President Ruthven, Regent Harry Kipke, or Henry Ford are present to argue case. Said intimidation is being used, that U of M authorities and big business are taking orders from someone (intimated Fascist). Said this meeting was only the opening gun, that President Ruthven will not have a comfortable night's sleep until these students are reinstated."[160] Yet the authorities' concern was ultimately as misplaced as the participants' enthusiasm. Despite optimistic reports of heightened interest in the dismissed students' cases in the immediate aftermath of the hearing, attention to the whole affair abated sharply by the end of November. Writing to Beatrice Kahn from Wisconsin, Forman observed, "Activity on the Michigan case has slowed down terrifically since the 'hearing' and probably will remain so until registration, where the situation will again arise for another campaign. I have tried to prod them, but it really is difficult to get them to concentrate on the expulsions, what with the national and international scenes the way they are, and the local campus situation in a bad mess—wages & house, N.Y.A. [National Youth Administration], negro discrimination, etc."[161]

The desperate eleventh-hour rush to secure a venue not only depressed turnout but also left MCAF with a sizeable deficit. MCAF wrote to the ACLU begging for support to cover its expenses: "When reactionary pressure took from us the use of the two-thousand–seat auditorium we had rented, and forced us to meet on a base-ball diamond in forty-degree weather, we necessarily expended a great deal of additional money to publicize the new meeting-place. The reduced attendance caused by the forty-degree weather out of doors made it impossible to fulfill our reasonable anticipations of covering all expenses through the

160. Ann Arbor Police report, VPSS, box 4, folder ASU, BHL.

161. Forman to Khan, letter dated November 30, 1940, CRC, series 8, box 76, folder Correspondence November 11–30, 1940, WRL.

collection."[162] While MCAF asked the ACLU for $150, in truth it appears to have incurred a deficit of over $400, making it difficult for MCAF even to compensate some of the attendees for their travel expenses.[163] By the winter of 1941, the movement to reinstate the dismissed students had for all intents and purposes vanished. By early 1941, new issues were beginning to occupy students' concerns: the ever-increasing likelihood of conflict with Germany and Japan and thus the possibility of conscription. But while the drive to reinstate the dismissed students created only a temporary—even illusory—mobilization among their supporters, it spurred a harsh and repressive response from the administration.

The Limits of Pluralism

On the same day of the open hearing in Ann Arbor's Island Park, President Ruthven was in Chicago at the National Association of State Universities' annual convention. Echoing his June commencement speech, Ruthven asserted that faculty members of state universities who tolerated criticism of the democratic form of government should quit. "Freedom of independent thinking, expresion [sic], and assembly in our schools is not license for students and faculty to work against the very form of government which allows such rights to exist," he said.[164] Ruthven proceeded to say that administrators and faculty needed to rid themselves

162. Letter to the American Civil Liberties Union [n.d. but after November 9, 1940], CRC, series 8, box 76, folder Correspondence—Dec. 1940, WRL.

163. See letter to Roger Baldwin, dated November 18, 1940, CRC, series 8, box 76, folder Correspondence—Dec. 1940, WRL. For MCAF's struggles to pay its speakers, see Ross to Jack Raskin, letter dated January 31, 1941, CRC, series 8, box 77, folder Correspondence—1941, WRL.

164. "Indiscriminate Criticism Not to Be Supported, Ruthven Declares," MD, November 10, 1940. See Paul Chandler's editorial response in Michigan Daily wherein he chides Ruthven for failing to define what he meant by "romanticism, sentimentalism, and indiscriminate tolerance." He also reminded Ruthven of a speech he gave in 1938 in which the president defended the values of a liberal education. See Chandler, "The Little Red Schoolhouse . . . ," MD, November 12, 1940.

of the notion that "romanticism, sentimentalism, and indiscriminate tolerance are essential constituents of democracy."[165]

Yet it was the students, not faculty, who continued to feel the brunt of Ruthven's hardline policy. Having been stripped of many of its members courtesy of the dismissals, the Michigan ASU was placed on probation by the university in December. The Michigan ASU held a "novelty party" on Friday night, November 8—the night before the open hearing—at the Michigan League and had unwisely failed to secure university approval.[166] Although the group was essentially let off with a warning, it was to run afoul of the administration again very soon—and for the final time. The ASU had secured permission to use space in the Michigan Union to sponsor a series of speeches on Monday, November 11. When it filed a request to use university space, it listed the overarching topic of the speeches as "Can Armistice Day Mark a Renewed Fight for Peace?" featuring Herbert Witt, executive secretary of the national ASU, George Axtelle, Stanley Nowak, and Harper Paulson as speakers.[167]

Although the event happened without an incident, the Michigan ASU's executive secretary, Margaret Campbell, received a letter a week afterward from Carl Brandt, secretary to the Lecture Policy committee accusing the ASU of misrepresenting the nature of the meeting.[168] "I am informed," Brandt wrote, "that speeches were made by you and other people which were in the nature of a protest to certain actions of the University that had nothing to do with the main purpose of the meeting."[169] He also contended that the Michigan ASU had changed speakers and had commenced a collection when, according to the requirements of the university's facilities usage, monies were not to be collected

165. "Indiscriminate Criticism," *MD*, November 10, 1940.

166. Rea to Norris, letter dated November 15, 1940, Ruthven, box 58, folder 12, BHL.

167. A copy of the request for permission is in Ruthven, box 58, folder 12, BHL.

168. Brandt to Campbell, letter dated November 16, 1940, Ruthven, box 58, folder 12, BHL.

169. Brandt to Campbell, November 16, 1940, Ruthven, box 58, folder 12, BHL.

at such occasions. Most likely, Brandt received this information from Stanley G. Waltz, manager of the Michigan Union, who had sent an informant named Frank Oakes to the November 11 meeting.[170] Oakes's report back to Waltz claimed that the turnout at the event was about two hundred and that, instead of just keeping to the meeting's stated purpose of advocating US neutrality, the event was also used to rally support for the dismissed students. At the meeting, Campbell affirmed in her speech that the Michigan ASU was determined to continue the fight and, according to Oakes's report, that "Some chap I do not know followed her to the platform and spoke more about the recent TRIAL for the dismissed students and stated that the TRIAL was only the beginning of the fight to secure reinstatement."[171] Oakes also reported that "then someone chimes in with the statement that the ASU knew that this fall the administration would be more reactionary than it had been last spring" and that Bert Witt, the head of the national ASU, made two caustic references about Ruthven.[172] In a letter accompanying Oakes's report, Waltz informed the Committee on Student Affairs that the Michigan ASU had broken faith with the university on multiple occasions, that this was the last straw, and that "we therefore respectfully request and urge that the local chapter of the American Student Union be removed at once from the list of approved student organizations."[173]

170. Waltz is mentioned in *The University of Michigan: An Encyclopedic Survey*, https://quod.lib.umich.edu/u/umsurvey/AAS3302.0004.001/472:3.2. See also "Waltz Called to Army Duty," *Ann Arbor News*, January 24, 1941, https://aadl.org/aa_news_19410124-waltz_called_to_army_duty. A Frank Oakes is mentioned in the *Michigan Alumnus*, August 21, 1943, 465.

171. See the report attached to the letter from Waltz to Dean Joseph Bursley, Committee on Student Affairs, dated November 25, 1940, Ruthven, box 58, folder 12, BHL.

172. The report attached to the letter from Waltz to Dean Joseph Bursley, Committee on Student Affairs, dated November 25, 1940, Ruthven, box 58, folder 12, BHL.

173. Waltz to Bursley, letter dated November 25, 1940, Ruthven, box 58, folder 12, BHL. The letter trail is incomplete here inasmuch as Brandt notified Campbell of the ASU's infractions on November 16. It seems likely that Waltz shared Oakes's report, which was dated November 11, with Brandt before he submitted it to the

Dean Bursley referred the matter to the Men's Judiciary Council that had the authority to investigate specific disciplinary problems upon the dean's request. In its communication with the Discipline Committee, the council concluded that the Michigan ASU had violated ten university regulations: specifically that it had failed to gain permission to host its novelty party in the Michigan League; that it misrepresented the natures of its novelty day meeting on November 8 and its armistice-themed meeting on November 11; that no accounting of the funds collected at both meetings were made to the dean of students; that members of the university staff could not secure full and frank cooperation with the ASU; that the ASU was unable to pay $50 in charges assessed against it by the dean of students; and that it had already been disciplined the previous year. The council recommended probation for one year, depriving the ASU of the privileges of an officially recognized student organization but "would still permit the University and the Office of the Dean of Students to have control over the American Student Union."[174]

One of the charges of which the Men's Judiciary Council found the Michigan ASU guilty had nothing to do with its social activities. The council referred to a letter that Harold Norris,[175] president of

Committee on Student Affairs, although why it took him a week to do so is not clear from the documentation.

174. Quaal to Discipline Committee, VPSS, box 4, folder ASU, BHL.

175. Harold Norris (1918–2013) became a professor at the Michigan State University College of Law where he taught constitutional law, criminal law, and women and the law for over thirty-five years. After finishing his bachelor's and master's degrees at Michigan (in 1939 and 1941, respectively), he served in the Army Air Corps during the Second World War and earned his Juris Doctor from Columbia University. He also served as president of the Detroit chapter of the ACLU from 1958 to 1961 before joining Michigan State. Norris was also a delegate to the Michigan Constitutional Convention, serving as the principal architect of the Michigan Bill of Rights, drafting provisions prohibiting racial and religious discrimination and co-authoring provisions creating the Michigan Civil Rights Commission. His obituary at https://www.law.msu.edu/news/2013/norris-notice.html states his birthday as April 7, 1918, which is the same date that he gives in his interview with the University of Michigan's "Discipline Committee: Interview with Harold Norris," *Meeting of the Disciplinary Committee, University of Michigan*, December 4, 1940, 11, VPSS, box 4, folder ASU, BHL.

the Michigan ASU chapter, had printed in the *Daily* on November 26, which the council claimed "oversteps the bounds of propriety and is a malicious attack on the University and the Board of Regents."[176] The "letter" was actually an editorial that Norris had written in response to the Men's Judiciary Council's defense of Ruthven's decision to dismiss the students. The council had argued in its *Daily* editorial that the dismissed students were representatives of a group that had indirectly forced the university into raising tuition to the detriment of all students on campus. The council's editorial submitted that the Michigan ASU's radicalism over the past several years had tarnished the university's reputation with the state government: "Unfortunately, the people of the state have confused our broadmindedness and tolerance toward radicalism with radicalism itself. For years, the authorities of our University have seen its name splashed across Detroit headlines such as 'Red Probe at U. of M.' they have seen and heard the State Legislature criticize and condemn us as a stronghold of communism, the Times Square of the Middle West, and a bulwark of atheism. They have watched our appropriations being slashed every year, thanks to the free tongue and free pen of our 'two per cent' [of students who are politically radical]."[177] The editorial proceeded to defend Ruthven's willingness to accept widespread criticism in the name of preserving the university's appropriations and to justify his dismissal decision. Indeed the text claimed that Ruthven had to forgo his commitment to academic freedom "until we could erase our undeserved reputation with our financial backers, the Legislature, and the people."[178]

Although the Men's Judiciary Council believed that Ruthven had sufficient cause to dismiss the students, the council members intended to back him even if the ASU's charges against the presi-

176. Quaal to Discipline Committee, VPSS, box 4, folder ASU, BHL.

177. "Men's Judiciary Council Explains Its Stand on Readmission Cases," *MD*, November 19, 1940.

178. "Men's Judiciary Council Explains Its Stand on Readmission Cases," *MD*, November 19, 1940.

dent were correct. "But if the reasons are political, as is charged," the editorial asserted, "we nevertheless back his [Ruthven's] move wholeheartedly as being necessary to the best interest of Michigan and ninety-eight percent of her students."[179]

In his rebuttal a week later, Norris dismissed the council's claim that Ruthven had nobly sacrificed the ideals of academic freedom for the greater good of maintaining harmonious relations with the state government.[180] He reminded the council that the president had made no specific charges and that he had not given the students any opportunity to defend themselves. Norris further argued of the danger in the university's and the council's belief that the voice of a minority should be suppressed for the majority's benefit. Norris then charged that the university's tuition hike was not due to a cut in the annual appropriations from Lansing that was, after all, only a reduction of 1% for 1940–41. He laid the blame for the tuition hike, which adversely affected lower-income students, instead on the Board of Regents itself, insinuating that the regents used the controversy of the dismissals to raise tuition in order to keep out-of-state and poor students from attending the University of Michigan. For good measure, Norris also referenced the inflammatory article published in the *Nation* in September 1940 stating that the "University's Board of Regents contains, among its eight members, Michigan's former head football coach, Harry Kipke, who as a candidate for his post received the aid of Ford's anti-union personnel director, Harry Bennett."[181]

Considering the efforts that the ASU and MCAF had already taken to publicize the dismissed students' cases nationally, the reference to Kipke and Bennett in an editorial in Michigan's own

179. "Men's Judiciary Council Explains Its Stand on Readmission Cases," *MD*, November 19, 1940. Given the stated opposition of the Men's Judiciary Council to the ASU in this November 19 editorial, Dean Bursley's decision to refer the disciplinary matter over to them sometime after November 25 was effectively a move to get a foregone recommendation for disciplinary action against the group.

180. Harold Norris, "A Reply to the Judiciary Council," *MD*, November 26, 1940.

181. Norris, "A Reply," *MD*, November 26, 1940.

student newspaper was simply too much for the administration. On December 4, the University Board in Control of Publications, also under the chairmanship of Dean Bursley, suspended the *Daily*'s managing director, Hervie Haufler, and its editorial director, Alvin Sarasohn, for one week from the paper. Moreover, the two students were required to write and publish an apology upon their reinstatement.[182]

On the same day that Haufler and Sarasohn received their suspension from the *Daily*, the Disciplinary Committee, composed of three faculty members, interviewed the Michigan ASU chapter's president, Harold Norris, and its executive secretary, Margaret Campbell, over the events of the past month.[183] Norris's interview with the committee came first, and it was a testy affair. The committee questioned him on his surname, whereupon Norris admitted that he had his name changed in Detroit probate court from Ossepow. He was asked about the ASU's failure to secure permission to use a room at the Michigan League for its novelty party on November 8. Norris claimed to have no knowledge of the arrangements or even of all the members of the chapter's executive committee. Then the committee brought up the group's misrepresentation of its armistice meeting on the eleventh of November. When the committee charged that raising the issue of the dismissed students was extraneous to the topic of warfare and neutrality, Norris replied that "to a great number of minds, the question of war and peace is related to the expulsion, and we felt that that was a consideration, and Miss Campbell in giving

182. "Student Editors Are Suspended," *Ann Arbor News*, December 4, 1940. The committee was chaired by Grover C. Grismore, professor of law. Other members included A. E. R. Boak of the history department; Axel Marin of the mechanical engineering department; and Dean Bursley as ex-officio member. See "'U' Discipline Faced by ASU," *Ann Arbor News*, December 5, 1940; and "ASU Placed on Probation," *Ann Arbor News*, December 7, 1940.

183. The transcriptions of each interview are located in VPSS, box 4, folder ASU, BHL.

the announcement felt it was proper."[184] The committee asked Norris about a new handbill produced by the ASU in the wake of his column that was named "A New Victimization!" concerning the immanent suspensions of Haufler and Sarasohn and that, the committee alleged, the Michigan ASU distributed leaflets at the Engineering Arch and at the Union in violation of university policy.[185]

Finally, the committee addressed the issue of Norris's editorial in the *Daily*. In particular, the committee asked that Norris clarify the implications he made about the tuition hike and, above all, his characterization of individual Board of Regents members as crooked. Norris explained that his point about the tuition raise was not to doubt the honesty on the part of the board but rather to affirm "the power and position they [the board members] have to get a tuition raise," which clearly discriminates "against certain sections of the population."[186] Asked if he had any basis for his belief, Norris replied, "Well, out-of-state students had to pay higher rates. I believe it is impossible to know how many students had the idea of coming to the University and had it changed when the tuition raise went into effect."[187] Finally, the committee asked about Norris's criticisms of Kipke, wondering how Norris could have stooped so low as to imply that Kipke's running a lunch concession at the Rouge plant was crooked. The committee also wondered what Norris meant with his claim that all of these things had connections to the University of Michigan. "There is a connection in that the tuition raise had to go through the Board of Regents

184. Interview with Harold Norris," *Meeting of the Disciplinary Committee, University of Michigan*, December 4, 1940, 9, VPSS, box 4, folder ASU, BHL.

185. A copy of this handbill is located in VPSS, box 4, folder ASU, BHL. The handbill apparently was circulated on campus on the very day of the Disciplinary Committee's meeting on December 4. See "Student Union on the Carpet," *Detroit Free Press*, December 5, 1940, VPSS, box 4, folder ASU, BHL.

186. Interview with Harold Norris," *Meeting of the Disciplinary Committee, University of Michigan*, December 4, 1940, 14–15, VPSS, box 4, folder ASU, BHL.

187. Interview with Harold Norris," *Meeting of the Disciplinary Committee, University of Michigan*, December 4, 1940, 14–15, VPSS, box 4, folder ASU, BHL.

and the expulsion had to go through the Board of Regents," Norris replied. Pressed further to explain this connection, Norris continued, "It is not a far-fetched implication that certain interests in the state of Michigan have certain interpretations of events and would like to see certain policies carried out."[188]

The interview ended when the committee could not get Norris to admit that he failed to ascertain the reasons for the board's decision to raise tuition. Norris was summarily asked to leave the meeting. After Norris's stormy interview, Campbell was grilled on what she knew (or did not) about the policies surrounding use of the university's facilities. She admitted to taking up a collection to defray the costs of using the Union for the armistice meeting on November 11. Moreover, Campbell also said that she had changed the nature of the program upon the recommendation of Preston Slosson, a professor of history who was one of the speakers that evening. Campbell was also asked about the ASU's "New Victimization!" handbill and especially whether she agreed with its assertion that the two *Daily* editors were suspended for exercising their right of free speech. Campbell was then queried about Norris's article itself and especially its insinuation that tuition had been raised to exclude certain students from the university. She was also asked about Norris's attacks on Kipke and the Board of Regents, which the committee claimed had no connection to the tuition hike or the dismissal of the students. "You are making two assertions," Campbell replied, "first, that Harry Kipke's connection with Ford and Bennett is a false attack, and second that they have no connection with the student expulsions."[189]

When the Discipline Committee pressed Campbell on Kipke, asking what she thought was the connection between the lunch concession he received and the fact that he was a regent, Campbell replied, "your connection with any institution, whether a uni-

188. Interview with Harold Norris," *Meeting of the Disciplinary Committee, University of Michigan*, December 4, 1940, 19, VPSS, box 4, folder ASU, BHL.
189. "Interview with Margaret Campbell," *Meeting of the Disciplinary Committee, University of Michigan*, December 4, 1940, 17, VPSS, box 4, folder ASU, BHL.

versity or a factory, usually makes your opinions conform." When asked if Campbell considered a suspension of the ASU an act of discrimination on the university's part, she concurred. The interview with Campbell then shifted into a discussion on the issue of burden of proof and inquired into the composition of the ASU, with the committee asking how many were in-state students and how many were out-of-state. Finally, the committee informed Campbell that its members had interviewed the two *Daily* editors and that both disavowed any connection with the ASU. The committee then suggested that the ASU itself was "a tool for outside influences. You not only think of the students on campus—but someone outside is thinking of you."[190] While the transcript does not reveal which outside influences the committee claimed were supporting the ASU, the insinuation was clear: the ASU was not within "the boundaries of pluralism." Rather it was clearly an organization steered by alien or "outside" elements.

It was hardly surprising, then, that three days after the Disciplinary Committee's interviews with Norris and Campbell, the University of Michigan's administration formally suspended the ASU. In addition, the university also revoked Campbell's graduate scholarship, ostensibly because she had changed her residence to St. Louis, Missouri, and was thus no longer eligible for this in-state academic award. Campbell herself claimed that she knew that her scholarship was to be withdrawn unless she "ceased biting the hand that fed her."[191] Campbell also linked the ASU's suspension to the dismissed students as being "all part of an attempt to stifle any voice which is expressive and speaks for peace."[192]

190. "Interview with Margaret Campbell," *Meeting of the Disciplinary Committee, University of Michigan*, December 4, 1940, 22, VPSS, box 4, folder ASU, BHL.

191. "ASU Notified of Probation by University," *MD*, December 7, 1940; and "Dean Yoakum Gives Views in Statement: Says Scholarships Were Discontinued Because Residence Changed," *MD*, December 8, 1940.

192. "ASU Notified of Probation by University," *MD*, December 7, 1940. Although Campbell's scholarship was revoked beginning in the Winter 1941 term, nonetheless, she remained an enrolled student at the university. The VPSS's archives contain

Ruthven received a renewed stream of letters from journalists and academics expressing outrage at the suspension of the *Daily* editors. "I am much disturbed by the statements in the accompanying newspaper clippings," one journalist and Michigan alumnus wrote, "which seem to suggest reactionary trends and lack of educational freedom at the university."[193] Another alumnus and former *Daily* reporter told Ruthven that the news that he had read in the New York papers about the suspensions disgusted him, especially in light of the fact that the editors had published the quote from the *Nation* article about Kipke's ties to Bennett and Ford. The alumnus chided Ruthven: "If your views are conservative, surely you don't think there is anything reprehensible in Ford connections and corporation law. And if you do realize how bad it is for students to be under the rule of a front man for the anti-Semitic, Hitler-medaled Mr. Ford, you couldn't have any objection to publishing the fact."[194] Yet, unlike the more voluminous response in the wake of the dismissed, the outrage over the *Daily* suspensions subsided quickly. Haufler and Sarasohn published their apology in the *Daily* in which they both distanced themselves from the now-suspended ASU and yet averred that the ASU had been felled by "a gang of reactionary Red-baiters [who] saw in America's present fifth-column jitters a chance to clean out the opposite camp and remove these 'annoyances' and deterrents."[195]

Unmentioned in their editorial remains the fact that a disproportionate number of students who were dismissed had been

a letter from her to Dean Bursley, dated October 4, 1941, requesting the reinstatement of the ASU. On her signature line, she is listed as president of the chapter. VPSS, box 4, folder ASU, BHL. Based on his MSU obituary cited above, Norris was able to complete his master's degree in 1941. The reason that these two students did not suffer the same consequences as the other students is unknown.

193. Fred Kelly to Ruthven, letter dated December 11, 1940, Ruthven, box 58, folder 10, BHL.

194. Ronald Goodman to Ruthven, letter dated December 17, 1940, Ruthven, box 58, folder 10, BHL. The text is underlined in the original.

195. Hervie Haufler and Alvin Sarasohn, "A Week's Reflections," *MD*, December 12, 1940, VPSS, box 4, folder ASU, BHL.

Jewish. By emasculating "Red" action on campus in the summer and fall of 1940, Ruthven had targeted many more Jewish students than Gentiles for outright dismissals. Indeed, most of the Gentile students (Cotton, Keats, Chapman) were merely warned or quickly reinstated and, in the case of Roger Lawn, were retained even though his father had attempted to persuade Ruthven into withdrawing him. No such reinstatements were offered to Jews who were deemed to be outsiders to the campus community, clearly beyond the bounds of pluralism. While not every politically active Jewish student who caught the administration's attention was removed (such as Copilowish and Norris), it remains a fact that the overwhelming number of those dismissed in 1940, as well as all of the students dismissed in 1935, were left-wing Jewish students from the East Coast. Naturally, the suspension of the ASU effectively closed one avenue for left-wing politics for Jews, African Americans, and Gentiles. However, our argument, that the administration identified Jews as the main culprits for causing the university trouble with their radical politics, is substantially borne out by the fact that among the students whom the University of Michigan's leadership decided to forgive by offering them a chance to return, Jews were massively underrepresented.

Moreover, there is sufficient documentation to show that Ruthven received reports from Kipke on student radicals that emphasized their Jewishness. While this does not prove that Bennett or Kipke or Ruthven were themselves antisemitic, it does show that the students' ethnic or religious (Jewish) and racial (African American) identity were characteristics that received emphasis in the reports that Kipke was sent and that he in turn forwarded to the president. Based upon the few examples that we have, it appears that the rumors on campus were correct that Kipke served as a conduit for Harry Bennett and Henry Ford to pressure the administration into dismissing students deemed unfit to remain in the university. And the students so deemed were by and large Jews from the East Coast—just as they had been five years earlier.

Coda: Kipke, Ford, and Ruthven—1944

Another example of the pressure that Ford and Kipke could bring to bear on the university occurred some years later. In January 1944, the *Daily* printed an unsigned editorial that attacked Henry Ford for his "fascist tendencies"; informed readers that Ford had hired German Nazis to work in his plants; reminded them of Ford's sponsorship of the antisemitic newspaper, the *Dearborn Independent*; mentioned that Ford had won accolades from Hitler including being bestowed the Grand Cross of the German Eagle; and averred that Ford was an active supporter of the America First Committee, which the unknown author claimed was Fascist-run.[196] Frederick C. Matthei, a prominent Detroit industrialist and future regent who had been an advocate for Willis Ward and was later a member of the University of Michigan's Board of Regents, wrote to the Regents excoriating the letter and the *Daily* for printing it. Kipke sent a telegram to Ruthven from Chicago in mid-February that read "ASSUME PROPER ACTION TAKE IN THIS CASE ALSO TO CURB FURTHER EDITORIALS OF THIS NATURE. WOULD APPRECIATE A REPORT OF ACTION TAKEN."[197] Ruthven rushed to assure Kipke that the Board in Control of Publications was taking clear action concerning the editorial. "It seems to me," the president wrote, "that regardless of how true the facts were the language was almost libelous. I am sure the Board [in Control of Student Publications] will consider all of these aspects of the situation."[198] Ultimately the president proposed to Kipke to

196. "In a Hurry by Nobody," *MD*, January 26, 1944. The article also claims that John Bugas, the former head of the FBI's Detroit office, which had solicited information on the dismissed students of 1940, was now employed by Harry Bennett in Ford's Personnel Department.

197. Matthei's letter and Kipke's telegram appear in Ruthven, box 36, folder 32, BHL. The all caps quotation is because this is a telegram. Kipke had expressed an interest in 1940 in exercising greater control over the *Daily* by packing more faculty members onto its oversight body, the Board in Control of Student Publications. See Ruthven's letter to Kipke, dated August 9, 1940, Ruthven, box 28, folder 20, BHL.

198. Ruthven to Kipke, letter dated February 16, 1944, Ruthven, box 36, folder 24, BHL.

reduce the autonomy of the student editors by placing the *Daily* under the control of the journalism department. But, Ruthven continued, "it is already known to the students where the pressure for action originates, and if they make an issue of this we may be reasonably sure that the labor unions will have something to say."[199] As the president here seems to acknowledge, students remained well aware that Ruthven's administration was subject to outside pressure, and, by reading such a vociferous attack on Ford as had appeared in the *Daily*, they also had a good idea of where this pressure originated. In that sense, the legacy of the 1940 dismissals persisted even when the dismissed students themselves had moved on.

Conclusion

There is no doubt that by the late 1930s and into the first two years of the 1940s, President Ruthven had come to restrict his much-vaunted pluralism. As this chapter demonstrated, there were a number of forces external to the University of Michigan that rendered the bliss of pluralism a lot costlier to the university and the president than it had been a decade earlier when Ruthven assumed this university's presidency. This is not to excuse the president's increasing intolerance toward students he deemed ill-fitting to the university. It is merely to explain Ruthven's edginess that he had barely displayed during his previous years in the demanding position of being the University of Michigan's president. It is patently obvious that Ruthven massively disliked—perhaps even disdained—communism and any ideology close to this worldview. More directly to his own concerns, he saw it as a clear threat to the comprehensive and, yes, tolerant worldview leading a great university's educational mission.

In so doing, Ruthven also bore antipathy toward anybody holding such views that Ruthven found repulsive and dangerous. With East Coast (in particular New York–area) Jews play-

---

199. Ruthven to Kipke, letter dated April 11, 1944, Ruthven, box 36, folder 24, BHL.

ing a prominent and disproportionate role among advocates of radical politics driven by such views, Ruthven quite clearly—even if inadvertently—came to pursue measures that discriminated against these people,. This meant that Ruthven, his administration, and thus the University of Michigan indulged in disciplinary steps that affected Jews more than any other ethnic or religious group among the student body. The fact that Jewish radicals bore the brunt of the president's policies is evident in that Gentile students who were Communists and radicals were not punished as severely as their Jewish peers.

This in no way means that Ruthven was an antisemite. Indeed, he was clearly not, given his ongoing support of Hillel and his high regard of Judaism as an integral part of Western civilization. Yet there can be no doubt that the president fell under the sway of people who undoubtedly were antisemites. While Ruthven was no friend to radical students, it is evident that the dismissals in 1940 occurred by dint of the pressure he was receiving from outside the university. Ruthven's actions to dismiss another, larger group of radical students than he did in 1935, demonstrated that the president had fortified, indeed restricted, the boundaries of pluralism at the University of Michigan.

CONCLUSION

A lthough the organizers of the mock trial hoped that it would spur more collective action against Ruthven and his administration, this event became the last gasp of radical student activism on campus. With the year-long suspension of the American Student Union (ASU), the administration effectively sidelined its prime antagonist. The chapter barely functioned for the brief time it existed following its reinstatement.[1] In the same week of November 1940 in which the open hearing occurred, Franklin Roosevelt won his third term for the presidency with many students and faculty turning their attention to the increasing likelihood of war. Moreover, by the end of 1940, the ASU was rapidly losing its remaining credibility on college campuses nationwide. Having advocated anti-fascist intervention for several years, the ASU radically reversed its stance and embraced isolationism following the Nazi-Soviet pact of August 1939. This volte-face split the ranks of the ASU between diehard Communists who hewed to the Stalinist line of non-intervention and those who still advocated

1. Margaret Campbell submitted a letter in October 1941 to Dean Bursley requesting its re-instatement. It was hosting speakers again in the Michigan Union by early November 1941. See Campbell to Bursley, letter dated October 6, 1941, VPSS, box 4, folder ASU, BHL; and "ASU to Hear Dr. Emerson," *MD*, November 6, 1941. The attack on Pearl Harbor and the US entry into the war ultimately ended whatever life was left in the group. The last mention of ASU in the *Michigan Daily* was a small announcement for a film screening in March 1942: "ASU to Present Show," *MD*, March 13, 1942.

militant opposition to fascism in all its guises.[2] Moreover, the ASU's new isolationist stance eroded whatever support or respect the organization had among the general student population. The *Michigan Daily*'s Elliott Maraniss was himself taken to task by history professor Preston Slosson in the pages of the student paper for having chastised British Prime Minister Neville Chamberlain's appeasement in Munich in September 1938 but then advocating for non-intervention regarding Poland in September 1939.[3]

As long as the campus chapters of the ASU clung to the Stalinist line of isolationism, students and faculty accused the organization of hypocrisy and reminded its remaining members of their previously strident anti-fascist interventionism. "Before the fall semester of 1940 was over," according to one historian, "the isolationist monopoly on student organizing came to an end. Inspired by England's courage in the Battle of Britain and worried by the fall of France, interventionist students on scores of campuses began to organize."[4] The ASU, and the strain of political radicalism that it embodied in the second half of the 1930s, receded in favor of a growing readiness to confront fascism and Nazism combatively. In a survey conducted by the University of Michigan's Bureau of Student Opinion in February 1941, when the United States was still neutral, Jewish students, far more than Protestants and Catholics, supported the idea that the United States should openly declare its allegiance to Great Britain and send armed forces aiding its cause. Jews more than respondents of other surveyed denominations also endorsed that "G.B. [Great Britain] gets everything she needs except men—even if its [sic] more than half our production and even if we have to give it to her."[5] In a subsequent survey in March, more Jewish students than Protestants or Catholics

2. See Cohen, *When the Old Left Was Young*, 278–321.

3. Maraniss, *Good American Family*, 141.

4. Schwartz, "Joseph P. Lash: Leader of the Student Movement on the Left," in *American Students Organize*, 44.

5. Survey dated February 24, 1941, Set C, Bureau of Student Opinion, SRA, box 8, BHL.

endorsed the propositions that US ships should transport goods to belligerents and that the United States should declare war on Germany if it appeared that Britain was about to lose.[6]

Still, as late as March 1941, Jewish students at Michigan remained ambivalent as to the United States' actual entry into the European war. In this they resembled Gentile students at the University of Michigan. The Bureau of Student Opinion queried Protestants, Catholics, and Jews as to their opinions on the extent to which the United States should involve itself in the European conflict.[7] Although a higher percentage of Jews (13.4%) in the survey than Protestants (6.4%) or Catholics (6.3%) wanted the United States to "declare ourselves allies [with Great Britain] and send our air force, navy, and army if necessary," Jews were far more likely to endorse the more limited objective of material provisioning without military assistance (63.4%) than either Catholics (42.4%) or Protestants (45.3%). Whereas 66.8% of Jewish students supported the Lend-Lease Act compared to 40.8% of Protestants and 45.3% of Catholics pursuant to a survey from February 1941, Jewish students at 43.3% were less likely to support food provisions for the five small democracies (Norway, Finland, the Netherlands, Belgium, and Poland) than either Protestants (48%) or Catholics (57.2%).[8] The data are crystal clear: even though Jewish students at the University of Michigan hardly spoke with a unified voice on the European war, their greater support of a more assertive policy than exhibited by either Catholic or Protestant students suggests that the Jews appreciated the threat of Nazism much more keenly than others.

The student-faculty Winter Parley held in January 1941 also reveals that attitudes, at least among the most politically engaged students on the Michigan campus, shifted in favor of some kind

6. Survey dated March 17, 1941, Set D, Bureau of Student Opinion, SRA, box 8, BHL.

7. "Summary of Student Opinion on the War," report dated April 11, 1941, SRA, box 8, BHL.

8. Survey dated February 24, 1941, Set C, Bureau of Student Opinion, SRA, box 8, BHL.

of enhanced American participation in the European war. While the issue of the dismissed students was relegated to one panel, the war was featured on three. There was some floor discussion on the dismissals, with one person stating "money behind school does not like the ASU or radical groups," but the panel session focused more on the question of academic freedom and how much such freedom the students actually enjoyed. However, by far, the greater and more substantive discussion focused on the European war and the vexing issue of American neutrality.[9] For Jewish students, the unfolding catastrophe overseas assumed an urgency that was quite unique and that was more important than the "political correctness" of the ASU. An editorial in the *B'nai B'rith Hillel News* explained, "But despite the fact that the return to Ann Arbor does shelter us from much of the chaos in the world, it is just impossible to shut our eyes to the gigantic political, social, and ethical changes that are occurring every hour of the day throughout the world. These catastrophic changes have caused confusion and uncertainty among all individuals and groups, regardless of hue."[10] As a result, Hillel's political engagement focused on organizing support for refugees fleeing Hitler's Europe. Reports of the ghettoization of Jews and their desperate migrations away from Nazi-held Europe appeared already in the *B'nai B'rith Hillel News* in late 1939.[11] Hillel was active over several years in soliciting funds for the United Jewish Appeal to assist refugees and meet "overseas emergencies."[12] In addition, an Ann Arbor Jewish Committee—composed of faculty, townspeo-

9. Winter Parley, January 1941, Blakeman, box 3, BHL. The quote is from page 2 of the section "The Future and the Student's Relation to It."

10. "What Hillel Can Do," *HN*, October 1940. For a survey of Hillel's activities during the 1940–45 period, please see Markovits and Garner, *Hillel at Michigan*, 155–97.

11. "Jews Penned in Huge Ghetto; Mass Migration Under Way," *HN*, December 1939.

12. "United Jewish Appeal Sets $23,000,000 for 1940 Quota to Meet Refugees and Overseas Emergencies" and "U.J.A. Chairmen List Ten of the Most Urgent Needs," *HN*, February 1940. See also "Campus, Townspeople Coordinate Forces as United Jewish Appeal Drive Opens," *HN*, May 1940.

ple, and students—played an important role in organizing relief efforts on a local scale.[13] Yet the plight of European Jews and the looming threat of war as well as domestic antisemitism did more than simply spur humanitarian efforts. It also appealed to Jewish unity. "There is a crying need for unity, particularly as concerns the preservation of Jewish rights," declared one Hillel editorial in April 1940.[14] This recognition of the need for more cohesiveness among Jewish students was borne out by Hillel's increasingly successful membership recruitment drives. By early 1941, Hillel boasted of having enrolled over 800 members out of a total 1,100 enrolled Jewish students at the University of Michigan, which meant that almost three-quarters of the university's Jewish students became Hillel members in these troubled times for Jews.[15]

Hillel, of course, was not the only space for Jewish life on campus, although it was surely the biggest, most prominent, and the best documented. Other groups like Zeta Beta Tau (ZBT) and Avukah remained active as the United States entered the war. For Avukah, the dream of a Jewish homeland persisted. In March 1942, the group sponsored a seminar on "Jewish realities" that featured discussions not only on settlement in Palestine but also on Jews in the war.[16] The organization continued its normal programming of talks, meetings, film screenings, picnics, and study sessions throughout the war years. In early 1946, Avukah changed its name to the Michigan chapter of the Intercollegiate Zionist Federation of America.[17] ZBT and its Michigan chapter also continued their

13. "Ann Arbor Jewish Group Aids Many Refugee Students," *HN*, November 1940. The committee was formed in the fall of 1939, see "Campus, Townspeople Unite as Effort to Raise Funds Enters Final Week," *HN*, January 1941; "Ann Arbor Jewish Committee Raised $4,300," *HN*, February 1941; and "United Jewish Appeal Drive Begins April 27," *HN*, March 1941.

14. "Jewish Unity Is Essential Need in Present Crises," *HN*, April 1940.

15. "Membership Drive Passes 800 Mark; Aims for 1,000," *HN*. The 1940–41 enrollment figures by denomination are in Smith, box 8, folder 6, BHL.

16. "Zionist Group Will Sponsor Seminar Here," *MD*, March 28, 1942.

17. "Avukah Given Permission to Change Chapter Name," *MD*, April 4, 1946.

existence during the war. The national organization emphasized especially the contributions that its members made to the war effort. Its quarterly journal, *Zeta Beta Tau Quarterly*, introduced a new feature "Service Men's Mail Bag" in its July 1942 issue that published letters from alumni fighting overseas. In the July 1944 edition, *Zeta Beta Tau Quarterly* proudly described both the challenges that the fraternity faced during wartime and its accomplishments.[18] Despite the wartime draft, only seven chapters on American college campuses had become inactive. During the conflict, ZBT established a Service-Men's Service which provided "our brothers overseas with food delicacies, newspapers, cigarettes, and books." To organize this, ZBT created a "Get Acquainted Bulletin" that listed the names and camp locations of its members. The fraternity also produced a newsletter for the members fighting overseas. "In many cases," the report noted, "one or two 4-Fs or 2-Bs took upon themselves the task of acting as 'postmaster,' collecting and mimeographing letters from all recent graduates and circulating the resulting bulletin among the entire group. In addition the chapters threw open their facilities and their social affairs to servicemen, ZBT and otherwise."[19]

Thus, Jewish social life continued at Michigan and other campuses throughout the war, even if fraternities and other organizations saw a reduction in the number of their members or their activities that they could afford to sponsor. The Michigan ZBT, which had fifty members in April 1941, retained thirty-two in December 1945, and won eighteen pledges (among these were nine ex-servicemen).[20] Hillel too continued to thrive; in November 1942, the Michigan chapter opened its new larger facility on

18. The information in this paragraph is taken from Herbert G. Ahrend, "History of Zeta Beta Tau—Dec. 7 1941 to Sept. 1944," *Zeta Beta Tau Quarterly*, July–September 1944, 14–15.

19. Ahrend, "History of Zeta Beta Tau—Dec. 7 1941 to Sept. 1944," *Zeta Beta Tau Quarterly*, July–September 1944, 14–15. 4-F and 2-B were categories denoting their recipients' inability to serve in the United States armed forces.

20. "ZBT Chapter Statistics," *Zeta Beta Tau Quarterly*, October–December 1945.

Hill Street where it carried out activities in support of the war effort, including housing Red Cross first aid stations and assisting the War Manpower Commission, as well as continuing its work aiding Jewish refugees.[21] Just like ZBT, Hillel, too, proudly highlighted the contributions that its members and alumni were making to the war effort.[22] By the end of the war, the Michigan Hillel boasted the largest membership in its history, comprising over 90% of the Jewish students on campus. [23] Jews continued to make their mark in sports in the early forties: Merv Pregulman from Lansing, Michigan, played for the Wolverines from 1941 to 1944 and achieved distinction as an All-American tackle in 1943. He then became a first-round draft pick for the Green Bay Packers the following year.[24]

However, with the demise of the ASU by early 1942, the space for political radicalism—and specifically Jewish radicalism—had closed for the duration of the war years. We have not been able to discover whether the university's personal interview practice persisted into the forties. The last extant copies of interview sheets in Ira Smith's files date from the spring of 1939, around the time Arlene Lazansky was pushing to convince the administration to overturn its rejection of her application. What we can say is that Ruthven's pluralist policy, however compromised by his actions in 1935 and 1940, remained in existence throughout the war years, even if it contained, in the words of one scholar, "ambiguities and fissures."[25] Edward Blakeman, now nearing his seventies,

21. "New Hillel Home Will Be Scene of War Activity," *HN*, November 1942. Hillel was so successful in its financial stewardship that it was able to pay off the mortgage in two years. See "Hillel Burns New Foundation Mortgage," *HN*, November 1944.

22. "Hillelites in the Armed Forces," *BBHN*, January 1943.

23. "Hillel Membership Campaign Hits Top," *HN*, December 1945.

24. https://footballfoundation.org/hof_search.aspx?hof=1680. Late in life, Pregulman established the Mervin and Helen S. Pregulman Scholarship for the University of Michigan School of Social Work, https://ssw.umich.edu/finaid/list/15575-mervin-and-helen-s-pregulman-scholarship.

25. Harrold, "'Mess of Pottage,'" 39.

had expressed concern of what he saw as the increasing sectarianism that emerged on campus with the arrival of the evangelical group named the Inter-Varsity Christian Fellowship and the appearance of a new director for the Student Religious Association (SRA), Frank Littel. Whereas Blakeman advocated the assimilationist and pluralist philosophy that had informed his long experience as Counselor of Religious Education—that religious experience should form the basis of social harmony and integration on campus—Littel believed that more emphasis needed to be placed in "explicit religion grounded in particular traditions."[26] For Blakeman religious pluralism was a means toward integrating a diverse campus. For Littel, in contrast, pluralism meant giving the campus's pastors, priests, and rabbis more ability to proselytize on campus for their own faiths rather than promoting a truly integrated campus culture. In Littel's view, Blakeman's approach was too centralized; true pluralism came with allowing religious organizations the freedom to pursue their own objectives on campus. Losing many battles to Littel, Blakeman left the University of Michigan in July 1948 to take a position at the Pacific School of Religion in Berkeley, California. Pluralism persisted at the University of Michigan, but in the postwar period, its meanings were changing.

Finally, the boundaries of pluralism remained: Ruthven's views toward campus radicals did not soften with the end of the war years. In the Cold War climate of the late forties, he again made an example in 1947 by curtailing the activities of two political groups, the American Youth for Democracy and the Michigan Youth for Democratic Action.[27] Four years later, Ruthven retired after serving as president of the University of Michigan for twenty-two years, to date the second longest tenure in the university's history after James Burrill Angell.

---

26. Harrold, "'Mess of Pottage,'" 43.
27. The documentation is in Ruthven, box 58, folder 6, BHL.

* * * * *

This book features the interaction of three stories, each of which is a major component of US history. First and foremost, we tell the story of Jews and their accommodation in American public life during the first half of the twentieth century. Specifically, we focus on Jewish students at the University of Michigan, one of the most renowned and pedigreed public universities in the United States. Second, we feature this university's policies, visions, and desires to outline what it believed constituted an enlightened and ecumenical world both within its own confines and, of course, in society at large. The University of Michigan thus became a locus for struggles of political orientation and ethnic and religious identities during a period of turmoil in the country, indeed the world. And last, we also tell a story as to how forces outside the university affected its navigation between the Scylla of succumbing to pressures of intolerance and outright exclusionist prejudice and the Charybdis of an activism that advocated policies and visions that were quite different from what the university extolled as its model.

Jewish accommodation and assimilation took multiple forms, including the formation of specifically Jewish organizations such as Menorah, ZBT, the Zionist societies (Michigan Zionist Society and Avukah) and above all Hillel, which to different degrees and with different emphases sought to foster their members' sense of Jewish identity but also their assimilation into the University of Michigan. As we have shown, Jewish students were largely successful at Michigan by integrating into the broader campus culture, as attested to by their participation in many campus activities and organizations, including sports. Jewish assimilation dovetailed with and supported President Ruthven's desire to build and promote a diversified campus community but one whose diversity was rooted in students' memberships within religious organizations and associations. In many respects, this was a profoundly liberal objective considering the times. Facing the changing demographics of student populations across the nation, Ruthven ultimately sought to enfold these new students within an ecumenical pluralist order. Far from the conservative image that he later acquired, Ruthven had a pluralist vision that sought to provide a space for diverse populations of students, including Jews, but in a way that "contained" anxieties about these new faces by situating them within a religious order and by promoting intercultural and interfaith dialogues among them. Thus, for example, Hillel received Ruthven's full support and active intervention in the 1930s, especially during the financially perilous dark days of the Depression, because, in the president's view, the organization represented a valuable locus for Jewish students to gather and flourish as Jews and thus solidify their Jewish identity. Moreover, Hillel also enjoyed Ruthven's support because he perceived the presence of such an organization as the creator and guarantor of a religious and cultural identity that comprised an essential ingredient of his vision of an ecumenically sound liberal education anchored in cultural pluralism.

The emergence of left-wing Jewish student activism on campus in the 1930s not only challenged fundamentally Ruthven's enlightened pluralist vision of higher education but it also posed a threat to Hillel and other Jews, who were afraid that the radicals' activities would lead to all Jews being associated with radicalism and communism. These students had good reasons to be worried because by the late thirties, Jews on the Michigan campus felt that the climate in Ann Arbor was becoming more antisemitic. Fostering further tensions on campus, Ruthven's policies augmented Jewish students' uncomfortable predicament at Michigan and made them—if even inadvertently—central to the controversies of the times. The President's policies first featured the discreet formation of interviews specifically for Jewish applicants from the East Coast in order to prevent potentially undesirable radicals to enroll as students at the University of Michigan. Ruthven then followed this preemptive measure with the dismissal of students in 1935 and again in 1940. Ruthven's moves, and the justification that he presented for them, show him trying to steer his vaunted vision of a pluralist campus between the provocations of the student radicals, largely but not completely Jewish, and the pressures from individuals like Bennett, Kipke, Dilling, and other who had powerful ties to major business and government interests who were hostile to political radicalism. Pluralism and tolerance, ultimately, had limits, and the result was that Ruthven was compelled to punish students for their political behavior.

In considering the history of Jewish students on the Michigan campus, we looked at them in several spaces. First, we considered their daily lives and activities and the manner and extent with which they assimilated into, and felt that they belonged to, the campus community. Then we shed light on the way the university's administration regarded these Jewish students either benevolently, especially with respect to Hillel, or less so, when considering the Jewish members of radical organizations. Finally, we also analyzed the attitudes of external actors whose power and influence shaped university policies and the administration's reaction to politically minded Jews. Only by considering the relations between Jewish students and the university on multiple levels could we gain a fuller understanding of what it meant to be a Jewish student at the University of Michigan in the formative years of their presence on campus.

In the final analysis, we wanted to know what it was like to be a Jewish student at the University of Michigan between 1897 and 1945. Specifically, we commenced our research by focusing on this university's continued pride in a claimed tolerance and integration of Jewish students when many of its peer institutions were less inclusive. After all, one continues to hear on the contemporary Michigan campus how the still-extant relatively large presence of Jewish students from the East Coast—New York in particular—hails from the university's historical tolerance and open-mindedness of the mid-1920s and 1930s, when East Coast universities—Harvard, Yale, Columbia among them—established various barriers of entry to Jewish applicants. Our final tally assigns the University of Michigan a fine grade, although not a perfect one. As demonstrated in chapter 1—in which we gauged Jewish life on the Michigan campus from the late nineteenth century until the mid-1920s by painstakingly assembling information from disparate sources since no official tally of Jewish students at Michigan existed at the time—Jewish students seemed well integrated into student life on campus. They participated in extracurricular activities, belonged to clubs, and ran for and won elective positions in student organizations. With the important exception of the world of fraternities, from which Jewish students were by and large excluded leading them to form their own, Jewish students seemed well integrated with and accepted by their Gentile peers and the University of Michigan as a whole.

Even when admissions policies at leading American universities—Michigan among them—started to change in the mid- to late 1920s, largely compelled by the desire to curtail the number of Jewish students in postsecondary education, Jewish applicants to and students at the University of Michigan seemed unaffected. However, this changed abruptly by the mid-1930s, when the university administration came to associate East Coast Jews—and those from the New York metropolitan area in particular—with radical politics and actions that the university deemed unacceptable. While never resorting to quasi-official quotas of Jews that its Medical School had pursued for years, the University of Michigan instituted elaborate screening mechanisms that aimed to exclude left-wing Jewish radicals from the East Coast, primarily New York City and its vicinity. As no such efforts befell any other applicants to the university, it is not too far-fetched to categorize this policy as at least borderline antisemitic or antisemitic in its effect, if not necessarily in its intent. Until the mid-to-late thirties, Jewish students on the whole remained largely unaffected by antisemitism on campus because of Hillel's protective cover and its explicit support of the university's anti-radical position. Moreover, it is important to mention the fact that many Jews, like the majority of students, focused on their studies rather than on the political issues of the day. Being Jewish at the University of Michigan throughout the 1930s was fine provided this did not entail any left-wing activities. As soon as it did, being Jewish became a handicap that Gentile left-wing radicals did not have. The University of Michigan's continued pride in its historical tolerance and pluralism has a legitimate foundation. Our study has not tried to dislodge this. Rather, a more nuanced understanding of this pluralism might well be appropriate and a clear demonstration of its boundaries—emphatically delineated in these pages—might only enhance this fine university's proud history and well-earned standing in American higher education and in American society as a whole.

In a sense, then, this book—just like its companion, *Hillel at Michigan 1926/27–1945: Struggles of Jewish Identity in a Pivotal Era*—centers its story on the constant tensions and innate contradictions of an ethnic or religious group's assimilation into, accommodation of, and acceptance by the societal mainstream. Moreover, it also focuses on how such a group maintains its distinct cultural traits and fosters its own sovereign voice. As such, both books have much relevance to contemporary conflicts in which issues of diversity, equity, and inclusion provide such contentious terrain at American universities. Although our story is almost exclusively about Jewish men, it still bears major relevance for other groups that currently face the struggle of how to maintain their distinct voices in the American symphony. However, there is one major difference: the tonality of the American symphony at the time of this book's story was much clearer and less cacophonous than it is today; joining the orchestra was more clear-cut than it is in our current era. Of course, this book's America was also a place that, in its manifest delineations and simple boundaries, was much less pluralist than it is today. Thus, the boundaries of a more pluralist country ought to enhance the boundaries of pluralism within an institution like the University of Michigan and hence make both more inclusive and more democratic.

APPENDIX 1: JEWISH STUDENT ORGANIZATIONS ON THE MICHIGAN CAMPUS BEFORE 1945

<u>Jewish Student Organization Chapters at the University of Michigan Before 1945</u>

Organization	*Dates of Existence*
Michigan Menorah	February 27, 1910[1] – Approx. 1923-24
Jewish Student Congregation	February 26, 1914[2] - After March 1926
Michigan Zionist Society (a/k/a Intercollegiate Zionist Association; Intercollegiate Zionist Society)	May 1916 – Mid-1923
Hillel	July 1926[3] - present
Avukah	Fall 1927 – April 1946[4]

1. Per Irving Katz, "A History of the Menorah Movement in the U.S., at U-M."
2. Per Stiefel, "Early Jewish Life."
3. "Hillel Foundation to Help Michigan," *MD*, July 11, 1926
4. Avukah changed its name to the "Student Zionist Federation" on April 6. See "Avukah Given Permission to Change Chapter Name," *MD*, April 4, 1946.

Jewish Fraternities and Sororities at the University of
Michigan Before 1945[5]

	Founding Date (where indicated) or
Fraternities	*Earliest Mention in Michigan Daily*
Zeta Beta Tau	May 19, 1912[6]
Pi Lambda Phi[7]	October 14, 1913
Phi Sigma Delta	April 5, 1919
Kappa Nu	January 16, 1920
Phi Epsilon Pi	November 22, 1921
Phi Beta Delta	May 3, 1922[8]
Tau Delta Phi	December 6, 1922
Sigma Alpha Mu	October 9, 1923

Sororities

Alpha Epsilon Phi	September 25, 1922
Phil Sigma Sigma	December 14, 1922[9]

5. The list of Jewish fraternities and sororities is derived from "104 Jewish Men and Women Are Pledged," *HN*, October 24, 1933.

6. Zeta Beta Tau's Michigan chapter's actual founding date is given in ZBT's 25th anniversary publication, *The First Twenty-Five Years, 1898-1923* (ZBT: 1923). The date provided above is from that publication, not the *Michigan Daily*.

7. In the *Michigan Daily*'s announcement, the fraternity was described as a "general fraternity" with no reference to its being specifically for Jews. "Senate Sets Date for Convocation." *MD*, October 14, 1913.

8. "New Fraternity Recognized Here," *MD*, May 3, 1922.

9. The initiation and installation session for this new sorority was held on December 14, 1922. See "Phi Sigma Sigma Installs Here," *MD*, January 5, 1923

Michigan Campus Chapters of Political Groups That Had
Prominent Jewish Members

Organization	Dates of Existence
National Student League (NSL)[10]	Fall 1932 – December 1935
Vanguard Club	September 1933 – After April 1935[11]
American Student Union (ASU)[12]	January 1936 – December 1940 (suspended) October 1941 (reinstated)- March 1942 (last mention in *Daily*)

10. "NSL Is Out of Existence as an Individual Unit," *MD,* January 12, 1936

11. The last mention of any club activities was in *MD*, April 30, 1935.

12. "NSL Is Out of Existence as an Individual Unit," *MD,* January 12, 1936

APPENDIX 2: AFTERLIVES

A lthough the dismissed (and warned) students' reactions
to their ordeal ranged from bewilderment to traumatic,
in most cases they picked up their lives and moved on. What is
striking, especially among the 1940 cohort, is how many of these
students would go on to have esteemed professional careers as
poets or social critics, professors or scientists. When he was conducting research for his doctoral dissertation in the early 1970s on
Ruthven's presidency, Peter Van de Water sought to track down as
many of the dismissed students from 1935 and 1940 as he could.
While he succeeded in locating many of them, the notes and documents that he deposited with the university archives, and that are
currently housed at the Bentley Historical Library, show that only
very few of them were willing to revisit the dismissal controversy.
Michelle McClellan provided us with her research photos of these
notes and, using them and the internet, we were able to sketch
out, at least, most of the students' subsequent life histories. Sadly,
Van de Water died in April 2014, just a year before we commenced
our project, so we were unable to avail ourselves of his knowledge
of Ruthven's presidency and the dismissal controversy beyond his
1970 dissertation and the subsequent book, *Alexander Grant Ruthven: Biography of a University President*, which was published seven
years later.

The life histories below, therefore, are as complete and exact
as we were able to achieve. In some cases, these students had
sufficiently prominent careers - such as Howard Moss and John

Creswell Keats – that tracing their biographies was relatively simple; others, however, involved more speculation. Van de Water's notes do not provide enough evidence to trace the subsequent life of Joseph Boyd, who was alive in 1970. George Stein, the graduate student whose fellowship was revoked in October 1940, is not mentioned in Van de Water's materials and we were unable to track down any additional information about him. Although we have shown that the dismissals, and the actions of Ruthven's administration in the mid- to late-1930s, demonstrated a disproportionate emphasis on East Coast Jewish students, we have decided to provide the life histories of all of the dismissed (and warned) students irrespective of ethnicity or religious affiliation.

- *A.S.M. and K.G.*

The 1935 Students

Van de Water's notes yield no insights into the subsequent life history of **Daniel Cohen**, who unsuccessfully sued the University of Michigan in 1936. Searches of ancestry and obituary sites have turned up nothing conclusive.

Joseph Feldman transferred to the University of North Carolina at Chapel Hill in 1935 and completed an English degree there in 1937. In his memoir, *Timebends*, Arthur Miller later recalled meeting him in New York City around 1940 where Feldman expressed an interest in becoming a stage designer. He told Miller that he had joined the Army Air Corps. Feldman's decision caught Miller, who recalled him as an avowed Communist, by surprise. Feldman later died fighting in Burma during the Second World War. *The Michigan Alumnus*, volume 56 (March 18, 1950), page 325, confirms that Feldman served as a Lieutenant in the U.S. Army Air Corps and died in service on January 18, 1944. Years later, Miller visited Joseph's mother at the Feldman Pharmacy at 96th and Madison in New York and, mentioning that he was a friend of her late son,

Mrs. Feldman showed him a photo of his gravestone in Burma. Joseph had been her only child and "her eyes began to fill with tears, and she turned away" from him. See Miller, *Timebends*, 98–99.

According to Van de Water's notes, **William Fisch** was living in West Englewood, New Jersey, in 1970 and "didn't grad [graduate]." Online searches have not yielded anything certain about his subsequent life.

Leon Ovsiew, whom Ruthven reinstated after receiving a contrite note for past activities and a promise of good behavior, enlisted in the army during the Second World War. Afterwards, he became a professor of education at Temple University, where he chaired the Faculty Senate Steering Committee. See Hilty, *Temple University*, 102. He authored four books on educational practice in his professional career: *Making the Core Work* (New York: Metropolitan School Study Council, 1951); *Budgeting for Better Schools* (co-authored with William Castetter; Englewood Cliffs: Prentice-Hall, 1960); *Modern Foreign Language Study in the Elementary Grades, a Feasibility Study* (ERIC Clearinghouse, 1962); and *Change Capability in the School District* (ERIC Clearinghouse, 1974). He died in 1989.

Aschler Opler was a graduate of Cherry Lawn School in Darien, Connecticut, before coming to the University of Michigan. He later worked for Computer Usage Company, the first independent company to market software. In the mid-1960s, he headed the Computer Usage Education subsidiary that published software books, including *Programming the IBM System/360* (1966), for which he was the co-author. Opler died in February 1969 and his obituary can be found in the *New York Times* on February 25, 1969.

Edith Folkoff married fellow Michigan student, Robert Warshow (1917–55). Warshow became a film critic for *Commentary* and author of seminal essays on film culture, which have been collected in *The Immediate Experience: Movies, Comics, Theatre, and Other Aspects of Popular Culture* (Cambridge: Harvard University Press, 1962). Warshow died suddenly of a heart attack at the age of thirty-seven and Folkoff, who suffered from multiple scerlosis, died only three years later. On Folkoff, see *Immediate Experience*, xii–xiii. Folkoff's death in October 1958 was listed in the *Michigan Alumnus* 65 (July 11, 1959) on page 399.

The 1940 Students

Hugo Reichard served in the US Army during the Second World War where he was awarded a Bronze Star. He ultimately earned a master's and PhD degree in English from Harvard. After teaching at Duke University from 1952 to 1956, he spent the remainder of his career in the English department at Purdue University and was an active member of numerous community associations. He died in July 1998. See https://www.southcoasttoday.com/article/19980812/NEWS03/308129995.

It is not entirely conclusive what happened to **Nathaniel Rinzberg**. According to Van de Water's notes, he changed his last name to "Brooks." However, in surveying the *Michiganensian* yearbooks for 1937-40, we found no mention of a Nathaniel Rinzberg or a Nathaniel Brooks. Van de Water's notes state that Nathaniel Brooks was living in Detroit as of 1970. The notes also mention "M.S.U." and "Wayne '57-'61," suggesting that he received further education. An obituary for a Nathaniel Brooks in the *Nashua Telegraph* (January 5, 2016) states that he had a "B.A. from the University of Michigan and later in life got his Masters in Social Work from Wayne State University." The obituary mentions that Brooks, like Rinzberg, was born in Brooklyn. He was 97 years old when he died at the beginning of 2016, which would have made 1918 his birth year and him a senior during the 1939-40 academic year. The similarity in the biographical details lead us to surmise that this Nathaniel Brooks was indeed Rinzberg although we have no other corroborating evidence that definitely links Rinzberg to Brooks save Van de Water's notes. If it was Rinzberg, then, according to his obituary, he worked as a journeyman tool and die maker and then, after obtaining his social work degree, "made significant contributions nationally in promoting services for senior citizens. He then moved on to become an executive in an organization devoted to improving the lives of the people of Detroit." See http://www.nashuatelegraph.com/obituaries-memorials/obituaries/2016/01/05/nathaniel-brooks/.

Information about **Yale Forman**'s later life is even less conclusive. An obituary for one Frances Forman from January 2009 describes her as the widow of Yale Forman. After a career in opera during her youth, "she subsequently worked in partnership with her husband in their business, Yale Forman Designs, a full service design and licensing firm serving the home furnishing industry." Van de Water's 1970 notes indicate that Forman lived in New York City at that time and that he had not completed his degree. Moreover, Yale's family, as shown in the letters sent to Ruthven pleading for his reinstatement, was in the garment trade in Bayonne, New Jersey. Thus, we conclude that it is likely, but not definitive, that this is the same Yale Forman; if so, he died in 1986, although our research has not turned up a specific obituary notice for him. For Frances Forman's obituary, see https://www.legacy.com/obituaries/nytimes/obituary.aspx?n=frances-forman&pid=122090811&fhid=2086.

Van de Water's 1970 notes show that **Howard Moss** was on the editorial staff of the *New Yorker*. In fact, Moss became a renowned poet and was the *New Yorker*'s poetry editor for forty years, according to his *New York Times* obituary. This obituary mentions that Moss graduated from the University of Wisconsin in 1943, which corroborates the fact that he was one of the three students (along with Forman and Rosenbaum) who transferred there in the fall of 1940. At the *New Yorker*, Moss helped to publish the early work of James Dickey, Anne Sexton, Richard Wilbur, Sylvia Plath, and Theodore Roethke. Moss' own *Selected Poems* won the National Book Award in 1971. He died of a heart attack in September 1987: https://www.nytimes.com/1987/09/17/obituaries/howard-moss-65-poetry-editor-of-the-new-yorker-40-years.html.

After also graduating from the University of Wisconsin in 1943, **Hilda Rosenbaum** (**Kahne**) earned a masters and a doctorate from Harvard. She taught at Wellesley College and Wheaton College, and also served as a dean of the Radcliffe Institute from 1966 to 1977. In 1985, she authored *Reconceiving Part-Time Work: New Perspectives for Older Workers and Women*. Her biographical information can be found at https://prabook.com/web/hilda.kahne/197212

Morris Gleicher, who was the only Jewish student on the "warned" list, became an economic analyst for the Michigan Employment Security Commission and eventually founded an advertising firm, MG Advertising (later MG Associates). He was also an advisor to Detroit Mayor Jerome Cavanaugh, president of the Michigan ACLU, and a consultant to many major political figures in Michigan before his death in October 1992. His archives are held at the Walter Reuther Library at Wayne State University: https://reuther.wayne.edu/files/UP001536.pdf.

Van de Water's notes indicate that **Joan Geiger** had died by 1970.

Abraham Stavitsky became a professor of microbiology at Case Western Reserve University. Following his dismissal from Michigan, he earned a Ph.D. in Bacteriology from the University of Minnesota in 1943 and a V.M.D. from the University of Pennsylvania in 1946. He was Professor at Case Western Reserve from 1962 to 1989 and then Emeritus Professor until 2012. He published over 200 research papers (the final one in 2013!) and died at the age of 96 in August 2015.

According to Robert Copp during the authors' interview in December 2015, **Roger Lawn** died in the Second World War. This is corroborated by the Fair Lawn, New Jersey's "Honor Roll of War Deceased," which lists a Roger Lawn as having died on May 20, 1944. Van de Water's 1970 notes also lists Lawn as deceased. See https://www.fairlawn.org/government/honor-roll-war-deceased.

After attending the University of Pennsylvania, **John Creswell Keats** fought in the Army Air Corps during the Second World War and then became a journalist and freelance writer. As his *New York Times* obituary states "his 13 books frequently delved into American obsessions with education, automobiles, suburbia and the like." Among these books were *A Crack in the Window* (1956) that attacked the suburbanization of America, and *The Sheepskin Psychosis* (1965) that criticized the expansion of higher education. In 1961 he won a Guggenheim Fellowship. He also wrote biographies of Howard Hughes and Dorothy Parker. See the *New York Times* obituary, dated November 24, 2000: https://www.nytimes.com/2000/11/24/arts/john-keats-79-a-writer-who-noted-american-foibles-and-obsessions.html.

Following his graduation from Howard University, **Kenneth DeHaney** attended McGill University in Canada and Guy's Hospital Medical School in London, according to a news article profiling his daughter, Dr. Aleeta Somers-DeHaney. Aleeta set up the Kenneth and Clover Somers-DeHaney Foundation in Montego Bay, Jamaica, which awards scholarships to students pursuing secondary education: http://www.jamaicaobserver.com/observer-west/-i-will-show-my-mother-that-i-can-do-better-_169054?profile=0.

Roy Cooley completed his medical studies at the University of Michigan and practiced family medicine in Pontiac, Michigan, for over fifty years, including as Chairperson of Family Practice at Pontiac General Hospital. He was a member of many organizations including the Oakland County Board of

Supervisors, the Pontiac City Building Authority, and served as Pontiac City Commissioner. His obituary is accessible at: https://www.legacy.com/obituaries/theoaklandpress/obituary. aspx?n=roy-van-cooley&pid=147749939.

Holden Hayden appears to have been in the armed forces, and specifically the Army Automotive Electrical School and the Atlanta Ordinance Base. Eventually, he was employed with the Pacific Gas & Electric Company, although when questioned on this by the California Senate Un-American Activities in August 1953, he invoked the Fifth Amendment. Witnesses claimed that Hayden was also an instructor at the California Labor School in San Francisco, which the committee deemed communist. See *Eighth Report of the Senate Fact-Finding Committee on Un-American Activities 1955*. (Sacramento: California State Senate, 1955), 403-04. As of 1970, according to Van de Water's notes, Hayden was a "freelance writer" although he had no address for him. Our research unearthed no other information about Hayden.

Robert Chapman stayed at Michigan where he took courses with W.H. Auden and participated in the Young Communist League before joining the Army Signal Corps. After earning his delayed bachelor's degree in 1947, Chapman earned a doctorate in English. After teaching English at colleges in New York and Pennsylvania, he was hired as an editor at Funk and Wagnalls and then Holt, Rinehart & Winston. Chapman also edited the fourth and fifth editions of *Roget's Thesaurus*. After teaching at Drew University from the mid-sixties to the mid-eighties, Chapman died in January 2002 at the age of 81. See his obituary in the *Los Angeles Times*: https://www.latimes.com/archives/la-xpm-2002-feb-24-me-chapman24-story.html

Margaret Cotton married a fellow Michigan student, Lawrence Clifton Vincent, a theatre major, and as of 1970 was living in Cleveland, Ohio. Her husband was head of the Theater Arts

Department of Cuyahoga Community College and she worked as an actor, stage manager, and director. According to Vincent's March 2013 obituary, she had predeceased him. See: https://lib-ebook.colorado.edu › sca › archives › interpreter205.

Philip Cummins, the brother-in-law of Eliott Maraniss, who withdrew from the university two weeks before his family received Ruthven's warning letter, struggled with mental health issues for the remainder of his life. He spent nearly twenty years in and out of an Ashville, North Carolina, psychiatric hospital before moving back to Ann Arbor in the late fifties. He died in 1992. His nephew, David Maraniss, wrote movingly about his uncle in *A Good American Family: The Red Scare and My Father* (Simon and Schuster, 2019) as well as in "Saving Uncle Phil," *Washington Post*, October 27, 2002. This article is an excerpt from Maraniss' earlier book, *Nothing to Hide: Mental Illness in the Family* (New Press, 2002).

BIBLIOGRAPHY

Archival Sources

Brackets refer to the abbreviated forms found in the footnotes.

Benson Ford Research Center, Dearborn, Michigan [BFRC]

Henry and Clara Ford Estate Records
Owen W. Bombard Interview Series

Bentley Historical Library, University of Michigan [BHL]

Alexander Ruthven Papers [Ruthven]
American Student Union Papers [ASU]
Arthur Stace Papers [Stace]
Board in Control of Intercollegiate Athletics [BCIA]
Committee on Student Discipline Records [CSDR]
Edward Blakeman Papers [Blakeman]
Harry Kipke Papers [Kipke]
Henry B. Joy Papers [Joy]
Hillel Collection [Hillel]
I. Leo Sharfman Papers [Sharfman]
Ira Smith Papers [Smith]
Joseph Herbert Papers [Herbert]
Library Clipping Files [Clippings]
Peter Van de Water Papers [Van de Water]
Student Religious Association Papers [SRA]
Vice President of Student Services Papers [VPSS]

Harlan A. Hatcher Library, University of Michigan [HHL]

John E. Pokorny Papers [Pokorny]

Temple Beth El Archives, Bloomfield Hills, Michigan [TBE]

Stern & Weiner Family Collection

Walter Reuther Library of Labor and Urban Affairs, Wayne State University [WRL]

Civil Rights Congress Collection [CRC]
Philip Slomovitz Collection
Maurice Sugar Collection [Sugar]

Newspapers/Journals

American Hebrew & Jewish Messenger
Ann Arbor News
Chicago Daily Tribune
Cornell Daily Sun
Detroit Free Press
Detroit Jewish Chronicle [Jewish Chronicle]
Detroit News
Detroit Times
Hillel News (aka B'nai B'rith Hillel News) [HN; BBHN]
Ludington [MI] Daily News
Michigan Alumnus
Michigan Daily [MD]
Michigan Today
Michigan Tomorrow
New Republic
New York Sun
New York Times
Pathfinder
Student Advocate
Student News
Trenton [NJ] Evening Times
USA Today

Washtenaw Post-Tribune
Zeta Beta Tau Quarterly

Primary Sources

Bennett, Harry. *We Never Called Him Henry*. New York: Fawcett, 1951.

Blakeman, Edward. "The Protestant View of Public Higher Education." n.d. Ruthven, box 7, folder 4, BHL.

Blakeman, Edward. "Report of Progress in Religious Education, University of Michigan." June 1938. Ruthven, box 21, folder 25, BHL.

Blakeman, Edward. "Toward a Religious Education at the University of Michigan." n.d. Ruthven, box 21, folder 25, BHL.

Dilling, Elizabeth. "Radicalism in the University of Michigan." n.d. Pokorny, box 2, Labadie Collection, HHL.

Michiganensian (the University of Michigan Yearbooks). 1897–1927, 1934, 1936–40.

Miller, Arthur. *Honors at Dawn*. Unpublished manuscript, 1937. University of Michigan, Special Collections Library.

Miller, Arthur. *Timebends: A Life*. New York: Grove Press, 1987.

Morgan, Kenneth O. The Student Religious Association 1937–1939." 1939. Ruthven, box 26, folder 28, BHL.

"The President's Report to the Board of Regents 1940–1941." Ann Arbor: University of Michigan, 1941.

Ruthven, Alexander. *Naturalist in Two Worlds: Random Recollections of a University President*. Ann Arbor: University of Michigan Press, 1963.

Van Paassen, Pierre, and James Waterman Wise, eds. *Nazism: An Assault on Civilization*. New York: H. Smith and R. Haas, 1934.

Vicary, James. "A Survey of the Relations of Jewish and Gentile Students at the University of Michigan." Student Religious Association, University of Michigan, 1940. SRA, box 8, BHL.

Secondary Sources

Adler, Richard, and Ruth Adler. *Jewish Ann Arbor*. Images of America. Charleston, SC: Arcadia Publishing, 2006.

Aminoff, Helen. "The First Jews of Ann Arbor." *Michigan Jewish History* 23.1 (January 1983).

Amann, Peter H. "Vigilante Fascism: The Black Legion as an American Hybrid." *Comparative Studies in Society and History* 25.3 (July 1983): 490–524.

Ann Arbor District Library. "Hugo Reichard and the Radicals of 1940." September 13, 2016. https://aadl.org/node/347740.

Austin, C. Grey. *A Century of Religion at the University of Michigan: A Case Study of Religion and the State University.* Ann Arbor: University of Michigan, 1957.

Baldwin, Neil. *Henry Ford and the Jews: The Mass Production of Hate.* New York: PublicAffairs, 2002.

Behee, John. *Hail to the Victors! Black Athletes at the University of Michigan.* Ann Arbor: Ulrich's Books, 1974.

Borst, Charlotte G. "Choosing the Student Body: Masculinity, Culture, and the Crisis of Medical School Admissions, 1920–1950." *History of Education Quarterly* 42.2 (Summer 2002): 181–214.

Brater, Enoch. "Early Days, Early Works: Arthur Miller at the University of Michigan." In *Arthur Miller's America: Theater & Culture in a Time of Change,* edited by Enoch Brater. Ann Arbor: University of Michigan Press, 2005.

Brinkley, Alan. *Voices of Protest: Huey Long, Father Coughlin and the Great Depression.* New York: Vintage, 1983.

Brinkley, Douglas. *Wheels for the World: Henry Ford, His Company, and a Century of Progress, 1903–2003.* New York: Viking, 2003.

Burleigh, Michael, and Wolfgang Wipperman. *The Racial State: Germany 1933–1945.* Cambridge: Cambridge University Press, 1991.

Cain, Timothy Reese. "Little Red Schoolhouses? Anti-Communists and Education in an 'Age of Conflicts.'" In *Little "Red Scares": Anti-Communism and Political Repression in the United States, 1921–1946,* edited by Robert Justin Goldstein, 105–133. New York: Routledge, 2014.

Cohen, Naomi W. "Antisemitism in the Gilded Age: The Jewish View." *Jewish Social Studies* 41.3/4 (Summer–Autumn 1979): 187–210.

Cohen, Robert. *When the Old Left Was Young: Student Radicals and America's First Mass Student Movement, 1929–1941.* New York: Oxford University Press, 1993.

Copp, Robert. "Michigan, Ford's Football." *New Republic,* January 6, 1941, 23–24.

Culver, Mary. "Harry Bennett: Hatchet Man, Architect, Artist, and Animal Lover." *Impression: Washtenaw Historical Society Newsletter* (2000).

Dash Moore, Deborah. *B'nai B'rith and the Challenge of Ethnic Leadership.* Albany: SUNY Press, 1981.

Davenport, Horace W. *Not Just Any Medical School: The Science, Practice, and Teaching of Medicine at the University of Michigan, 1850–1941.* Ann Arbor: University of Michigan Press, 1999.

Demsky, Aharon, Y.A. Raif, Joseph Tabory, and and Edwin D. Lawson, eds. *These are the Names: Studies in Jewish Onomastics*. 3 vols. Ramat Gan, Israel: Bar-Ilan University Press, 2001.

Diggins, John Patrick. *Mussolini and Fascism: The View from America*. Princeton, NJ: Princeton University Press, 1972.

Dillard, Angela D. *Faith in the City: Preaching Radical Social Change in Detroit*. Ann Arbor: University of Michigan Press, 2007.

Dunbar, Willis F. and George S. May. *Michigan: A History of the Wolverine State*, 3rd ed. Grand Rapids: Wm. B. Eerdmans Publishing, 1995.

Fermaglich, Kristen. "The Social Problems Club Riot of 1935: A Window into Antiradicalism and Antisemitism at Michigan State College." *Michigan Historical Review* 30.1 (Spring 2004): 93–115.

Goldberg, Harvey E. "Names in Their Social Contexts: An Anthropological Perspective." In *These Are the Names: Studies in Jewish Onomastics*, edited by Aaron Demsky, Joseph A. Reif, and Joseph Tabory. Ramat Gan, Israel: Bar-Ilan University Press, 1997.

Gorr, Shmuel (Rabbi). *Jewish Personal Names: Their Origin, Derivation, and Diminutive Forms*. Bergenfield, NJ: Avotaynu, 1992.

Greenberg, Murray. *Passing Game: Benny Friedman and the Transformation of Football*. New York: PublicAffairs, 2008.

Greene, Daniel. *The Jewish Origins of Cultural Pluralism: The Menorah Association and American Diversity*. Bloomington: Indiana University Press, 2011.

Harrold, Philip. "'A Mess of Pottage': The Debate over Religious Pluralism at the University of Michigan, 1944–1948." *Michigan Historical Review* 24.2 (Fall 1998): 37–54.

Higham, John. "Anti-Semitism in the Gilded Age: A Reinterpretation." *Mississippi Valley Historical Review* 43.4 (March 1957): 559–78.

Higham, John. *Send These to Me: Immigrants in Urban America*. Rev. ed. Baltimore: Johns Hopkins University Press, 1984.

Higham, John. "Social Discrimination against Jews in America, 1830–1930." *Publications of the American Jewish Historical Study* 47.1 (September 1957): 1–33.

Hilty, James W. *Temple University: 125 Years of Service to Philadelphia, the Nation, and the World*. Philadelphia: Temple University Press, 2009.

Hollinger, David A. "Academic Culture at Michigan, 1938–1988: An Apotheosis of Pluralism." In *Intellectual History and Academic Culture at the University of Michigan: Fresh Explorations*, edited by Margaret A. Lourie. Ann Arbor: The Horace H. Rackham School for Graduate Studies, University of Michigan, 1989.

Hollingsworth, Peggie J. *Unfettered Expression: Freedom in American Intellectual Life*. Ann Arbor: University of Michigan Press, 2000.

Hook, J. N. *Family Names: How Our Surnames Came to America*. New York: Macmillan, 1982.

Jeansonne, Glen. *Gerald L. K. Smith: Minister of Hate*. Baton Rouge, LA: Louisiana State University Press, 1997.

Jeansonne, Glen. *Women of the Far Right: The Mothers' Movement and World War II*. Chicago: University of Chicago Press, 1996.

Johnson, Christopher H. *Maurice Sugar: Law, Labor, and the Left in Detroit, 1912–1950*. Detroit: Wayne State University Press, 1988.

Jospe, Alfred. "Jewish College Students in the United States." *American Jewish Year Book* 65 (1964): 131–45.

Jospe, Alfred. *Jewish Students and Student Services at American Universities: A Statistical and Historical Study*. Washington, DC: B'nai B'rith Hillel Foundations, 1963.

Kaganoff, Benzion C. *A Dictionary of Jewish Names and Their History*. Lanham, MD: Rowman and Littlefield, 1996.

Katz, Irving I. "A History of the Menorah Movement in U.S., at U-M." *Detroit Jewish News*, March 9, 1979.

Katz, Irving I. *The Beth El Story with a History of the Jews in Michigan before 1850*. Detroit: Wayne University Press, 1955.

Kruger, Brian, dir. *Black and Blue: The Story of Gerald R. Ford, Willis Ward, and the 1934 Michigan-Georgia Tech Football Game*. Stunt3 Multimedia, 2012.

Larsen, Grace H., and Henry E. Erdman. "Aaron Sapiro: Genius of Farm Cooperative Promotion." *Mississippi Valley Historical Review* 49.2 (September 1962): 242–68.

Lassman, Peter. *Pluralism*. Cambridge, UK: Polity, 2011.

Lendvai, Paul. *Antisemitism without Jews: Communist Eastern Europe*. Garden City, NY: Doubleday, 1971.

Levine, David O. *The American College and the Culture of Aspiration, 1915–1940*. Ithaca, NY: Cornell University Press, 1986.

Levinger, Lee J. *The Jewish Student in America: A Study Made by the Research Bureau of the B'nai B'rith Hillel Foundations*. Cincinnati, OH: B'nai B'rith, 1937.

Lieberson, Stanley. "Jewish Names and the Names of Jews." In *These Are the Names: Studies in Jewish Onomastics*, edited by Aaron Demsky, Joseph A. Reif, and Joseph Tabory. Ramat Gan, Israel: Bar-Ilan University Press, 1997.

Lipstadt, Deborah. *Denying the Holocaust: The Growing Assault on Truth and Memory*. New York: Penguin, 1994.

Lucas, Christopher J. *American Higher Education: A History*. 2nd ed. New York: Palgrave Macmillan, 2006.

Luxemburg, Rosa. *Briefe an Freunde*. Edited by Benedikt Kautsky. Hamburg: Europäische Verlagsanstalt, 1950.

Maraniss, David. *A Good American Family: The Red Scare and My Father*. New York: Simon and Schuster, 2019.

Markovits, Andrei S., and Kenneth Garner. *Hillel at Michigan 1926/27–1945: Struggles of Jewish Identity in a Pivotal Era*. Ann Arbor: Maize Books, 2016.

McWilliams, Carey. *A Mask for Privilege: Anti-Semitism in America*. Boston: Little, Brown, 1948.

Mizruchi, Susan L. *The Rise of Multicultural America: Economy and Print Culture, 1865–1915*. Chapel Hill: University of North Carolina Press, 2008.

Nowak, Margaret Collingwood. *Two Who Were There: A Biography of Stanley Nowak*. Detroit: Wayne State University Press, 1989.

Oren, Dan A. *Joining the Club: A History of Jews at Yale*. New Haven: Yale University Press, 1985.

Peckham, Howard H., Margaret L. Steneck, and Nicholas H. Steneck. *The Making of the University of Michigan, 1817–1992*. Ann Arbor: University of Michigan Press, 1994.

Rockaway, Robert A. "To Speak Out Without Malice: An Interview with Philip Slomovitz, Jewish Journalist." *American Jewish History*, vol. 80, no. 1 (Fall 1990): 5-20.

Rubin, Jeff. "The Road to Renaissance, 1923–2002." B'nai B'rith Hillel Foundation, n.d. https://www.hillel.org/docs/default-source/historical/the-road-to-renaissance---hillel-history-1923-2002.pdf.

Sahlins, Peter. *Boundaries: The Making of France and Spain in the Pyrenees*. Berkeley: University of California, 1991.

Sanua, Marianne R. *Going Greek: Jewish College Fraternities in the United States, 1895–1945*. Detroit: Wayne State University Press, 2003.

Sanua, Marianne R. *"Here's to Our Fraternity": One Hundred Years of Zeta Beta Tau, 1898–1998*. Hanover, NH: Brandeis University Press and University Press of New England, 1998.

Sanua, Marianne R. "Jewish College Fraternities in the United States, 1895–1968." *Journal of American Ethnic History* 19.2 (Winter 2000): 3–42.

Schrecker, Ellen W. *Many Are the Crimes: McCarthyism in America*. Princeton, NJ: Princeton University Press, 1998.

Schrecker, Ellen W. *No Ivory Tower: McCarthyism and the Universities*. New York: Oxford University Press, 1986.

Schwartz, Eugene G. "Joseph P. Lash: Leader of the Student Movement on the Left." In *American Students Organize: Founding the U.S. National Stu-*

dent Association after World War II, edited by Eugene G. Schwartz. Westport, CT: American Council on Education/Praeger, 2006.

Smith, Patti F., and Britain Woodman. *Vanishing Ann Arbor.* Charleston, SC: History Press, 2019.

Soderstrom, Robert M. *The Big House: Fielding H. Yost and the Building of Michigan Stadium.* Ann Arbor: Huron River Press, 2005.

Solberg, Winton U. "The Early Years of the Jewish Presence at the University of Illinois." *Religion and American Culture: A Journal of Interpretation* 2.2 (Summer 1992): 215–45.

Steinberg, Stephan. *The Academic Melting Pot: Catholics and Jews in American Higher Education.* New Brunswick, NJ: Transaction Books, 1977.

Stepan-Norris, Judith, and Maurice Zeitlin. *Talking Union.* Urbana: University of Illinois Press, 1996.

Steward, Tyran Kai. "At the University but Not of the University: The Benching of Willis Ward and the Rise of Northern Racial Liberalism." *American Studies* 55.3 (2016): 35–70.

Stiefel, Barry. "Early Jewish Life at the University of Michigan." *Michigan Jewish History* 46 (Fall 2006; Tishrei 5767): 17–23.

Stockton, Ronald R. "McGuffey, Ford, Baldwin, and the Jews." *Michigan Historical Review* 35.2 (Fall 2009): 85–96.

Synnott, Marcia Graham. *The Half-Opened Door: Discrimination and Admissions at Harvard, Yale, and Princeton, 1900–1970.* 1979. New Brunswick, NY: Transaction Publishers, 2010.

Tobin, James. "The Doves of 1940." *Michigan Today,* March 16, 2015.http://michigantoday.umich.edu/the-doves-of-1940/.

Tuttle, William M., Jr. "American Higher Education and the Nazis: The Case of James B. Conant and Harvard University's 'Diplomatic Relations' Germany." *American Studies* 20.1 (Spring 1979): 49–70.

Van de Water, Peter E. *Alexander Grant Ruthven of Michigan: Biography of a University President.* Grand Rapids, MI: Eerdmans, 1977.

Vinyard, JoEllen. *Right in Michigan's Grassroots: From the KKK to the Michigan Militia.* Ann Arbor: University of Michigan Press, 2011.

Wallace, Max. *The American Axis: Henry Ford, Charles Lindbergh, and the Rise of the Third Reich.* New York: St. Martin's, 2003.

Warren, Donald. *Radio Priest: Charles Coughlin, the Father of Hate Radio.* New York: Free Press, 1996.

Watts, Stephen. *The People's Tycoon: Henry Ford and the American Century.* New York: Knopf, 2005.

Webber, Alan, and Jonathan Sacks. *The B'nai B'rith Hillel Foundation: 1953–1993.* London: B'nai B'rith Hillel Foundation, 1993.

Wechsler, Harold S. *The Qualified Student: A History of Selective College Admission in America*. New York: Wiley, 1977.

Wechsler, Harold S. "The Rationale for Restriction: Ethnicity and College Admission in America, 1910–1980." *American Quarterly* 36.5 (Winter 1984): 643–67.

Wechsler, James. *Revolt on the Campus*. New York: Covici, Friede, 1935.

Woeste, Victoria Saker. *Henry Ford's War on Jews and the Legal Battle against Hate Speech*. Stanford, CA: Stanford University Press, 2012.

Zeitlin, Solomon. "Jewish Learning in America." *Jewish Quarterly Review* 45.4 (1955): 582–616.

Unpublished Dissertations, Theses, and Papers

Gongora, Alan. "The Changing Function of Public Education: Selective Admissions at the University of Michigan, 1920–1940." BA honors thesis, University of Michigan, 1999.

Horowitz, Susan. "Peace, Protests, and Parties: The Radical Student Movement against War and Fascism in America, 1933–1939." BA honors thesis, University of Michigan, 2005. Department of History, Senior Honors Theses, BHL.

Kaplan, Leah Melanie. "A Forgotten History: The 1930's Student Movement." BA honors thesis, Dickinson College, 2011. Department of History, Senior Honors Theses, BHL.

LaLonde, Kristine. "Student Activism and the Student Newspaper: The University of Michigan in the 1930s." BA honors thesis, University of Michigan, 1991. Department of History, Senior Honors Theses, BHL.

Magnuson, Roger R. "The Concern of Organized Business with Michigan Education, 1910 to 1940." PhD diss., University of Michigan, 1963.

Stefanick, Adam. "Personality and Power in the Ford Motor Company Hierarchy: The Story of Harry Bennett, 1916–1945." BA honors thesis, University of Michigan, 2011.

Steward, Tyran Kai. "In the Shadow of Jim Crow: The Benching and Betrayal of Willis Ward." PhD diss., The Ohio State University, 2013.

Van de Water, Peter E. "Peace Maker: President Alexander G. Ruthven and His Relationship to His Faculty, Students, and Regents." PhD diss., University of Michigan, 1970.